RUDMAN'S COMPLETE GUIDE TO CIGARS

Theo Rudman

D0733837

TRIUMPH
B O O K S
CHICAGO

Published in the United States by:
Triumph Books
644 South Clark Street
Chicago, Illinois 60605
Telephone: (312) 939-3330
Fax: (312) 663-3557

Published by:
Good Living Publishing
P.O. Box 5223, Helderberg, 7135, Cape,
South Africa
Telephone: (27) (21) 905-3600
Fax: (27) (21) 905-2188

Cover design by Salvatore Concialdi
Cover photographs by John Thoeming

Typeset in South Africa by Creda Press and in the
United States by Graffolio
Printed in the United States of America

1995 Edition, February 1995
1996 Revised Edition, October 1995
1996 Edition Reprinted, December 1995
Third Edition, October 1996
Fourth Edition, September 1997

ISBN 1-57243-245-4

FOREWORD

In the foreword to the earlier editions of my "Complete Pocket Guide to Cigars" I said I wanted, inter alia, to list every size, of every model, of every brand, of every cigar, of every country. With this third issue I think I have achieved that rather daunting ambition, as the book now itemises more than 4 000 different cigars from 24 different nations.

Of course, scores of new models are brought out each year; but, due to the rapport I have established with the trade, these are immediately identified for inclusion in the next "Guide".

In this third edition I have introduced new sections and comprehensively updated existing ones, particularly "Cigar Shops of the World" which now lists many hundreds of leading outlets spread over the globe, so that the traveller, wherever he may be, can go straight to where he can satisfy his passion for one of the abiding joys of life.

I have tried to make the book all-embracing, covering every aspect of matters affecting cigars and cigar-smokers — leaf growth and selection, manufacture, smoking qualities, storage, ageing, details of accessories and, of course, the more than 250 pages of model-by-model analysis. This includes nearly 700 personal evaluations, as well as the most comprehensive listing of Cuban cigars.

Such a wide coverage of cigar-related information is just not available elsewhere under one cover.

The "Guide" may be used as an instruction manual as a reference book, or just as pleasurable reading. It is interesting and informative and should appeal to cigar tyro and aficionado alike. I believe it enriches the cigar world.

Good smoking!

Acknowledgements

Once again to Richard DiMeola of Consolidated Cigars for his hospitality and untiring patience in replying to my endless stream of faxes.

To Danny Kolod, owner of Cousin's Cigar Company in Cleveland, for his friendship and assistance in supplying me with brand information.

To Richard Perelman, author and publisher of Perelman's Pocket Cyclpedia of Cigars, although a direct competitor, for his hospitality during my recent visit to Los Angeles and for his assistance in obtaining information on brands not in my previous editions. A true gentleman.

To Ben Rapaport, owner of Antiquarian Tobacciana, for his comments and supply of valuable historical material as well as permission to use his select Bibliography of 20th Century Cigar Literature.

To Anton Graf of Austria Tabak for his assistance.

To Simon Chase of Hunters & Frankau for permission to quote freely from their newsletter, "Cigar World" and various publications.

To Kevin Minnie and Brad Wilmott of L. Suzman Distributors in Johannesburg for their assistance, support and encouragement.

To all those too nuermous to mention, who supplied me with names of various cigar shops as well as cigars for evaluation, and for the benefit of their experience and advice in interviews and correspondence.

To Tommy Bell and Brian Taylor who, once again performed production miracles.

And, again, to Christine, my wife, for her support of this project which, inevitably impacts considerably on her life.

Contents

CUABA

Four sizes - all hand-made and all figurados
Quality: superior

Launched in UK, November 1996. Only the second new Cuban brand since Cohiba. The name comes from the Taino Indians, who were the original inhabitants of Cuba. They called their cigars cohibas, which they lit with a particular kind of bush that burns well, and still grows on the island. The Tainos called this bush the Cuaba.

All four sizes are *figurados,* bulbous in the middle with pointed ends. The only Havana brand to consist entirely of *figurados,* the shape that made Havanas world famous at the end of the 19th century. Gradually the fashion changed to *parejo* or parallel sided cigars and by the late 1930s this shape had virtually disappeared. Carlos Izquiero Gonzalez, 60, who has spent his whole life in tobacco, was one of the few remaining rollers who could still create a *figurado.* In 1995 he assembled and trained a team of 14, mostly women, to recreate the rare *figurado* sizes for Cuaba. Cigars made before April 1997 were made without mould, causing each one to be slightly different. These have already become collector's items.

Distinctive beautiful, dark oily wrappers. Ideal for ageing.

EXCLUSIVOS*****
Diameter: 18.3mm/46 Length: 145mm/5 5/8 ins
Beautifully made. Slow, even burning. Fairly strong, but smooth and mellow with lots of flavour. Elegant. After dinner cigar for connoisseur.

GENEROSIS*****
Diameter: 16.67mm/42 Length: 132mm/5 1/8 ins
Wonderful rich flavours, with coffee undertones. Smooth. For the connoisseur.

TRADICIONALES*****
Diameter: 16.67mm/42 Length: 120mm/4 3/4 ins
Although small in size, not small in flavour. Smooth, good finish. For the connoisseur.

DIVINOS*****
Diameter: 17.1mm/43 Length: 101mm/4 ins

Surprising flavour for a small cigar. A worthwhile quick smoke. For the connoisseur.

VERGAS ROBAINA

Five sizes - all hand-made
Quality: superior

Launched in Spain in June 1997. Only the third new Cuban brand since Cohiba. Second in under 12 months. Will be exclusive to Spain for about six months.

Brand named after one of Cuba's finest farmers, Don Alejandro Robaina, 78, head of one of the most renowned tobacco growing families in Cuba. He has run their plantations since 1950. The family's tobacco farming tradition dates back to mid 19th century. Brand launched in recognition of the craftsmanship of the Robainos and, more particularly, of Don Alejandro himself.

Filler comes from San Luis region in famed Vuelta Abajo. Wrapper comes from the famous Veja Alejandro itself. Produced in the Jose Marti (H. Upmann) Factory.

DON ALEJANDRO (double corona - *prominente* - hand-made)★★★★★
Diameter: 19.5mm/49 Length: 194mm/7 5/8 ins
Smooth, oily wrapper. Ideal for ageing. Mild strength with medium body. Spicy, with coffee undertones. Wonderful end to the day. For connoisseur.

UNICOS (torpedo - *pirmide* - hand-made)
Diameter: 20.6mm/52 Length: 156mm/6 1/8 ins.

CLASICO (lonsdale - *cervante* - hand-made)★★★★★
Diameter: 16.67mm/42 Length: 165mm/6 1/2 ins
Dark, oily wrapper. Ideal for ageing. Good draw. Slow, even burning. Full bodied. Spicy, with touch of coffee. Good after dinner cigar. For connoisseur.

FAMILIAR (corona - *corona* - hand-made)
Diameter: 16.67mm/42 Length: 140mm/5 1/2 ins

FAMOSOS (robusto royal - *hermoso No 4* - hand-made)
Diameter: 19.1mm/48 Length: 127mm/5 ins

C A N A R Y   I S L A N D S

ARMENTER RESERVA

Hand-made. Quality, good. All Canary Islands tobacco. Distributed by Armenter Cigar Holding, New York.

NO 7	191mm/7 1/2 ins x 19.8mm/50
NO 6	178mm/7 ins x 18.3mm/46
NO 5	168mm/6 5/8 ins x 16.67mm/42
NO 4	143mm/5 5/8 ins x 16.67mm/42
NO 3	191mm/7 1/2 ins x 19.8mm/50

CARA MIA

Hand-made. Quality, good. Connecticut shade wrapper. All Canary Island tobacco. Distributed by Metaco, New York.

PYRAMIDE	179mm/7 ins x 20.6mm/52
CHURCHILL	179mm/7 ins x 19.8mm/50
TORO	152mm/6 ins x 19.8mm/50
LONSDALE	165mm/6 1/2 ins x 16.67mm/42
CORONA	140mm/5 1/2 ins x 16.67mm/42

CAPOTE

Hand-made. Distribution in USA by Mike's Cigars, Bay Harbour, Florida.

NO 1	178mm/7 ins x 19.8mm/50
NO 2	152mm/6 ins x 19.8mm/50
NO 3	165mm/6 1/2 ins x 17.1mm/43
NO 4	140mm/5 1/2 ins x 15.5mm/39

GLORIA PALMERA

Hand-made. Quality, superior. Connecticut shade wrapper. Filler is a blend of tobacco from Brazil, Canary Islands and Dominican Republic. Distributed by Compania de Tabacos Del Mediterranea, Madrid, Spain.

DOUBLE CORONA	191mm/7 1/2 ins x 19.8mm/50
TORO	152mm/6 ins x 19.8mm/50
ROBUSTO	127mm/5 ins x 19.8mm/50
LONSDALE	165mm/6 1/2 ins x 17.1mm/43

GOYA

Hand-made. Quality, good. Made by CITA, Tobacos de

Canarias. Distributed in USA by Mike's Cigars, Bay Harbour, Florida.

GRAN CORONA	184mm/7 1/4 ins x 19.8mm/50
REALES	152mm/6 ins x 19.8mm/50
CETRO	168mm/6 5/8 ins 17.1mm/43
CORONA	140mm/5 1/2 ins x 17.1mm/43

LA FAVORITA

Hand-made. Quality, superior. Connecticut shade wrapper. Filler is a blend of tobacco from Brazil, Canary Islands and Dominican Republic. Distributed in USA by Arango Cigar.

DOUBLE CORONA	191mm//7 1/2 ins x 19.8mm/50
TORO	152mm/6 ins x 19.8mm/50
ROBUSTO	121mm/4 3/4 ins x 19.8mm/50
LONSDALE	165mm/6 1/2 ins x 17.1mm/43

LA PALMA DE ORO

Hand-made. Distributed in USA by Cuban Cigar Factory, San Diego.

DOUBLE CORONA	171mm/6 3/4 ins x 19.8mm/50
ROBUSTO	127mm/5 ins x 19.8mm/50
DON RICARDO	171mm/6 3/4 ins x 18.3mm/46
CAFE	140mm/5 1/2 ins x 17.5mm/44
DON JORGE	159mm/6 1/4 ins x 19.8mm/50
SUPERIOR	191mm/7 1/2 ins x 21.4mm/54
PIRAMEDES	171mm/6 3/4 ins x 20.6mm/52

PROFESOR SILA

Hand-made. Quality, superior. Cuban seed Canary Island filler and binder. Connecticut shade wrapper. Generally, mild and aromatic. Distributed by Las Palmas Tobacco Co., Fairfax, Virginia.

MAJESTAD	203mm/8 ins x 19.8mm/50
EXCELENCIA	165mm/6 1/2 ins x 17.9mm/45
PRESIDENTE	137mm/5 3/8 ins x 17.9mm/45
ROBUSTO	118mm/4 5/8 ins x 19.8mm/50
PRINCIPE	185mm/7 5/16 ins x 15.1mm/38

VARGAS

Hand-made. Quality, good. All Canary Island tobacco. Distributed by Marcos Miguel Tobacco Corp., Dallas.

CHURCHILL	191mm/7 1/2 ins x 19.8mm/50
PRESIDENTES	171mm/6 3/4 ins x 18.3mm/46

SENADORES	140mm/5 1/2 ins x 18.3mm/46
CAPITOLIOS	130mm/5 1/8 ins x 17.5mm/44
ROBUSTOS	121mm/4 3/4 ins x 19.8mm/50
DIPLOMATICOS	140mm/5 1/2 ins x 14.3mm/36

COSTA RICA

BAHIA

Hand-made. Quality, superior. Ecuadorian wrapper. Nicaraguan binder and filler, aged for five years. Cigars also aged for several months after rolling. 1989 vintage rolled in June 1996, released in February 1997. Production 490 000. Distributed by Tony Borhani Cigars, La Jolla, California, who specialises in setting up humidors in wine trade.

DOUBLE CORONA	203mm/8 ins x 19.8mm/50
CHURCHILL	175mm/6 7/8 ins x 19.1mm/48
ESPLENDIDO	152mm/6 ins x 19.8mm/50
ROBUSTO★★★★	127mm/5 ins x 19.8mm/50

Mild to medium bodied. Good flavours with a hint of sweetness. Good balance and finish. To follow meal. For discerning smoker.

| NO III | 152mm/6 ins x 18.3mm/46 |
| NO IV★★★★★ | 140mm/5 1/2 ins x 16.67mm/42 |

Firm draw. Flavour develops. Spicy with creamy finish. Smooth. Daytime smoke. For connoisseur.

DOMINICAN REPUBLIC

ABREU ANILLO DE ORO

Hand-made. Quality, superior. Connecticut shade wrapper. Dominican filler and binder. Distributed by Mike's Cigars, Bay Harbour, Florida.

PRESIDENTE	203mm/8 ins x 19.8mm/50
CHURCHILL	165mm/6 1/2 ins x 18.3mm/46
TORITO	127mm/5 ins x 19.8mm/50
CORONA	178mm/7 ins x 17.5mm/44
ESPECIALES	127mm/5 ins x 10.3mm/26
PANETELA	191mm/7 1/2 x 15.1mm/38

BOHIO

Hand-made. Quality, superior. Connecticut shade wrapper. Dominican binder and filler. Distributed by T&R Tobacco Sales Co., St. Albans, New York.

PRESIDENTE	191mm/7 1/2 ins x 19.8mm/50
CHURCHILL	178mm/7 ins x 18.3mm/46
CORONA	152mm/6 ins x 17.5mm/44
PETIT CORONA	140mm/5 1/2 ins x 16.67mm/42
ROBUSTO	127mm/5 ins x 19.8mm/50
PIRAMIDES	152mm/6 ins x 20.6mm/52

CABALLEROS

Hand-made. Quality, superior. Connecticut shade wrapper. Dominican filler and binder. Distributed by Metaco, New York.

CHURCHILL★★★★   178mm/7 ins x 19.8mm/50
Medium-bodied. Spicy. Creamy finish. Good draw. Medium to full-bodied. For discerning smoker.
DOUBLE CORONA   171mm/6 3/4 ins x 19.1mm/48
ROTHCHILD★★★★   127mm/5 ins x 19.8mm/50
Well-made. Medium-bodied. Spicy.
CORONA★★★★   146mm/5 3/4 ins x 17.1mm/43
Good draw. Well made. Mild to medium-bodied. Daytime smoke. Ideal for beginners.
PETIT CORONA   140mm/5 1/2 ins x 16.67mm/42

CANONABO

Hand-made. Quality, superior. All Dominican filler and binder. Connecticut shade wrapper. Named after heroic Cibao Indian chief, who died in 1495 as a prisoner of the Spanish. Owned by Palm Business Services, Miami.

GRAND PREMIER	191mm/7 1/2 ins x 19.89mm/50
GUANINES	152mm/6 ins x 17.5mm/44
NABORIES	140mm/5 1/2 ins x 16.67mm/42
CACIQUES	191mm/7 1/2 ins x 15.1mm/38
NITAINOS	127mm/5 ins x 143mm/36
PETIT PREMIER	114mm/4 1/2 ins x 19.8mm/50
HELENNAS	127mm/5 ins x 11.9mm/30

CARBONELL

Hand-made. Packed in boxes of 10 and 20. Distributed by Howard House Tobacco, Celine, Ohio.

PIRAMIDE GIGANTE	203mm/8 ins x 27mm/68
PIRAMIDE	191mm/7 1/2 ins x 16.67mm/42
PIRAMIDE BREVA	140mm/5 1/2 ins x 22.2mm/56
GIGANTE	254mm/10 ins x 22.2mm/56
SOBERANO	216mm/8 1/2 ins x 20.6mm/52
TORO	140mm/5 1/2 ins x 19.8mm/50
PRESIDENTE	191mm/7 1/ 2 ins x 19.5mm/49
CHURCHILL	191mm/7 1/2 ins x 18.3mm/46

CORONA	165mm/6 1/2 ins x 17.5mm/44
PALMA EXTRA	178mm/7 ins x 16.67mm/42
PALMA	165mm/6 1/2 ins x 16.67mm/42
PALMA SHORT	140mm/5 1/2 ins x 16.67mm/42
PANETELA GRANDE	191mm/7 1/2 ins x 15.1mm/38
PANETELA	152mm/6 ins x 14.3mm/36
PANETELA THINS	178mm/7 ins x 12.7mm/32
DEMI TASSE	127mm/5 ins x 11.9mm/30
PALMARITOS	101mm/4 ins x 11.1mm/28

CARLOS TORANO

Hand-made. Quality, superior. Connecticut shade wrapper. Mexican binder. Dominican and Nicaraguan filler. Also available in Europe. Cuban, Carlos Torano is credited with introducing Pilolo Cuban seed from Cuba in the Dominican Rep. in the mid 1960s. Distributed by Torano Cigars, Miami.

CARLOS I	152mm/6 ins x 19.8mm/50
CARLOS II	171mm/6 3/4 ins x 17.1mm/43
CARLOS III	191mm/7 1/2 ins x 20.6mm/52
CARLOS IV	146mm/5 3/4 ins x 17.1mm/43
CARLOS V	152mm/6 ins x 18.3mm/46
CARLOS VI	178mm/7 ins x 19.1mm/48
CARLOS VII	121mm/4 3/4 ins x 20.6mm/52
CARLOS VIII	165mm/6 1/2 ins x 14.3mm/36

CIMERO

Hand-made. Quality, superior. All Dominican tobacco. Distributed by Jonathan Drew Inc., New York.

CHURCHILL	178mm/7 ins x 19.8mm/50
TORO	152mm/6 ins x 19.8mm/50
ROBUSTO	127mm/5 ins x 19.8mm/50
LONSDALE	175mm/6 7/8 ins x 18.3mm/46
CORONA	140mm/5 1/2 ins x 16.67mm/42
CETROS	152mm/6 ins x 17.5mm/44
DEMI TASSE	127mm/5 ins x 13.5mm/34

CUSANO HERMANOS

Hand-made. Quality, superior. Connecticut shade wrapper. Dominican binder and filler. Distributed by Dom Rey Cigar, Boston.

CHURCHILL	175mm/6 7/8 ins x 18.3mm/46
CORONA	152mm/6 ins x 17.5mm/44
ROBUSTO	127mm/5 ins x 19.8mm/50
BULLET	102mm/4 ins x 19.8mm/50

CUSANO ROMANI

Hand-made. Quality, superior. Available with Connecticut, maduro and Indonesian wrappers. Dominican binder and filler. Distributed by Dom Rey Cigar, Boston.

PYRAMID   165mm/6 1/2 ins x 21.4mm/54

DANIEL MARSHALL DOMINICAN RESERVE

Hand-made. Quality, superior. Connecticut wrapper. Mexican binder. Dominican filler. Top humidor manufacturer, has now added a small but, select range of Dominican and Honduran cigars to compliment impressive range of humidors. Natural pairing - a class cigar with a class humidor. Black and silver band indicates Dominican range. Made by MATASA. Distributed by D. Marshall Inc., Tustin, California.

CHURCHILL*****   178mm/7 ins x 19.1mm/48
Good consistent construction. Slow, even burning. Cool, smooth. Good flavour. Spicy. For connoisseur.
ROBUSTO*****   127mm/5 ins x 19.8mm/50
Good, consistent construction. Cool, smooth, with loads of flavour. Light to medium strength. Spicy. For discerning smoker.
CORONA   152mm/6 ins x 17.1mm/43

DON ABREU

Hand-made. Quality, superior. Connecticut shade wrapper. Dominican binder and filler. Distributed by Andre Suarez Ltd., Miami Beach.

PRESIDENTE	203mm/8 ins x 19.8mm/50
EJECTIVOS	191mm/7 1/2 ins x 19.8mm/50
DOUBLE CORONAS	191mm/7 1/2 ins x 19.5mm/49
TORPEDOS	165mm/6 1/2 ins x 21mm/53
BIG TOROS	165mm/6 1/2 ins x 19.8mm/50
CORONAS	178mm/7 ins x 17.5mm/44
CHURCHILL	165mm/6 1/2 ins x 18.3mm/46
CORONITAS	165mm/6 1/2 ins x 17.5mm/44
GENERAL	140mm/5 1/2 ins x 16.67mm/42
TOROS	127mm/5 ins x 19.8mm/50
PETIT	127mm/5 ins x 18.3mm/46

DON ALBERTO COMANDANTE

Hand-made. Quality, superior. Indonesian wrapper. Dominican binder and filler. Distributed by Don Alberto Cigar Co., Miami.

CHURCHILL	203mm/8 ins x 19.1mm/48
DOUBLE CORONA	165mm/6 1/2 ins x 18.3mm/46
ROBUSTO	127mm/5 ins x 19.8mm/50

DON ALBERTO GRAND CRUZ

Hand-made. Quality, superior. Indonesia maduro wrapper. Dominican binder and filler. Owned by Don Alberto Cigar Co., Miami.

PRESIDENTE	203mm/8 ins x 19.8mm/50
CORONA	178mm/7 ins x 17.5mm/44
PIRAMID	165mm/6 1/2 ins x 21.mm/53
ROBUSTO	127mm/5 ins x 19.8mm/50

DON ALBERTO ORO DE HABANA

Hand-made. Quality, superior. Connecticut shade wrapper. Dominican binder and filler. Owned by Don Alberto Cigar Co., Miami.

CHURCHILL	203mm/8 ins x 19.1mm/48
CORONA	178mm/7 ins x 17.5mm/44
DOUBLE CORONA	165mm/6 1/2 ins x 18.3mm/46
PIRAMID	165mm/6 1/2 ins x 21mm/53
ROBUSTO	127mm/5 ins x 19.8mm/50

DON ALBERTO SANTIAGO

Hand-made. Quality, superior. Connecticut shade wrapper. Dominican binder and filler. Owned by Don Alberto Cigar Co., Miami.

PRESIDENTE	203mm/8 ins x 19.8mm/50
CORONA	178mm/7 ins x 17.5mm/44
DOUBLE CORONA	165mm/6 1/2 ins x 18.3mm/46
ROBUSTO	127mm/5 ins x 19.8mm/50

DON BARCO

Hand-made. Quality, superior. Indonesian wrapper. Dominican binder and filler. Distributed by Tampa Rico Cigar Co., Tampa, Florida.

GALEON	191mm/7 1/2 ins x 19.8mm/50
CAPITAN	127mm/5 ins x 19.8mm/50
ADMIRAL	152mm/6 ins x 19.8mm/50
MARINERO	171mm/6 3/4 ins x 18.3mm/46

DON MANOLO

Hand-made. Quality, good. Sumatran wrapper. Dominican binder and filler. Also available with maduro wrappers. Distributed by Capone Cigar.

CHURCHILL	178mm/7 ins x 19.8mm/50
PYRAMID	152mm/6 ins x 21.4mm/54
ROBUSTO	140mm/5 1/2 ins x 19.8mm/50
CORONA	152mm/6 ins x 17.5mm/44

DON MIGUEL

Hand-made. Quality, superior. All Dominican tobacco. Available with maduro wrappers. Distributed by Andre Suarez Ltd., Miami Beach.

PRESIDENTS	203mm/8 ins x 19.8mm/50
EJECUTIVOS	191mm/7 1/2 ins x 19.8mm/50
DOUBLE CORONAS	191mm/7 1/2 ins x 19.5mm/49
TORPEDOS	165mm/6 1/2 ins x 21mm/53
BIG TOROS	165mm/6 1/2 ins x 19.8mm/50
CORONAS	178mm/7 ins x 17.5mm/44
CHURCHILL	165mm/6 1/2 ins x 18.3mm/46
CORONITAS	165mm/6 1/2 ins x 17.5mm/44
GENERAL	140mm/5 1/2 ins x 16.67mm/42
TOROS	127mm/5 ins x 19.8mm/50
PETIT	127mm/5 ins x 18.3mm/46

ESPANOLA

Hand-made. Quality, superior. Connecticut shade wrapper. Dominican binder and filler. Exclusive to JM Tobacco, Los Angeles.

PRESIDENTE	178mm/7 ins x 19.8mm/50
CHURCHILL	171mm/6 3/4 ins x 19.8mm/50
SASSOUN	152mm/6 ins x 19.8mm/50
ROBUSTO	127mm/5 ins x 19.8mm/50
EXCELLENTE	175mm/6 7/8 ins x 18.3mm/46
CORONA	140mm/5 1/2 ins x 16.67mm/42
TORITO	152mm/6 ins x 14.3mm/36

ESPANOLA RESERVE

Hand-made. Quality, superior. Connecticut shade wrapper. Dominican binder and filler. Exclusive to JM Tobacco, Los Angeles.

FABULOSO	203mm/8 ins x 20.6mm/52
BELICOSO	140mm/5 1/2 ins x 20.6mm/52
DOUBLE CORONA	191mm/7 1/2 ins x 19.8mm/50
TORO	152mm/6 ins x 19.8mm/50
ROBUSTO	127mm/5 ins x 19.8mm/50
CHURCHILL	178mm/7 ins x 19.1mm/48
CORONA GRANDE	152mm/6 ins x 17.5mm/44
EXCELLENT	165mm/6 1/2 ins x 16.67mm/42

PETIT CORONA   127mm/5 ins x 16.67mm/42
DEMI TASSE   114mm/4 1/2 ins x 74.3mm/36

FAT CAT

Hand-made. Quality, good. Dominican grown Cuban seed filler and binder. Sumatra wrapper. In spite of the name is a serious cigar. Owned by Fat Cat Cigars Ltd., Sunrise, Florida.

TORPEDO   165mm/6 1/2 ins x 20.6mm/52
CHURCHILL   179mm/7 ins x 19.8mm/50
ROBUSTO   127mm/5 ins x 20.6mm/52

LA FLOR DOMINICANA

Hand-made. Quality, superior. Connecticut wrapper. Dominican binder and filler. Exclusive to Premium Imports, Coral Gables, Florida.

PRESIDENTE   203mm/8 ins x 19.8mm/50
MAMBISES   175mm/6 7/8 ins x 19.1mm/48
ALCALDE   165mm/6 1/2 ins x 17.5mm/44
INSURRECTOS   140mm/5 1/2 ins x 16.67mm/42
MACEO   127mm/5 ins x 19.1mm/48
MACHETEROS   102mm/4 ins x 15.9mm/40
CHURCHILL RESERVA ESPECIAL
          175mm/6 7/8 ins x 19.5mm/49
FIGURADO   165mm/6 1/2 ins x 20.6mm/52
ROBUSTO RESERVA ESPECIAL
          127mm/5 ins x 19.1mm/48
BELICOSO RESERVA ESPECIAL
          140mm/5 1/2 ins x 20.6mm/52
DIPLIMATICO   127mm/5 ins x 11.9mm/30

LA HABANERA

Hand-made. Quality, superior. Connecticut shade wrapper. Dominican binder and filler. Distributed by Don Alberto Cigar Co., Miami.

CHURCHILL   175mm/6 7/8 ins x 18.3mm/46
DIPLOMATICOS   152mm/6 ins x 17.5mm/44
ELEGANTE   175mm/6 7/8 ins x 16.67mm/42
EMPERADORES   140mm/5 1/2 ins x 19.8mm/50
ESPECIALE   127mm/5 ins x 12.3mm/30
PRESIDENTE   191mm/7 1/2 ins x 19.8mm/50
PURITANOS   146mm/5 3/4 ins x 16.67mm/42
SELECTOS   178mm/7 ins x 14.3mm/36

LA PRIMERA

Hand-made. Quality, superior. Ecuadorian wrapper.

Dominican binder. Blend of Nicaraguan and Dominican filler. Launched October 1996. Made by Manufactura de Tabacos SA (MATASA), owned by renowned Manuel Quesada. Distributed in USA by SAG Imports, Miami.

PRESIDENTE	216mm/8 1/2 ins x 20.6mm/52
CHURCHILL	178mm/7 ins x 19.8mm/50
TORO	152mm/6 ins x 19.8mm/50
CETRO GRANDE	171mm/6 3/4 ins x 17.5mm/44
ROTHSCHILD*****	127mm/5 ins x 19.8mm/50

Well made. Medium body, rich flavours. Good balance and finish. For discerning smoker.

PETIT CORONA	146mm/4 3/4 ins x 17.1mm/43

MONTERO

Hand-made. Quality, superior. Connecticut seed wrapper. Dominican binder and filler. Made by Tabacos Dominicos. Distributed by Tropical Tobacco, Miami.

PRESIDENTE	191mm/7 1/2 ins x 19.8mm/50
TORPEDO	178mm/7 ins x 21.4mm/54
CHURCHILL	175mm/6 7/8 ins x 18.3mm/46
TORO*****	152mm/6 ins x 19.8mm/50

Well-made. Slow, even burning. Smooth. Medium body. Good balance and finish. For discerning smoker.

CETRO	152mm/6 ins x 17.5mm/44
ROBUSTO	127mm/5 ins x 19.8mm/50

PANOREA

Hand-made. Quality, superior. Connecticut shade wrapper. Dominican binder and filler. Distributed by CEI Group, Northfield, Illinois.

CHURCHILL	178mm/7 ins x 19.8mm/50
BELICOSO	159mm/6 1/4 ins x 20.6mm/52
LONSDALE	165mm/6 1/2 ins x 17.1mm/43
ROBUSTO	127mm/5 ins x 19.8mm/50
CORONA	140mm/5 1/2 ins x 17.1mm/43

PREMIUM DOMINICAN SELECTION

Hand-made. Quality, good. Available with Connecticut, Cameroun and maduro wrappers. (Note ring gauge of Giant and El Cid.) Distributed by Antillian Cigar Corp., Miami.

GIANT	229mm/9 ins x 24.6mm/62
SUPER SOBERANOS	216mm/8 1/2 ins x 20.6mm/52

PRESIDENTE	203mm/8 ins x 19.8mm/50
EL CID	178mm/7 ins x 23.8mm/60
CHURCHILL	178mm/7 ins x 19.5mm/49
REGULARES	152mm/6 ins x 19.8mm/50
NO 1	171mm/6 3/4 ins x 17.1mm/43
NO 3	171mm/6 3/4 ins x 15.1mm/38
NO 4	140mm/5 1/4 ins x 15.1mm/38
ROTHSCHILDS	121mm/4 3/4 ins x 19.5mm/49
SUPER FINO	152mm/6 ins x 13.9mm/35

PUEBLO DOMINICANO

Hand-made. Quality, good. All Dominican tobacco. Each cigar is named after a pueblo in the Dominican Republic, except the Siglo V, which commemorates the 500 years of Dominican history. Brand established 1996. Owned by Pueblo Dominicano Imports, Austin, Texas.

BARUHONA	203mm/8 ins x 19.8mm/50
SAN PEDRO	114mm/4 1/2 ins x 20.6mm/52
SANTO DOMINIGO	152mm/6 ins x 19.8mm/50
LA ROMANA	140mm/5 1/2 ins x 18.3mm/46
SIGLO V	171mm/6 3/4 ins x 18.3mm/46
SANTIAGO	133mm/5 1/4 ins x 16.67mm/42
SAMANA	102mm/4 ins x 16.67mm/42

RICOS DOMINICANOS

Hand-made. Quality, superior. Connecticut shade wrapper. Dominican filler and binder. Also available with maduro wrappers. Made by MATASA. Distributed by SAG Imports, Miami.

CHURCHILL	178mm/7 ins x 19.8mm/50
TORO	152mm/6 ins x 19.8mm/50
BREVA	140mm/5 1/2 ins x 17.5mm/44
CETRO LARGO	171mm/6 3/4 ins x 17.5mm/44

ROMANTICOS

Hand-made. Quality, superior. Dominican filler and binder. Connecticut shade wrapper. Distributed by S & T Cigars, Coral Gables, Florida.

MARC ANTHONY	203mm/8 ins x 20.6mm/52
VALENTINO	178mm/7 ins x 19.8mm/50
CYRANO	152mm/6 ins x 20.6mm/52
CLEOPATRA	146mm/5 3/4 ins x 17.1mm/43
EROS	127mm/5 ins x 19.8mm/50
VENUS	127mm/5 ins x 14.3mm/36

SERENDIPITY

Hand-made. Quality, superior. Connecticut shade wrapper. Dominican filler and binder. Distributed by Mike's Cigars, Bay Harbour, Florida.

PRESIDENTE	203mm/8 ins x 19.8mm/50
CHURCHILL	165mm/6 1/2 ins x 18.3mm/46
TORITO	127mm/5 ins x 19.8mm/50
CORONITA	165mm/6 1/2 ins x 17.5mm/44

SIGLO 21

Hand-made. Quality, superior. Ecuadorian wrapper. Dominican filler and binder. Created to celebrate the new millenium. Made by Puros de Villa Gonzalez SA. Distributed by Swisher Intl.

21 - 1	114mm/4 1/2 ins x 19.8mm/50
21 - 2	165mm/6 1/2 ins x 17.5mm/44
21 - 3	152mm/6 ins x 19.8mm/50
21 - 4★★★★	178mm/7 ins x 19.1mm/48

Uneven burn. Mild. Herby flavours. Daytime smoke.

21 - 5	203mm/8 ins x 19.8mm/50

TABANTILLAS

Hand-made. All Dominican tobacco. Distributed by Indianhead Sales.

TABANTILLAS A	254mm/10 ins x 19.8mm/50
GRAN DUQUE	203mm/8 ins x 19.8mm/50
HAVANA CLUB	184mm/7 1/4 ins x 15.1mm/38
1866 NO 1	171mm/6 3/4 ins x 15.1mm/38
TORERRO	152mm/6 ins x 19.8mm/50
CONDADO REAL	140mm/5 1/2 ins x 18.3mm/46
NO 4	133mm/5 1/4 ins x 16.67mm/42
ROMERO	114mm/4 1/2 ins x 20.2mm/52

VALDRYCH

Hand-made. Quality, superior. Produced with blends of Olor Dominicano and Piloto Cubano tobacco. Sun grown wrapper. A medium strength, full-bodied range with attractive, dark wrappers. Close in flavour, texture and quality to that of genuine Havana. All tobacco is aged for at least three years. If not properly humidified wrappers become particularly fragile. Good, consistent construction throughout range.

QUISQUEYA REAL	254mm/10 ins x 19.8mm/50
MONUMENTO★★★★★	203mm/8 ins x 19.8mm/50

Good draw, even burning. Smooth. Full-flavoured. To follow good meal. This cigar is an occasion!

CABALLERO	197mm/7 3/4 ins x 15.1mm/38
TAINO	152mm/6 ins x 19.8mm/50
CONDE	114mm/4 1/2 ins x 20.6mm/52
CARLOS*****	114mm/4 1/2 ins x 19.8mm/50

Good draw. Medium strength with lots of flavour. Spicy. Good balance. For the connoisseur.

1904****	171mm/6 3/4 ins x 18.3mm/46

Firm, but good draw. Slow, even burning. Smooth. Short finish.

FRANCISCO	140mm/5 1/2 ins x 18.3mm/46

Good draw. Burns a little unevenly. Makes long, white ash. Good balance and finish. Hint of coffee. To follow meal. For discerning smoker.

ANACAONA****	140mm/5 1/2 ins x 16.67mm/42

Burns and draws well. Smooth. A little more complexity would make this a stunning cigar. Daytime smoke.

SUBLIME	102mm/4 ins x 16.67mm/42

VICTOR SINCLAIR

Hand-made. Quality, superior. Legend has it that this is the cigar that, in 1838, was appreciated by members of the Agricultural and Sporting Club of St Simons Island. Connecticut shade wrapper. Owned by Victor Sinclair Inc., St Simons Island, Georgia.

CHURCHILL	192mm/7 1/2 ins x 19.8mm/50
ROBUSTO NO 1	140mm/5 1/2 ins x 19.8mm/50
ROBUSTO NO 2	114mm/4 1/2 ins x 19.8mm/50
LONSDALE	152mm/6 ins x 17.5mm/44
PYRAMID	179mm/7 ins x 21.4mm/54
CORONA	152mm/6 ins x 18.3mm/46

VICTOR SINCLAIR GRAND RESERVE

Hand-made. Quality, superior. All with maduro wrappers. Packed in boxes of 10 or 15. Owned by Victor Sinclair Inc., St Simons Island, Georgia.

PANETELA	179mm/7 ins x 15.1mm/38
FIGURADO	127mm/5 ins x 18.3mm/44
BELICOSO	146mm/5 3/4 ins x 20.6mm/52
PYRAMID	152mm/6 ins x 21.4mm/54

YUMURI

Hand-made. Quality, good. Dominican filler and binder. Connecticut shade wrapper. Distributed by Brown Leaf Co., Miami.

CHURCHILL	178mm/7 ins x 19.1mm/48
LONSDALE	178mm/7 ins x 17.1mm/43
TORO★★★	152mm/6 ins x 19.8mm/50

Well-made. Slow, even burning. Mild. Daytime smoke. Ideal for beginners.

CORONA	140mm/5 1/2 ins x 17.1mm/43
ROBUSTO	121mm/4 3/4 ins x 20.6mm/52

H O N D U R A S

AL CAPONE

Hand-made. Quality, superior. Brazilian wrapper. Nicaraguan binder and filler. Exclusive to Swisher Intl.

CORONA GRANDE	171mm/6 3/4 ins x 17.1mm/43
ROBUSTO	121mm/4 3/4 ins x 19.8mm/50

BALLENA SUPREMA DANLI COLLECTION

Hand-made. Quality, superior. Connecticut shade wrapper. Mexican binder. Filler is blend of Dominican Piloto from Cuban seed and Mexican San Andres Morron. A range with full flavour. Distributed by pipe tobacco specialist McClelland Tobacco Co., Kansas City, Missouri.

CAPITAN (PYRAMID)	178mm/7 ins x 21.4mm/54
ENCANTO	203.2mm/8 ins x 19.8mm/50
VENTAJA	178mm/7 ins x 17.5mm/44
ALMA	178mm/7 ins x 18.7mm/47
CONSUELO	127mm/5 ins x 19.8mm/50

DA VINCI

Hand-made. Quality, superior. Ecuadorian wrapper. Dominican binder. Cuban seed Honduran, Nicaraguan and Dominican filler. Distributed by Brimar Group, Dallas.

RENAISSANCE (TORPEDO)	178mm/7 ins x 21.4mm/54
LEONARDO	216mm/8 1/2 ins x 20.6mm/52
GINEVRA DE BENCI	178mm/7 ins x 19.1mm/48
MONALISA★★★★★	152mm/6 ins x 19.8mm/50

Well-made. Good draw. Slow, even burning. Good complexity with medium bodied. To follow meal. For discerning smoker.

CECILIA GALLERANI	152mm/6 ins x 17.1mm/43
MADONNA	127mm/5 ins x 19.8mm/50

DANIEL MARSHALL HONDURAN RESERVE

Hand-made. Quality, superior. Connecticut shade wrapper. Honduran binder. Honduran and Nicaraguan filler.

Top humidor manufacturer, has now added a small but
select range of Honduran and Dominican cigars to compliment impressive range of humidors. Black, gold and
white band donates Honduran range. Natural pairing -
a class cigar with a class humidor. Distributed by D.
Marshall Inc., Tustin, California.

CHURCHILL	178mm/7 ins x 19.8mm/50
CORONA	152mm/ 6 ins x 17.5mm/44
ROBUSTO*****	127mm/5 ins x 19.8mm/50

Good draw. Slow, even burning. Cool. Medium strength
with good balance of spicy, creamy flavours. Enjoy this
when you can get it. For discerning smoker.

DON FIFE

Hand-made. Quality, superior. Connecticut and Ecuadorian wrappers. Cuban seed Honduran binder and filler.
Owned by Don Fife, Cigars Corp., Miami.

CHURCHILL	178mm/7 ins x 19.1mm/48
NUMERO 1	178mm/7 ins x 17.1mm/43
DOUBLE CORONA	165mm/6 1/2 ins x 17.5mm/44
CORONA GORDA	152mm/6 ins x 19.8mm/50
PETIT CETRO	140mm/5 1/2 ins x 17.1mm/43
PETIT	114mm/4 1/2 ins x 11.9mm

DON TONIOLI

Hand-made. Quality, superior. Ecuadorian wrapper.
Nicaraguan binder and filler. Tobacco aged for four years.
Cigars also aged for several months after rolling.
Distributed by Tony Borhani Cigars, La Jolla, California,
who specialises in setting up humidors in wine trade.

SUPER TORPEDO	191mm/7 1/2 ins x 25.4mm/64
TORPEDO	152mm/6 ins x 20.6mm/52
CHURCHILL	178mm/7 ins x 18.7mm/47
ROBUSTO	127mm/5 ins x 19.8mm/50
CORONA EXTRA	146mm/5 3/4 ins x 18.3mm/46

ELEGANTE BLEND

Hand-made. Quality, good. Connecticut seed Ecuadorian
wrapper. Dominican and Honduran filler. Distributed by
Tampa Rico Cigar Co., Tampa, Florida

ESPECIAL	178mm/7 ins x 19.1mm/48
CENTIMO	178mm/7 ins x 17.5mm/44
PETIT CETRO	152mm/6 ins x 16.67mm/42
QUEEN	127mm/5 ins x 19.8mm/50

EL INCOMPARABLE

Hand-made. Quality, superior. Distinctive presentation. Imbued with 25 year old Springbank Single Malt Whisky. Owned by Frenchman, Jean-Claude Marty. Made by Tobacos de Plasencia in Danli. Distributed in USA by Music City Marketing, Nashville.

CHURCHILL★★★★★   203mm/8 ins x 19.1mm/48
Well-made. Attractive, smooth, oily wrapper. Slow, even burning. Smooth. Wonderful complexity. A luxurious smoke for the connoisseur.
TORPEDO   179mm/7 ins x 22.2mm/56
CORONA   152mm/6 ins x 17.5mm/44
ROBUSTO   114mm/4 1/2 ins x 19.8mm/50

FLOR DEL CARIBE

Hand-made. Quality, superior. Available in natural or Maduro wrappers. All Honduran tobacco. Made by Villazon for Arango Cigar.

SOVEREIGN   178mm/7 ins x 20.6mm/52
SUPER CETRO   178mm/7 ins x 18.3mm/46
DUQUES★★★★   140mm/5 1/2 ins x 16.67mm/42
Medium to full-bodied. Hint of cinnamon. Well-made. Ideal to follow meal. Underrated—deserves being discovered. Good value.

GILBERTO OLIVA

Hand-made. Quality, superior. Connecticut shade wrapper. Dominican and Nicaraguan Cuban seed filler. Named after patriarch of old Cuban tobacco family. Made by Gilberto Oliva in Tobacos de Plascencia Factory. Distributed by Oliva Cigar Co., Smyrna, Georgia.

CHURCHILL★★★★   178mm/7 ins x 19.8mm/50
Dark. oily wrapper. Has good ageing potential. Medium-bodied. Smooth. Creamy finish.
VIAJANTE★★★★   152mm/6 ins x 19.8mm/52
Slow, even burning. Smooth. Mild. Good finish.
TORPEDO★★★★★   152mm/6 ins x 19.8mm/52
Well-made. Smooth. Good complexity with touch of sweetness. Buy if you see it. For discerning smoker.
NO 1★★★   165mm/6 1/2 ins x 17.5mm/44
Some disturbing flavours. Spicy.
ROBUSTO★★★★★   140mm/5 1/2 ins x 19.8mm/50
Slow, even burning. Smooth. Well-made. Medium bodied. Spicy. To follow light meal. For discerning smoker.

LA DILIGENCIA

Hand-made. Quality, superior. Connecticut shade wrapper. Dominican binder. Dominican, Honduran and Nicaraguan filler. Distributed by Swisher Intl.

PRESIDENTE	216mm/8 1/2 ins x 20.6mm/52
CHURCHILL	178mm/7 ins x 19.1 mm/48
TORO	152mm/6 ins x 19.8mm/50
GRAN CORONA	152mm/6 ins x 17.5mm/44
ROBUSTO	121mm/4 3/4 ins x 19.8mm/50

LA GIANNA

Hand-made. Quality, superior. Ecuadorian wrapper. Nicaraguan binder and filler. Distributed by Gary Scott Intl., Massachusetts.

CHURCHILL	178mm/7 ins x 19.5mm/49
ROTHCHILD	127mm/5 ins x 19.8mm/50
TORPEDO	152mm/6 ins x 21.4mm/54
NO 2	159mm/6 1/4 ins x 17.5mm/44

ROYAL HONDURAS

Hand-made. Quality, superior. Indonesian wrapper. Dominican binder. Honduran filler. Exclusive to Antillian Cigar Corp., Miami.

CZAR	203mm/8 ins x 19.8mm/50
SOVEREIGN	178mm/7 ins x 19.1mm/48
KINGS (TORPEDO)	156mm/6 1/8 ins x 21.4mm/54
PRINCE	178mm/7 ins x 17.5mm/44
MAJESTY	127mm/5 ins x 19.8mm/50
JOKER	140mm/5 1/2 ins x 16.67mm/42
PRINCESS (PYRAMID)	127mm/5 ins x 15.1mm/38
KNIGHT	152mm/6 ins x 19.8mm/50

VIRTUOSO TORANO

Hand-made. Quality, superior. Ecuadorian wrapper. Nicaraguan binder. Honduran, Nicaraguan and Mexican filler. Owned by Torano Cigars, Miami.

PRESIDENTE	203mm/8 ins x 20.6mm/52
DOUBLE CORONA	152mm/6 ins x 19.8mm/50
ROBUSTO	121mm/4 3/4 ins x 20.6mm/52
LONSDALE	178mm/7 ins x 17.5mm/44
CETROS	152mm/6 ins x 17.1mm/43

VSOP

Hand-made. Quality, superior. Connecticut shade and Sumatra wrapper. Honduran binder and filler. Distributed by CEI Group, Northfield, Illinois.

CHURCHILL	178mm/7 ins x 19.8mm/50
TORPEDO	152mm/6 ins x 21.4mm/54
LONSDALE	165mm/6 1/2 ins x 16.67mm/42
ROBUSTO	127mm/5 ins x 19.8mm/50
CORONA	140mm/5 1/2 ins x 16.67mm/42

INDONESIA

CELESTINO VEGA

Hand-made. Quality, superior. Indonesian wrapper and binder. Filler is blend of tobacco from Indonesia, Dominican Rep. and Pennsylvania. Available in conventional boxes or unique triangle boxes. Distributed by Caribbean Cigar Co., Miami.

CHURCHILL	178mm/7 ins x 19.8mm/50
CUBAN PERFECTO	152mm/6 ins x 19.1mm/48
CUBAN CORONA	165mm/6 1/2 ins x 16.67mm/42
CUBAN PANETELLA	178mm/7 ins x 11.1mm/28
SUPER ROTHCHILD	152mm/6 ins x 19.8mm/50
ROTHCHILD	127mm/5 ins x 19.8mm/50
SENATOR	89mm/3 1/2 ins x 19.1mm/48
PETIT CORONA	121mm/4 3/4 ins x 15.9mm/40
SENORITA	105mm/4 1/8 ins x 12.7mm/32
TESORITA	92mm/3 5/8 ins x 7.9mm/20

MEXICO

BALLENA SUPREMA SAN ANDRES COLLECTION

Hand-made. Quality, superior. Connecticut shade wrapper. Mexican filler and binder. Distributed by pipe tobacco specialists, McClelland Tobacco Co., Kansas City, Missouri.

ESPERANZA	178mm/7 ins x 19.8mm/50
CONCORDIA	178mm/7 ins x 19.1mm/48
PATRON (TORPEDO)	165mm/6 1/2 ins x 20.6mm/52
CORDURA	127mm/5 ins x 20.6mm/52
CORTES****	178mm/7 ins x 16.67mm/42

Burns evenly. Nutty. Hint of harshness.

LA DALMATA

Hand-made. Quality, superior. Sumatra wrapper. Mexican binder and filler. Distributed by Dalmation Cigar Co., New York.

| CHURCHILL | 178mm/7 ins x 19.8mm/50 |
| TORO | 152mm/6 ins x 19.8mm/50 |

| CORONA GRANDE | 152mm/6 ins x 17.5mm/44 |
| ROBUSTO | 127mm/5 ins x 19.8mm/50 |

N I C A R A G U A

CARLIN

Hand-made. Quality, superior. All Nicaraguan tobacco. Distributed by Arango Cigars and Swisher Intl.

GIGANTE	203mm/8 ins x 20.6mm/52
CHURCHILL	178mm/7 ins x 19.1mm/48
TORO	152mm/6 ins x 19.8mm/50
CORONA	140mm/5 1/2 ins x 17.1mm/43
ROBUSTO	121mm/4 3/4 ins x 20.6mm/52

GRAND NICA

Hand-made. Quality, superior. All Nicaraguan tobacco. Distributed by Torano Cigars, Miami.

GIGANTE	203mm/8 ins x 21.4mm/54
CHURCHILL	178mm/7 ins x 20.6mm/52
TORPEDO	165mm/6 1/2 ins x 21.4mm/54
LONSDALE	165mm/6 1/2 ins x 19.8mm/50
TORO	152mm/6 ins x 19.8mm/50
ROBUSTO	127mm/5 ins x 20.6mm/50

HUGO CASSAR SIGNATURE SERIES

Hand-made. Quality, superior. Indonesian wrapper. Nicaraguan binder and filler. Owned by Hugo Cassar Cigars, Moorpark, California.

GIANT	203mm/8 ins x 21.4mm/54
CHURCHILL	178mm/7 ins x 19.1mm/48
TORO	152mm/6 ins x 19.8mm/50
ROBUSTO	121mm/4 3/4 ins x 20.6mm/52
LONSDALE	171mm/6 3/4 ins x 17.5mm/44
CORONA	140mm/5 1/2 ins x 16.67mm/42

SEBASTIAN RESERVA

Hand-made. Quality, superior. Connecticut, Sumatra and Cuban seed wrapper. Nicaraguan binder and filler. Distributed by Armenter Cigar Holding, New York.

NO 1	216mm/8 1/2 ins x 20.6mm/52
NO 2	203mm/8 ins x 21.4mm/54
NO 3	191mm/7 1/2 ins x 19.8mm/50
NO 4	178mm/7 ins x 21.4mm/54
NO 5	175mm/6 7/8 ins x 19.1mm/48
NO 6	165mm/6 1/2 ins x 17.5mm/44

NO 7	152mm/6 ins x 16.1mm/41
NO 8	143mm/5 5/8 ins x 19.1mm/48
NO 9	140mm/5 1/2 ins x 20.6mm/52
NO 10	114mm/4 1/2 ins 20.6mm/52

VEGAS GRAN RESERVA

Hand-made. Quality, superior. Colorado Sumatra wrapper. Nicaraguan binder and filler. Distributed by Andre Suarez Ltd., Miami Beach.

CHURCHILL	178mm/7 ins x 20.6mm/52
PIRAMIDE	165mm/6 1/2 ins x 18.3mm/46
DOUBLE CORONA	152mm/6 ins x 19.1mm/48
PANETELA	152mm/6 ins x 15.1mm/38
CORONA	140mm/5 1/2 ins x 17.5mm/44
ROBUSTO	127mm/5 ins x 20.6mm/50

SOUTH AFRICA

SERENGETI

Hand-made. Quality: Superior. Dry cigar. Leaf from Indonesia. Established in 1995 in Roodepoort, in Province of Gauteng, near Johannesburg, by Tom and wife, Jon, van der Marck, Hollanders, new residents in South Africa. He has 32 years experience as tobacco buyer and blender with Dutch, Swiss, German, and American companies. Company previously called Gauteng Cigar Co.

Rolled in tradition that made Holland famous in 1940s and 1950s, now all but disappeared. This is a range for connoisseur of dry cigars.

CORONA KUDU***** 140mm/5 1/2 ins x 15.8mm/40
Mild to medium-bodied. Good balance, flavour and finish. Elegant. Well-made.
ROBUSTO GRANDE RHINO*****
165mm/6 1/2 ins x 19.5mm/49
Mild to medium-bodied. Good balance, flavour and finish. Elegant. Well-made. Good daytime smoke.
CORONA BUSHBUCK*****
140mm/5 1/2 ins x 15.8mm/40
Medium-bodied. Good flavours with coffee undertones. Long creamy finish. Well-made.
ROBUSTO GRANDE BUFFALO*****
104 mm/4 1/8 ins x 15.8mm/40
Medium-bodied. Good flavours with coffee undertones. Long creamy finish. Well-made. Good daytime smoke. Wrappers from Java.

UNITED STATES OF AMERICA

COJIMAR by DON RENE DE CUBA

Hand-made. Quality, superior. Connecticut shade wrapper. Dominican Piloto Cuban seed filler and binder. Named after the small Cuban fishing village that inspired Hemingway's classic novel, *The Old Man and the Sea*. Brand established March 1996. Owned and distributed by The Cigar Connection, Miami Beach.

PRESIDENTE	203mm/8 ins x19.8mm/50
TORPEDO	152mm/6 ins x 21.4mm/54
LAGUITO	171mm/6 3/4 ins x 15.1mm/38
CORTADITOS****	171mm/6 3/4 ins x 15.1mm/38

Wrapper features two attractive shades of both maduro and Colorado claro in barber pole construction that adds additional dimension of flavour. Mild. Well-made. For discerning smoker.

SENORITAS	127mm/5 ins x 11.9mm/30
CORONITA	171mm/6 3/4 ins x 17.5mm/44
TORO	40mm/5 1/2 ins x 19.84mm/50

DOMINO PARK

Hand-made. Quality, superior. Ecuadorian wrapper and binder. Nicaraguan and Dominican filler. Made by Caribbean Cigar Co., Miami.

PRESIDENTE	03mm/8 ins x 20.6mm/52
CHURCHILL	178mm/7 ins x 19.8mm/50
CORONA	165mm/6 1/2 ins x 16.67mm/42
ROBUSTO LARGA	152mm/6 ins x 19.8mm/50
ROBUSTO	127mm/5 ins x 19.8mm/50

DON RENE

Hand-made. Quality, good. Dominican and Nicaraguan filler. Honduran binder. Ecuadorian wrapper. Made by Cigar Connection, Miami Beach.

PRESIDENTE	216mm/8 1/2 ins x 19.8mm/50
CHURCHILL	184mm/7 1/4 ins x 19.8mm/50
TORPEDO	165mm/6 1/2 ins x 21.4mm/54
LANCERO	178mm/7 ins x 15.1mm/38
CORONA	165mm/6 1/2 ins x 17.5mm/44
TORO	140mm/5 1/2 ins x 18.3mm/46
CORONITA	140mm/5 1/2 ins x 16.67mm/42
ROBUSTO***	140mm/5 1/2 ins x 19.8mm/50

Good draw. Slow, even burning. Mild to medium strength with good flavour. Every-day smoke. Ideal for beginners.

SENORITAS	127mm/5 ins x 11.9mm/30

EL IMPERIO CUBANO

Hand-made. Quality, good. Ecuadorian wrapper. Made by Antillian Cigar Corp., Miami.

TORPEDO****	159mm/6 1/4 ins x 21.4mm/54

Well-made. Slow, even burning. Medium-bodied.

CHURCHILL	171mm/6 3/4 ins x 19.1mm/48
TORO	152mm/6 ins x 19.8mm/50
ROBUSTO	127mm/5 ins x 19.8mm/50
LONSDALE	171mm/6 3/4 ins x 17.1mm/43
CORONA	140mm/5 1/2 ins x 17.1mm/43

FLOR DE FLOREZ

Hand-made. Quality, superior. Honduran Cuban seed filler and binder. Connecticut shade wrapper. Good value. Named after family patriarch, Carlos Florez, who operated a tobacco plantation in pre-Castro Cuba. Made by Flor de Florez Dist., Inc., Hoboken, New Jersey.

PRESIDENTE	178mm/7 ins x 19.5mm/49
CETROS	165mm/6 1/2 ins x 17.5mm/44
CORONA	152mm/6 ins x 19.5mm/49
ROTHSCHILD	124mm/4 7/8 ins x 18.7mm/47
BLUNT	127mm/5 ins x 16.67mm/42

FLOR DE FLOREZ CABINET SELECTION

Hand-made. Quality, superior. Nicaraguan Cuban filler and binder. Ecuadorian wrapper. Made by Flor de Florez Dist., Inc., Hoboken, New Jersey.

GIGANTE*****	191mm/7 1/2 ins x 19.5mm/49

Well-made. Slow, even burning. Dark, oily wrapper. Full-bodied with complex, spicy flavours. To follow meal for connoisseur.

SIR WINSTON	178mm/7 ins x 18.7mm/47
GRAN PANATELA*****	178mm/7 ins x 15.1mm/38

Dark, oily wrapper. Well-made. Good draw. Surprisingly good burning for this size. Medium-bodied. Earthy, spicy flavour. Good balance and long finish. Pleasant aroma. Is worth the time. For the connoisseur.

BELICOSO	165mm/6 1/2 ins x 20.6mm/52
FLOREZ-FLOREZ	140mm/5 1/2 ins x 18.3mm/46
CORONITAS	127mm/5 ins x 16.67mm/42
ROBUSTO	127mm/5 ins x 19.8mm/50

FREE CUBA

Hand-made. Quality, superior. Java wrapper. Nicaraguan binder. Cuban seed. Dominican filler. Made by Caribbean Cigar Co., Miami.

PERFECTO	165mm/6 1/2 ins x 19.1mm/48
TORPEDO	165mm/6 1/2 ins x 21.4mm/54
CHURCHILL	184mm/7 1/4 ins x 19.8mm/50
DOUBLE CORONA	191mm/7 1/2 ins x 18.3mm/46
CORONA	165mm/6 1/2 ins x 16.67mm/42
ROBUSTO LARGO	152mm/6 ins x 19.8mm/50
ROBUSTO	127mm/5 ins x 19.8mm/50
MINIATURE	127mm/5 ins x 14.3mm/36

HAVANA SUNRISE

Hand-made. Quality, superior. Medium to full bodied. Good consistent construction throughout range. Made by Havana Sunrise Cigar Co., Miami.

PRESIDENTE	203mm/8 ins x 20.6mm/52
CHURCHILL	190mm/7 1/2 ins x 19.84mm/50
LANCERO	190mm/7 1/2 ins x 15.08mm/38
PYRAMID	178mm/7 ins x 23.8mm/60
HAVANA*****	171mm/6 3/4 ins x 18.3mm/46

Well-made. Good draw. Slow, even burning. Good balance between strength and flavour. Complex flavours. Appreciate this cigar if you can get it. For the connoisseur.

EMPERADOR	159mm/6 1/4 ins x 21.4mm/54
DOUBLE CORONA	152mm/6 ins x 19.1mm/48
CORONA	152mm/6 ins x 17.5mm/44
TORPEDO*****	152mm/6 ins x 21.4mm/54

Dark, oily wrapper. Good draw. Slow, even burning. Cool. Well-made. Rich flavour with good complexity. Good finish. Ideal after-dinner cigar for the connoisseur.

ROBUSTO	127mm/5 ins x 19.84mm/50
PANETELA-CACHE	127mm/5 ins x 11.1mm/28

INDIAN TABAC

Hand-made. Quality, good. Ecuadorian Sumatra wrapper. Mexican binder. Honduran and Nicaraguan filler. Made by Indian Tabac.

CHIEF	191mm/7 1/2 ins x 20.6mm/52
BUFFALO*****	152mm/6 ins x 20.6mm/52

Even burning. Cool. Medium strength. Well balanced. Good finish. A cigar that will bring happiness even in the darkest circumstance. Appreciate it if you can get it. Scarce.

WARRIOR	152mm/6 ins x 16.67mm/42
TEEPEE (PYRAMID)	152mm/6 ins x 20.6mm/52
BOXER	114mm/4 1/2 ins x 19.8mm/50
ARROW	140mm/5 1/2 ins x 13.5mm/34

ISLAND AMARETTO

Hand-made. Quality, good. Amaretto flavoured. Medium filler. Made by Caribbean Cigar Co., Miami.

GRAN BELLA	178mm/7 ins x 18.3mm/46
BELLISSIMA	127mm/5 ins x 15.1mm/38

MAESTRO

Hand-made. Quality, good. All have maduro wrappers. Mexican and Honduran filler. Factory established 1994. Made by Cuban Cigar Factory, San Diego, California.

NO 1	152mm/6 ins x 21.4mm/54
NO 2	165mm/6 1/2 ins x 20.2mm/50
NO 3	121mm/4 3/4 ins x 20.6mm/52

MORRO CASTLE

Hand-made. Quality, superior. Ecuadorian wrapper. Nicaraguan binder and filler. Made by Caribbean Cigar Co., Miami.

PERFECTO	165mm/6 1/2 ins x 19.1mm/48
TORPEDO	165mm/6 1/2 ins x 21.4mm/54
CHURCHILL	184mm/7 1/4 ins x 19.8mm/50
DOUBLE CORONA	191mm/7 1/2 ins x 18.3mm/46
CORONA	165mm/6 1/2 ins x 16.67mm/42
ROBUSTO LARGO	152mm/6 ins x 19.8mm/50
ROBUSTO	127mm/5 ins x 19.8mm/50
MINIATURE	127mm/5 ins x 14.3mm/36

REY DEL MAR

Hand-made. Quality, superior. Connecticut shade and maduro wrapper. Dominican filler. Owned by Caribbean Cigar Factory, Miami.

CHURCHILL	178mm/7 ins x 19.1mm/48
PIRAMIDES	165mm/6 1/2 ins x 17.5mm/44
PETIT CORONA	152mm/6 ins x 15.1mm/38
CORONA	140mm/5 1/2 ins x 17.1mm/43
ROBUSTO	114mm/4 1/2 ins x 20.6mm/52

RUM RUNNER

Hand-made. Quality, good. Rum flavoured. Medium filler. Made by Caribbean Cigar Co., Miami.

PIRATE	178mm/7 ins x 18.3mm/46
BUCCANEER	140mm/5 1/2 ins x 17.5mm/44
WENCH	127mm/5 ins x 15.1mm/38

TRADITIONALES

Hand-made. Quality, good. Connecticut shade wrapper.

Mexican and Honduran filler. Factory established 1994.
Made by Cuban Cigar Factory, San Diego, California.

PRESIDENTE	197mm/7 3/4 ins x 20.6mm/52
CUBAN ROUND LARGA	184mm/7 1/4 ins x 20.2mm/50
TORPEDO	178mm/7 ins x 20.2mm/50
EL CUBANO	171mm/6 3/4 ins x 17.5mm/44
HAVANA	152mm/6 ins x 18.3mm/46
CORONA	146mm/5 3/4 ins x 16.67mm/42
MONTECRISTO	140mm/5 1/2 ins x 20.6mm/52
ROBUSTO	127mm/5 ins x 20.2mm/50

WEST INDIES VANILLA

Hand-made. Quality, good. Vanilla flavoured. Medium
filler. Made by Caribbean Cigar Co., Miami.

CARMELLA	178mm/7 ins x 18.3mm/46
CARMELITA	127mm/5 ins x 15.1mm/38

V E N E Z U E L A

SABANA

Hand-made. Quality, good. Ecuadorian wrapper.
Venezuelan filler and binder. Distributed in USA by
Inversione Housto de America, Houston.

NO 3	146mm/5 3/4 ins x 18.3mm/46
NO 2	140mm/5 1/2 ins x 16.67mm/42
NO 1	40mm/5 1/2 ins x 15.1mm/38
ESPECIAL	114mm/4 1/2 ins x 15.9mm/40

BRAZIL

CANORENO No 20**
Well-made. Slow, even burning. Medium bodied, complex with hint of sweetness. Smooth. An elegant daytime smoke for discerning smoker.

DON PEPE Double Corona**
Unusual silky, Colorado wrapper for Brazilian cigar. Good draw. Slow even burning. Mild to medium bodied. Well-made.

CANARY ISLANDS

DUNHILL Corona Grandes*
Good draw. Well-made. Slow, even burning. Light to medium bodied. One dimensional. Ideal for beginner or early morning smoke for experienced smoker.

COSTA RICA

BAHIA Robusto***
Good draw. Slow, even burning. Full bodied with range of spicy, peppery flavours. Well-made. A quality, medium strength cigar.

BAHIA No 4**
Firm draw. Slow, even burning. Well-made. Medium bodied with good complex flavours.

TROYA No 81**
Easy draw, burns a little hot. Smooth. Medium to full bodied. Daytime smoke for beginners and experienced smokers alike.

DOMINICAN REPUBLIC

AGUILA Brevas 46**
Good, consistent construction. Cool. Slow, even burning. Light bodied. Touch of sweetness. Value for money.

AGUILA Petit Gordo**
Well-made. Good draw, slow, even burning. Flavourful. Not for the beginner.

ASHTON 8-9-8**
Well-made. Good draw, slow, even burning. Medium to strong, with rich flavour and touch of sweetness. Smooth,

good finish. A daytime smoke for beginners and experienced smokers alike. Good value.

AVO "XO" Intermezzo★★★★★
Beautifully-made with oily wrapper. Smooth. Medium bodied with attractive integrated flavours. A cigar to be appreciated.

BUTERA ROYAL VINTAGE Cedro Fina★★★★
The finely made cap adds to an already excellently made cigar. The flavour does not match the construction. Short finish. Good morning cigar to start the day.

BUTERA ROYAL VINTAGE Dorado 652★★★★★
Good, consistent construction. Good draw. Even burn. Smooth. Complex, full flavoured. Long finish. For the connoisseur.

CARLOS TORANO Carlos V★★★★
Well-made. Sometimes burns unevenly. Medium bodied. Spicy and peppery. Long finish.

CARRINGTON No 3★★★★
Slow, even burning. Smooth. Medium strength. Discreet flavours. Well-made for this size. Good daytime smoke. Ideal for beginners.

DIAMOND CROWN Robusto No 2★★★★★
Attractive wrapper. Good, consistent construction. Good draw. Slow, even-burning. Smooth. A wonderful cigar. For the connoisseur.

DIAMOND CROWN Robusto No 5★★★★★
Attractive wrapper. Wonderful draw. Mild with full flavours. Hint of spice and caramel. Smooth. A delight to smoke.

DOMINICAN ORIGINAL Fat Tub★★★★
Not just for laughs. It is worth smoking. Easy draw, cool, slow burning. Mild.

DON MARCOS Monarch★★★★★
Well-made. Cool, even burning. Medium to full bodied strength with loads of flavour. A cigar that can be appreciated.

FONSECA 2-2★★★★★
Extremely well-made. Slow, even burning. Mild, with creamy flavours. A pleasant, quick, daytime smoke. For discerning smoker.

FONSECA 7-9-8★★★★
Well-made, consistent construction. Smooth. Even-burning. A light cigar. Smoke for beginner.

FONSECA 8-9-8★★★★★
Firm, but good draw. Slow, even-burning. Mild, but flavours build up as cigar is smoked. Long finish. For discerning smoker.

H. UPMANN Coronas Brevas★★★
Well-made. Good draw and burning qualities. Bland.

H. UPMANN Demi Tasse★★★
Good draw. Slow, even burning. Medium bodied with robust flavours. Daytime smoke.

H. UPMANN Monarch★★★★★
Good draw. Slow, even burning. Smooth. Rich, creamy flavours. Good balance between strength and flavour. Good consistent construction.

H. UPMANN Petit Corona★★★
Easy draw. Flavours increase as cigar smoked. Consistent construction. Value for money.

HUGO CASSAR DIAMOND SELECTION Corona★★★★
Slow, even burning. Peppery. Full bodied. To follow a meal.

JOSE MARTI Jose Marti★★★
Well-made. Rich, spicy flavours. Becomes slightly bitter.

JOSE MARTI Creme★★★★
Medium bodied. Tones of wet hay. Even burn.

JOSE MARTI Robusto★★★★
Well-made. Good draw. Slow, even burning. Mild. Good balance. Daytime smoke.

JUAN CLEMENTE Corona★★★★★
Extremely well-made and consistent. Wonderful draw. Slow, even burning. Cool. Good balance. Lovely flavours. Daytime smoke for discerning smoker.

JUAN CLEMENTE Demi-Corona★★★★
Well-made with good draw. Slow, even burning. Has rich flavours, unusual for this size.

LA AURORA Robusto★★★★
Easy draw. Cool burn. Medium bodied. Good flavour with caramel finish. (New size).

LA DIVA Robusto★★★★★
Medium bodied. Lots of flavour with caramel undertones. Well-made. Good draw. Slow, even burning. Smooth. After dinner cigar for discerning smoker.

LAMB'S CLUB Churchill★★★
Full bodied. Spicy and earthy.

LAMB'S CLUB Corona Extra★★★
Good draw. Even burn. Full bodied, spicy.

LEON JIMENES No 2★★★★
Good draw. Smooth. Full bodied with complex flavours.

LICENCIADOS Excellentes★★★★
Smooth. Slow, even-burning. Full flavoured. Daytime smoke for discerning smoker.

LICENCIADOS Wavell★★★★
Good draw. Mild to medium bodied with pleasant flavours. Daytime smoke.

LOS LIBERTADORES Insurrectos★★★★
Good, consistent construction. Spicy, with touch of sweetness. Mild, but flavourful. Daytime smoke.

MATCH PLAY Cypress★★★★
Firm draw. Cool. Medium bodied. Touch of sweetness.

MATCH PLAY Prestwick★★★★★
Fine, dark, oily wrapper. Good, consistent construction. Smooth. Fruity with hint of sweetness. For connoisseur.

MATCH PLAY Troon★★★★
A well-made pyramid. Burns cool and evenly. Good balance and finish. Mild, pleasant, daytime smoke.

MATCH PLAY Turnberry★★★★★
Well-made. Attractive, oily wrapper. Good draw. For discerning smoker.

MONTERO PRESIDENTE★★★★
Good, consistent construction. Excellent draw. Smooth. Slow, even burning. Mild, but with loads of flavour. Good finish. Ideal for beginner or casual smoker.

NAT SHERMAN EXCHANGE SELECTION Academy No 2★★★★
Good, consistent construction. Good draw. Slow, even burning. Cool, light bodied. Daytime smoke.

NAT SHERMAN LANDMARK SELECTION Hampshire★★★★★
Attractive, dark, oily wrapper. Well-made. Good draw. Slow, even burning. Smooth. Good balance between strength and flavour. Unusually powerful cigar for this size. An after-dinner cigar for discerning smoker.

OPUS X (Fuente Fuente Opus X) Petit Lancero★★★★
Well-made. Medium bodied. Full, spicy flavour. Short finish.

OPUS X Reserva D'Chateau★★★★★
Beautiful, oily wrapper. Medium bodied. Good flavour.

Spicy with touch of sweetness. To follow a meal. This cigar is an occasion!

OPUS X (Fuente Fuente Opus X) Robusto★★★★★
Dark, oily wrapper. Extremely well-made. Good draw. Slow, even burning. Smooth. Full bodied, creamy. Probably the best Dominican robusto. For a special occasion for the connoisseur.

P & K GUARDSMEN No 2★★★
Inconsistent construction. Lots of flavour with honeyed undertones. Light to medium bodied. Value for money.

PARTAGAS No 10★★★★★
Well-made. Good draw. Slow, even burning. Complex, full flavours. Ideal after dinner cigar. (Re-evaluation—see page 239.)

PETERSON Churchill★★★★
Mild to medium bodied. Discreet flavours. Daytime smoke.

PETERSON Corona★★★★
Good draw. Mild strength, but lots of complex flavours. Ideal for beginner.

PETERSON Petit Corona★★★
Well-made with attractive wrapper. Slow, even-burning with subtle flavours. Morning smoke.

PLEIADES PLUTTON★★★★★
Good, consistent construction. Good draw. Cool. Floral aromas. Good after dinner cigar.

PRIMO DEL REY Seleccion No 2★★★★
Firm draw. Good burning qualities. Mild to medium bodied. Good balance and finish. Daytime smoke.

PRIVATE Stock No 8★★★★
Acceptable draw. Slow, even burning. Full bodied. Good flavour with touch of spice. For the connoisseur.

ROMEO Y JULIETA Vintage III★★★★★
Excellent, consistent construction. Good draw. Slow, even burning. Complex, full flavours with cedar undertones. Ideal to smoke with an espresso. For the discerning smoker.

ROYAL JAMAICA Petit Corona★★★
Medium bodied with earthy flavours. Ideal for the beginner and value for money. Daytime smoke.

SAVINELLI EXTREMELY LIMITED RESERVE No 3 Lonsdale★★★★
Beautiful, oily wrapper. Medium bodied, spicy. Good draw.

SAVINELLI EXTREMELY LIMITED RESERVE
No 6 Robusto★★★★★
Fine Colorado wrapper. Extremely good, consistent construction. Draws well. Slow, even burning. Fairly mild, but has loads of spicy flavours. A cigar you would wish would go on forever. Difficult to get, so treasure the moment when you smoke it.

TROYO No 27 Corona★★★★
Good, Consistent Construction. Easy draw. Mild to medium bodied. Good finish. Complex flavours.

HONDURAS

ASTRAL Besos★★★★
Attractive wrapper. Full bodied. Robust. Not for beginner.

ASTRAL Perfeccion★★★★
Well-made. Medium bodied. Smooth. Good balance.

BACCARAT Petit Corona★★★★
Good draw. Cinnamon and coffee undertones. Good balance. Fine finish. Ideal daytime smoke for beginner and experienced smoker alike. Value for money.

BACCARAT Polo★★
Inconsistent construction. Mild. Lacks punch.

BANCES Brevas★★★★
Good, consistent construction. Medium bodied. A pleasant smoke. Value for money.

BANCES Corona-Immensas★★★★
Good draw, even burning. Medium bodied. Spicy. Daytime smoke.

BANCES Presidents★★★★★
Well-made. Good draw. Full flavour. Hint of cinnamon and coffee. For experienced and casual smoker alike. Value for money.

BELINDA Breva Conserva★★★★
Good draw. Slow, even burning. Medium bodied, spicy with treacle undertones. Good finish. Value for money.

BELINDA Cabinet★★★★
Good, consistent construction and draw. Slow, even burning. Smooth. Cinnamon and coffee undertones. Extremely good value for money.

C.A.O. Churchill★★★★★
Well-made. Even burning. Flavours improve all the time. Good balance between strength and flavour. Medium

strength. The size and quality make this cigar ideal for a special occasion.

C.A.O. Corona★★★★
Good draw. Slow, even burning. Medium bodied. Touch of cinnamon. Good finish.

C.A.O. Corona Gorda★★★★★
Dark, oily wrapper. Good, consistent construction. Slow, even burning. Smooth. Medium bodied. Good balance between strength and flavour. For discerning smoker.

C.A.O. Petit Corona★★★
Attractive, oily wrapper. Slow, even burning. Full, nutty flavour. Good finish. Ideal for beginner.

C.A.O. Robusto★★★★
Good draw. Medium strength. Full flavour with nutty undertones. Smooth. To follow a meal for discerning smoker.

C.A.O. Triangulare★★★★
Good draw. Slow, even burning. Smooth. Full bodied with spicy, full flavours. For beginner and experienced smoker.

CAMACHO Nacionales★★★
Draws and burns well. Cinnamon and caramel flavours. Good everyday smoke. Value for money.

CAMORRA IMPORTED LIMITED RESERVE Capri★★
Inconsistent construction. Medium bodied. Caramel undertones. Harsh.

CAMORRA IMPORTED LIMITED RESERVE Genova★★★
Inconsistent draw. Fairly strong, robust. Full flavours. Not for beginner.

CAMORRA IMPORTED LIMITED RESERVE Roma★★★★
Mild with creamy, nutty undertones. Daytime smoke. Ideal for casual smoker.

CERVANTES Senadores★★★
Medium strength. An everyday smoke. Good value.

CUBA ALIADOS Rothchild★★★
Burns unevenly. Lacks punch. A boring smoke. An inexpensive cigar.

DON LINO Panetelas★★
Hard draw. Harsh, slightly bitter.

DON LINO Peticetro★★★★
Well-made. Mild with character. Good balance. Ideal for beginner.

DON LINO Rothchild★★★★
Dark, oily maduro wrapper. Well-made. Full flavours with hint of chocolate and caramel. After-dinner cigar for connoisseur.

DON LINO ORO Toro★★★
Good draw. Slow, even burning. Medium bodied. Hint of caramel. Daytime smoke.

DON TOMAS Epicures★★★★★
Good draw. Slow, even burning. Smooth. Full, spicy flavours. Big punch for a small cigar.

EL REY DEL MUNDO Corona★★★★★
Good, consistent construction. Good draw. Rich flavours with long finish. Good complexity.

EL REY DEL MUNDO Originale★★★★★
Medium strength. Rich, full flavour with touch of cinnamon. Smooth. Well-made.

EL REY DEL MUNDO Rectangulare★★★★
Good, consistent construction. Slow, even burning. Medium strength with full, complex flavours.

EVELIO Corona★★★★
Fairly strong. Loads of flavour. Smooth. Good finish.

EVELIO Double Corona★★★★★
Medium strength. Full bodied, spicy with creamy finish. Well-made. To follow meal or with port or cognac.

EVELIO Robusto★★★★★
Well-made. Good draw. Slow, even burning. Good balance. Medium bodied. Spicy. For discerning smoker.

EVELIO Robusto Larga★★★★★
Good, consistent construction. Slow, even burning. Good balance and finish. Medium to full bodied. Worth the time it takes.

EVELIO Torpedo★★★★★
An attractive, well-made cigar. Good balance and finish. Fairly mild, subtle. For discerning smoker.

F.D. GRAVE & SON Churchill★★★★
Good draw. Slow, even burning. Full, earthy flavours.

F.D. GRAVE & SON Corona Grande★★★★
Dark, oily wrapper. Good draw. Burns unevenly. Rich, full flavour. Robust.

F.D. GRAVE & SON Lonsdale★★★★
Good draw. Slow, even burning. Full, earthy flavours. The extra ring gauge improves this cigar.

FELIPE GREGORIO Belicoso (torpedo)★★★★
Dark, oily wrapper. Medium strength. Rich, full, complex flavours with coffee and caramel undertones.

FELIPE GREGORIO Sereno★★★★
Slow, even burning. Medium bodied. If reasonably aged, a satisfying smoke.

FLOR DE PALICIO No 1★★★★
Medium strength with complex flavours. Good finish. Value for money.

HABANA GOLD Corona★★★★
Good draw. Slow, even burning. Smooth. Mild. Good finish. Early morning smoke.

HABANA GOLD Double Corona★★★
Medium bodied with rich, spicy flavours. Smooth. Cool smoke.

HABANA GOLD Presidente★★★★
Hard draw. Full earthy flavours. Daytime smoke, but will take a lot of time. Ideal for beginners to this size.

LAS CABRILLAS Cortez★★★
Good draw. Mild.

LAS CABRILLAS Magellan★★★★
Good draw and consistent construction. Even burning. Medium bodied. Dry finish. Everyday smoke.

LA DILIGENCIA Gran Corona★★★
Well-made. Consistent construction. Mild, touch of pepper. Daytime smoke.

LA FONTANA VINTAGE Da Vinci★★★
Good draw. Well-made. Mild cigar. Creamy. Touch of sweetness.

LA NATIVE Cetros★★★
Indifferent construction. Medium strength. Full flavour with chocolate and cinnamon undertones.

LA NATIVE Moderno★★★
Good, consistent construction. Uncomplicated, medium flavours. Because of price, ideal for everyday smoking.

LEMPIRA Churchills★★★★
Good draw. Well-made. Slow, even burning. Spicy. Good balance.

MAYA Churchills★★★★
Mild with good flavour. Ideal for beginner or casual smoker. Value for money.

MAYA Coronas★★★★
Medium strength with tons of flavour. Cool. Good finish. Ideal to smoke with cognac or scotch.

NESTOR VINTAGE 454★★★★
Medium bodied. Good draw. Slow, even burning. Doesn't have complexity one would expect from this ring gauge.

NESTOR VINTAGE 654★★★★★
Oily wrapper. Medium strength with lots of flavour. Good balance. For discerning smoker. Ideal for ageing.

NESTOR VINTAGE 747★★★★
Slow, even burning. Smooth. Creamy, with touch of cinnamon. Good finish.

NORDING Corona★★★
Medium strength and flavour. Smooth. Good finish.

PETRUS TABACAGE 89 Double Corona★★★★★
Maduro. Black, oily wrapper. Well-made. Slow, even burn. Smooth. Rich, earthy flavours. Robust. A big smoke.

PETRUS TABACAGE 89 Palma Fina★★★★
Firm draw, but acceptable. Slow, even burning. Robust, earthy flavour. Has "punch" for a thin cigar.

PUNCH Cafe Royal★★★★★
Well-made. Good balance. Medium bodied. Hint of cinnamon on finish. For discerning beginner and experienced smoker alike.

PUNCH Rothschilds★★★
Loose construction. Burns hot, creating harshness. Not in same class as others evaluated in this range.

PUNCH DE LUXE Coronas★★★★
Good draw. Medium strength, full, rich flavours. Touch of sweetness. Cinnamon undertones. For discerning smoker.

PUNCH GRAN CRU Monarcas (tube)★★★★
Good, consistent construction. Slow, even burning. Good complexity. Ideal for beginner and experienced smoker alike.

PUNCH GRAN CRU Robustos★★★★
Well-made. Good balance. Touch of cinnamon. Lacks complexity for this ring gauge.

PUROS INDIOS Churchill Especial★★★★
Good draw. Slow, even burning. Smooth. Full bodied. Good balance. To follow meal. Not for beginner.

PUROS INDIOS Figurin★★★
Well-made. Burns well. Don't expect much from this cigar. You could be in for a long, boring smoke. Lacks punch for cigar of this size. A cigar for showing, not smoking.

PUROS INDIOS Nacionales★★★★★
Good, consistent construction. Good balance between strength and flavour. Creamy. For discerning smoker.

PUROS INDIOS Petit Perla★★★★★
Good draw. Slow, even burning. Well-made. Surprising flavour for a small cigar. Elegant. Good finish.

PUROS INDIOS Rothschild★★★★★
Attractive, oily wrapper. Good draw. Slow, even burning. Full bodied. Spicy. To follow meal.

SANTA ROSA Regulares★★★★
Don't judge this cigar too quickly. Flavour soon builds up with good complexity. For everyday smoking. Good value for money.

TESOROS DE COPAN Corona★★★
Medium bodied. Full flavour. Good draw. Will benefit with ageing.

THOMAS HINDS HONDURAN SELECTION Churchill★★★★★
Slow, even burning. Well-made. Rich, spicy flavour. Good finish. For discerning smoker.

THOMAS HINDS HONDURAN SELECTION Corona★★★
Earthy, wet hay flavours. Attractive aroma. Ideal for beginner.

THOMAS HINDS HONDURAN SELECTION Presidente★★★★
Medium bodied. Smooth. Spicy with creamy finish.

THOMAS HINDS HONDURAN SELECTION Royal Corona★★★★★
Firm, but good draw. Well-made. Medium strength. Full, complex flavours. Ideal for beginner and experienced smoker.

THOMAS HINDS HONDURAN SELECTION Torpedo★★★
Easy draw. Burns unevenly. Medium bodied. Earthy with cinnamon undertones. Daytime smoke.

V CENTENNIAL Cetros★★★★★
Well-made. Good draw. Slow, even burning. Medium strength. Lots of spicy, creamy flavours. For discerning smoker.

V CENTENNIAL Churchills★★★★
Attractive wrapper. Well-made. Spicy, hint of cinnamon. Smooth. Good finish.

V CENTENNIAL Numero 1★★★★★
Good draw. Slow, even burning. Good balance between strength and complex flavours.

VIRTUOSO TORANO Double Corona★★★★★
Well-made. Good smoking qualities and balance between strength and flavour. Wonderful after-dinner cigar.

VIRTUOSO TORANO Presidente★★★★
Good, consistent construction. Slow, even burning. Smooth. Good balance between strength and flavour. Touch of caramel and cinnamon. Fine ending to good meal.

VIRTUOSO TORANO Robusto★★★★★
Good consistent construction. Has complexity with nutty undertones. Long finish. Good introduction to this size for beginner.

ZINO Connoisseur No 100★★★★
Firm draw. Slow, even burning. Mild to medium bodied. Complex flavours develop. Good finish. For discerning smoker.

ZINO Mouton Cadet No 1★★★★★
Good, consistent construction. Good complexity. Spicy. Good balance. Elegant.

ZINO Mouton Cadet No 6★★★★★
A well-made cigar. Good burning qualities. Smooth, creamy. Good finish. For discerning smoker.

ZINO Veritas★★★★★
Silky, oily wrapper. Well-made. Medium bodied. Good flavour with chocolate undertones. Good finish. For discerning smoker.

M E X I C O

CRUZ REAL No 2★★★★
Even burn. Spicy. Medium bodied. Daytime smoke.

HUGO CASSAR PRIVATE COLLECTION Robusto★★★★
Good draw. Spicy. Uncharacteristically strong for a Mexican cigar. After-dinner smoke.

N I C A R A G U A

CASA DE NICARAGUA Gigante★★★★
Full, complex flavours, hint of caramel. Long finish. Medium strength.

CASA DE NICARAGUA Petit Corona★★★★
Good draw. Spicy, full flavour. Medium strength. A good example of this size. Ideal for beginner and experienced smoker. Good value.

JOYA DE NICARAGUA No 6★★★★
Good draw. Slow, even burning. Mild and smooth. Good morning smoke for experienced smoker. Ideal for beginner. Value for money.

JOYA DE NICARAGUA Presidente★★★★★
Lovely draw. Slow, even burning. Smooth. Full bodied, with tons of spicy flavour. Hint of sweetness. To follow meal. Well-made.

PANAMA

JOSE LLOPIS No 4★★★★
Smooth, silky Connecticut wrapper. Good draw. Slow, even burning. Smooth. Complex, creamy flavours. Well-made. Ideal for beginner and experienced smoker alike.

PHILIPPINES

CALIXTO LOPEZ Palma Royale★★★★★
Good, consistent construction. Good draw. Slow, even burning. Medium to full bodied, robust, with range of spicy flavours. Lots of complexity. An excellent cigar. Exceedingly good value. Buy when you can.

DOUBLE HAPPINESS Bliss★★★
Unique, twisted bun on tuck end (foot). Uneven burn. Subtle, medium bodied. For the beginner. A good-looking cigar, but construction not up to its looks.

DOUBLE HAPPINESS Rapture★★★★
Good draw. Consistent, good construction. Slow, even burning. Rich, earthy flavours. Not for the beginner.

FIGHTING COCK Texas Red (square)★★★
Medium bodied. Peppery with touch of sweetness. Not for beginners.

FLOR DE MANILA Cetro Largo★★★
Medium bodied. Spicy and peppery.

UNITED STATES OF AMERICA

CALLE OCHO Gordito Largo★★★★★
Attractive, oily wrapper. Good draw. Slow, even burning. Consistent construction. Light to medium strength with loads of flavour. Good complexity. For discerning smoker.

HAVANA CLASSICO Malelcon★★★★★
Appealing, oily wrapper. Good, consistent construction. Easy draw. Slow, even burning. Smooth. Medium strength with lots of complex flavours. Good balance.

It will take time, but will be worth it. For discerning smoker.

LA PLATA MADUROS Magnificos★★★★
Rich, full flavour with touch of sweetness. For the bold, experienced smoker.

ROLANDO NUMERO No 2★★★
Drawing quality not consistent. Mild. Complex flavours.

ROLANDO BLEND Robusto★★★
Firm, acceptable draw. Full bodied, robust. Lacks refinement.

SIGNATURE COLLECTION BY SANTIAGO CABANA Churchill★★★★★
Well-made. Medium bodied. Spicy, full flavours with undertone of wet hay. Good balance and finish.

TOPPER Old Fashioned (perfecto)★★★★
Oily maduro wrapper. Milder than it looks. Medium bodied. Good, creamy flavours. Slightly sweet aroma. Probably best value for money.

UPDATED Cigar Shops

The following cigar shops are an addendum to the shops beginning on page 87:

AUSTRALIA

MELBOURNE

New listing:
Alexander's Cigar Divan, Lower Ground Level, Crown Ltd, 8 Whiteman Str., Southbank. Tel: (61)(3)9292-7842 Good range of top Havanas. Kept in ideal conditions. Knowledgeable service. Nearby is cigar club and bar named Fidels.

BAHRAIN

MANAMA

New location:
Casa del Habano, Hotel Le Royal Meridien, Shop No. 8, Manama. Tel: (973)58 0400.

CYPRUS

New listing:
Casa del Habano Limassol, Riga Fereau Str., No. 4, Limassol. Tel: (357)(5)74 7341.

New Listing:
DUBAI
Casa del Habano, Dubai Intercontinental Hotel, Shopping Arcade, P.O. Box 267, Dubai, UAE. Tel: (971)(4)22 5008.

New listing:
EGYPT

CAIRO
Casa del Habano, Hotel Semiramis Intercontinental. Tel: (202)354-9608.

GREECE

ATHENS

New listing:
Casa del Habano, 1-3 Spyromiliou Str., 10564. Tel: (30)(1)323-5325.

HONG KONG

Updated:
Cohiba Cigar Divan, The Lobby, Mandarin Hotel. Tel: (552)2522-0111 Ext. 4074. Twentieth-century recreation of cigar divan. Large range of Havanas. Manager: Teddy Lam.

New listing:
IVORY COAST

ABIDJAN
Afrique Tabacs, 20 Ave. Fanchet D'Esperey, Plateau, 04 B.P. 748 Tel: (225)21 6300.

LEBANON

BEIRUT

New location and listing:
Casa del Habano, Achrafie, Cassine Sq., Notre Dame Centre. Tel: (961)32 8568

Casa del Habano, Zalka Highway, Arz Centre, Abu Jande Blvd. Tel: (961)(1)74 15 03

NETHERLANDS

AMSTERDAM

Updated:
P.G.C. Hajenius, 92-96 Rokin. Tel: (31)(20)623-7494. Wonderful atmosphere. Large humidor with wide selection of cigars from many parts of the world, including Havanas. Have range under own name, which is probably the top brand made in Holland. Wide range of accessories, pipes, tobacco and humidors. Regarded as one of the most beautiful cigar shops in the world. Built in 1914, based on original Dutch tobacco house. Lavish use of carved wood, marble, crystal chandeliers. Interesting and extensive museum. Extensively refurbished in September 1997, when private lockers and library added. Situated in what was centre of Amsterdam tobacco industry. Patronised by Prince Bernhard. Bought in 1983 by Ritmeester Group. Managers: Max

Leenheers and Dik Nooy. Latter has worked in store for more than 30 years.

New listings:
PHILIPPINES

MAKATI CITY
Tabas at the Peninsula Hotel, Shop 12, Makati Tower, Cnr. Ayola Makati Aves. Tel: (632)867-1597. Large range of Havanas and non-Cuban cigars. Has elegant library-styled lounge. Owner: Katrina Panlilio.

MANILA
Tabas at the Sofitel, Lobby, Hotel Sofitel Grande Boulevard Manila, 1990 Roxas Blvd. Tel: (632)526-7388. Good range all types cigars, accessories and books. Owner: Katrina Panlilio.

SAN JUAN
Tabas on Wilson, 215 Wilson Str., Greenhills. Owner: Katrina Panlilio.

SAUDI ARABIA

JEDDAH

New listing:
Casa del Habano, Palestine Td., Al Hamra. Tel: (966)(2)665 8227.

No longer available:

Hotel Sands Shop

Hotel Sofitel Shop

New listings:
RIYADH
Casa del Habano, Prince Sultan Str., Olaya. Tel: (966)(1)465 6037.

Casa del Habano, Palestine Rd., Al Hamra. Tel: (966)(2) 665 8227.

SOUTH AFRICA

CAPE TOWN

Updated:
Sturk's Tobacconists, 54 Short Market Str. (opposite famous Green Market Square flea market). Tel:(27)(27) 23-3928. Established 1873. Specialises in pipe tobacco. Blends on site in Victorian blender. Good selection cigars. Owner: Abe Bravo, has lifelong experience in cigar trade.

New listing:
Vaughn Johnson's Wine Shop, Pier Head, Dock Rd., Waterfront. Tel: 419-2121. Small but good range of Havanas. Enthusiastic and knowledgeable owner, Vaughn Johnson.

New listing:
SOMERSET WEST
Curiosity Hut, Shop 78, Somerset Mall. Tel: (27)(21)851-1095. Owner: Freddie Eckley.

SWITZERLAND

GENEVA

Updated:
Davidoff, 2 rue de Rive. Tel: (41)(22)728-9041. Perhaps world's greatest, certainly most famous, cigar shop. A must for every aficionado. Wide selection of top Havanas and non-Havanas, impressively stored. Superb range of accessories, humidors, and pipes. Knowledgeable and friendly staff. Manager: Thomas Mathys.

Gerard Pere et Fils, Noga Hilton Hotel, 19 Quai du Mont-Blanc. Tel: (41)(22)732-6511. Another great cigar shop, family enterprise. Most recent addition to ranks of master cigar dealers. Impressive cedar-lined shop. Carries enormous stock of Havanas in superb condition. Connoisseurs should look out the "Selection Gerrand". Unusual range accessories. Written beautifully produced books—*The Connoisseurs Guide to Havana Cigars and Havana Cigars*, available in English, French, German, and Spanish. Top quality service. Owner: Vahe Gerard.

Gresel Cigars is now Raffi Cigars. 2-4 Place Longmalle, 1204 Geneva. Tel: (41)(22)311-9740. In addition to Havanas, has excellent range of non-Cuban cigars. Carries lonsdale, corona, and panatella especially made for them by Moyo de Monterrey in Honduras.

ZURICH

New listing:
La Casa del Habano, Bleicherweg. 18 CH-8002. Tel: (41)(1)202-1211.

No longer available:
Durr

New listing:
TURKEY

ISTANBUL
Casa del Habano, Nispetiye Cad 32/A, 1, Levant. Tel: (90)(212)282 7113.

New listings:
THAILAND

BANGKOK
Circle, 26/27 Ruam Rudee Village, Sol Ruam Rudee, Pleenchit. Tel: (662)650-8047. Good range Havanas. Lounges and restaurant cover three floors. Private lockers for hire. Manager: Dejnatee Saengjakara.

Davidoff, Hilton Hotel, 2 Wireless Rd., Lampini, Pratanwen. Tel: (662)253-0123.

Pacific Cigar, Oriental Hotel, 48 Oriental Ave. Tel: (662) 267-1596. Recreation of cigar divan. Good range Havanas. Manager: Joe Thanilvejjakul.

Perfect Evening, Sip 'n' Puff Lobby, 20/12-15 Ruamradee Village, Sai Ruamrudee Ploenchili Rd. Tel: (662) 255-1084. Graces three floors. Main floor features comfortable furniture creating atmosphere for small groups to enjoy Havanas while sipping fine wines. Private cigar smoking and meeting rooms on second floor. Owners: Tan Chandraviroj and Piya Jittalan.

Siam Havana Cigar Co., 2nd Flr. Lobby, Dusit Thani Hotel. Tel: (662)233-5259. Good range all types cigar and accessories. Manager: John Lindgren.

UNITED STATES

WASHINGTON D.C.

New listings:
The Cigar Vault, 1500 Wilson Blvd. Arlington-Rosslyn. Tel: (1)(703)276-7225. Walk-in humidor. Large range of over 100 brands. Good selection accessories and humidors. Good, knowledgeable service. Four stories, equally well-stocked in various parts of city. Owned by Potomac Retail Ent. Store manager: Bill White.

The Cigar Vault, 2341 Jefferson Davis Hwy., 109 Arlington-Crystal City. Tel.: (1)(703)413-8727.

The Cigar Vault, 6242-C, Little River Turnpike, Alexandria-Landmark. Tel: (1)(703)750-9532.

The Cigar Vault, 2820 Prince William Pkwy., Woodbridge-Potomac Mills.

History of Cigars and Tobacco

The present virulent campaign against smoking, particularly cigar smoking, is not new. The punishment of being insulted, vilified, forced to put out the offending cigar or banished from a restaurant, is nothing compared to what adherents suffered in 17th century Turkey.

Murad IV, Sultan of Turkey, who began his reign in 1622, penalised smokers by cutting off their noses and ears.

Around the same time, the Moslem hierarchy decreed that the use of coffee and tobacco offended the Koran and was therefore punishable by decapitation.

In 1624 Pope Urban VIII ex-communicated anyone "chewing, smoking or sniffing" tobacco.

In puritanical England, the smoking habit continued to expand in spite of the efforts of Oliver Cromwell's roundhead troops to tear up tobacco plants and punish smokers by flogging.

As recently as 1907 the Japanese shogun of Tokugawa sentenced smokers, among other punishments, to confiscation of their property and 50 days, imprisonment.

In 1645, Czar Alexander of Russia decreed that all smokers be deported to the cold waste lands of Siberia. It was not long before he further proclaimed torture and even death for smokers.

However, persecution against tobacco ended in Russia when Peter the Great, who became an adherent after a visit to England, unbanned smoking and then imposed a tax to benefit the treasury, a practice followed by many governments to this day. Towards the end of the Century the Russian monarchy established a tobacco monopoly in Siberia.

The use of tobacco in pharmacopeia helped spread its fame internationally, as it was believed to have many curative properties.

This was substantiated by an ordinance published in Persia in 1635 that prohibited the sale of tobacco except by pharmacists.

It is not clear from where the word tobacco derives. Some say it was a corruption of Tobago, the Caribbean island, where tobacco was found by the discoverers of America. However, this is probably incorrect as the island was only discovered by Columbus during his third voyage in 1498. Tobago refers to the pipe used by the natives. Others believe it stems from the Tabasco province of Mexico. However, this, too, is unlikely as Tabasco was named by Hernan Cortés in 1519 for the Cacique, who governed it and fought against the Spaniards during the conquest of Mexico.

There is also much dispute about the origin of the word cigar. Some historians believe that this comes from sik'ar, the Mayan Indian word for smoking, while other hold that believe it derives from the Spanish word *cigarro* (cigarrar) which means to roll. One of the most popular forms of cigars made in Seville from Cuban leaf, towards the end of the 17th century, was the *cigale* which in Spanish means locust, so named because of its similarity in colour and shape to that of a large locust.

The first cigars (or Havanas), as discovered by Christopher Columbus in 1492, were smoked by native Indians of Cuba and were made from raw, twisted leaves of cured tobacco. Dried corn (maize) husks were used for wrappers.

The first cigars made in similar fashion to those of today were produced by the State tobacco monopoly, Tabacalera, in Seville, Spain in the early 18th century. It was then that the idea of constructing a cigar with filler, binder and wrapper was invented. Because of the cost of tobacco, they were only smoked by the wealthy. The idea was exported to Cuba and in 1740, a Royal Decree created a tobacco monopoly in Cuba, called the Royal Trading Company of Habana (*Real Compãnia de Comercio de la Habana*). Hence Cuba's cigar industry was, largely, created by the Spanish. This monopoly was interrupted during the English occupation, but was restored in 1764.

In the middle of the 18th century cigars were exported to Holland and, soon after, to Russia. There, in 1762, Catherine II, having murdered her husband, Peter III, ruled as absolute monarch and Empress of All the Russias. Contemporary historians state: ". . . although of great ability, she had all the vices of her time and station."

One of those "vices" (apart from homicide, of course) was doubtless her embracing the habit of smoking cigars. However, being a fastigious lady, she did not want nicotine to stain her fingers, so she had strips of silk placed around her smokes. This became widely adopted as the cigar band we know today.

By the end of the century cigar production had spread from Spain into France and Germany but it was not until the first quarter of the 19th century that the manufacture of "segars", as they were then called, started in Britain, an 1821 Act of Parliament governing such production.

Manufacture in England had become necessary because Wellington's troops, returning in 1812 from Portugal, had become used to "segars" in the Iberian Peninsula, and were increasingly turning to that form of smoking in preference to the pipe — a trend rapidly to spread to the general public.

Local output was also stimulated by duties levied on imported cigars, with the result that only 15 000 units were imported in the early twenties. However, the superior quality of the overseas article could not be gainsaid and, despite expense, the imported cigar became a status symbol. By 1840 importation had risen dramatically to 13 million.

By that time, too, cigar factories had been established in Italy and Switzerland, so the whole of Europe, from Portugal to Russia, and including the British Isles, could then be said to be "cigar territory".

It was not long before the demand for cigars from Cuba, then a Spanish colony, outstripped the demand for *Sevillas* as the Spanish version was called. The production of Cuban cigars was originally a Spanish state monopoly, but, in 1821 a royal decree allowed the unfettered growth and sale of tobacco in Cuba. This decree gave a boost to the industry and new producers emerged throughout the island. From then on the Spanish Crown obtained its entire supply of cigars from Cuba. Every year the present King, Juan Carlos, receives a gift of Cuba's premier cigar. This used to be the legendary Cohiba brand but it is now believed to have been surplanted by a box of 100 of the unique Trinidad cigar, named after one of Cuba's most beautiful historical cities. Spain remains the largest importer of Havana cigars, these reaching about 30 million in 1989. However this figure has dropped off slightly because of the fall in production in Cuba since 1991.

Towards the end of the 19th century and in the early 20th century new shapes evolved, inspired, to some extent, by prominent British smokers. During the 1880s,

London financier Leopold de Rothschild commissioned the famous Hoyo de Monterrey factory in Cuba to make a short cigar with a large ring size so that he could enjoy the richest flavour possible without having to take the time to smoke a full-length cigar. This size is still popular today.

Early in this century the Earl of Lonsdale commissioned his own cigars of a distinctive length and shape, and packed in boxes replete with his portrait. He chose the Rafael Gonzales factory in Havana to produce this exclusive article which soon moved into the public domain and, today, the "Lonsdale" is in world-wide demand as a popular cigar size.

By the middle of the 19th century smoking had become so universal as to require the establishment of "smoking" rooms in hotels and clubs and "smoking" compartments on trains. Skull caps in bright colours and smoking jackets were introduced to obviate the aroma of cigars clinging to normal wear. The dinner jacket, or tuxedo, is called "Le Smoking" in French-speaking countries to this very day.

This growth of the cigar was effected in Britain against the active disapproval of an unamused Queen Victoria and it was only after the accession of King Eward VII that the after-dinner pronouncement: "Gentlemen, you may smoke" became de rigueur.

This is probably the reason why King Edward cigars are not only, the most popular in Britain but also, since the Second World War, probably the top selling cigar in the world.

The first plantations to grow leaf for pipe smoking were established in Virginia in 1612, and in Maryland in 1631. The cigar itself only arrived in America in 1762. Then a British naval officer, Colonel Israel Putnam, returned to his home in Connecticut from Cuba where he had been a officer in the British army, bringing back a selection of Havana cigars and large amounts of Cuban tobacco. He became a general during the American Revolution.

It was not long before cigar factories were established in Connecticut, New York and Pennsylvania. It was at one of the Pennsylvania factories in Conestoga that a long cigar was produced called, as a result of its origin, a "stogie". Later this name was to apply to any working man's cigar. Production of tobacco, from Cuban seed, was started around 1825, with good results, Connecticut tobacco today providing some of best wrapper leaf to be found outside Cuba. By this time Cuban cigars themselves were being imported into the United States and concurrently local production was taking off, its most expensive products being made from Cuban tobacco. These were called Havanas, just as the Cuban product was, the name Havana having become a generic term.

However, it was only after the Civil War that the American industry began to attain and show signs of the size and importance it was to develop by the 1970s.

President Ulysses S Grant and writer Mark Twain both, in their own way, helped to publicise the cigar which was becoming a status symbol in the United States. As branding became important, cigar bands were developed, many of the early ones remaining largely unchanged to this day. Partagas, Par Larranaga and H Upman were the first trademarks to be registered, in the first half of the 19th century, for Cuban cigars. The famous Henry Clay cigar, named after the Senator, was launched towards the end of the century as a premium cigar product.

An early American connoisseur of Havana cigars was John Quincy Adams, one of New England's most aristocratic leaders and the sixth President of the United States from 1825 to 1829.

Production in the United States received a major impetus when Cubans in large numbers left the island to escape the iron grip of the Spanish conquerers. Most of them made their way to the nearest part of America facing Cuba — Florida, mainly in Tampa and Key West — where their natural skills resulted in the production of "Tampa" cigars every bit as good as the "Havanas" of their homeland.

By the end of the 19th century there were more than 7 000 cigar factories in the United States, the pick of them, some 500, being in Florida.

As a result, cigar consumption peaked in 1907, thereafter to fall off gently due to the advent of cigarettes.

At the end of 1919, Thomas Riley Marshall, a Democrat and Woodrow Wilson's vice-president, tired of listening to a Republican Senator ramble at length about the country's needs, uttered the immortal quote; "What this country needs, is a really good five cent cigar." This ambition was to take nearly 40 years to realise, when homogenised tobacco was developed by pulverising the leaf, and then forming it into thin sheets.

This saved wastage and, together with machine rolling, invented in the 1920s, resulted in lower prices.

During the Second World War Cuba was unable to supply the United Kingdom with sufficient cigars and, as a result, some were imported from Jamaica, a crown colony in the Caribbean.

Machine-made cigars represented 10 percent of total production in the United States and rose to 98 percent by the end of the 1950s.

Cuba, anxious not to be outdone by these low-cost competitors, started producing machine-made cigars itself. This had a dramatic effect of making available a machine-made Havana at half the price of a hand-made one. This, more than anything else, served to popularise the Havana in the United States.

In 1961, as a result of the disastrous Bay Of Pigs venture, where Cuban exiles with the help of the United States government tried to overthrow the government of Fidel Castro, President Kennedy declared an embargo on all the importation of goods from Cuba. This naturally caused a tremendous surge in the price of stocks of pre-embargo Havanas and also on price factors, gave the local industry a temporary shot in the arm.

For nearly 30 years, due largely to the anti-smoking lobby, cigar consumption in the United States has declined from a peak of over nine billion of all types of cigars in 1964, to a little over two billion in 1992. The next three years saw an increase of over 60 percent for premium cigars, with most producers experiencing back-orders from two to six months. Consumption in 1995 was 2.5 billion, of which about 161 million were premium cigars.

Except in the sanctuary of their own homes, tobacco shops, or in a declining number of cigar-friendly restaurants and bars, it is becoming increasingly difficult for cigar smokers in the United States to enjoy their cigars unhindered. Just as in Victorian England, cigar smoking is again frowned upon in public. History certainly has a way of repeating itself, although we have yet to suffer the punishment meted out to smokers in Europe two to three hundred years ago. However, there is no doubt that the personal liberties of smokers are being infringed. There are even criticisms of cigar smoking in cigar-friendly restaurants, in restricted smoking areas, at private dinner parties, or at functions in hotels or convention centres. Anti-smokers have said that the staff in such establishments should not have to breathe in the smoke, even though their work place is their own free choice.

Cigar smokers mainly show restraint under this duress. However the time has come to take action and fight back. It may be too late in cities and towns that already prohibit all smoking, but there is still action that can be taken. Patronise only cigar-friendly restaurants. If cigarette smokers complain about your cigar, argue your cause as their cigarettes are much more harmful to health than your cigar. If it is the aroma to which they really (which is all they can, under the circumstances) object, then one is dealing very much with personal preferences. Some non-smokers enjoy cigar aroma, just as others enjoy the smoke from a wood campfire that has pine cones on it. Argue that it is hypocritical for restaurants to allow cigarettes but not cigars.

Growing Cigar Tobacco

CULTIVATION

Due to cross-breeding different strains and varieties, since the 18th century, the tobacco plant, *Nicotiana tabacum* now not only maximises leaf production but also develops desirable physical and chemical properties which enable cigars of high and consistent quality to be manufactured.

The mature tobacco plant can attain a height of six feet (two metres) or more, and comes from seeds which are so small that Linnaeuse, the great Swedish botanist, once counted 40 320 seeds in a single tobacco pod.

Seeds are raised in flat nursery beds under carefully controlled conditions. They are covered with cloth or straw to shade them from the scorching sun. This covering is gradually removed as they begin to germinate at a temperature of about 18 degrees C (65 degrees F). Within six weeks they attain a height of between six and eight inches (15 to 20 cms) and are ready to be planted out in rows, in the tobacco fields. Potash is used to enhance disease resistance while nitrates encourage leaf growth. Each square yard of nursery bed produces enough seedlings for about 200 square yards of soil in the plantation.

After 45 to 50 days of continued hoeing and pest control, the plant reaches its maximum height. To encourage concentrated growth and flavour in the leaves, the tobacco grower or *veguero* as he is known in Cuba, plucks out the tip of the stem, thus preventing development of the flower head.

The leaves on the stem of the tobacco plant are divided into three parts: the top or *Corona*, the *Centro* or middle and *Libre De Pie* or bottom, all of which are harvested. As buds appear they are removed by hand to prevent the stunting of leaf and plant growth, as well as denying the leaves additional flavour. This process is called *desbotonar* in Spanish. Most plants will have yielded, by harvest time, between eight and 12 oblong leaves, the largest being up to 18 inches long (roughly 46 cms).

The growing season is inevitably a worrying time for the *veguero* due to the large variety of natural hazards that can ruin his crop. Even the best run plantations or *vegas* are operated on the assumption that about 15 percent of the crop will be destroyed by pests and diseases. Dry weather is essential and fields are never irrigated. Morning dew and the occasional brief, light shower provide all the moisture the plants need. Violent storms, hailstorms and hurricanes that are prevalent in the Caribbean (although fortunately not often during the growing season) can ruin the crop within a few short hours.

Plants for the all-important wrapper for the best cigars are grown under muslin or cheesecloth sheets, called *tapados*, which are supported on tall wooden poles. The leaves have to be protected from direct sunlight to retain a smooth, elastic, silky and even texture. This elasticity provides the leaf with the ability, when moisturised, to stretch without tearing. A high-quality wrapper is smooth with thin, fine veins, and, if there is no wastage, due to rejection, the average wrapper plant can cover up to 32 cigars.

TOBACCO HARVEST

When the right moment arrives to remove the leaf from the stem, it is pressed with the index finger and carefully detached with a single movement of the hand.

Leaves selected as wrappers are stacked one on top of the other to form a bundle of 25 and are called a *gavilla* or hand. Leaves are picked in six phases, called *libre de pie* (at the base), *uno y medio* (one-and-a-half), *centro ligero* (light centre), *centro fino* (thin centre), *centro gordo* (thick centre) and *corona* (top). All leaves except the bottom section, *libre de pie*, can be used for wrappers. However the best quality leaves are obtained from the centre of the plant. Top leaves *(corona)* are usually too oily to be used for wrappers, except for some domestic consumption, and normally serve as filler leaves. Reaping each section can take around a week.

Wrapper leaves grown under cover have six classifications: *ligero* (light), *seco* (dry), *viso* (glossy), *amarillo* (yellow), *medio tiempo* (half texture) and *quebrado* (broken). Those leaves grown in the full sunlight are divided into *volado, seco, ligero* and *medio tiempo* (categories). In addition leaves are classified by size into large, average and small, and by physical condition, into healthy, broken and unhealthy. The last two are types used for cigarettes or short filler machine-made cigars.

After picking, leaves are cut and bundled into *gavillas* or hands. About 300 leaves at a time are packed into oval baskets and covered with mosquito netting or sack-cloth for their trip to the curing barns, known as *casas de tabaco* for air curing before fermentation.

These barns must run in an East-West direction, so that the sun will heat only the ends of the building in the early morning and late afternoon. In the Remedius District in Cuba, the curing barns are entirely covered with palm leaves. In the Partido, Semi-Vuelta and Vuelta Abajo Districts some of the barns are built in this way, but usually the sides are boarded and the roofs thatched with palm leaves.

Temperature and humidity in the barn are important factors. Therefore, barns are tightly closed in normal weather. The doors at each end and windows on the sides are only opened if outside weather conditions affect the temperature and humidity inside the barn.

Inside the barn leaves are strung with large needles and thread onto four metre long poles, called a *cujes*. When fully loaded with between 50 and 55 pairs of leaves, each *cuje* is hoisted up horizontally, allowing the air to circulate evenly. The leaves are then left to cure for around 50 days. During this process they slowly turn from bright green, to yellow and then to light brown. Barns become a kaleidoscope of tones and aromas as new fragrances mingle with older, riper ones.

Once cured the leaves are removed from the humid environment of the *cuje* sorted into bundles by type, and then transported to the *escogida* or grading room which is normally close to the plantation.

The leaves are now separated, then dampened and aired before going to the opening room, where they are graded into classes and tied into bunches of 50 in preparation of the all-important fermentation process.

LEAF FERMENTATION

Fermentation can take place (depending on the country or the factory concerned) in small wood barrels stored in dark rooms, cupboards, or in four to five feet deep pits in the ground, or simply by stacking bundles of leaves on the floor of the *escogidas* in large piles.

In Cuba the following fermentation process is followed. Bunches of tobacco leaves are packed in long piles, called *ilones* about three feet (one metre) high in the fermentation house. Usually there is sufficient moisture present in the natural, hot, humid climate to start the first fermentation, which lasts up to 30 days. During this process the piles are constantly watched. When the temperature exceeds 35 degrees C (95 degrees F), the piles are broken up and the leaves allowed to cool before the pile is rebuilt with the outer leaves in the inside and the inside leaves on the outside. This reduces the oiliness in the leaves, resulting in a more uniform colour.

When this process is complete the leaves undergo a *moja* or moisturising. Wrappers are sprinkled with pure water, while fillers and binders are dampened with a tobacco extract, made from water and tobacco stems. Care is taken not to apply too much moisture as this can cause spotting and rotting.

The leaves then undergo an initial classification. The thick stems are stripped out and the leaves are then fully classified according to size, colour, texture and type.

These leaves are then re-bundled and stacked into much larger piles or bulks, called *burros*. These *burros* are at least six feet or two metres high.

During this second fermentation, which lasts up to 60 days, the leaves reach temperatures of 42 degrees C (108 degrees F). A long sword-like thermometer is thrust into the bulk to check temperature. This fermentation, as with the first one, is monitored 24 hours a day and the leaves turned to ensure even processing.

During each fermentation the tobacco undergoes a chemical change enhancing flavour and aroma. At the same time nicotine, tar, ammonia, acidity and other impurities are reduced, making it much more palatable than normal cigarette tobacco.

According to Tobacco Encyclopedia, "Nicotine decreases by between 10 and 90 percent. Soluble carbohydrates are eliminated and there is a considerable reduction of nitrogen compounds which result in the obvious release of gaseous ammonia. The ph becomes more alkaline during fermentation. The extent of all changes is dependent on the severity of the process which, however, is very complex and still understood incompletely."

In Cuba most leaves used in good quality hand-rolled cigars undergo two fermentations, and, in the case of the top line Cohiba, as many as three.

After fermentation the tobacco is rested for a few days on airing racks.

When fully recovered, the leaves are packed into solid packages, or *tercios*, made from the bark of the Royal Palm tree, called *yaguas*, where they are stored, in some cases, for up to three years. During storage, the leaves undergo an ageing or maturing process, which further refines their aroma and flavour.

After that the *tercios* are transported to the cigar factories in Havana.

Having to finance this valuable crop for so long adds considerably to the cost of the Havana. Such factors plus the expense of the slower hand-making process, really make the Havana excellent value for money.

DISEASES AND PESTS

One of the dangerous diseases that face the tobacco grower is blue mould. This feared fungus, arising from adverse temperature and moisture conditions, destroyed the entire Cuban tobacco crop in the 1979/1980 season. At times, due to financial problems, Cuba had not been able to afford to buy sufficient fungicides, as was the case in 1979/1980. The effect was to close Cuba's tobacco processing factories for two years.

The tobacco crop is also vulnerable to climatic hazards, such as heavy rains, strong December winds and hurricanes, which provide ideal conditions for the spread of this mould, that starts on the underside of the leaf where it has been carried by airborne spores.

BABILLA

A rot which occurs in the middle of bunches of seedlings when they have been pulled for transplanting into the fields while wet from rain, dew or irrigation water. This disease manifests itself during the second day after pulling in the form of a spittle-like substance found on the lower parts of the stems, which will not take root if planted in this condition.

BIBIJAGUA (Atta insularis Guerin)

The giant ant of Cuba, which often causes serious damage in tobacco seedbeds. This pest is to tobacco what the locust is to wheat.

BLUE MOLD (Peronospora tabasina)

Also known as downy mildew. This feared fungus, arising from adverse temperature and moisture conditions, can destroy an entire tobacco field in days.

It is characterised by the appearance of brown necrotic spots on the leaves which, soon, develop a bluish-grey coating. Eventually the leaves dry out and droop.

In Honduras, the 1995/96 crop experienced a particularly severe attack.

CANDELILLA (Phthorimea operculella Zeller)

A tobacco leaf borer, also known in Cuba as *furro de catre* and in the USA as the potato tuber moth. This borer is not a serious pest in Cuba.

CHINCHITA DE LA HOJA DEL TOBACCO (Cyrtopeltis varians Dist.)

This small bug is commonly found on Cuba's tobacco plants.

GRILLITO DE LA TIERRA (Anurogyllus abortivus)
A cricket which damages tobacco in Cuba.

HIERBA ZOSA (Orobanche ramosa L.)
A parasitic plant, also known as hemp broomrape, which lives on tobacco roots and feeds off their sap.

WHITE MOLD (Moho blanco)
A light grey thread-like fungus that appears on leaves that have been rained upon after the tobacco has been fully dried and the laths separated in the curing barn. This will cause the tobacco to rot if care is not taken.

PUDRICIÓN NEGRA
This black leaf rot appears after heavy rains and shows the same characteristics as the black rot which occurs in the seedbeds. It appears in the form of large, wet, dark green spots on the bottom and lower middle leaves, finally destroying the principal leaves on the plant where there is little light and air. Infected plants should be pulled up and removed.

SAHORNE
Also known as chafing and is a type of rot which attacks tobacco leaves that are exposed to excess moisture during the curing period.

SAND DOWN
A chlorsis caused in the Vuelta Abajo fields by a deficiency of magnesia in the soil. Characterised by yellowish, roughly rounded variegated spots, surrounded by green lines. Found on small plants, rarely on full-grown ones.

TABACO SENTIDO
This name applies to spoiled tobacco that has rotted in the bulk due to being placed there when too wet or because the temperature was allowed to rise too high. This form of rot may also occur in the *casilla* or in the petuning process, under similar conditions.

PINTA DE AJONJOLI (Cercospora nicotianae)
Also known as sesame spot, leaf spot or frogeye disease. Identified by, roughly, circular spots, brown at first, but becoming whitish as they grow larger. Generally in the form of concentric rings which darken from the perimeter to the centre. Sometimes attacks the crown leaves, usually found on lower and lighter leaves when the weather is hot and humid. Just a few hours of south wind are enough to start an attack of this fungus.

PINTA DE HIERRO

Also called iron spot because of the rusty colour of the leaf spot. Is found mainly on the upper leaves of the plant. Does little damage and usually found on tobacco in dry years.

PUDRICJÓN (Rhizoctonia specifica)

Rot is caused by this fungus and attacks the young plants in the seedbed or soon after they have been transplanted, when the weather is hot and humid and south winds prevail. Difficult to control.

PUDRICIÓN DEL TALLO

This stem rot, sometimes known as black shark, is identified by yellowish spots on the lower part of the stem, mainly in the section containing the bottom and lower middle leaves. This spot turns greyish or dark in colour and increases in size as it wilts the leaves and turns them yellow, occurring before the disease entirely circles the stem, causing the plant to die. Not common in Cuba, but prevalent in some Central American growing areas. Often appears during rainy years on low, wet lands.

With all these natural enemies, it is nothing short of a miracle that a crop can be brought to fruition. This is possible only due to the expertise, vigilance and hard work of the grower.

Structure of a Cigar

A cigar has three components: the filler, the binder and the wrapper.

FILLER

The biggest mass of a cigar is the filler and, in the case of hand-made cigars, usually it is strips of tobacco cut to the length of the cigar, known as long leaf.

Short leaf indicates smaller, cut-up pieces normally used for machine-made cigars. Long leaf is more expensive and, therefore, kept for premium (high grade) cigars, although many excellent cigars are made from short filler.

There are three different types or styles of leafs in use for the filler blend. These are:

LIGERO — These are leaves grown from tobacco during seasons of abundant rainfall, and is so called because it has little oil, but is full flavoured. When this type of tobacco is dampened for grading, only a small amount of water can be used. It must always be handled in dry weather and baled with the minimum of delay. It gives the cigar its strength and flavour.

Full-bodied *ligero* leaves need to mature for two to three years.

A cigar will burn unevenly if *ligero* leaf, with its slow-burning qualities, is too near the wrapper, so the buncher must ensure that it is placed in the centre of the cigar.

SECO (dry, thin) — This is one of the weather classifications of tobacco in Vuelta Abajo and Partido (districts in Cuba). *Seco* tobacco includes leaves with less oil or gum, little body, without juice and are lighter in colour with, probably, less flavour. They give the cigar its sublety. These need to be matured for about 18 months.

VOLADO (high) — This is another name, in the Remedius District in Cuba, for the grade also known as *permanente*. In Vuelta Abajo it is the least gummy or oily grade of tobacco, with little flavour. These leaves usually, only require about 12 months of maturation before use.

The filler normally consists of a blend of two to four different styles of leaves, depending on the diameter (or ring size as it is known). Blends provide variation in tastes, aromas and characteristics for differing brands. Here, as in size, which we will discuss later, one is again reminded of the fact that a cigar is not just a smoke perse, but each one is a very individual thing.

A full-bodied cigar, like a Bolivar, will have a higher proportion of *ligero* in its filler than will a mild cigar such as a Fonseca, where more *seco* and *volvado* are used. Small, thin cigars or cigarellos usually have no *ligero* leaf in them at all. To maintain a consistent house style, blends of tobacco from different harvests and plantations are used, thus requiring a large stock-holding of matured leaf.

There is also the "short leaf" or "chopped" filler which is small, finely chopped-up pieces, similar in appearance to that found in cigarettes. This method is often used in the better grades of Dutch-type dry cigars.

Less expensive cigars often use "scrap" filler, the left-overs from all the above styles.

BINDER *(CAPOTE)*

This binder encloses the filler and gives the cigar its proper shape and size. Leaves used for this purpose usually have the tensile strength to hold the cigar together. In many cases the binder is selected almost entirely for its physical properties and may have indifferent smoking qualities. However, in the best Havanas, care is taken to ensure that it imparts a complementary flavour to the filler and wrapper. They require around 12 months of maturation.

A characteristic of a premium cigar is that it is made entirely of natural leaf and has no chemical additives. This is in contrast to many less expensive, mass-market, machine-made cigars which use homogenised binders made from leaf particles and cellulose.

WRAPPER *(CAPA)*

The quality of the wrapper is crucial in any cigar and, generally, can account for anything up to 70 percent of the tobacco by value, while being only 10 percent by weight. A good wrapper should have flavour and steady-burning qualities. A smoker examines a cigar for appealing appearance, texture and aroma. This is where a good wrapper justifies its high cost. If the wrapper is not smooth, silky or oily and does not have an appealing aroma, the smoker will reject it and the sale will be lost.

Wrappers must be elastic and without coarse veins. They have to mature for at least 12 to 18 months, really good ones for even longer. Wrappers of hand-made non-Cuban cigars can come from Cameroun, Connecticut, Costa Rica, Ecuador, Honduras, Mexico, Nicaragua or Sumatra.

Hand-made Cigars

ROLLING CIGARS

Once *tercios* (bales) of leaf arrive at the factory they are opened by labourers called *zafadores*. Before going to the rolling table the leaf is moisened with water to make it pliable.

The actual rolling is done by skilled workers called *torcedores* who sit in rows at long, narrow work benches. They are then given batches of leaves that have been expertly prepared and graded. Each batch represents the correct blend of tobacco to produce one day's production. A good Cuban *torcedor* can roll between 100 and 150 cigars a day, depending on the size. *Torcedores* are able to make a variety of sizes and shapes, but usually specialise, for long periods of time, in one type of cigar.

The *torcedor* prepares the filler by laying the different types of tobacco on top of each other to form the required blend. With great skill the leaves are folded or concertina'd along their length, but not rolled, to allow a passage through which smoke can be drawn when the cigar is lit. This can only be properly achieved by hand. Sometimes the leaves are folded in half, as if they were the pages of a book. This is easier with the thicker sizes. This style of arranging the filler is sometimes called the "book" style or "booking". Some aficionados believe this folding method tends to produce a heavy concentration of filler leaves along the folds (or spine of the book) with the result that the taste of each tobacco in the blend is not evenly distributed. It can also cause the cigar to burn unevenly down the side.

The filler is then placed on the binder leaf and rolled by hand, to form a "bunch", which is simply a cigar without its wrapper.

These are placed in a 10 bunch wooden mould, each mould being shaped to the exact size of the cigar the roller is making. Moulds when filled are stacked in a press and the bunches squeezed into shape. Depending on the size of the bunch and the practice of the factory, bunches can remain in the press from 15 to 60 minutes.

In Cuba the entire cigar is made by the same *torcedor*. This differs from other countries, particularly in the Dominican Republic, where bunchers and wrapper rollers work in specialist teams — one buncher usually supplying two rollers.

The *torcedor* then selects a wrapper leaf, places it upside-down so that, when rolled, the smooth outer surface of the leaf will be showing. He trims it to the right size with a sharp semi-circular blade called a *chaveta*. The cigar is then rolled, even pressure being applied. *Torcedores* (cigar-makers) will roll the leaf tip into the foot or tuck of the cigar, to ensure full flavour. The leaf is rolled from the base of the cigar upwards, so that the wrapper does not unwind, and is then fixed with a tiny drop of Tragacanth vegetable gum, which is colourless and flavourless. Then a small round piece of tobacco is cut from the remaining wrapper, ensuring that the colour matches the wrapper, and is gummed in place over the head of the cigar.

In the case of some cigars such as the Montecristo Especial, the Cohiba Especial and the Cohiba Lanceros, a different method of sealing the head of the cigar is employed. Here, the head is sealed by twisting the end of the wrapper itself to form a small tail (*rabo de cochina*). This is known as the "flag" method or sometimes curly head or pigs tail, and is a highly skilled process only used on the best hand-made cigars and never on machine-made ones.

Finally, the cigar is placed in the wooden groove of a small hand operated guillotine, kept on the *torcedor's* rolling bench, and cut to the correct length.

The construction of a cigar is crucial to its smoking enjoyment. If it is under-filled, it will draw easily, but burn too fast and get hot and harsh as a result. If it is over-filled, it will have drawing difficulties or be "plugged". "Plugging" can also arise if the leaves of the filler are not folded correctly.

Quality control is affected in most factories by weighing the finished cigars and measuring the length and girth in a ring gauge. If the cigar has the right diameter but is underweight, then it is under-filled; overweight, it is over-filled.

In the Consolidated Cigar Corporation factory in the Dominican Republic suction machines test every bunch for quality of draw before the wrapper is applied. Bunches that fail this test are reworked.

Although more small cigars are usually made in a day than larger sizes, they are, in many ways, more difficult to produce. This is not only because of the additional dexterity required by the *torcedore* but also because of the difficulty of fitting more than one or two leaves into the filler blend so the wrapper and binder augment the slightly reduced taste of the filler. It is also easier for the natural channels created in the folds of the filler to get "plugged" with small pieces of tobacco or to become twisted and closed, thereby interfering with the draw.

However, it is also difficult to construct a large bunch so that all of the different leaves in the filler are equally distributed along the entire length of a long cigar. But, if this is not done, then one particular tobacco will dominate aroma and taste.

Torcedores who make large sizes get paid more than those who only make smaller ones. In Cuba there are seven grades of cigar rollers. A grade four, who only makes small or less complicated shapes gets paid less than a grade seven, which is the highly skilled category. The first three grades perform other functions besides rolling, such as sorting and stemming. Grade four personnel make only cigars up to and including the petit corona size. Coronas and larger are made by grade five rollers and those in grades six and seven make difficult, specialist shapes such as figurados and any cigars that do not have parallel sides, (torpedos, for example). Each of the top factories have their own training schools so that new blood is steadily introduced. It takes at least about a year to learn to roll a cigar. Skilled rollers develop after five to six years, while it takes more than 20 years for a cigar roller to become a master *torcedor*. The grading system even affects the seating arrangements in the factory, with the top grade *torcedors* sitting in the front and the lower grades at the back of the room. Large and complicated shapes cost more, because they use more tobacco and the cigar-maker gets paid more per cigar. This system applies to all the major cigar-producing countries.

There are around 70 different cigar sizes or shapes made today. At the H Upmann factory in Cuba the average production per person of the large Montecristo A is around 50 to 60 cigars.

The average cigar factory is hot, the air being filled with the pungent aromas of tobacco, cedar oil and sweat. The monotony of cigar-rolling is broken, in many plants, by radio broadcasts. In Cuba the 19th century practice of having a *lector de tabaqueria* reading out aloud, from a *galeria* or platform, passages from the works of Spanish writers such as Cervantes and

Unamuno, as well as translations of Dickens and Shakespeare, still continues. However, recently the subject matter has changed, stories and poems of Che Guevara and Jose Marti and other heroes, as well as editorials from Granma, the Party newspaper. The *lector* or reader is paid a small amount collected from each of the rollers.

In Cuba a cigar-rolling school for women was opened in 1961 in the El Laguito factory, which today is the exclusive producer of the Cuban flagship range, Cohiba. Until then few female rollers existed because many of the cigar factory owners believed that their hands were not strong enough to shape cigars properly. It was also thought that their presence would distract the men. However, many fine *torcedors* in Cuba today are women.

HANDLING THE NEWLY-CREATED CIGAR

Generally, hand-made cigars undergo the following procedure after rolling and trimming: further quality checks; fumigation; drying out in the ageing room; colour grading; banding or packing into cellophane tubes; labelling and finishing; and, finally, packing and storing in the warehouse prior to shipment.

After weighing and checking for proper size and shape, cigars are tied with a soft ribbon in bundles of 50, called a *media rueda* or half-wheel. A slip of paper is attached to the bundle with its pedigree — name of the roller, the supervisor responsible for quality inspections, details of types of tobacco used, shape of the cigar and or its brand. This is done in case any cigar in the bundle does not meet the required standard and the coding will identify what and where it went wrong. The *torcedor's* name is essential, as any rejected cigars are deducted from the maker's pay.

The *media rueda* is then placed in a vacuum fumigation chamber to kill any pest or eggs that may have been laid in the tobacco and which can possibly incubate and hatch later. Sometimes the fumigation process is not totally efficient and that is why it is wise for the consumer to store his or her cigars in a humidor with a temperature of not much more that 20 °C (70 °F). Incubation of most bugs takes place in temperatures of 25 °C (75 °F) and over.

DRYING AND AGEING CIGARS

During manufacture the tobacco has to be quite wet to prevent cracking and breaking. This excess moisture content has now to be removed for about three weeks to make the cigar smokeable. This is done by placing the bundles in a special temperature-controlled cedar cabinet, called an *escaparate*. Apart from extracting the excess moisture, this period allows the flavours of the different tobaccos to marry together, as the alcohol and fruit does in the long ageing process of a fine vintage port. These cabinets usually hold around 18 000 cigars.

Super premium cigars are aged for longer periods. The Dunhill range of vintage cigars, launched with 1986 tobaccos, ages for at least three months; the Ashton Cabinet selection, Fuente Hemingway and Chateau Fuente ranges for at least six months; the limited edition Don Carlos cigar from Fuente and J R Ultimate cigars, for more than a year; while the Dominican range from Davidoff is aged for a minimum of 18 months.

Havana cigars used to be aged for about three weeks. Today except for a few brands, including the flagship Cohiba range, most Havanas are aged in 100-year-old cedar cupboards for only a week. This is because of the need for Cuba to turn her tobacco crop into cash as soon as possible.

Smoking a fresh or green cigar is a different experience as even the best cigar is harsh when smoked too young. Therefore, unless one is buying from established merchants who specialise in ageing cigars for their clients (such as Alfred Dunhill in New York and San Francisco, Nat Sherman in New York, Alfred Dunhill, James Fox, Robert Lewis and Desmond Sautter in London), it is best to age the cigars in your humidor for three to six months before lighting up. Some traditionalists believe a cigar should either be smoked within three months of manufacture or after one year.

One does not usually experience the problems of cigars that are too fresh from Honduras or the Dominican Republic.

It must be remembered that just as with good wine, you sometimes find a bottle that is not up to standard and may be undrinkable due to it being "corked", a similar "catastrophe" can happen with cigars when the filler is too tight (making the draw too hard) or too loose (resulting in a fast, hot and, therefore, harsh smoke). If one has to discard a cigar too often because of any one of such problems then it is time to consider avoiding that particular brand. But before doing so it is advisable to talk to the tobacconist where the cigars were bought so that he can give feedback to the supplier.

CLASSIFYING BY COLOUR

After ageing and drying, the cigars are taken to the *escogida* which is the selection and packing depart-ment, where they are graded by colour and then boxed. There are over 65 different shades. When the selector has grouped the cigars by hue and tone, they go to the packer, who matches them even further to present them in chromatic harmony. The darkest cigar is positioned on the left and the lightest on the right. Cigars with unsightly veins are removed. It is a great source of pride for both the cigar-maker and the cigar-smoker to be able to see the same shade of wrapper on each offering. This does not make the cigars smoke any better, but it is an indication of the pride each company takes in its product, with the resulting assurance of the quality of the rolling.

When cigars have been grouped into the same colour hues, they are then banded. Each band is put on by hand at exactly the same height on every cigar. Opening a box of cigars and seeing the same shade of wrapper on each cigar and bands that all line up perfectly is a beautiful sight.

THE CIGAR BAND

Around the year 1750 cigars were exported to Holland and later to Russia. There, Empress Catherine II had her cigars decorated with silk bands so that her royal fingers would not become stained while she was smoking. This inspired Dutchman Gustave Bock, a manufacturer of Cuban cigars, in the middle of the 19th century, to affix a paper band with his logo, on his products to distinguish his brand from the many others on the market. This forced other producers to follow suit and cigar bands are still widely in use today.

However the band is only used on cigars sold in flat boxes. A number of shapes, particularly the robusto or Rothschild, are packed in "Cabinet Selection" cedar wood boxes, containing either a bundle of 25 or, sometimes, 50 loosely packed cigars tied together with a silk ribbon, and these have no bands. This half-wheel or *media rueda* was in fact the way all cigars were packed before the introduction of the cigar band.

Particularly when it was fashionable for gentlemen to wear white evening gloves, the band played a role in protecting the smoker's gloves from becoming stained.

Some older brands have fancier, elaborate bands with plenty of gold foil. However, many products aimed at the most discerning part of the market (such as Dunhill, Cohiba and Montecristo) have just simple and elegant bands.

Those on non-Cuban cigars with Havana brand names tend to be similar to the Cuban originals, although they vary in small details such as often including the date of origin of the brand in the space where the Cuban version has the word "Habana".

Some Havanas use more than one design on the band. For instance Romeo and Julieta, on its Churchill sizes have an elegant gold band, whereas the other sizes have red, gold and white ones.

THE CIGAR BOX

The two types of cigar boxes available are mostly made by hand. One is the cedar plywood "dress box", in which much of the wood is covered by paper which has been heavily printed with labels and separate edging designs. Then there is the cedar "cabinet box" which, if it is the flat type, uses European brass hinges and nails that will not rust in a humidor. Sometimes these boxes have fancy brass clasps, known as a broach. Such cabinet boxes also come in square shapes to accommodate the ribbon-tied bundle or half wheel and has a sliding lid.

The Montecristo A is packed in a varnished black box. Such boxes are usually stamped with the brand logo and do not carry any sort of label other than the government seal.

Most Caribbean cigars are packed in boxes from Honduran-grown African cedar. Cuba also imports the heavier cedar from Honduras. All of Habanos SA's (formerly called Cubatabacco), (the State-owned export monopoly) cigar boxes are made locally. Cedar for cabinet boxes can also come from Nicaragua, Mexico and the United States, while Brazil, South Korea and Taiwan produce that wood for the dress boxes.

Many cigar companies print their own labels, ranging from four-colour ones down to simple single colour offerings. The first full coloured label was produced in Cuba by cigar-maker Ramon Allones, an immigrant from France, for the brand he started in 1837.

After filling and checking, the box is nailed shut and tightly sealed with a green and white label to guarantee that the cigars are genuine Havanas, or *puros Habanos*. The word *puro* means pure, but it has also become a synonym for cigar. This seal, introduced in 1912 by the Cuban government, includes a reproduction of the Cuban emblem and has a partial view of a tobacco field as a guarantee to the legitimacy of the product. Its texts are in Spanish, English, French and German. Today a few other countries have their own seal for cigar exports. Honduras has both green and brown labels, while green seals are used on boxes from the Philippines and Nicaragua. An olive green manu-facturers warranty (not government) seal is placed on cigars from the city of La Romana in the Dominican Republic.

Since 1985, Cubatabaco has attempted to provide the consumer with a little more security by introducing, in that year, on the underside of the box, the Cubatabaco stamp, plus (since 1989) the legend, stamped in black, *"Hecho en Cuba. Totalmente a mano"* ("Made in Cuba. Totally hand-made").

If the box only states *"Hecho en Cuba"* then this indicates that the cigars are made by machine. Some-times you can be lucky and find hand-finished (machine bunched/hand-finished) cigars inside.

If the legend is *"Hecho a mano"* ("Made by hand") the cigars are probably hand-finished, rather than fully hand-made, if made in or after 1989. However, older boxes of hand-made cigars will also have the legend *"Hecho a mano"*.

Only buy pre-1989 cigars, where you don't have the *"Totalmente a Mano"* guarantee, from reputable cigar merchants.

Cigars made before the Revolution in 1959 are commonly known as "pre-Castro" and, until 1962 (year of US embargo), have the words "Made in Havana, Cuba" printed on the bottom of the box.

Many boxes often have a hyphenated code stamped on them in a different colour. The first part is the code to indicate in which factory the cigars were made. Here are some of the codes:

BM: Briones Montoto, formerly Romeo Y Julieta,
EL: El Laguito, the Cohiba factory,
FPG: Francisco Perez German, formerly Partgas,
FR: Fernando Roig, formerly La Corona,
JM: Jose Marti, formerly H Upmann.
HM: Heroes Del Moncado, formerly El Rey Del Mundo.

These factories are in Havana.
In addition there are at least two factories in the provinces outside Havana.
These are:

VSC: Villa Santa Clara,
SS: Sancti Spiritus.

Often these letters are followed by a numeral, which designates the specific factory in the particular town.

Cigars made in these factories are seldom sold in Europe, which demands consistent quality.

The second part of the code relates to the date of manufacture.

Each letter designates a number, from 1 to 0.

DATE CODE

```
N I V E L A C U S O
1 2 3 4 5 6 7 8 9 0
```

The remaining four letters refer to the date. The first two letters of this relate to the month and the second two to the year.

For example the blue stamp "FPG ONSA" would indicate that this box was made in the Francisco Perez German (Partagas) factory and made in January, '96.

Until recently this date code was regarded as secret by Habanos SA and "Cigar Insider" was the first to publish the code in February 1996.

Most brands are made in more than one factory, as each factory tends to specialise in certain sizes.

The majority of machine-made cigars are made in the Fernando Raig (La Corona) factory, which is the biggest factory in Cuba.

The colour of the contents also used to be stamped underneath. Sometimes this stated the colour in full, such as "claro" and sometimes it just used a "C". But, apparently, this practice has been stopped for the time being, maybe because colour identification was quite often inaccurate.

With non-Havanas care should be taken to differentiate between hand-made, hand-rolled and hand-packed. Hand-made is self-explanatory; hand-rolled means the cigar has been machine-made with only the wrapper added by hand; hand-packed, or "*Envuelto a mano*", means you are dealing with an entirely machine-made product.

American produced boxes have the code "TP", which means tobacco products, followed by a number identifying the manufacturer. Cigars imported into the United States do not carry such a code.

In the case of "vintage" cigars, the vintage on the front of the box refers to the year of harvest of the tobacco used, not the year of manufacture.

Machine-made Cigars

There is a tremendous difference in price (and, usually, quality) between premium and mass-market cigars. This is due to the fact that premium cigars are largely hand-made while mass-market cigars are machine-made, although there are some exceptions to this rule that will be discussed later in this chapter. This is illustrated by the fact that, in Cuba, the output of a good cigar roller or *torcedor* is 100 to 150 cigars per day, depending on size. In Honduras the output by hand can be as high as 500 to 700 cigars per day per team of three, but such figures are dwarfed by machines which can produce easily around 10 000 cigars per eight hour shift!

To achieve this scale of output machines, with few exceptions, have to use homogenised binders, which are made from leaf particles and cellulose.

Homogenised filler is made from tobacco stems and fibres, mixed with water and cellulose, to make an amorphous material, which comes off a drying belt in the form of rolls, not unlike paper. The majority of all mass-market cigars are made from homogenised binders and most of these use homogenised wrappers as well. Notable exceptions are the Dutch-made La Paz and the De Heeren van Ruysdael ranges, which are machine-made but use only natural leaf and have no chemical additives.

It is fairly easy to identify a homogenised (HTL) wrapper, as it appears to have a flat finish in contrast to the natural wrapper which has a definite, oily-like texture and visible fine veins. Homogenised wrappers come in any colour, as artificial colouring is often added. Just as colouring is added to the wrapper, so are rum, vanilla and a whole host of other flavourings sometimes added to the binder.

As is the case with most mechanised products, machine-made cigars are more consistent and uniform in construction than hand-made cigars. The additives in the homogenised tobacco also control the burning rate more readily and ensure a mild smoke.

There is a distinct difference between mass-market machine-made cigars and premium machine-made cigars. Notable exceptions are the excellent short filler cigars, La Paz and De Heeren van Ruysdael from the Dutch EBAS Group, and the Muniemaker, Bouquet Special, Judges Cave and Cueto brands from the American F D Grave and Son Company in Connecticut.

There is a wide range of the dry, Dutch-type European variety of good machine-made cigars. These include, the range from Villiger, Gallaher, Henry Winterman, Ritmeester, Willem II, Schimmelpenninck, Christian of Denmark and Agio. Most dry cigars are machine-bunched, using a blend of many types of tobacco. Often they are dusted with a chemical powder to give wrappers a more uniform colour. The word "gemateered" refers to this process. Dutch cigars are meant to be smoked "dry". But this is Holland "dry", so a little humidifying may be necessary in really dry climates such as in the central region of the United States and on the Highveld in South Africa.

Cubatabaco (now Habanos SA), Cuba's cigar export sales group, markets excellent machine-made cigars produced entirely from Havana tobacco and these are really good value for money. Of the 32 Cuban brands being exported, 20 of them included at least a few machine-made cigars. Some examples are: Bolivar Demi Tasse and Regentes; Partgas Culebras and Petit Bouquet; Belinda Petit Coronas; Flor de Cano Petit Coronas; H Upmann's Petit Upmann; and most of the Caney and Troya ranges. The H Upmann and La Corona factories, where all Cuban machine-made cigars are manufactured, are known now by the post revolutionary names of Jose Marti and Fernando Roig respectively.

Machine-bunched & Hand-finished Cigars

Often, only price enables one to tell the difference between a machine-bunched & hand-rolled cigar and a true hand-rolled one, as the draw is much the same. Machine-bunched cigars, made since the 1950s because they are usually less expensive, are often described as "hand-made" cigars. This is because a great deal of hand labour goes into each product; therefore, they do represent exceptionally good value.

The draw is as good as that of hand-made cigar, often even better, because a machine is more consistent in forming the bunch than a human.

What is not generally known is that Cuba produces a large number of machine-bunched and hand-finished cigars. These sometimes have short filler.

A typical way of making this cigar would be to feed the pre-blended filler leaf into a machine that automatically bunches it. While this is happening another worker places a rough-cut binder leaf over a template, where upon a mechanised blade trims the leaf precisely to the required form. The binder is then picked up mechanically and glued with clear gum arabic to hold the filler leaf, which is rolled into the binder before the finished bunch tumbles gently onto a conveyor belt. This is then picked up by hand, trimmed, and placed into the cigar moulds and pressed. After that the machine-bunched cigar is treated exactly like a hand-made one. It goes to the hand-roller who applies the wrapper the same way as he would for a totally hand-made product. The cigar then follows the standard steps of manufacture, including the quality inspection, colour-sorting and ageing processes.

Smoking for Pleasure

SELECTING YOUR CIGAR

A lot has been said and written about selecting the size of a cigar to suit the shape of your face or the size of your frame, but I do not subscribe to this. I believe that quality, flavour and aroma are the only criteria for choosing a cigar.

The size of a cigar is most important.

Whenever you try a new brand it is a good idea to buy just one cigar. Most tobacconists sell cigars singularly as well as by the box, although buying by the box can of course, often entitle one to a discount, I suggest the beginner should start by exploring the small cigars from Holland or Denmark. These include the range from Villiger, Gallaher, Henry Winterman, Ritmeester, Willem, Schimmelpenninck, Christian of Denmark and Agio. These are inexpensive and in most cases, represent good value. These mild cigars have a pleasant aroma. An excellent transition to cigars with more body would be small cigars from Jamaica, Philippines and the Dominican Republic.

Before reaching the goal of Havanas it would be a good idea to progress to the small cigars from Honduras and Nicaragua, as these (particularly, Joyo de Nicaragua) are, in my opinion, closer in body to cigars from Cuba than those from any other country.

When starting on real Havanas I recommend that the tyro experiments with the thin panatela size range. An excellent place to start, if price is no object and if outlets are available, would be the Davidoff No. 2, but, La Gloria Cubana Medaille D'Or No. 4, the Hoyo De Monterey and Hoyo du Gourmet, may prove more practical choices.

Coronas, which are the most popular size in the world, are the middle of the road, allowing not too much smoke on each draw, while the length is such that it provides the right quantity (time) for most people. A good selection here would be the Montecristo No. 1 to No. 5 range, but excluding the gargantuan No. 2, La Flor de Cano Coronas, Diplomaticos No. 3 and, again, if money be no object, the flagship Cohiba Corona Especial. Under "Strength and Flavour" I will deal more fully with the effects size has on the cigar.

The intermediate cigar-smoker will, by this time, not only have experimented with different brands and different sizes from different countries, but will have done this at different times of the day. He will be looking to see what cigar suits him best for given times and given occasions. Generally indicated is a small cigar in the morning, a medium-bodied and medium-size one after lunch and a bigger, full-bodied cigar to follow a heavy dinner. The occasion also affects the smoker's choice. A large Cohiba Esplendido Havana or a Arturo Fuente Masterpiece from the Dominican Republic, would be suitable for a special celebration, such as the birth of a child or the closing of a good business deal.

STRENGTH OF DIFFERENT TOBACCO

A general guide to the strength of cigars from various countries may now be helpful for the beginner. I suggest we rate countries on a scale of one to five. One would be extremely mild and five very strong. Two and three would be the middle of the road, covering, for example, most of the cigars from the Dominican Republic.

BRAZIL: Dark, rich and smooth. Has a natural, slightly sweet flavour: 4.
CAMEROUN: Heavy aroma with a spicy taste: 3 to 4.
DOMINICAN REPUBLIC: Usually smooth, mild and slow-burning. Popular in the USA: 2 to 3. Honeyed, earthy and floral tones are common.
ECUADOR: Good flavour, but mild: 2 to 3.
HAVANA: Medium to full-bodied: 4 to 5. Earthy, coffee, spicy and honeyed tones are often found. Note: apart from local manufacture, the tobacco is often used as part of the filler blend in many European (but not American) dry cigars.
HONDURAS: More full-bodied than those from Dominican Republic. Nearly as rich as tobacco from Cuba, but with a slightly different flavour: 3 to 4. Much spicier, with pronounced cinnamon.
JAMAICA: Mild and subtle: 2.
MEXICO: Not a particularly refined taste, and not particularly consistent, ranging from from very mild up to full bodied and coarse: 1 to 4.
NICARAGUA: Full bodied and aromatic. Wrappers are slightly sweet: 3 to 4.
SUMATRA: Very mild but spicy: 2.

CIGAR SIZES

There are over 70 possibilities. Some of the Havana ranges are confusingly extensive and cover hand-made and machine-made models. The four Cuban brands with the biggest range are Partagas, with a staggering 58; Romeo Y Julieta, with 46 H; Upmann 42; and Punch, close behind, with 39.

Non-Cuban ranges are usually much smaller, with hand-mades, mostly, being limited from six to 10 different sizes.

There are many minor variations in the standard sizes from brand to brand and this can sometimes cause confusion — a confusion which is increased when some brands use size names such as Churchill, Rothschild or Corona, for cigars which are not technically those sizes. The Primo Del Rey Churchill (6 1/2 in/165mm × 16.27mm/41) from the Dominican Republic is actually a Lonsdale, whose standard size is 6 1/2 in/165mm × 16.67mm/42.

A comprehensive list, in metric and non-metric measurements, is provided to assist you in this important task of selecting the right shape and size to suit you and the occasion.

Cigars are measured in inches in the USA and in millimetres in Europe and countries using metric measurement. The thickness of the cigar is measured by the "ring gauge". In the United States this is expressed in 1/64th of an inch. It is not used in Europe, where the thickness is measured in millimetres. Hence, if a corona-size cigar is described as 5 1/2 × 42 in the United States it will translate to 142mm × 16.67mm in Europe. For example:

POPULAR NAME	SIZE
gigante	D18.65mm/47 L 235mm/9 1/2 in
double corona	D19.45mm/49 L 194mm/7 5/8 in
churchill	D18.65mm/47 L 178mm/7 in
torpedo	D20.64mm/52 L 156mm/6 1/8 in
corona grande	D17.07mm/43 L 170mm/6 3/4 in
corona grande	D17.46mm/44 L 162mm/6 3/8 in
corona grande	D18.65mm/47 L 158mm/6 1/8 in
corona grande	D17.46mm/44 L 145mm/5 11/16 in
corona grande	D17.46mm/44 L 143mm/5 5/8 in
corona extra	D18.26mm/46 L 143mm/5 5/8 in
figurado	D20.64mm/52 L 140mm/5 1/2 in
robusto royal	D19.05mm/48 L 127mm/5 in
robusto royal	D18.26mm/46 L 137mm/5 3/8 in
figurado	D17.86mm/45 L 134mm/5 1/4 in
robusto/rothschild	D19.84mm/50 L 124mm/4 7/8 in
lonsdale	D16.67mm/42 L 165mm/6 1/2 in

lonsdale	D16.67mm/42 L 155mm/6 1/8 in
corona	D16.27mm/41 L 150mm/5 7/8 in
corona	D15.87mm/40 L 146mm/5 3/4 in
corona	D15.87mm/40 L 142mm/5 3/4 in
corona	D16.67mm/42 L 142mm/5 9/16 in
corona	D17.46mm/40 L 145mm/5 11/16 in
corona	D16.67mm/42 L 135mm/5 5/16 in
petit corona	D15.87mm/40 L 140mm/5 1/2 in
petit corona	D17.46mm/44 L 132mm/5 3/16 in
petit corona	D15.87mm/40 L 130mm/5 1/8 in
petit corona	D16.67mm/42 L 129mm/5 1/16 in
petit corona/figurado	D17.46mm/44 L 127mm/5 in
petit corona	D15.87mm/40 L 129mm/5 1/16 in
petit corona	D15.87mm/40 L 126mm/5 in
petit corona	D15.87mm/40 L 123mm/4 7/8 in
corona	D16.67mm/42 L 110mm/4 5/16 in
corona	D15.87mm/40 L 116mm/4 9/16 in
corona	D15.87mm/40 L 117mm/4 5/8 in
half corona	D15.87mm/40 L 102mm/4 in
gran/long panetela	D15.08mm/38 L 192mm/7 9/16 in
long paneta	D14.29mm/36 L 128mm/5 5/16 in
panetela	D13.10mm/33 L 178mm/7 in
panetela	D15.08mm/38 L 166mm/6 9/16 in
panetela	D15.48mm/39 L 160mm/6 5/16 in
panetela	D13.89mm/35 L 159mm/6 1/4 in
panetela	D14.68mm/37 L 155mm/6 1/16 in
panetela	D15.08mm/38 L 152mm/6 in
panetela	D13.89mm/35 L 143mm/5 5/8 in
slim panetela	D13.10mm/33 L 170mm/6 3/4 in
slim panetela	D12.70mm/32 L 152mm/6 in
slim panetela	D11.11mm/28 L 175mm/6 7/8 in
culebras	D15.48mm/39 L 146mm/5 3/4 in
short panetela	D15.08mm/38 L 134mm/5 1/4 in
short panetela	D15.08mm/38 L 127mm/5 in
short panetela	D14.29mm/36 L 127mm/5 in
short panetela	D15.08mm/38 L 110mm/4 5/16 in
short panetela	D14.29mm/36 L 115mm/4 9/16 in
short panetela	D14.68mm/37 L 98mm/3 7/8 in
short panetela	D13.89mm/35 L 117mm/4 9/16 in
short panetela	D13.89mm/35 L 110mm/4 5/16 in
belvedere	D15.48mm/39 L 125mm/4 15/16 in
belvedere	D14.30mm/36 L 125mm/4 15/16 in
panetela	D13.89mm/35 L 127mm/5 in
small panetela	D13.49mm/34 L 125mm/4 15/16 in
small panetela	D11.51mm/29 L 126mm/5 in
small panetela	D13.49mm/34 L 117mm/4 9/16 in
small panetela	D12.70mm/32 L 100mm/3 15/16 in
small panetela	D12.30mm/31 L 108mm/4 1/4 in
small panetela	D11.90mm/30 L 100mm/3 15/16 in
small panetela/cigarillo	D10.83mm/26 L 121mm/4 3/4 in
cigarillo	D10.32mm/26 L 115mm/4 1/2 in
cigarillo	D11.51mm/29 L 106mm/4 3/16 in

(In the cigar directory later in this book, all cigars are listed in both units of measurement.)

FLAVOUR AND TASTE

The soil in which tobacco seed is grown enormously influences the flavour of the leaf. In fact, the same seed grown in different areas, even if similar in climate and altitude, will produce tobacco with distinctly different taste characteristics. That is what happened when, after the Castro revolution in Cuba, all the cigar businesses were taken over by the State. The previous owners left, with little or no possessions except, in many cases, small quantities of best quality Cuban tobacco seed and they started new cigar businesses in several other countries, often using the same brand names that they had before. Although, in some cases, the resultant quality was excellent, the flavour and style of tobacco were still quite different from that of Cuba.

Personal preference for most things is subjective and taste and flavour are no exception. All the tongue can taste is bitter, sweet, salt and sour. Terms commonly used to describe cigars are spicy, floral, fruity, woody, aromatic and green, which are all aroma-related, a function of the nose. Other terms often used are harsh, heavy, medium, light, dusty, mellow, strong and subtle, which are terms to describe texture. Rich, complex, fresh, character and lively are related to impression. Because of this personal subjectiveness, it is difficult to generalise on taste and aroma.

AROMA

The purpose of ageing a cigar is to marry or blend the different aromas of the different leaves together with those of the cedar cigar box or the cedar-lined humidor. Fragrance and aroma are present in the oil of the leaf, particularly that of the wrapper. If the wrapper has little or no oil, there is little to be gained in ageing that cigar. This also applies to a cigar that started out with a good, oily wrapper; but, due to bad storage (lack of sufficient humidity or too great a temperature) has dried out.

The aroma or bouquet of a cigar should never be confused with its strength. A cigar could be mild and rich in aroma or, on the other hand, be strong with little or no aroma. Bouquet or aroma will effect the smoker's sense of taste and smell, while the strength of the cigar will affect his throat. If the cigar is too strong for a particular smoker, he will experience harshness on the back of his throat.

Because the nose has a wider range than the palate or tongue, aroma is a most important quality in a cigar. The burning ability can also have a profound effect on enjoyment.

Many believe size affects strength. In reality size has little influence on strength. Strength and flavour come, largely, from the filler blend. The strength of a cigar leaf can be altered during curing, from a pale-green light leaf (light in both colour and taste) to a deep chocolate brown heavy "mudoro" leaf, which is much stronger. So choosing a cigar that is the right strength for you can really only be achieved as a result of experimentation — and that is an almost endless journey of surprise and delight making cigar smoking one of the more civilised pleasures in life.

And remember that your own strength criteria may well vary according to your mood, the time of day and whether the smoke is pre or post prandial. A good tobacconist will have a selection of open boxes of cigars to be sold singly so that you can easily keep a selection of brands and sizes to suit your needs.

SELECTING THE CORRECT LENGTH

Length determines the quantity you wish to smoke at any one time. Often you may think a particular cigar is too strong, but it may just be that the cigar is too long, ie too large, for the occasion, and that you have had enough before you have reached its end. Sometimes, when in the right mood or occasion, one can drink a whole bottle of wine; but, at other times, a glass or two is appropriate. The same applies to a cigar.

SHAPE AND THICKNESS

All cigars fall into two categories *parejos* being straight or parallel-sided and *Figurados* covering all the irregular shapes. The main groups in the *parejos* category are coronas, churchills, lonsdales, robustos, also known as rothchilds, panetelas and cigarillos.

For almost a hundred years the corona size had been the most popular. Classic size for a Cuban corona is 5 9/16 ins/142mm × 16.67mm/42. Londales are the same ring gauge as coronas (16.67mm/42, but longer, up to 165mm/6 1/2 ins.) The traditional size for a churchill is 7 ins/178mm × 18.65mm/47, and for a robustos 5 7/8 ins/124mm × 19.84mm/50.

Panetelas are much thinner. Their ring gauges vary from 11.51mm/29 to 15.48mm/39. The length can be anything from 4 9/16 ins/117mm (small panetela) to 7 ins/178mm (long panetela). Cigarillos are short very thin cigars, with ring gauges from 7.9mm/20 to 11.51mm/29. Length can range from 85mm/3 3/8 ins to 106mm/4 3/16 ins.

There are six major *figurado* shapes. These are:

Torpedo, has a pointed closed head, an open foot or tuck with a bulge in the middle; *Pyramid*, also has a pointed closed head and widens steadily to an open foot or tuck; *Belicos*, is a pyramid shape with a round head rather than a point; *Perfecto*, has both ends closed, with a bulge in the middle; *Diademas*, is a large cigar, usually 203.2mm/8 ins or longer, with an open foot or tuck and pointed head; *Culebras*, comprises three thin cigars plaited together with a thread. This is undone and the cigars are smoked individually.

Each shape can be appropriate for differing occasions.

The thickness of the cigar, measured in either millimetres or, in the United States, in "ring size" or "ring gauge", contributes to the richness and coolness of the smoke. Generally, a well-rolled, thicker cigar, provides a much easier draw. This gives a large, satisfying amount of smoke, with less effort, so the cigar can be smoked slower and, therefore, cooler.

The coolness of the smoke is of paramount importance. If you are used to taking a big pull on the cigar to obtain a big mouthful of smoke, then you will probably, be more comfortable with a cigar with a bigger ring gauge, as a big pull on a thinner cigar, makes the smoke hot and harsh. A sign that this is happening is when the lighted part becomes long and pointed.

A thinner cigar may suit those who like a smaller volume of smoke per draw, but if it is fairly tightly packed, you will find it necessary to draw too hard to get a satisfying quantity of smoke, and this can result in a hot smoke. In such cases, try drawing in a little air with the smoke. Do not be afraid to experiment with cigars of different thicknesses to find the one most satisfying for you. To encourage this, a number of manufacturers are packaging their cigars in packs of five, even the prestige Havana Cohiba range are now being offered in this new trend.

A cigar should be the correct size for the amount of time available to smoke it. Bear in mind that a long thin cigar may smoke for the same time as a short, thick cigar. Remember too, that you only smoke between two-thirds and three-quarters of the cigar, that is, up to the cigar band as the build-up of tars and juices can make the remaining section rather bitter.

WRAPPER COLOURS

The next step is consideration of the wrapper. There are about 65 different shades of these wrappers. The cigar smoker likes to see the same shade of wrapper on each cigar. This does not make the cigar smoke any better, but it is an indication of the pride each company takes in its product, with the resulting assurance of the quality of the rolling.

Within the wide spectrum of shades there are seven basic colours, namely:

CLARO CLARO: At one time the majority of cigars on the American market used to come in this shade which, as a result, became known as AMS, or American Market Selection. It is also known as CANDELA. The light greenish brown colour is achieved by fixing the chlorophyll with rapid high temperature drying that also reduces the natural oils and flavour. Such wrappers can taste slightly sweet.

CLARO: a pale ginger or yellowish brown colour. Often found on Havana brands like H Upman and American brands using Connecticut Shade wrappers. This is the colour of the classic mild cigar.

COLORADO CLARO: A light tawny brown, sometimes called "natural". It is frequently grown in the full sun as are the Cameroon wrappers commonly found on Dominican Partagas.

COLORADO: Reddish-brown and called EMS, or English Market Selection. Used to appeal most to the English market, but today has gained tremendous popularity in the United States. It has the rich flavours and subtle aromas. Its colour normally indicates well-matured cigars.

COLORADO MADURO: Collage brown, medium strength and very aromatic. Has the rich flavour found in many premium Honduran cigars.

MADURO: Coffee brown and comes from the Spanish word for "ripe" and refers to the extra length of time needed to produce a rich, dark brown wrapper. It is sometimes thought of as the traditional Cuban colour and should be oily and silky with strong flavour and mild aroma. The full-bodied Cuban Bolivar is normally this colour, as are Mexican wrappers. It is also occasionally referred to as SMS, or Spanish Market Selection.

OSCURO: Means dark and is blackish brown. It is also called negro (black) in tobacco-producing countries. It is usually left longer on the plant and is longer matured. This colour can be produced artificially by "cooking" the leaves in ovens or pressure cookers. These wrappers are strong, with little aroma and come mainly from Brazil, Mexico, Nicaragua and the sun-grown Connecticut Broadleaf.

OPENING A NEW BOX

Be careful when opening a new box. If it is a dress box, the lid will be nailed down. Do not run a knife along the front split to ease up the lid as you can damage cigars on the top layer. Rather use a flat rounded tool on each side of the single nail, after slitting the label or government seal that may also keep the box shut. Many guillotine cutters have such a device with a small slit or notch that can be inserted around the nail enabling the lid to be prized open without going too far into the box and, thus, protecting the top layer.

THE FINAL CHOICE

Before making the final choice, it is important to consider the cigar's physical appearance and condition. Take a close look at the wrapper. In a premium cigar, this should be free from discolouration and evenly rolled. Occasionally one will find spots on premium cigars. These arise from drops of rain on the tobacco leaf, before it is picked, and the sun's magnification through those drops bleaching out the colour. Such spots are harmless and do not affect the taste or burning qualities of the cigar. Blemishes and discolorations on the wrapper are common on many bundle cigars, a category which will be discussed later.

Except in the case of the dry Dutch (European) cigar, the wrapper should not be dry and dead, but rather have some texture and an oily sheen, particularly in the case of the darker wrappers. This is an indication that the tobacco has been properly cured. Preferably the veins should be visible, albeit fine. They should run as parallel as possible to the length of the cigar, as this ensures that the cigar will burn evenly. This will indicate that it has been properly rolled. If the wrapper is beginning to unravel or crack, it has been stored in conditions that are too dry.

A loosely-packed cigar will indent easily when pressed, feel lighter than one that is more tightly rolled and will, probably, provide an easier draw. However, if too loose it will burn too quickly and, therefore, be hot and harsh.

If there is no give over the entire length of the cigar then it is probably overfilled and will be hard to draw. Hardness in just one spot can indicate that the cigar is "plugged", which, again, affects the draw. If the cigar is, indeed, "plugged" (a fault in construction), you can try kneading the hard spot in the hope of breaking up the blockage. However, there is a major probability that you will damage the wrapper and if that happens then either throw the cigar away or try taking it back to your tobacconist.

Rolling a cigar next to your ear to hear a crackle as an indication that the cigar is too dry, serves no useful purpose. All it does is risk damaging the delicate wrapper. In any case even if the cigar has been kept at a perfect, humidity, you will still hear a faint crackle.

If you examine the foot (the end to be lighted) you will be able to see if the filler has been "booked". That is, the filler will show in straight lines, instead of appearing to flow around in curves.

THE CIGAR BAND

The bands on non-Cuban cigars with Havana brand names tend to be similar to the Cuban originals, although they vary in small details that often include the date of origin of the brand in the space where the Cuban version has the word "Habana".

Should you leave a cigar band on or take it off? This is an oft-asked question. I think the answer really lies in the circumstances or company in which the cigar is smoked. In Britain many consider it "not done" to advertise the brand you are smoking. In the rest of the world the band is usually left on although sometimes it is removed after the cigar has been smoked part of the way.

Care must be taken if the band is to be removed, as quite often, a drop of the glue that joins the band may have oozed out on to the delicate wrapper. This may then tear when the band is taken off. If you are going to remove the band it is probably safer to do so after the cigar has been lit and smoked for about 20 percent of its length as the heat of the smoke will loosen any offending drop of glue. Never slide the band off down the length of the cigar as it will, most likely, dig in and tear the wrapper.

BUNDLE CIGARS

One part of the cigar business that is growing enormously is that of "bundle" cigars. These originally appeared in the early 1960s as good "value for money" smokes. They were a means of using the manufacturer's "seconds", in that there were small blemishes on what were otherwise, good wrappers. Further cost was saved by eliminating the colour sorting process and the costly cedar box. Such offerings are wrapped in bundles of 20, 25 and 50 bandless cigars. These bundles often retail cheaply and include cigars from Honduras, Dominican Republic, Mexico, Jamaica, and recently, Nicaragua. Bundle cigars have become so popular, that manufacturers now plan specifically for that trade.

Originally such cigars often did not match in colour or in taste. Some were machine-made, some hand-made, and the quality was often inconsistent. However, major firms such as Villazon, Consolidated and General Cigar are no longer packing "seconds" in bundles, but are manufacturing specifically for that market and these cigars have the same consistency as the standard product.

There is a growing supply of bundle cigars from Honduras, its Indian Head bundles, made with a long filler, particularly representing good value. The Fuente factory makes what is probably the most expensive cigar in the bundle category, with an outstanding blend of all long-leaf filler. This is of high quality, packaged without the expense of a box.

One draw-back of buying bundles is that one is unable to examine individual cigars because they are all totally enclosed in cellophane. The one thing you can do is to check that those on the outside of the pack have not been damaged.

CUTTING

All hand-made cigars are sealed at the head, that is, the end to be cut and go into your mouth. The cigar has, during manufacture, been sealed with a thumb-nail sized round piece of tobacco which has been cut from wrapper leaf thus ensuring that the colour matches the wrapper itself.

There are several ways to cut the end off the cigar. Mechanical cutters range from simple and inexpensive models (around $3/£1.75) to elaborate, gold-plated ones, costing anything up to $100/£57, for those encorporated with a lighter.

Some smokers prefer to bite the end off, or pinch it off with their fingernail, which often can result in a large rough opening which may cause the wrapper to unroll and ruin the cigar, or to use a sharp knife. Whatever method you choose, it is important that the cut be clean and level, otherwise you can have difficulties with the draw. A popular method is to use a small, portable guillotine, with either a single or double blade. My favourite is a small pair of cigar scissors, that can be sharpened when necessary.

You should aim to cut off only the part of the cap that actually covers the end, so that the rest of the seal remains, creating a thin ring that will stop the wrapper from unravelling. If the whole cap is removed the wrapper will, almost certainly, unravel.

Some people use a cutter that takes a "v" shaped wedge out of the end. For a long time this was considered a most effective method, as it created a two-sided surface to provide an adequate draw and bitter juices and tars were kept away from the tongue. However there are two main disadvantages to this method, few clippers are capable of making a clean v-type cut without damaging the end, and a v-cutter cannot effectively handle sizes thicker than a 47 or 48-ring gauge.

Yet another method is to pierce the end with a cigar drill or piercer. This is not recommended as it gives a narrow opening, with the edges of the filler compressed and can cause a concentration of hot oils and smoke on the tongue.

Many machine-made cigars are cut before they are packaged. This is particularly the case with the dry Dutch or European cigars. The cutting, v-wedging and piercing methods are often to be found in these "ready-to-smoke" cigars.

LIGHTING THE CIGAR

An old-fashioned practice is that of licking the whole cigar before lighting it. This stems from times before humidors were common-place. But even then it was pointless, as it is impossible to humidify a cigar (remember, the filler and binder also need moisture) by simply licking the outside wrapper.

Petrol (gasoline) lighters or cardboard matches should never be used to light a cigar. The smell of the fuel from the lighter and the chemicals and wax on the cardboard can affect the aroma. Use a butane lighter, wooden matches (preferably special long slow-burning ones available from quality tobacco shops) or a cedar wood taper (made from the thin sheets of cedar wood found in most boxes of premium Havanas). When using a match make sure the sulphur has completely burnt off, otherwise this will make your first few draws unpleasant.

It is important to light the cigar properly, so take your time when doing it. The ritual of lighting a cigar adds as much to enjoyment as feeling and smelling it do at selection.

When lighting, the foot should be held just above the tip of the flame and at about 45 degrees to it. Then, rotate the cigar, slowly, gently and evenly, toasting the entire end until it is completely charred.

At this stage, hold the cigar horizontally, with the end about half an inch (one cm) from the flame and begin gently to draw, gradually lighting the entire foot. It is important to have an even burn, so do not forget to rotate the cigar. To facilitate an even light, blow on the glowing end. When you first do this, you will be able to see clearly those areas that still need to be lit. Drawing quickly on the cigar will increase the temperature which, in turn, introduces a harshness that will spoil the cigar's flavour.

SMOKING THE CIGAR

Now draw to enjoy the rich, full flavour and aroma. Do not inhale. You will get sufficient pleasure from the taste and aroma simply by swirling or holding the smoke in your mouth for a few minutes. A cigar should be smoked slowly. It should not be pulled on or puffed too frequently as this will lead to overheating and will spoil the flavour. When a cigar is well-made the wrapper, binder and filler will burn in harmony. If this does not happen you will not get the maximum enjoyment from that cigar. A clear sign that the wrapper is not burning at the same rate as the binder and filler is when a heavy, pronounced black ring appears around the cigar, just below the actual burning part.

The flavour of the cigar changes as you smoke down its length, the smoke filtering through the tobacco and intensifing the flavour as the cigar grows shorter.

Sometimes, even with a top brand, you will find that the cigar will start to burn unevenly, one side faster than the other. When this happens you can clip the burning end straight. This treatment only helps for a short while, but it is all you can do. Assuming the cigar has been lit properly, this phenomenon can be caused by any of the following problems — incorrect humidification, poor burning quality tobacco, a booked filler, or a fault in the actual construction of the cigar. The two most common reasons are incorrect humidification and poor construction of the cigar. Although you can't do much about the other problems you can at least ensure that your cigars are properly humidified.

To achieve maximum satisfaction it is important for the cigar to burn at its optimum temperature and speed. So it is necessary to develop a pace that will suit you and, at the same time, allow the cigar to burn at its slowest effective rate, without going out. It is not the end of the world if the cigar does, in fact, go out. We all relight cigars. But, remember, when drawing the flame over the burnt end you suck in some of the carbonised tobacco and each time you relight the cigar, it gets a little harsher. If you allow the cigar to get cold, the oils and tars will concentrate and saturate the rest of the tobacco and on relighting will affect the taste.

If you are not going to finish the cigar and intend to continue smoking it later, then it is best to blow out the smoke before laying it down and then to knock off the ash after it has gone out. It would also be better to cut off a portion just behind the burnt end. This is not quite the same as a fresh smoke, but, if it's a good cigar, why waste it?

A lot has also been said and written about keeping the ash on a cigar. Long ash on a premium cigar indicates a healthy wrapper and a well-formed long-leaf filler bunch. Many believe that long ash cools the smoke, but I do not think this has ever been proven. Experiment for yourself.

Long ash on a cigar certainly looks attractive. Sometimes, if there is a soft spot in the filler, the ash will fall off unexpectedly at that point. It is not possible to get long ash on machine-made, short-filler cigars, so short ash is normally taken as an indicator of a short filler.

When you reach the last third of the cigar, the build-up of tars and juices will make this remaining section harsh, with a rather bitter aftertaste. When this happens it is time to abandon the cigar. It is not necessary to stub it out, as is done with cigarettes. It will go out soon enough if left in the ashtray. But it is a good idea to dispose of the dead stubs as soon as possible, as their pungent, stale aroma will permeate the room. I keep a medium-size ashtray (or a small bowl may be used) in my sitting room and a further small bowl at the bottom of my wardrobe, half filled with bicarbonate of soda. This absorbs, overnight, the heavy cigar aromas. The bicarbonate of soda only needs to be changed every six months or so, but should be stirred around with the finger every two or three weeks.

Storing Cigars

TEMPERATURE AND HUMIDITY CONTROL

There is no question about it, a cigar has to be stored under the right conditions to get the best out of it. Even if you only buy a small quantity of cigars on a daily or weekly basis, it is still essential that they have been stored correctly by your tobacconist. Other than the Dutch or European dry types, only buy from a shop that keeps its cigars in a humidor containing both a thermometer and a precision hygrometer (humidity gauge). When cigars are left at normal room temperature and humidity levels, they may lose their moisture and condition in a relatively short time. However, cigars can be seriously damaged if the humidity exceeds 80 percent and the temperature goes above 80 degrees F or 25 degrees C.

TOBACCO BORER

Although all tobacco should have been fumigated, it is still sometimes possible for the larvae of the dreaded *Lasioderma serricorne Fabr.* or tobacco beetle as it is known in the United States, to escape warehouse fumigation and lie dormant in the leaf of your cigar. It can stay there until the ideal conditions allow it to hatch and it will then wreck havoc on your cigars. Unless it is treated the whole box will become infested and ruined. If there are neighbouring boxes they, too, can suffer infestation. This tiny, horrific creature will usually create a small tunnel to the surface of the cigar, which is sufficient to completely ruin it. Occasionally the beetle will eat a deep trough along the length of the wrapper before moving on to your next prized possession.

The only way to deal with this problem is to throw out all damaged cigars and then to thoroughly clean and aerate your humidor. Place all undamaged cigars in a plastic ziplock bag. After sealing, put it in the freezer for three days. Then remove the cigars and thaw them out slowly, preferably in a refrigerator first and then in a normal room, until the whole body of the cigar has reached room temperature. But be careful — if you thaw too quickly, the wrappers will split. If done properly, your cigars will be back to normal and the dreaded enemy will have been destroyed.

IDEAL TEMPERATURE AND HUMIDITY

Ideally, cigars should be stored at between 65 and 70 percent relative humidity (RH), with the temperature up to about 70 degrees F, or 21.1 degrees C. In hot, dry climates a cigar can dry out within a couple of days. Many people, particularly in the United States, believe the ideal storage conditions are a 70/70 mix (70 percent RH and 21.1 degrees C).

The British taste, however, is for a much dryer cigar. Top British merchants store at a humidity level of between 60 and 65 percent (see "To Smoke Wet or Dry" chapter). Years ago stock used to be kept by merchants at between 55 and 60 percent RH. One such British merchant once said: "A dry, aged cigar gives you the taste of pure tobacco, not simply water."

The ideal is for your cigar to be neither too dry nor too damp. If a cigar is far too moist, it will feel damp to the touch and, in extreme cases, there will be small bubbles on the wrapper.

The real humidity on your cigars is affected by the temperature in your humidor. The hygrometer could be reading 70 percent, but your cigars could be dry, if the temperature is below 70 degrees F (21.1 degrees C).

RH is the volume of moisture (water vapour) in the air, relative to the maximum amount it could hold at that temperature. Therefore, if the temperature inside the humidor is 74 degrees F (23.3 degrees C), the hygrometer should read 61 percent RH. Conversely, if the temperature drops to 66 degrees F (18.9 degrees C), the RH reading should be 80 percent.

RH has little meaning without knowing the temperature. So install a thermometer together with the hygrometer.

Free humidity/temperature conversion charts, together with instructions are available from Coast Creative Services, P.O. Box 113, Julian, California 92036, USA. Telephone/fax: (1)(619) 765-3455.

Sometimes cigars develop a "plume", also called "bloom". This is a whitish dust on the surface of the wrapper and arises from the crystallisation of oils in the cigar tobacco. Plume, which can evolve over a long period in the dark, moist confines of a humidor, is not harmful and can be brushed off with a soft brush, a dry tissue or sponge. Some smokers even believe it is beneficial to a cigar's taste.

Mould, however, has a bluish tint and will mark the wrapper. It can also be removed like plume, but is a sign that your cigars are being stored in too hot and/or humid conditions. If you allow mould to remain and do not reduce the humidity in which your cigars are stored, the cigars will begin to smell musty thus seriously affecting your smoking enjoyment.

STORING CIGARS IN HUMIDORS

If you are a regular smoker then it is worthwhile investing in a good quality humidor. This should be able to hold a realistic number of cigars. They come in all sizes, storing from 25 up to even 200 cigars. Your humidor should approximate to your usual brand. If you wish to store up to 25 Churchill size cigars then a humidor that can store 25 coronas will not suffice.

It is preferable to have a humidor that has been lined with cedar wood, as its spicy aroma is ideal for intermingling with tobacco aromas. If it is a high quality container it will come with a hygrometer (a gauge for measuring the level of humidity) as well as a humidifier (a device for putting moisture into the air in your humidor). These devices range from those that work on sponges, chemical compounds to even plain bottles containing water.

A humidor should always be measured against its ability to provide a constant performance over a long period. Which means that it should not warp or crack over the years. And make sure the lid closes tightly. Remember that the humidor will only provide the correct humidity inside if it is stored in an environment not exceeding 75 °F or 24 °C and preferable around 70 °F or 21 °C.

Humidors come in a wide range of finishes and wood — from painted exteriors in different colours, lacquers in either matte or gloss finishes. A humidor should not overwhelm its surroundings. It should be both handsome and functional.

DIRECTORY OF HUMIDOR SUPPLIERS IN THE USA

The following is a brief list of some humidor suppliers in the United States, with telephone numbers where additional information can be obtained.

ALBEE AMERICAN ARTS — Tel: (909) 780-7892.

CAO International Inc. — Tel: (615) 352-0587.

CLUB IMPORTS — Tel: (800) 292-2582 for retailer information.

M. CORNELL IMPORTERS INC. — Tel: (612) 633-8890.

DANIE MARSHALL INC. — Tel: (714) 973-8660. Fax: (714) 550-0631.

DAVIDOFF OF GENEVA (CT) INC. — Tel: (800) 328-4365 or (203) 323-5811.

DUNHILL OF LONDON STORES — Tel: (800) 776-4053.

HOLLCO ROHR — Tel: (800) 247-6653 for retailer information.

MASTRO DE PAJA USA, INC. — Tel: (800) 886-7252 or (813) 961-5788.

MICHEL PERRENOUD — Tel: Nat Sherman's at (800) 221-1690.

MIKE'S CIGARS DISTRIBUTORS INC. — Tel: (800) 962-4427 or (305) 538-6707

NAT SHERMAN — Tel: (800) 221-1690 or Fax: (212) 246-8639.

SAVINELLI — Tel: (919) 481-0511 for retailer information.

DUTCH OR DRY CIGARS

The Dutch-type cigars that are so popular in Europe, and South Africa are meant to be smoked "dry". These include, among others, the range from Villiger, Gallaher, Henry Winterman, Ritmeester, Willem, Schimmelpenninck, Christian of Denmark and Agio. These cigars will perform well if stored in areas with a humidity level of between 55 and 60 percent.

Dry cigars also come from Germany, Switzerland and Denmark and with a variety of tobacco for the filler including that of Cuba, Indonesia, Mexico, Java, Cameroun and Mexico. The lighter and milder tasting wrappers come from Sumatra and the darker, spicy ones from Brazil. The former are the most popular but the darker cigars are often smoked after dinner or on special occasions. As stated in the chapter on machine-made cigars, many of these dry cigars are made with homogenised leaf (HTL).

One reason why this type of cigar is not as popular in the United States as it is in Europe is that, although smaller, often costs much the same as a larger cigar from Honduras or the Dominican Republic. However, some isolated larger sizes of the Dutch dry smokes do exist and a Christian of Denmark Corona can last a full hour.

REFRIGERATING CIGARS

Often the question is asked if there is benefit in storing cigars in a refrigerator. And the answer must be a clear no, unless the only available storage space is much colder, hotter or dryer than a refrigerator. Then they should go in for a short time, until more suitable conditions can be obtained. If cigars are to be stored in a refrigerator they must be put inside a sealed plastic ziplock bag otherwise they will absorb adjacent food flavours.

The average temperature in a normal household refrigerator is about 35 °F or 10 °C — far too cold, inhibiting any maturing or development of the tobacco and resulting only in slow deterioration.

So the answer is, under all normal circumstances, refrigerators are to be avoided!

RESTORING DRY CIGARS

There has been much discussion and argument over whether cigars can be restored to their normal state once they have dried out. If a cigar has become dry and the wrapper has not cracked and unravelled, then it can be restored. But this must be done slowly and patiently. If the wrapper has actually broken then the cigar should be discarded. If it has completely dried out, it will fall apart between your fingers regardless of how gentle and careful you are.

Remember, that although dry cigars could be brought back to an acceptable smoking condition, they will probably never be as good as they originally were. There are several ways of treating dry cigars, depending on their condition.

They must be removed from any cellophone wrappers, cedar or aluminium tubes before any restoration process. If they are not excessively dry, the box with its lid open should be placed inside a large walk-in humidor or, if one is not available, in a cellar or similar dampish location, where they can be exposed slowly to dampness, as close to 70 percent humidity as possible.

After two or three days the top and bottom rows should be interchanged and should remain in that position for another two or three days.

If you do not have a walk-in humidor or cellar then you can probably undertake a similar process using two ziplock plastic bags. Firstly, puncture the smaller bag with many little holes and then insert the open box and close the bag. Place that bag, now containing the cigars, into a larger ziplock bag containing a wrung-out slightly damp sponge. Seal the second bag. This method of using ziplock bags has been suggested by Lew Rothman, owner of JR Tobacco of America, one of the world's largest retailers.

After four to six days the cigars should be removed from their box and exposed to the full humidity. Sometimes small water bubbles may appear under the wrapper, but there is nothing to fear as long as you give the cigars a 25 percent rotation every two or three days. Complete the process until the cigars have been fully rotated at least twice, providing even exposure to the humidity. By this time any bubbles will have disappeared. This process can take up to three weeks.

I have practised this "quarter-turn" method for more than 10 years now and it works!

At the end of the treatment the wrappers will again look and feel smooth with only the normal gentle crackling sound when the cigars are pressed between fingers. They can then be returned to their original box.

If you use the ziplock bags, ensure the wrung-out sponge is just damp, not excessively wet.

When the cigars are not too dry they can sometimes be restored by simply wrapping the closed box in a damp (not wet) towel for about two weeks.

After treatment it is best to leave cigars for six to 12 months for the three components (filler, binder and wrapper) again to equilibrate before smoking. Just check on their condition every three months.

It takes only a few weeks for a cigar to become dry in adverse conditions, but it takes a few months to restore them to a smokable condition.

Incidentally it is best not to mix cigars of different brands, particularly Havanas and non-Havanas, but to store them separately.

RESTORING EXTREMELY DRY CIGARS

If you provide extremely dry cigars with too much humidity, too quickly, then the wrappers will split. It is best to keep them in their box in a large or walk-in humidor or ziplock bag for about a month before opening the lid. Then they can be removed and then undergo the previously described rotation method.

If you buy your cigars from reputable tobacconists, who do not allow their cigars to get out of condition, the need for such tiresome processes will not arise.

Ageing Cigars

The wrapper has the biggest single effect on the ageing or maturing potential of a cigar. Experiments have been undertaken with cigars from the same area of cultivation, with similar tobacco and production techniques but using different shades of wrappers. In the same storage conditions over the same period of time they have reacted differently. Darker, oily wrappers, with shades of Colorado Claro and Colorado, proved to have better ageing potential than the lighter Claro Claro or Claro wrappers.

Ageing cigars is much like maturing wine. Laying it down will not improve a bad wine. It has to be good in the first place, with good fruit, sufficient alcohol, acid and tannins. If it is light-bodied with little fruit and tannins it is better to drink it early.

Many cigar producers believe their cigars are ready to be smoked once they have left the factory, however, a large number of retailers feel that it is probably best not to smoke fine hand-made cigars for a year or longer. Some importers and top-flight retailers still age quality hand-made cigars for anything up to two years.

George Gershell, Consolidated Cigar's leaf expert with 35 years experience and a senior vice-president, was adamant during a memorable dinner with him and two other senior executives of the company, during my recent visit to the company's head office in Fort Lauderdale, Florida, that it is impossible for the tobacco to undergo another fermentation once the cigar has been made. Both he and Richard DiMeola, the company's Chief Operating Officer, questioned the cigar's ability to become more mellow with maturing and ageing. (See Chapter "Consistency the Keynote" by Richard DiMeola).

Again, like wine, proper ageing will only take place in good storage conditions. In Continental Europe and North America ideal conditions are 70 percent humidity and temperatures of between 18 and 20 degrees C or 65 to 70 degrees F. In the United Kingdom, where there is a preference for a dryer taste, the humidity is normally a little lower at between 60 and 65 percent.

How long should one age cigars and for how long can one?

The first is a matter of personal preference. But many experts believe that, under the right storage conditions, cigars will reach their peak in six to 10 years. However, if you are storing cigars for longer periods, you should smoke one periodically to see whether or not you like its development. Although they probably will not improve after 10 years of ageing, some cigars, under the right conditions, can still be a wonderful smoke up to 50 years of age.

The winter 1993/94 issue of the magazine, *Cigar Aficionado* carried a most informative article entitled, "Smoking History" which discussed cigars up to 60 years old.

If you are going to age cigars, you will need an effective humidor. The size or number of humidors will depend on the quantity of cigars you have. Before placing them in your humidor, you will need to take the cigars out of any cellophane or aluminium they may be in.

Although the intention of the cellophane and aluminium tubes is to keep the cigars fresh and in perfect condition, in practice they lose their aroma and become dull and dry if kept in tubes for periods of a year or so. But after proper humidifying they can recover. Many experts believe that keeping cigars in tubes for long periods delays the ageing process and that they need to breathe if the final stage of fermentation is to take place.

The tube is useful for carrying the cigar to smoke after a lunch or dinner, particularly if you only wish to take one of the larger sizes, such as a Churchill, which would otherwise require a large cigar case. It is also convenient if you have to extinguish it, such as upon entering a lift or elevator. Often you will still be able to smoke it later.

Another problem with cigars in tubes is that, as we normally only see one cigar at the time we take it out of the tube, just before smoking it, we do not get an opportunity to appraise the general standard and uniformity in colour of the whole box. However, be assured that after the cigars have been dried, they are grouped by hue and tone, and packed in chromatic harmony in each box, tubes or no tubes. Cigars with unsightly veins are always removed.

It is a great source of pride for both the cigar maker and the cigar smoker to be able to see the same shade of wrapper on each cigar. This does not make the cigars smoke any better, but it is an indication of the pride each company takes in its product, with the resulting assurance of the quality of the rolling.

Except for the large Churchill sizes the majority of machine-made cigars are packed in aluminium tubes or cellaphane. A notable exception is the Cohiba range where the Lanceros, Panetalas and Especiales are packed in cellophane.

VINTAGE CIGARS

A fairly new category of interest for the aficionado is the vintage cigar. It is made with specially selected tobaccos, all from the same year of growing (vintage). Often, although not always, it is aged longer.

Only years of exceptional quality are chosen. As premium hand-made cigars are only produced from leaf at least three years old, the maker is able to determine that the tobacco is of the highest quality, before the cigar is made.

The first brand to follow this practice was Dunhill, who launched their Aged Cigar Series in 1990 from tobacco from the 1986 Dominican Republic vintage. Dunhill and Macanudo are among a few brands that prominently display the actual vintage year on the box. The date thus shown is the year the tobacco was grown and not the year of manufacture or release.

The current Dunhill vintage on sale is 1989. The last vintage was 1987 and some of these can still be found in a few retailers.

I believe that 1990 and 1991 were excellent years in the Dominican Republic and, as a result, more premium cigars have joined the vintage ranks. These cigars are normally packed in boxes with special labels and bands that set them apart from the normal non-vintage category. They are also among the most expensive on the market. The four sizes from the Juan Clemente "Club Selection" vintage edition, the Vintage Cabinet I to IV models in the Macanudo Vintage series and the Number 1 to 3 models in the Ashton Cabinet Selection Vintage Limited Edition, are all certainly worth the extra cost.

The Hoyo De Monterrey Excalibur and Punch Grand Cru ranges from Villazon are not called vintage but are made of selected tobacco and are of excellent quality.

Cigar Smoking Etiquette

Always allow sufficient time to fully enjoy the cigar of your choice. A corona will probably need a good 30 minutes, whereas a robusto or Rothchilds size may require a little longer, perhaps 45 minutes if you are a slow puffer. Any of the Churchill sizes will demand an hour or, sometimes, slightly more. These larger sizes are normally much more appropriate for relaxed late night smoking. The smaller cigars, such as petit coronas and cigarillos are popular today, as they are quick to smoke, in tune with the hectic pace of a working day.

For me, smoking a cigar is really taking a break from the hurly-burly of life. Enjoying a fine cigar while listening to appropriate music and sipping a glass of fine port, is a wonderful opportunity to contemplate what you have accomplished during the day and what still needs to be done. In leisure hours, you can relax, focus your senses on your cigar, and fully appreciate the exotic tastes and aromas of a fine hand-rolled product.

In Japan where social etiquette is largely based on tradition and dictates behaviour to a larger extent than Western countries, a subordinate cannot smoke a cigar larger than that of his superior without transgressing social etiquette.

Cigars should not be smoked during a meal. Their heavy, rich aroma can easily interfere with one's ability to enjoy the fine flavours of good food.

It is good manners to respect the comfort and rights of non-smokers.

While I smoke in the living area of our home, I never do so in any of the bedrooms. Because, as attractive and pleasant as the aroma of a lighted cigar can be, just as unpleasant is the smell of stale smoke and used cigars. While I believe cigar smokers have a right to their pleasure, not only in their own homes, but also in certain public places, it is good manners to be sensitive and aware of the reaction of non-smokers. It is not wise or kind to blow smoke in the face of a non-smoker.

If you wish to enjoy a cigar in a restaurant and you are in the smoking area, it is still polite to wait for the other diners at your table, and even those at adjoining tables, to finish their meal before lighting up.

If you smoke during the day while working, you may find yourself with a good cigar in hand and the need to use a lift or elevator, where, in many parts of the world, smoking is not allowed. Then you will find that the carrying of an empty large aluminium tube is quite useful. This will enable you to place your smoke in the tube for re-lighting or discarding later.

When offering a cigar to guests it is not good manners to take one out of the box or humidor. It is better to offer the open container so that they can make their own selection. If the humidor is too large to take to your guests, then they should be invited over to make their own selection.

However, when offering a new box to guests (after opening by the method described in "Opening A New Box") press gently on the rounded end of the cigars, thereby lifting the foot or cut end, enabling it to be easily removed without damage. Lay this cigar across the others and offer the box.

Never allow anyone with sharp finger-nails to remove a cigar from the tightly packed box as sharp nails can often ruin the wrapper of either the chosen one, or of those on either side. This could prove to be very costly.

A cherished gift for many a cigar smoker, is a box of fine hand-made cigars. Sir Winston Churchill, war-time prime minister of Great Britain received large quantities of Havanas. General Ulysses S Grant, 18th president of the United States and the Union general who brought the Confederate Army to its knees, received more than 10 000 boxes of premium brands after the battle of Fort Donelson. Heads of states and political leaders in many countries receive cigars from visiting dignitaries.

The now non-smoking President Fidel Castro (he hasn't smoked for over nine years) still appreciates the value of a fine cigar and he had his best makers produce a special and unique brand, called "Trinidad", after one of Cuba's most beautiful historical cities, exclusively to present to visiting dignitaries. The Trinidad is identical in shape to the Cohiba Lanceros, being long and thin, measuring 15.08 mm/38 ring gauge and 190 mm/7 1/2 inches. It is packed in a simple cedar box of 100 cigars and the El Laguito factory, where the famous Cohiba range is also made, produces about 20 boxes a month.

Cigars always make a warm and welcome gift to a cigar smoker.

To Smoke Wet or Dry?

Humidification has dominated the Havana cigar trade in Britain over the past 20 years. In the mid-1970s there were two or three Havana retailers in Britain who kept their cigars humidified. Today there are hundreds.

Traditionally the British preferred dry Havana cigars, while the reverse was the case on the Continent.

Shortly before the Second World War, the late Zino Davidoff displayed a sign in his Geneva shop advising customers that all his cigars were humidified at 72 percent. A similar sign in the window of one of a leading London cigar merchant, would then probably have resulted in that merchant going out of business with customers avoiding his shop like the plague.

It was common practice in those days for British importers to place their cigars in drying rooms before delivery to retailers. The unique feature of the British trade was that they aged their cigars, usually for a minimum of five years, before permitting them to be sold to smokers.

To gain full benefit from ageing and maturing, Havanas must be kept at a significantly lower humidity, no higher than 50 percent, and then be allowed gradually to lose some of the moisture content which they originally contain. (See "Drying and Ageing Cigars".)

In the early part of this century Alfred Dunhill conducted "exhaustive research", in conjuction with the National Physical Laboratory, into the effects of varying temperature and humidity on fine Havana leaf.

These experiments, started before the First World War and completed shortly after it, led Dunhills to set up a complex series of condition-controlled cigar rooms.

First, the cigars recently imported from Havana, and judged too "green" to smoke, were placed in "The Maturing Room" and allowed to recover slowly from the rigours of their journey. Then they were transferred into either "The Keeping Room", where they were maintained at a comparatively low level of humidity, or into "The Humidor" where the "humid warmth of the Cuban climate was scrupulously reproduced".

Dunhills have operated a humidor ever since at 30, Duke's Street in St. James and for the past 30 years all their cigars have been kept humidified.

There are those who mourn the passing of the traditional British dry cigar for, fully aged and matured, it offered a refined delicacy of flavour that is not generally available today.

The reasons for its demise were largely commercial. After all, these days who could afford to sit on their stocks of valuable Havanas for five years before selling them? However, the smoker played his part too. The explosive growth in foreign travel in recent years introduced even the most dyed-in-the-wool British smoker to wet cigars and, in the end, he decided that he preferred them.

No doubt he was also influenced by the spread of central heating to nearly every home, office and shop in the country, which threatened to dry out his precious cigars to a much greater extent than was ever intended by Alfred Dunhill and the like. The British trade responded slowly to the change in consumer taste. Most shops were content to leave their Havanas unprotected on open shelves in the belief that the cigars were drying out in the way that customers wanted them. There was, of course, a world of difference between the classic British dry cigar, which had been aged and matured under controlled conditions, and those that had simply been left to desiccate at random. Smokers soon made this clear.

From the end of the 1970s retailers started to install humidors, and those who did prospered.

One of the first was Desmond Sautter in his Mount Street shop opposite the world famous Connaught Hotel. This shop now boasts three separate humidified areas, but the first was a glass walled room sited opposite the entrance, which was installed in 1979.

Sheffield Wine Merchant Michael Menzel recently installed a floor-standing humidified cabinet and business jumped by between 30 percent in the first six months after making the switch from ordinary counter display cabinets.

Smoking and Health

Much has been said and written about smoking and health. Since the first US Surgeon General's Report "Smoking and Health" in 1964 (the Terry Report) it is pretty well accepted that smoking is bad for one's health. However, according to *Dr Frank G Colby, no component or group of components, found in smoke, has ever been proved to be the cause of disease in man.

"Not a single experiment has been able to induce lung cancer resembling human lung cancer in labaratory animals through smoke inhalation, although in many cases the smoking conditions were unreasonably drastic, involving amounts comparatively many times the lifetime intake of even the heaviest of human smokers.

"This also applies to animal experiments involving other diseases alleged to be associated with smoking.

"Most of the allegations against smoking are based on 'statistical associations' found in epidemiological associations.

"Despite this, a large majority of the medical profession and the public, smokers and non-smokers alike, believe that smoking 'causes' various chronic diseases, such as lung cancer and/or cardiovascular diseases and/or chronic respiratory diseases, etc."

Critics condemn all forms of smoking as being equally hazardous to health. They make no distinction between cigarette and cigar smoking. Yet the differences are huge.

All tobacco leaf for premium cigars, which virtually include all hand-made and a few of the top machine-made cigars, undergoes two and, in some cases, three natural fermentations before the cigar is made. The process is described in detail in the section on "Leaf Fermentation" in the chapter "Growing Cigar Tobacco".

During the first fermentation, which lasts for up to 30 days, a temperature of 35 °C is maintained. During the second, and more powerful fermentation, a temperature of 45 °C (115 °F) is held for up to 60 days.

Some of the best cigars, such as Cohiba from Cuba, use tobacco that undergoes a further fermentation.

According to Tobacco Encyclopedia, Nicotine decreases by between 10 and 90 percent. Soluble carbohydrates are eliminated and there is a considerable reduction of nitrogen compounds which result in the obvious release of gaseous ammonia. The pH becomes more alkaline during fermentation.

Therefore, cigar tobacco is, as a result, not only more palatable than cigarette tobacco, but also has far fewer impurities that can affect health.

Another big factor when considering the effect cigar smoking has on the lungs, is that the cigar smoker usually does not inhale the smoke, which should only be swirled around the inside of the mouth to experience the flavour and aroma.

The anti-smoking lobby often claims that the effects of passive smoking are just as harmful to health as direct smoking. Therefore, the results of the first comprehensive research on how much tobacco smoke non-smokers really inhale from passive smoking is staggering. Released by an independent research laboratory, this reveals the amount to be, at the most, the equivalent of one cigarette a week.

The results of this survey, published towards the end of 1994, suggested that the health risks from passive smoking are, in fact, non-existent.

Scientists at the research laboratory, Hazelton Europe, attached air sampling devices to 255 non-smoking volunteers for 24 hours. The survey, sponsored by the Centre for Indoor Research, an organisation founded principally by the American chemical industry, with some money from tobacco interests, also showed that non-smokers breathe in 100 times more air pollution from other sources, such as petrol fumes.

A senior lecturer in toxicology at University College, London, said that the research suggested that passive smoking was an unlikely cause of lung cancer, as it was found that many of the volunteers were exposed to the equivalent of just five cigarettes a year and that even the highest exposure was equal to only 50 cigarettes a year.

The head of the research team, Dr Keith Phillips, said in an interview that he was more concerned about the ill effects of filling up his car with petrol than sitting in a smoky pub.

In my opinion, what minimal ill effects cigar smoking may have are more than off-set by the pleasure brought to the smokers. These mostly use the occasion as a break in the day, when their main focus is on keeping the cigar burning slowly and savouring the flavours and aromas. For many, this is a form of meditation when they shake off the many daily pressures, slow down, and relax with one of the truly great pleasures in life.

*An authoritative, detailed, article on this subject, entitled "Smoking and Health by Dr Frank G Colby Ph. D., Chemical Engineer and Associate Director of Scientific Issues in the Research and Development Department of RJ Reynolds Tobacco Co., Winston Salem, NC, USA, appears in Tobacco Encyclopedia, published by Tobacco Journal International.

Some Major Names in the Industry

AGIO SIGARENFABRIEKEN NV

Agio Sigarenfabrieken NV is a family enterprise, established in 1904 by Jacques Wintermans. Head office is in Duizel, Holland, where the processing of filler tobacco and the packaging and the worldwide dispatch of its products take place.

The company's rapid growth, combined with shortage of manpower in the Dutch Kempen, led to the establishment of a subsidiary in Geel, Belgium, in 1961. This is where all its cigars are currently produced.

The marked rise in wages in Holland and Belgium and the need to remain competitive internationally, led to relocation of its more labour intensive activities to countries where labour costs are relatively low. Hence subsidiaries were established in Malta in 1973, in Sri Lanka in 1985, and in the Dominican Republic in 1990. These companies process the binder and wrapper onto bobbins for their own cigars and for other manufacturers.

The group employs about 2 500 people worldwide,

producing about one billion cigars a year, of which about 500 million are exported under its own brand names to more than 100 countries outside Europe.

BRANDS

Machine-made (No. of models indicated in brackets):

Agio (11)	Balmoral (17)
Panter (7)	De Huifker (6)

CONSOLIDATED CIGAR CORPORATION

In 1918 Julius Lichtenstein, president of leaf specialists, American Tobacco Co., through sensitive and complicated negotiations, brought together six independent cigar manufacturers, and formed them into an amalgamation. At the time all of them were in competition in localised markets with various regional brands. Full co-operation among the six was slow to crystallise and it wasn't until 1921 that Lichtenstein grasped the reins of what was to become the Consolidated Cigar Corporation.

One of the original six, G H Johnson Cigar Co., had a cigar brand called Dutch Masters. It was decided to make this trademark the company flagship and, through constant promotion and national advertising in print and TV, Dutch Masters was built into what is today one of the biggest dollar volume cigar brands in the USA.

In 1926 Consolidated Cigar bought the GHP Cigar Co., owners of the El Producto brand, promoted by comedian George Burns who, until his death at the age of 100, early in 1996, smoked an average of 10 of those cigars a day.

There were further acquisitions under Julius Lichtenstein, who was finally succeeded in 1945 by Alfred Silberman. When Alfred died in 1948, his son, the legendary "Buddy" Silberman, became president.

The company acquired Muriel cigars from P. Lorriland & Co. in 1956. Through use of the now famous, "Pick me up and smoke me sometime", commercials with Edie Anton, (succeeded in the 1970s by a new Muriel girl, Susan Anton) the brand is today one of the major ones, in units, in the USA.

In 1968 the company was acquired by the huge multi-national corporation, Gulf & Western.

Consolidated Cigar entered the premium, hand-made cigar business through the formation of Cuban

Cigar Brands in the Canary Islands in conjunction with Pepe Garcia, whose factory in Cuba was nationalised by the Castro regime. It then bought Moro Cigar Co., and its Primo del Rey trademark. In the early 1970s the company became a factor in the pipe tobacco industry with the purchase of Slikliff Tobacco Co., manufacturer of Mixture 79 and other pipe tobacco brands.

Gulf and Western sold Consolidated Cigar in 1983 to five of its senior managers. Only 16 months later it was resold to MacAndrew K Forbes, the holding company controlled by Ronald Perelman, chairman of Revlon Inc. He installed Theo Folz, in July 1984, as president and chief executive.

Under Folz, a new structure and culture began to emerge, with emphasis on product quality and humanism. In 1986, he engineered the acquisition of the assets of the American Cigar Co., including Antonio y Cleopatra, La Corona and Roi-Tan cigars, as well as distribution for Sail and Flying Dutchman pipe tobacco, made in Holland by Theodorus Niemeyer Royal Factories. In addition, the company bought Milton Sherman Tobacco Co., and the pipe tobacco brands of Iwan Ries & Co.

In November 1988, Folz and five members of top management, together with Vestar Capital Partners, purchased Consolidated Cigar from MacAndrew L Forbes. Within two-and-a-half months of closing the deal, the company made three more acquisitions, Te-Amo cigars and other brands from Te-Amo/Geryl Corp., Royal Jamaica Cigars from Jamaica Tobacco Co., and Century Tobacco Company's pipe tobacco products.

Corporate headquarters was moved to Fort Lauderdale, Florida, where general policy decisions are made today although more autonomy for local decision-making has been given to on-site management.

In 1991 successful negotiations were concluded with Cuban Cigar Corporation (CCC), a company owned together by Consolidated Cigars and Cifuentes International, which marketed Montecristo and H. Upmann outside Cuba and the giant Spanish monopoly, Tabacalera SA.

Early in 1993 the group was repurchased by MAFCO Holdings Inc., Ronald Perelman's personal company. There was no change in personnel, responsibilities or direction of the company.

In 1995 the group produced over 45 million cigars —

25 million in the Dominican Republic, of which about four million were machine-made; 12 million in Honduras and about eight million in Mexico.

Total production of mass market machine-made cigars in the USA is around one billion.

Consolidated Cigar employs about 2 500 people. It has wholly-owned production facilities in Honduras, Puerto Rico, Pennsylvania, Virginia and the Dominican Republic and affiliations for production in Mexico and Holland. Leaf supplies are obtained from growers in most parts of the world.

Distribution in the USA is conducted through its own field sales organisation selling through a network of tobacco and candy distributors, direct-buying retail chains and speciality tobacco shops.

BRANDS

Machine-made (No. of models indicated in brackets):

Backwoods (3)	Super Value (4)
Harvester (2)	Supre Sweets (4)
1886 (1)	Dutch Masters (8)
El Producto (9)	Dutch Treats (5)
La Corona (1)	Antonio Y Cleopatra (4)
Roi-Tan (6)	Ben Franklin (2)
Muriel (11)	Rustlers (3)
Muriel Sweet Little Cigars (1)	Supre Sweets
Dutch Masters Collection (4)	
Super Value Pipe Tobacco Cigars (2)	

Hand-made in Dominican Republic:

H. Upmann (27)	Flamenco (1)
Don Diego (14)	Playboy by Dan Diego (5)
Primo Del Rey (20)	Henry Clay (3)
Cabanas (4)	Santa Damania (5)
Primo Del Rey Club Selection (4)	
H. Upmann Cabinet Selection (3)	
H. Upmann Chairman's Reserve (4)	
La Corona Vintage Selection (4)	

Hand-made in Mexico:

Te-Amo (18)	El Triunfo (7)
Te-Amo Segundo (7)	Matacan (10)
New York, New York by Te-Amo (6)	

Hand-made in Honduras:

Las Cabrillas (7)	Don Mateo (12)
Riata (11)	Tulas (6)

La Llorona (6)   Republicana Dominica (8)

CULBRO CORPORATION

In 1907 the Cullman Family started to grow tobacco in Connecticut from Cuban seed. By the late 1950s it owned and farmed 1 800 acres of tobacco.

In 1961 the son, Edgar M. Cullman Sr., was instrumental in forming a group that was to become Culbro Corporation, of which he was currently chairman, to buy General Cigar Company. At that time Culbro owned the following mass-market brands Robert Burns, White Owl, William Penn and Van Dyck, and had a combined turnover of about $30 million. It then bought General Cigar for about $25 million.

Shortly afterwards General Cigar took over Gradiaz, Anis makers of the premium Gold Label Cigar range. In 1969 it acquired the Temple Hall factory in Jamaica, which owned the Macanudo brand, sold mainly in the UK, but not in the US market. Temple Hall also made Creme De Jamaic cigars.

General Cigar, after reformulation, launched Macanudo ("the greatest" in Spanish) in the USA. Distribution was mainly to restaurants, and in 1970 the company backed this with considerable advertising. Macanudo was probably the first brand to receive such strong advertising support, making it the country's largest selling premium cigar with sales of over 12 million in 1995. Today 20 percent of production is in the Dominican Republic and 80 percent in Jamaica.

In 1974 the company bought the prestigious Partagas brand from Ramon Cifuentes, a Cuban refugee, who owned Partagas in Cuba before Castro came to power.

This was probably the first purchase by an American company of a Cuban brand name since the Cuban embargo. Production started in Jamaica but switched in 1979 to the Dominican Republic. Present sales are about half of that of Macanudo.

In 1976 the company established a leaf-processing operation in the Dominican Republic, handling all types of tobacco but specialising in wrapper leaves. Three years later the company expanded this limited activity into a full-fledged cigar manufacturing operation. Cigars are made in teams of one buncher supplying two rollers.

In 1991 the company registered the brand Cohiba in the USA and, to protect the registration, began limited marketing of three sizes. The original Cuban Cohiba brand was created by the present regime and is the flagship of Habanos SA, the Cuban cigar monopoly.

General Cigar engineered, under the supervision of its president, Austin Mc Namara, what is considered to be one of the greatest marketing achievements in the cigar industry, with the launch, in November 1995, of the Partagas 150 Signature Series. It was presented as a one-off special edition with a rare 18 year-old Cameroon wrapper. Although the six models retailed at between $5-50 and $12-00 and total production was more than one million cigars, it sold out almost immediately.

In 1996 Edgar M. Cullman Jr. succeeded his father as CEO, while retaining the titles of president and chief operating officer of Culbro Corporation. In that year the group opened in New York the first of a planned string of Club Macanudos — comprising a cigar bar and restaurant. Available were about 25 cigar brands, private humidor lockers and a club room with backgammon, chess tables, televisions, telephones, fax machines and a stock ticker. This concept was the brain-child of Cullman Jr.

Culbro, a public company quoted on the New York Stock Exchange, also has investments in landscape nurseries, industrial packaging machinery, labelling systems and real estate development.

BRANDS

Hand-made in Dominican Republic (No. of models indicated in brackets):

Partagas (18)	Macanudo
Canaria D' Ora (7)	Ramon Allones (7)

Hand-made in Jamaica:

Macanudo (32)	Jamaican Pride (7)
Temple Hall (12)	

Hand-made in USA:

Robert Burns (3)	Wm. Penn (4)
White Owl (14)	Tijuana Smalls (3)
Garcia y Vega (22)	Tiparillo (4)

DAVIDOFF OF GENEVA

Legendary Zino Davidoff was son of Henri Davidoff, a cigarette maker and merchant who, in 1911, immigrated to Switzerland from Russia and grew up working in his father's tobacco store in Lausanne. Later went to tobacco plantations in Bahia, Brazil and Cuba, to gain practical experience in all aspects of cigar-making.

On returning he developed the business, opening a shop on corner of Rue de Rive and Rue de La Fontaine in fashionable Geneva, which was the Mecca of Europe's rich and famous.

In 1970 Zino Davidoff, then 65, sold to large import-export Max Oettinger Company based in Basel, Switzerland. This company was founded in 1875 and was one of the earliest importers of cigars from Havana, Brazil and Jamaica into France, Germany and Switzerland.

Davidoff remained in the business to assist Ernst Schneider, present director general of the company, who internationalised trading by opening a chain of 45 stores (some corporate owned, some franchised). Has nearly 2 000 appointed stockists in 33 countries, of which around 80 in the USA. Group employs nearly 1 300 people worldwide.

Has a licensing agreement with Lancaster, the German fragrance house whose lines include Davidoff Cool Water. Also markets large range of cigar accessories, including luxury clothing, largely to defend the Davidoff trademark. This includes Davidoff Cognac Extra, which is produced in association with Hennessy and positioned between Le Paradis and Hennessy "XO". In spring 1996 launched a second cognac, Davidoff Classic, comparable to a VSOP.

In 1960 it launched Davidoff range of cigars, made in Cuba until 1990, due to a dispute over quality, it switched production to Tabacos Dominicanos in Dominican Republic. Has since bought an undisclosed percentage of this company.

The first brand to be made in that country was the then new brand, Griffin's. Also has exclusive distribution rights to the Avo range of cigars.

On January 14, 1994 Zino Davidoff died in Geneva, aged 87.

In 1995 group turnover was $1.36 billion (£0.91 billion). Cigars and accessories accounted for 40 percent of income, cigarettes 37 percent and 23 percent from Cognac, cosmetics and other diversified products.

BRANDS

Hand-made in Dominican Republic (No. of models indicated in brackets):

Davidoff (15)   Avo (13)
Davidoff Grand Cru (4)   Avo "XO" (3)
Griffin (8)

Hand-made in Honduras:
Zino (11)   Zino Connoisseur (3)
Zino Mouton Cadet (6)

Machine-made in Holland:
Zino (6)

EBAS GROUP

The Ebas group was established in 1989 as a result of merger between three companies — the famous Dutch ones of La Paz and Willem II and the strong German manufacturer, Arnold Andre. The group produces more than one billion cigars a year. Each brand has kept its own identity within the group, which employs almost 2 000 people, spread out over many countries. La Paz, Willem II and Clubmaster are the main international lines.

La Paz was established in 1814 by Mr van der Pas, a small cigar maker in the South of Holland. La Paz is particularly known for its Wilde Cigars, recognised by the unique uncut foot or tuck, a style developed in the late 1960s.

Willem II was founded in 1916 by the tobacco merchant, Hendrik Kersten, whose descendants established the brand internationally.

Clubmaster came from the German company, Arnold Andre, which was founded in 1817 in Osnabruck as Firma Gebruder Andre-Zigarrenfabrik; but in 1876, was renamed Arnold André-Zigarrenfabrik. Its main factory is in Konigslutter from where, in 1973 the Clubmaster brand was launched.

The Ebas group is active in nearly 100 countries on all continents.

BRANDS

Machine-made (No. of models indicated in brackets):

La Paz (23)   Justus von Maurik (11)
Willem II (23)   Elisabeth Bas (5)
Clubmaster (18)   Arnold André (5)

Montague   Fellows
Wings

EL CREDITO

El Credito was established in 1928 in town of San Antonio de los Bancos in Cuba by Ernesto Carillo snr., father of present owner, Ernesto Carillo jr who became a leading politician and member of the senate. Over the years the family acquired several tobacco farms in the Pinar del Rio region.

Family fortunes changed after Fidel Castro came into power in 1959. Carillo snr., was arrested several times and his farms, factory and warehouses were confiscated. In 1960 the family fled Cuba, with but few possessions, to go to America.

With the financial assistance from a relative already in the USA, Carillo snr. opened the Pan American Restaurant in Miami, in what today is known as Little Havana. After several ventures in the catering and other industries Carillo snr. in 1967 began working with tobacco again, becoming a cigar roller for Tropicana Cigar Company. In 1969, he restarted El Credito Cigars, employing one Cuban refugee to make cigars while he bought tobacco and sold the end product.

His son worked in the business after school and in between gigs as a budding jazz musician. After marrying at the age of 19 another Cuban refugee Elena, he attempted to make the big time as a musician in New York, working during the day for cigar merchant, Nat Sherman, and playing at night in clubs.

He returned to the family business, learning whatever he could about cigar-making from his father, particularly, the art of tobacco blending.

Carillo snr. died in 1980 and the business was taken over by his son. Today it markets four brands and employs 42 rollers, who each make the entire cigar to facilitate quality control. About one-third of present production of about 1,4 million cigars, across all brands, is sold direct to consumers, either through the mail or to the endless stream of visitors, who crowd into the minute sales area in the factory. The success of this policy may be judged by the fact that, in 1995, the company had back-orders equal almost to one year's production.

To overcome the critical shortage of skilled workers in Miami, Carillo expanded his operation to the Dominican

Republic in 1996 by leasing a two-floor, 32 000 sq ft factory, built to his specification. Annual production in the Dominican Republic is expected to reach one to one-and-a-half million cigars by the end of 1997.

Production in Miami continues, but additional output has been obtained by moving each brand in phases to the new factory. Quality and blends will remain the same. Three new lines, Los Statos de Luxe, Dos Gonzales and El Credito (seconds of La Gloria Cubana brand) were marketed during 1996.

El Credito plans to launch the La Gloria Cubana Special Selection range until early 1997.

BRANDS

Hand-made (No. of models indicated in brackets):

La Gloria Cubana (19)	Dos Gonzales
El Rico Habana (8)	La Gloria Special Selection
La Hoya Selecta (8)	

HUNTERS & FRANKAU

In 1840 Joseph Frankau, a German immigrant, established J. Frankau & Co in London and obtained the agency for the Cuban H. Upmann Cigars. At that time it was listed in contemporary trade directories as trading in the odd combination of leeches, sponges and cigars.

The Frankau fortunes prospered and Joseph was able to send his son Arthur to Eton and Oxford, from which the boy emerged well prepared to build on his father's success. Arthur died in his mid-50s, leaving the company in the hands of his son Gilbert whose interests lay in literature rather than commerce.

The Havana trade was thrown into a turmoil in 1903 when US tobacco magnate, J. R. Duke, attempted to corner the market through his Havana Tobacco Company.

The Frankaus stood shoulder to shoulder with the Upmann Family and other "independent" Cuban manufacturers against the American invader. They survived but soon afterwards Gilbert Frankau was infuriated when the Upmanns, with whom J. Frankau had never signed an official agreement, entered into an arrangement with other British importers to distribute certain sizes of the brand.

The first World War further damaged the relationship and in 1916 Gilbert sold J. Frankau & Co. to a rival concerned called Braden & Stark. However, when in 1922, due to the stock market crash in Europe, the H.

Upmann Cigar Factory went into liquidation, J. Frankau & Co seized the opportunity and bought the factory and the brand, creating a local Cuban company called J. Frankau SA.

The British-based Frankau company was an importer, not a manufacturer, so it appointed two Spaniards, Jose Salaun and Francisco Fernandez along with German, Paul Meller, to manage the factory on its behalf.

In 1931 a new name appeared on the British scene — Freeman. The Cardiff-based J. R. Freeman company had been making cigars in Britain since 1839. At this time it was managed by D. G. Freeman, grandson of the founder. Keen to develop into fine cigars, "D.G.", best known for his Manikin and King Six brands of popular cigars, decided to buy J. Frankau & Co from Braden & Stark and thus acquired the H. Upmann factory and the rights to the brand worldwide.

From experience of buying tobacco in Cuba "D. G." knew the Menendez family who were in the leaf business. He was aware that Alonzo Menendez had just set up a manufacturing company with Pepe Garcia, the former manager of Partagas. In 1935 he sold the H. Upmann factory and name to the partners for $250 000 (£100 000), J. Frankau & Co. retaining the right to market the brand in the UK for 80 years.

Because of the Second World War, British companies were not allowed to spend US dollars, except on war materials and, as a result, could not import cigars from Cuba until 1953. Therefore, J. Frankau had virtually no business and, as a result, set up a cigar factory in Jamaica as a joint venture with Menendez Garcia. This factory, with two main brands — El Trovador (which doesn't exist today) and La Invicta — soon became one of the biggest factories in Jamaica.

Another British company, Melbourne Hart, which had the UK agency for Punch, set up a similar joint venture project with the Cuban manufacturers of Punch. This company also produced Macanudo, which became the most successful Jamaican brand.

In 1947 the Freeman family sold its UK business (J. R. Freeman & J. Frankau) to Gallaher's and, in 1953, handed its interest in the Jamaican factory to its management.

The sale to Gallaher's included Robert Freeman ("DG's" son) appointment to its main board as director of sales and marketing. He remained on the board until

1953 and was compensated for loss of office (which would have been taxed at 98 percent), by being allowed to acquire J. Frankau at a nominal price.

A year later he bought the Hunter's business, which was called John Hunter, Morris & Elkin, then the oldest importer of Havanas in the UK. For a time the two companies were run separately as importers — J. Frankau imported H. Upmann and Hunters had the Ramon Allones and famous Montecristo brands.

In 1957 the two companies went into partnership with a big tobacco leaf broker, Siemssen Threshie. The businesses were put together and launched as a public company called Siemssen Hunter.

The Freeman family had an important share in the public company, but over the years this gradually reduced to about seven percent.

In the 1960s his son, Nicholas, joined J. Frankau after qualifying as a Chartered Accountant. He put the two companies together, creating Hunters & Frankau as the company is known today. He also started a cigarette and pipe tobacco company called William P. Solomon Ltd, which had the agencies for RJR, Lorillard, Lygett & Myers and Edgeworth.

In 1970, Nicholas became managing director of the public holding company, Siemssen Hunter. Robert Freeman became the non-executive Chairman and, because of lack of growth in the tobacco industry, Nicholas diversified the public company's activities to include educational publishing. By 1973, over 60 percent of the company's income was from publishing and the rest from tobacco.

The group consisted of Siemssen, Threshie the tobacco leaf brokers which operated in Africa and India, Hunters & Frankau importing cigars and William P. Solomon importing American cigarettes.

The education publishing division was run by John Selwyn Gummer, who is now UK Minister of the Environment in the Tory government.

When Nicholas became Managing Director, the group's stock traded at 12½p (pence) ($19c). By 1973 the value soared to 124p ($1,86). He gained the reputation of being somewhat a whiz kid.

However, after the British stock market crash in 1974, Nicholas determined not to remain involved in public companies and, by 1979, had rescued the company sufficiently to sell it profitably to another UK public company.

At the same time he spear-headed a management buyout of the cigar division, which was Hunters & Frankau, with the financial backing of Hambros, a well-known British investment bank.

This resulted in Nicholas controlling Hunters & Frankau. He then formed a new holding company, Hunters & Frankau Group Ltd., with 57 percent of the stock. About 38 percent was held by Hambros Bank and David (DAB) Baxter, who retired, in 1994, as managing director of Hunters & Frankau.

By the late 1980s it controlled nearly 40 percent of the imported Havana market in the UK. Then, in 1990, the group acquired a small business, Knight Brothers, which had the Romeo y Julieta agency. Three years later it took over one of the biggest Cuban cigar importers in the UK, Joseph Samuel & Sons, whose main brands were, Bolivar, Punch and Hoyo de Monterrey. This made Hunters & Frankau the sole distributor for all Cuban brands in the UK. In 1990 a Cuban government owned investment company acquired a significant percentage of Hunters & Frankau Ltd., the group's main trading division. This investment company holds a large number of Cuba's overseas investments in a wide range of commodities. Cuban Sergio Morera is joint managing director of this company.

In the late 1970s Hunters & Frankau acquired a controlling interest in Pan American Cigars, who were importing approximately 5 million Royal Jamaican Cigars per year into the US. This company was subsequently sold to Lane Limited. In the late 1980s the Pacific Cigar Company was formed, based in Hong Kong. Having secured the rights to Havana cigars for the Asia Pacific region, the business was sold to David Tang in 1991.

Hunters & Frankau also has the exclusive local agency for Agio Dutch cigars, Villiger from Germany, Don Ramos made in Honduras by Villazon & Co and Santa Damians from Consolidated Cigars. Another Company within the group, DB International Limited based in Woking, UK which represents the worldwide export business for General Cigar. This includes Macanudo, Partagas, Jamaican Pride, White Owl, Robert Burns, Garcia y Vega, Wm. Penn and Tijuana. Also within the Hunters & Frankau Group is Premium Cigar Limited which is the agent for Davidoff in the UK.

The group imports around 20 million non-Cuban

cigars, a little over five million Havanas and in 1995/96 had a turnover of about £22 million ($33 million).

A substantial challenge the group has had to confront in the 1990s was the British Conservative government's policy to increase the tax by three percent on all tobacco products through the Retail Price Index (RPI). This, with price increases from Cuba, translated into a retail price increase of between seven and 12 percent in 1996.

That year, Habanos SA launched a new brand, Cuaba, exclusive to the UK. This brand has four sizes, all in figurado shapes, based on the old style of Havanas from the 19th Century, which largely disappeared during the 1930s. This should expand and add excitement to the British Havana market.

M&N CIGARS

This company was founded in 1895 in Cleveland, Ohio, USA by Julius C. Newman, who emigrated from Austria-Hungary at the age of 14. When he went to vote for the first time he told the registration officer that he had no middle name. The official, there and then, opted for "Caeser" and he was soon known as "J.C".

Early in life he became an apprentice to a small cigar maker in Cleveland. He remained with the company, until 1894 when he became unemployed due to a countrywide slump.

Not taking kindly to being an economic victim, he started his own factory in the barn on his family's property, with capital of $65. This was enough to buy tobacco to fulfil his first order of 2 500 cigars.

By 1903 J. C. Newman owned the largest cigar factory in Cleveland. At that time brands include A-B-C and Dr Nichol, which used both domestic and imported tobacco in the bunch, with wrappers from Sumatra. When prices from Sumatra soared, he experimented with a Connecticut broadleaf wrapper for a new brand — Judge Wright — which soon became a popular five-cent cigar.

Later in the 1900s the company opened two new factories near Cleveland and bought cigar-making machines, which were still in their infancy, and cost the then astronomical amount of $4 000 each.

In 1921 recession halted the company's prosperity and all factories except the original one were closed. The company then merged with another important manufacturer in Cleveland, Mendelsohn Cigar Factory. This merger created the name, Mendelsohn and Newman Cigar Manufacturing, with J.C. as president and Grover Mendelsohn as vice-president, hence M&N Cigar Manufacturers.

Around this time, his son, the present 79 year-old company chairman, Standford Newman, joined the firm on a part-time basis. M&N survived the depression by continuing to be innovative and was the first maker to package cigars in cellophane, instead of the then popular foil. A small cigar called Little Cameo was introduced, with an all-Cuban leaf filler and binder and wrapper from Connecticut leaf.

In the late 1930s J.C. bought out his partner and by 1946, the company was making more than 250 000 cigars a day in two shifts.

In 1954 M&N leased part of a factory in Tampa, Florida, and Stanford ran this operation. Later that same year the company moved its entire operation to Tampa, where it had been ever since.

J.C. died in 1958, and the company was inherited by Stanford, his brother, Millard, and their two sisters. Soon afterwards M&N bought the Cuesta-Rey brand, which became a big line in drugstores and supermarkets, due to innovative polythene packaging that kept the cigars fresh for up to one year.

Because of the Cuban embargo the company started buying Cameroon wrappers in 1963. By 1986 it was selling, almost exclusively, machine-made cigars, including the most successful Cuesta-Rey 95 brand. By this time Stanford had been joined by his two sons, Eric, now president, and Bobby, present executive vice-president, sales.

Stanford then seriously looked at the possibility of including cigars from the Dominican Republic or Honduras. Fortuitously, he met the legendary Carlos Fuente Sr, owner of the prestigious Tabacalera A Fuente Factory in the Dominican Republic, and a deal was struck whereby M&N manufactured machine-made cigars for Fuente and the latter produced hand-made cigars for the Newmans. By 1992 all Cuesta-Rey models were transferred to hand-made production in the Dominican Republic.

In 1990 FANCO was established, a joint venture between the two families, to distribute all M&N cigars and many from the Fuente Family in the United States. In 1995 this company sold around 26 million cigars from the Dominican Republic and about 15 million machine-made from Tampa.

Today M&N employs about 150 people in its large, three-storey building, which also houses FANCO. Hand-made cigars are made, too, in Nestar Plasencia's Tobacos de Oriente Factory in Honduras.

In 1995 M&N launched the Diamond Crown cigar, from the Dominican Republic, to commemorate the company's 100th anniversary. In November, the same year, it produced a complimentary range of four sizes of Diamond Crown humidors, made in Norton, Massachusetts, USA, by Reed and Barton Corporation, who have been making quality, hand-crafted chests for more than 100 years. A full range of Diamond Crown accessories is envisaged.

BRANDS

Machine-made in Tampa (No. of models indicated in brackets):

Cuesta-Rey (6)   Rigoletto (6)

Hand-made in Dominican Republic:

Cuesta-Rey (5)   Rigoletto (3)
La Unica (5)   Diamond Crown (5)
Cuesta-Rey Cabinet Selection (5)
Cuesta-Rey Centenial Collection (12)

Hand-made in Honduras:
Don Jose (5)

SCHIMMELPENNINCK

In 1924 the Van Schuppen brothers went into partnership with their uncle, Geurts, who owned a small cigar factory with 21 employees. This factory was just one of the many family companies that existed in Holland at that time, all manufacturing cigars to their own specifications. The family trio soon introduced the brand, Schimmelpenninck, named after a famous governor of Holland in the early 19th century.

The 1930s began a policy of mechanisation which, with more attractive packaging and improved sales methods, resulted in the company becoming one of the larger factories in Holland. During this period a new factory was built.

Although the trend of the Dutch cigar industry, at that time, was to manufacture cheap mass products, Schimmelpenninck concentrated on premium quality products and that is still the basis of the company's policy.

About 90 percent of total production is exported to some 160 countries, the group making, for example, about 40 percent of all dry cigars sold in the USA. Its "Duet" is the world's best selling thin panetela. Today, Schimmelpenninck is owned by Rothmans International Tobacco Products, based in Amsterdam, Holland.

BRANDS

Machine-made (Models indicated in brackets):
Schimmelpenninck (23)

SWISHER INTERNATIONAL INC.

This company established in 1861 by David Swisher, a merchant trading out of Newark, Ohio, who received the then small cigar business in settlement of a debt. Initially, cigars were only a sideline for Swisher and his four sons compared with many products that they hawked across the Midwest from their "rolling stores" or wagons. Today, however, Swisher International accounts for about one-third of the cigar sales in the United States and is one of the country's largest exporters, selling its products in over more than 70 countries.

In 1888 one of David Swisher's four sons, John H, persuaded his brother Harry to join him in buying their father's company, and Swisher Brothers was formed. By 1895 the business had grown into three factories employing some 1 000 people, who hand-rolled more than 300 000 cigars a day.

In 1913 John bought out Harry and took in his son Carl and J. J. Swisher & Son was established. A decade later the company moved its operations to Jacksonville, Florida, which had a good climate, shipping facilities and proximity to raw materials and markets. Company headquarters has remained in Jacksonville ever since.

In 1923 Swisher became the first firm to order the rolling machines that transformed the business by mass producing cigars that were superior in uniformity, appearance and quality. These "fresh work" machines went into operation in 1924 and, by the end of that decade, the company was the world's largest cigar manufacturer and the facility in Jacksonville was the largest cigar factory in the world under one roof.

During that same period, because of its investment in

money-saving machinery, the company was able to cut the price of its King Edward cigar from five cents each to two for five cents. Sales soared and, by 1940, it was the biggest selling brand in the world.

In the following years the group expanded by opening other facilities in nearby tobacco growing areas for handling, processing, storing and shipping the huge quantities of leaf needed in Jacksonville.

In 1958 Swisher Sweets were introduced and, by 1969 the company was making a total of 4 million cigars a day, exporting to 47 countries. Because of the growing popularity of the little, cigarette-sized cigar, the company, in 1985 decided to enter that market by successfully introducing the Swisher Sweets Little Cigar.

BRANDS

Machine-made (No. of models indicated in brackets):

King Edward (12)	Keep Moving (1)
Swisher Sweets (10)	Dexter Londres (1)
Optimo (6)	As You Like It (4)
Sante Fe (3)	Al Capone (2)
El Trelles (5)	Pedroni (1)

Swisher Sweets Mini Cigarillo from Holland (1)

Hand-made from Honduras:

Bering (15)	La Diligencia (5)
Tiburon (3)	La Primadora Bundles (6)

Hand-made from Dominican Republic:

Carlin (5)	Don Julio Bundles (5)
Pleiades (11)	

Hand-made from Nicaragua:

For de Jalapa (5)	Sabrosa Bundles (5)

Hand-made from Canary Islands:
Penamil (9)

TABACALERA

Tabacalera was established in 1636 by the Spanish government as a tobacco monopoly and then rented to the private sector. After the 1936-1939 Spanish Civil War, the government reassumed a majority stake and now has 52 percent, with 38 percent controlled by private foreign investors and the remaining 10 percent by Spanish ones.

This giant conglomerate consists of more than 20 companies. Non-tobacco investments include olive oil (Koiped), sugar (Ebro Agricalas), dairy industry (La Lactaria) and pension funds.

The tobacco sector covers both cigarette and cigar production and imports. The group itself produces 2,5 billion packs of cigarettes (industry standard is 20 per pack) and approximately 350 million cigars. Its cigar business is worth around $300 million (£200 million) a year.

In addition Tabacalera has several, usually equal partnerships, including BAT (British American Tobacco), R.J. Reynolds and private investors in the Canary Islands, which together, produce about four billion packs (80 billion) of cigarettes per year.

Major brands of cigarettes include the second biggest line in Europe, Ducados (about 1,3 billion packs) and Fortuna (about one billion). The group accounts for almost 95 per cent of the cigarette market in Spain and also exports to France and other European countries. The group manufactures cigarettes in Poland and exports to Russia and some other former republics of the Soviet Union. The group intends to expand in other European Market countries.

Tabacalera is involved in all sectors of the tobacco industry, including leaf growing and processing, through two of its subsidiaries, CETARSA and INTABEX Holding Worldwide. It makes both hand-made and machine-made cigars in the Canary Islands through CITA. These brands include Penamil, Goya, Condal and La Fama. Tabacalera also makes machine-made cigars in Spain. Most brands include an important percentage of Cuban tobacco. In Spain it makes only machine-made cigars.

The group is a major buyer of Cuban tobacco, accounting for between 75 and 85 percent of total bulk tobacco exports from Cuba worth some $70 million (£465 million). Including its own production, the group distributes more than 600 million cigars a year. Of the 34 million hand-made cigars, five million are produced by Tabacalera.

Most of the five million hand-made cigars made in the Canary Islands contain Cuban leaf. The leading brands are Condal and Penamil. This Penamil, imported into the USA by Swisher Int, contains no Cuban leaf because of the US trade embargo against Cuba.

The group's main machine-made brand is Farais with

an output of about 250 million cigars, or over 60 percent of production. It contains a high percentage of Cuban leaf and is the group's top machine-made product, the Farais Centenario, the premium cigar in the range, has a Cuban leaf wrapper.

Spain is the largest importer of Cuban cigars, amounting to some 28 million in 1996 representing about half of Cuba's exports of hand-made cigars and about 10 percent of its machine-made ones. The value of these imports is in excess of $35 million (£25 million).

The first cigars made in similar fashion to those of today were produced by Tabacalera in Seville in the early 18th century. It was then that the idea of constructing a cigar with filler, binder and wrapper was invented. The process was exported to Cuba and, in 1740 a Spanish Royal Decree created a tobacco monopoly in Cuba, called the Royal Trading Company (Real Compania de Comercio de la Habano). As a result, Cuba has maintained strong cigar trade ties with Spain, even when it was under the economic influence of the former Soviet Union. These ties endured even with a Communist Castro in power in Cuba and a fascist Franco dictatorship in Spain.

The premium Montecristo brand controls almost 50 percent of total consumption of Cuban cigars in Spain. Of this, the No 4, which is a petit corona accounts for about 50 percent, followed by the No 2 (torpedo). The next most popular brand is Fonseca, and then Partagas, with the 8-9-8 being leading model in this range. Partagas has sales of close to three million.

Because of the small tax on tobacco products and the narrow profit margins, both with wholesalers and retailers, Spain has significantly low prices for Havanas.

Due, largely, to the break-up of the Soviet Union the Cuban tobacco industry has a critical shortage of foreign currency to buy fertiliser, pesticides, muslin cloth for wrappers and other agricultural requirements. This has resulted in a sharp decline in production since the early 1990s. To overcome this, Tabacalera designed an aid package. The group advanced about $25 million (£16,6 million) to finance the 1995/96 crop. Agricultural requisites to this value were bought by Tabacalera and shipped to Cuba. The Spaniards ensured that farmers, co-operatives and other growing concerns received those goods.

Tabacalera has formalised plans with the Cubans to

almost double production within the next three years. These plans have included incentives, paid in US dollars, to farmers and workers if they surpass their target. This could mean that the group will import around 54 million cigars before the end of this century.

Soon after the take-over of Cuba by Fidel Castro, businesses in that country were confiscated without compensation. The Cuban government took over the cigar factories using the existing brands. The former Cuban cigar business owners, however, set up factories in different countries and continued to use these brand names. Over the years some of these were sold by the original owners to various American companies and the value of the trademarks increased due to the resultant considerable increase in sales.

In 1987 Tabacalera started negotiations with the various non-Cuban owners who were selling outside the USA. Successful negotiations were concluded in 1991 with Cuban Cigar Corporation (CCC), a company owned together by Consolidated Cigars and Cifuentes International, who marketed Montecristo and H. Upmann outside Cuba. It is rumoured, although no confirmation could be obtained from either party, that Tabacalera paid CCC $10 million for these trademarks for use outside the USA and the Dominican Republic.

Tabacalera agreed to allow the Cubans to use these trademarks on Cuban made cigars as if they were the owner, without paying any royalty. In return, they provide Tabacalera with their best tobacco leaf for its own production.

However, before this deal was concluded, SEITA (the French tobacco monopoly) had secured rights from Habanos SA (formerly Cubatabaco) to produce the mini-Montecristo. Then in November 1994 this was replaced with the rights to produce the Cohiba Mini Cigarillo, with Tabacalera producing the Montecristo Mini in Spain.

In 1995 Tabacalera entered into negotiations to acquire from Culbro Corp in the USA, 51 percent of its General Cigar Company, for a price of about $100 million. The Spanish group, with a strong position in the European Economic Union and owning an important subsidiary in the Far East, Companias Philippinas, was looking for a presence in the United States, the third biggest cigar market.

This deal, had it materialised, would have been beneficial to both groups. General Cigar, with strong distribution in the USA, would have been able to launch Tabacalera's range of cigars hand-made in the Canary Islands and, in return, could have introduced General's Macanudo and other ranges. However, towards the end of 1995, it fell through.

Before approaching Culbro Corp Tabacalera had spoken to other American companies without success. It is understood that feelers to American companies are continuing at the time of going to press.

According to a 1996 report in financial newspaper, "Expansion", Tabacalera is on a US State Department blacklist of 39 Spanish companies with application of the Helmes-Burton legislation.

In 1995/96 this huge group's turnover was in excess of $7 billion (£5,6 billion) and profit about $150 million (£100 million).

In June 1996 Mr Cesár Alierta, replaced Mr Pedro Perez as chairman. Mr Alierta, who has law and MBA degrees, was previously founder and chairman of Beta Capital, a stock exchange and securities company. He has also been a member of the Permanent Commission Board of the Madrid Stock Exchange.

BRANDS

Machine-made in Spain (No. of models indicated in brackets):

Cariges (2)	Farais (7)	Tarantos (1)
Ducados (4)	Finos Cortados (1)	Vegafina (2)
Entrefinos (4)	Montecristo Mini (1)	

Hand-made in the Canary Islands:

Condal	Goya
Penamil	La Fama

TABACALERA A FUENTE INC.

This company was first established in 1912 in what is now Tampa, Florida, USA by the Cuban born father of the present chairman, Carlos Fuente Sr., together with various partners. In the mid-1920s the original factory burned down, the first of six such misfortunes to beset the Fuente family.

During the 1940s a new start was made from a factory in his house, working with his wife and mother. This was a family operation with his brothers and daughter coming to the factory after returning home from their full-time employment elsewhere.

The present patriach, Carlos Fuente Sr., was born in

that industry with both he and his brother rolling cigars after school.

After another fire in 1948 the family moved its operation to Nicaragua where yet a further fire destroyed their factory in 1977. This was rebuilt however and a second factory was established in Honduras. Amazingly this, too, was destroyed by fire in 1979.

In 1979 the family attempted to produce hand-made cigars in Tampa, Florida with Vietnamese and Cuban labourers. When this enterprise failed the Fuentes seriously considered abandoning the industry altogether. The only options facing the family were to sell up or to move, once again, to another country.

After considering various alternatives a move was made to the Dominican Republic in 1980, where the government was going out of its way to attract industries with incentives and plentiful, cheap labour. At this stage total annual exports of Dominican cigars were only 11 million.

Today the Fuentes have three factories in the Dominican Republic and employ over 1 000 people and they are probably the biggest cigar producer in that country. In 1996 total production is expected to be close to 35 million cigars — almost half of the country's total output.

In 1986 the Fuentes struck a deal with the Newman family, who owned M&N in Tampa, Florida, whereby the latter manufactured machine-made cigars for the Fuento and they in turn made hand-made cigars for the Newmans.

In 1990 FANCO was established as a joint venture between the two families to distribute all M&N cigars and many from the Fuente family in the United States. In 1995 this company sold around 26 million cigars from the Dominican Republic and about 15 million machine-made from Tampa.

A major development was the purchase, in 1992, of various farms, three new tobacco barns, and materials for a revolutionary shade-wrapper growing operation. This multimillion dollar investment was the brainchild of Carlos Fuente Jr., the present chairman of the group. In 1996, nearly 70 acres was planted for tobacco, about half for wrappers under shade and the balance sun-grown for binders. The 85 acre farm where wrappers are grown is now called Chateau De Le Fuente and is about a 45 minute drive from Santiago, in the country's interior. These distinctive, rich-tasting wrappers are only used on Fuente cigars and not sold to other producers.

The company today employs more than 1 000 people, nearly half of whom are cigar rollers.

The main brand is Arturo Fuente, mainly using Cameroon wrappers. Top priced range is the Opux X launched late 1995, retailing for between $7 and $12, depending on size. This has the new Cuban seed Dominican shade wrapper. The company also makes a number of brands for other producers and distributors.

BRANDS

Hand-made in Dominican Republic (No. of models indicated in brackets):

Arturo Fuente (16)   La Unica (5) (for M&N)
Don Carlos (3)   *Diana Silvius (4)
Opus X (7)   *Ashton (18)
Montesimo (7)
Arturo Fuente Chateau Series (3)
Arturo Fuente Hemingway Series (4)
Cuesta-Rey Cabinet Selection (5) (for M&N)
Cuesta-Rey Centerial Collection (8) (for M&N)
Diamond Crown (5) (for M&N)
*Savinelli Extremely Limited Reserve (6)

*Produced for other companies.

TABACOS DE PLASENCIA

This company originated in 1965 as a tobacco farm in the famed Jalapa Valley in Nicaragua, launched by the father of the present owner, Nestar Plasencia. The family business prospered until 1979 when the revolutionary Sandinisto regime seized the farm. The family fled to the town of Danli, just 20 miles from the Nicaraguan border, in neighbouring Honduras. The patriarch, who died in 1983, took this opportunity to encourage his son, Nestor, to take charge and rebuild the business.

Today Placencia Jr. believes Nicaragua and Honduras come closest to matching the natural qualities found in Cuba.

In 1990, when the government in Nicaragua changed, the family reclaimed its original farm and, in 1992, continued operating in both countries. The farm in Nicaragua which has 300 acres under cultivation is called Plasencia Tabacos de Nicaragua and the family's Segovia Cigar factory, opened in 1993, with a second following in Esteli in 1995. The company now makes more than 40 000 cigars a day, owns a second farm and three big warehouses in Ocotal, and employs a total of some 1 500 people.

During 1995 the original Honduran company was split into four individual firms, one of which was a box company, producing 1 200 hand-made cedar boxes a day. Another was the 1 000 acre farming operation, situated in the Jamastram Valley, retaining the name Tabacos de Plasencia and supplying most of the leaf used in the group's cigar output.

The third was the Classification and Exportation Company, which handles the selection, stripping and fermentation of the tobacco from two factories, one in Danli and one in Moroceli.

The fourth company in the Honduran group is the actual cigar making company, Fabrica de Tabacos Oriente (Tobaccos of the West), which operates two factories in Danli, one in Moroceli and one in El Paraiso, called Fabrica Tobacco de Caribe. The output of this factory goes exclusively to Tropical Tobacco in Miami.

It produces 110 000 cigars a day in Honduras, employing about 4 500 people.

The group produces about 70 percent of its own tobacco. The balance is imported from Dominican Republic, Ecuador and its own farm in Costa Rica.

In Honduras, tobacco is grown in two crops, the first, in September is for wrappers and the second, planted towards the end of May, is for filler. In 1997 the group plans to plant both Connecticut and Cuban seed tobacco under shade cloth — 150 acres in Honduras and 60 acres in Nicaragua.

What was once an essentially family business now only involves Plasencia and an uncle. However, he has hopes that, in time, his four children — three sons and a daughter — will join when they complete their studies.

The group is one of the biggest cigar producers in Honduras and is, probably, the largest in Nicaragua. In 1995 the group produced more than 33 million cigars, under 30 labels, in both countries. Production in 1996 was set to increase considerably. It also owns Tabacos de Valle SA., a 150-acre farm in Costa Rica.

BRANDS

Hand-made in Honduras (No. of models indicated in brackets):

Thomas Hinds (8)   *Maya (13)

*V Centennial (8)
Nestor 747
*Particulares (13)
*Lempira (7)
*Mocha Supreme (8)
*Beiring (14)

*Walgreen's
*La Diligencia (5)
*Solo Aroma (14)
*Indian Head (22)
Evelio (6)

Hand-made in Nicaragua:
La Finca (9)
*Don Juan (8)
*Flor de Jalapa (5)
*Sabroso (5)

*Puro Nicaragua (11)
Torcedor (5)
MiCubano (6)
Primera de Nicaragua

*Produced for other companies.

TABACOS DOMINICANOS SA

Founded in 1984 by Dominican born Henke Kelner. The first of two factories, called Tabadom, was established on outskirts of Santiago in the Dominican Republic. In 1996 over six million Davidoff cigars were made in this factory.

The second factory, later built in Villa Gonzalez, in 1996 produced the following brands: Avos (two million), The Griffin's (700 000), Paul Gamirians (700 000) and Troya (300 000).

Has about 1 200 acres (575 hectares) of tobacco under its control, through long-term contracts. Has started experiments with growing both shade and sun-grown tobacco for wrappers.

Firm is partly owned by the giant Swiss-based Max Oettinger Company, owners of the Davidoff brand, and employs nearly 600 people. At present does not own its own brand.

BRANDS

Hand-made (No. of models indicated in brackets):
Davidoff (20)
Avo (13)
Avo "XO" (3)
Griffin (8)

Paul Gamirians (PG) (16)
Troya (8)
Troya Clasico (2)

VILLAZON & CO

Established in Tampa, Florida, USA, by Frank Llaneza, Villazon in 1970 merged with Danby-Palicio, a company owned by Dan Blummenthall and Fernando Palicio. This company possessed the Franscisco G.

Bances brand and, in 1965 started making the Hoyo de Monterrey and Punch cigars in Tampa. Villazon was then owned equally by Frank Llaneza and his brother and Joe and Dan Blummenthall.

The company continued to make machine-made cigars in Tampa and moved its hand-making operation to Honduras, where today it is one of the two biggest producers in that country. Cuban tobacco was used in its cigars until 1975. The company owns its own box-making factory in Honduras and also has tobacco farms. The importing company, James B. Russell, is totally owned by Villazon & Co., and handles cigarettes, pipe tobacco and accessories.

In 1995 the group produced about 26 million hand-made and about 50 million machine-made cigars in Tampa, Florida.

BRANDS

Hand-made in Honduras (No. of models indicated in brackets):

Hoyo De Monterrey (21)	Punch Deluxe (4)
Excalibur (8)	Punch Gran Cru (7)
Bances (11)	Flor Del Caribe (4)
Punch (16)	Bermejo (2)

Machine-made in Tampa:

Lord Beaconsfield (6)	Villazon Deluxe (5)
Pedro Iglesias (3)	Topstone (10)
Villa de Cuba (3)	

VILLIGER

Villiger was founded in 1888 by Jean Villiger, grand-father of the present owners. Jean Villiger is still a family owned business. When Jean Villiger died in 1902 at 40, his widow, Louise, took over the running of the company. She expanded operations and, in 1910, founded a sister company in Tiengen, Germany.

When Louise retired, her sons, Hans and Max, ran the cigar factory. The present owners are the two sons of Max-Heinrich, in charge of the German operation, and Kasper, handling the business in Switzerland.

At present Villiger has four factories in Switzerland and Germany and employs about 900 people. It produces over 450 million cigars and cigarillos of which nearly 100 million are exported to 70 countries.

The company maintains a prudent policy of holding stock for up to three years of all types of tobacco so that one crop can be omitted if the quality is not up to standard.

EEC countries are supplied by factories in Germany, UK and France being the most important outlets, followed by Holland, Belgium, Italy and Greece. Other countries are supplied by Switzerland. The most important non-EEC markets are USA, Australia, South Africa, Saudi Arabia, Hong Kong and Cyprus. The products are sold in numerous duty free shops, on aircraft, ships and in diplomatic shops.

Also makes pipe tobacco and bicycles.

US importer: Tampa Products Co., Tampa, Florida, USA.

BRANDS

Machine-made (No. of models indicated in brackets):

Villiger Export (2)	Villiger Menorca (1)
Villiger Pamela (1)	Villiger Jewells (1)
Villiger Kiel (4)	Braniff (5)

Buying in Duty-free Shops

I have generally found that duty-free shops in Europe and Southern Africa, including the Indian Ocean Islands, are well stocked with the Dutch or dry European cigars, particularly Christian of Denmark, Ritmeester, Villiger, Wintermans and Willem II. The European duty-free shops usually have a good selection of hand-made cigars, particularly Havanas. However, on one trip last year I found the duty-free shop at Geneva completely out of Havanas, while at Heathrow the stock was fairly low. By comparison the duty-free at Schiphol Airport in Holland was well-stocked with Cuban cigars.

The problem with many duty-free shops is that they do not keep cigars in properly humidified conditions.

However, there are some outstanding retail cigar shops in most of the major European cities and you can apply for a VAT and duty refund, which you receive later by mail. However, in some countries, such as France, you can only apply for a VAT refund if your purchases exceed a certain amount.

The rent in many airports is extremely high, much more than that in many high street shops. If you are able to get the VAT and duty refund, you may find that many duty-free shops are not competitive.

In Spain where the normal retail prices of Havanas are particularly low, those in the duty-free shops are only about 10 percent lower.

In France, duty-free prices are, on average, between 15 and 30 percent lower and in Switzerland, between 20 and 40 percent.

Duty-free prices in Mexico vary between 20 and 50 percent lower than normal retail levels.

However, Havanas in the duty-free shops in South Africa are a particularly good buy.

Incidently, the normal retail prices of Havanas, generally, are considerably lower than in the UK and most European countries, except Spain, due to low taxes.

Cigar Shops of the World

This list includes more than 250 cigar shops in 24 countries. I have not included just specialist cigar shops, as these are relatively few, but also shops that, in addition to other merchandise, have a good selection of cigars. Where possible, the names of the proprietors or managers have been stated.

AUSTRALIA

MELBOURNE

Benjamins Fine Tobacco, Myer Hse Arcade, 250 Elizabeth Str. Tel: (61)(3) 663-2879.
Good humidor.

Daniels Fine Tobaccos, 300 Lonsdale Str., Melbourne Central. Tel: (61)(3) 663-6842.
Well-stocked humidor. Large range of open boxes for single sales.

SYDNEY

Alfred Dunhill, 74 Castlereagh Str. Tel: (61)(2) 231-6842.
Range of top Havanas. Knowledgeable service. "Laying down" facilities for clients.

TOORAK

J & D of Alexanders, Shop 7, Tok H Centre, 459 Toorak Rd. Tel: (61)(3) 827-1477.

B R A Z I L

SÃO PAULO

Casa del Habana, Brasil, (Bobi Chen), Alameda Lorena 1521, Cerqueira Cesar 1424-002, São Paulo.

B A H R A I N

MANAMA

La Casa Del Habano Bahrain, (Faieq Al Zagani) P.O. Box 120, Manama. Tobacco Road, Government Rd., No. 5. Tel: (973) 25-3356.

B E L G I U M

BRUSSELS

Zabia 8-10 Rue Lebeau. Tel: (32)(2) 512-9422.
Owned by Davidoff, but stocking most top brands. Good shop. Knowledgeable and patient service.

C A N A D A

CALGAREY

Cavendish & Moore, Penny Lane Market. Tel: (1)(403) 269-2716.
Well-stocked humidor. Good selection Havanas.

MONTREAL

Blatter and Blatter 365, President Kennedy Str.
Tel: (1)(514) 845-2028. Good selection of cigars from all over the world.

TORONTO

Havana House, 8, Cumberland Str. Tel: (1)(416) 927-7703. Well-stocked humidor. Smoking lounge. Part of nationwide chain.

Havana House, 87, Avenue Rd. Tel: (1)(416) 927-9070. Well-stocked humidor. Smoking lounge.

WINDSOR

Havana House, 473 Oulette Ave. Tel: (1)(519) 254-0017. Well-stocked humidor. Smoking lounge.

VANCOUVER

R.J. Clark Tobacconist, 3, Alexander Str. Tel: (1)(604) 687-4136. Wide selection cigars.

WINNIPEG

Havana House, 185 Carlton Street. Tel: (1)(204) 942-0203. Well-stocked humidor. Smoking lounge.

CYPRUS

Tobacco Boutique Shop, Hilton Hotel, 3 Makurios Ave. Tel: (357)(2) 37-77770.

CUBA

HAVANA

Casa del Habano, Partagas Cigar Factory, Industria No 520, Habana Vieja. Tel: (53)(7) 33-8060.

Casa del Habano, Tobacco Museum, Mercaderes E/Obispo y Cerapia.

Casa del Tabaco, Guitart-Habana Libre Hotel, Cnr 23rd St. and L. St., Vedado. Tel: (53)(7) 30-5011.

Casa del Tabaco. 5TA Y 16, Cnr 5th Ave. and 16th Str., Miramar. Tel: (53)(7) 33-1185.

Tienda del Tabaco, Comodoro Hotel, Cnr 3rd Ave. and 84th Str., Miramar. Tel: (53)(7) 33-5551.

Tienda del Tobaco, Hostal Valencia, Cnr Oficios and Baratillo Strs., Habana Vieja.

FRANCE

BORDEAUX

La Regence, 10 Cour du Juillet. Tel: (33)(56) 81-6344.

LYON

Le Khedive, 71 Rue de la Republique. Tel: (33)(78) 37-8695. Fine shop. Excellent cigar cellar. Supplies leading restaurants in Lyon.

PARIS

La Casa del Habano Paris (Louis Gerard Biret), 17 Bis, Blvd. Pasteur. Fax: (33)(1) 406-12390.

La Civette, 157 rue Saint Honore. Tel: (33)(1) 42 61-6107. Well-stocked humidor. Wide range accessories. Helpful service.

La Tabagie, 10 rue du Depart. Tel: (33)(1) 45 386518. Good humidor. Modern, perhaps too clinical for traditionalists. Knowledgeable staff.

Les Quatre — Temps, Centre Commercial des Quatre — Temps. La Defense. Tel: (33)(1) 477-47528. Wide range Havanas in good cellar. Caters mainly for businessmen.

Tabac George — V, 22 Avenue George — V. Tel: (33)(1) 474-34475. Inconspicuous shop. Cigar-smokers' paradise. Ideal rendezvous for enthusiasts. Staff hospitable, knowledgeable.

SAINT-TROPEZ

Chez Fuchs, 7 Rue des Commercants. Tel: (33)(93) 97-0125.
Luxury shop. Sophisticated cellar.

GERMANY

AACHEN

*Pfeifenn — Schneiderwind, Inh. W. Offermanns, Kramestr. 13-15.

AUGSBURG

*Herbert Mayer KG, Nr 7 Tabakwaren, Herren-Geschenke, Steingasse 7.

BAD REICHENHALL

*Eduard Akermann, Inh. M. Cesinger, Ludwigstrasse 20.

BERLIN

Kadewe Hertie Gmbh, Tauentziestr. 21-24. Tel: (49)(30) 21210.

Kaernbach Pipes & Tobacco, Muthesiusstrasse 9. Tel: (49)(30) 791-8912.

*Tabak L Pulver, Inh. R. Fischer, Rheinstrasse 42.

BREMEN

*Pfeifen-studio, Roland von Bremem, Inh R. Bechtloff, Herdentorsteinweg 37.

DORTMUND

*Zigarren — Henneke, Horder Tabakborse, Alfred-Trappen-Strasse 10.

DRESDEN

Hantsch Erico, Wilsdrufferstrausse 8. Tel: (0351) 495-5776.

DUSSELDORF

*Dusseldorfer, Pfeifen — Center Linz bach, Graf-Adolf-Strasse 78. Large store.

Tabac Benden, Konigsallee 60. Tel: (49)(211) 13-1956.

TH Kleen, Conrad-Adenauer-Platz 14. Tel: (49)(211) 36-4160.

ESSEN

*Pfeifen, Schilde GmbH, Kastanienallee 14.

FRANKFURT

Duske and Duske, Neuer Jungfernstieg 9-1. Tel: (49)(40) 349-4699.

Pfeifen Jimm, Jung fernsteig 26. Tel: (49)(40) 34-5187.

*Tabac-Fischer Munchener Strasse 22. Tel: (49)(69) 23-5885. Small well-stocked shop, mainly hand-made non-Havanas. Friendly old worldly service. Knowledge-able and helpful proprietor.

GIESSEN

*Otto Wagner, Tabakwaren, Bahnhofstrasse 106.

HAMBURG

*Ferdinand Tesch Wwe., Colonnaden 10.

HANAU

Pfeifen-Stube Heck, Rosenstrasse 15.

HANNOVER

Zigarren & Pfeifenhaus, Konig & Schubert oHG, Lavesstrasse 71.

HEIDELBERG

Tabak Bieler KG, Hauptstrasse 106.

HEILBRONN

Herbert Bieler KG, Hauprasse 106. Tel: (49)(6221) 22-384.

Tabak Sasse, Am Wollhaus 3.

Zigarren Grimm, Sofienstr 11. Tel: (49)(6221) 20-909.

HERNE

Pfeifen-Bresser, Berliner Strasse I.

KASSEL

Pipe Shop and Exquisit D, Inh. K. Doering, Wolfs-schlucht 1.

KOBLENZ

Pipe House, Inh. Jurgen Wilde, Jesuitengasse.

KÖLN

Cigarrendepot Steffany, Neumarkt 18-24. Tel: (49)(221) 257-7224.

Pfeifen Heinrichs, Martinstrasse 16-20 Tel: (49)(221) 258-2201.

*Tabac-Collegium Cöln Koster GmbH, Richartzstrasse 12.

LEIPZIG

Kahlers Tabakshop, Petersstrasse 20. Tel: (49)(341) 29-3005.

Margit Wartig, Wintergartenstrasse 7. Tel: (49)(341) 29-8230.

MAINZ

*Ziggarren-Hofmann, Fustrasse 2.

MARBURG

*H. Knau, Inh. F. Zadra, Gutenbergstrasse 7.

MEMMINGEN

*H. Sturm, Inh. Franz Sturm, Kalchstrasse 7.

MUNICH

Max Zechbauer, Residenzstrasse 10. Tel: (49)(89)

29-6886 or 2901.
Excellent stock. Wide range European dry cigars. Wonderful environment. Many items of interest for enthusiast and collector alike. Owner Max Zechbauer has done much in restoring Bavarian reputation for taste in cigars.

*Pfeifen-Huber, Inh Georg Huber, Im Tal 22.

Wilhem Bader, Marienplatz 8. Tel: (49)(89) 22-3006.

MÜNSTER

Wilhelm-Fincke, Inh Hans Fincke, Hammer Strasse 63.

NUREMBURG

*Drexer's Tabakstube, Kaiserstrasse 32.

OFFENBACH

*Zigarrenhaus, K. Heck KG, Frankfurter Strasse 37.

OLDENBURG

Hermann Paraat, Haarenstrasse 18.

PFORZHEIM

Tabak Sigrist, Dillisteiner Strasse 7.

SCHORNDORF

Tabac Hirschmann, Inh. W. Wagner, Markplatz 25.

SIEGEN

Siegner Tabakstube, Inh. Friedrich Giesler, Am Bahnhof 11.

STUTTGART

Alte Tobakstube, Inh. Peter Knylim, Schillerplatz 4. Tel: (49)(711) 29-2729. Large, well-stocked store.

Pfeifen-Archiv, Calwer Passage. Tel: (49)(711) 29-0701.

ULM

Cigarillo, Inh Rolf Vennermann, Platzgasse 54.

WIESBADEN

Pfeifenhaus Zander, Kirchgasse 54.

WURZBURG

Pfeifen Roesch, Dominikanerplatz 3d.

* All John Aylesbury specialist cigar shops. Each shop owner has share in the John Aylesbury cigar manufacturing business in Germany.

GREECE

ATHENS

Balli, 1-3 Spyromiliou Str. Tel: (30)(1) 322-1907. Good range. Reasonable prices.

Smoker's House, 57 Stadiou Str. Tel: (30)(1) 324-9034. Small selection Cuban cigars. Reasonable prices.

The Tobacco Shop, 12 Zisimopoulou, Glyfada. Tel: (30)(1) 894-2306. Large selection Cuban cigars, accessories and humidors.

HONG KONG

Cohiba Cigar Divan, The Lobby, Mandarin Hotel. Twentieth-century recreation of cigar divan.

KOWLOON

Davidoff, Peninsula Hotel Lobby.
Sophisticated shop. Wide range cigars and accessories.

IRELAND

DUBLIN

J.J. Fox, 119 Grafton Str. Tel: (353)(1) 70-0533. Owners of oldest cigar shop in London, now operating as James J. Fox and Robert Lewis in St James. Dublin shop carries good range of cigars.

ITALY

ROME

Carmigani, 41-42 Via de la Colona, Antonia. Tel: (39)(6) 79-5449.

Sincato, 34 via de la Colona Antonia. Tel: (39)(6) 785-5508.

LEBANON

BEIRUT

La Casa del Habano, P.O. Box 11-52-84.

NETHERLANDS

AMSTERDAM

Davidoff, Van Baerlestraat 84. Tel: (31)(20) 671-1042. Good selection of well-stored cigars and accessories.

John N. Andringer. Reguliersbreestraat 2. Tel: (31)(20) 623-2836. Well-stocked small shop. Established in 1902. Top quality cigars. One of 100 shops in Holland that stock their own brand of quality Compaenen Green and Red Series. Owner: John Andringer is most knowledgeable.

P.G.C. Hajenius, 92-96 Rokin. Tel: (31)(20) 23-7494. Wonderful atmosphere. Large humidor with wide selection of cigars from many parts of the world, including Havanas. Have range under own name, which is probably the top brand made in Holland. Wide range of accessories, pipes, tobacco and humidors. Regarded as one of the most beautiful cigar shops in the world. Built in 1914, based on original Dutch tobacco house. Lavish use of carved wood, marble, crystal chandeliers. Interesting and extensive museum. Situated in what was centre of Amsterdam tobacco industry. Patronised by Prince Bernhard. Bought about 13 years ago by Ritmeester Group. Managers: Pim Bakker and Dik Nooy. Latter has worked in store for more than 30 years.

Van Coeveden BV. Leidstraat 58. Tel: (31)(20) 624-5150. One of 17 Davidoff stockists in Holland. Good range top quality Dutch cigars and Havanas. Owner: Ed Schild.

SAUDI ARABIA

JEDDAH

Hotel Sands Shop, Al Toubaishi Str., Al Hamra. Tel: (966)(2) 66-9202.

Hotel Sofitel Shop, Sofitel-Al Hamrah, Palestine Str. Tel: (966)(2) 665-3873.

La Casa del Habano, (Nabil Turk), 353, Rue de La Tour, Centra 127. Fax: (966)(1) 46-86-7519.

SOUTH AFRICA

BELLVILLE

Cock 'n Bull, 20 Tyger Valley Centre. Tel: (27)(21) 948-2400. Part of four well-stocked gift shops. Has small selection of mainly non-Cuban cigars.

BLOEMFONTEIN

*Wesley's, Shop 14, Sanlam Plaza. Tel: (27)(51) 48-4658. Owner: Kallie Joubert.

CAPE TOWN

Cock 'n Bull, C40 Cavendish Square, Claremont. Tel: (27)(21) 61-1432. Owner: Ankie Roux.

Cock 'n Bull, 143 Victoria and Alfred Waterfront. Tel: (27)(21) 21-1860.

Both part of a chain of four well-stocked gift shops, carrying small selection of mainly non-Cuban cigars.

Scottish Piper, 119 Victoria Wharf Shopping Centre, V & A Waterfront. Tel: (27)(21) 418-5511.
Small range of Havanas and non-Havanas. Owners: Derry and Jan Trail.

Sturk's Tobacconists, 54 Short Market Str. (opposite famous Green Market Square flea market). Tel: (27)(27) 23-3928. Established 1873. Specialises in pipe tobacco. Blends on site in Victorian blender. Good selection cigars. Owner: Falkie Berger, has 35 years experience.

*Wesley's, 5A Upper Level, Gardens Shopping Centre. Tel: (27)(21) 45-1890.
Small but good range of premium cigars. Offers mailing service. Owner: Chris Horrel.

*Wesley's, 7 Plazza level, Golden Acre. Tel: (27)(21) 21-5090. Small but good range of premium cigars. Offers mailing service. Pleasant and knowledgeable service. Owner: Chris Horrel.

DURBAN

*Wesley's, Shop 234, The Pavillion, Westville. Tel: (27)(31) 265-0735. Owners Tony and Alexia Zografos.

Zoggy's, 87 Gardiner Str. Tel: (27)(31) 304-0866. Owners: Eelco and Sharon Otter.

EAST LONDON

*Wesley's, 10A, Vincent Park Centre. Tel: (27)(431) 57-873. Owners: Paul and Val Hammond.

JOHANNESBURG

*The Baron, Westgate Centre. Tel: (27)(11) 768-1480. Mainly a gift shop, has walk-in humidor. Good range of European type cigars.

*The Baron, Killarney Mall. Tel: (27)(11) 646-1654.

*The Baron, Fourways Mall. Tel: (27)(11) 465-6449.

*The Baron shops are owned by Gary Reimers and his son, Claude.

J.J. Cale Tobacconists, Sandton City Shopping Centre. Tel: (27)(11) 783-6311. Good range cigars and accessories. Mainly full box sales. Owners: Jim Stephen and Leo Barnard.

Scottish Piper, Eastgate Centre, Bedfordview. Tel: (27)(11) 616-6465.

Smoker's Den, Bedford Centre, 52 Smith Str., Bedford Gardens. Tel: (27)(11) 616-7301.

*Wesley's, Bank City, Pritchard Str. City. Tel: (27)(11) 833-2510. Offers humidor exchange service to restaurants. Owner: Elaine Wood.

*Wesley's, G39 Garden Pavilion, Carlton Centre, City. Tel: (27)(11) 331-1050. Small but good range of premium cigars. Owner: Colin Wesley.

*Wesley's, Shop 170, Rosebank Mall. Rosebank. Tel: (27)(11) 788-7413. Small but good range of premium cigars. Owner: Colin Wesley.

NELSPRUIT

*Wesley's, 22C Bester Brown Centre. Tel: (27)(1311) 53-308. Owner: Floris Engelbrecht.

PLETTENBERG BAY

Cock 'n Bull, The Square. Tel: (27)(4457) 30-335.
Part of chain of well-stocked gift shops. Has small selection of mainly non-Cuban cigars. Owner: Ankie Roux.

PORT ELIZABETH

*Wesley's, 24 Shoprite Checkers Mall. Greenacres. Tel: (27)(041) 34-2036. Owners: Sue and Jullian Brits.

POTCHEFSTROOM

M & H Curiosity Hut, Pick 'n Pay Centre. Tel: (27)(148) 24-254.

PRETORIA, CITY CENTRE

Tobacco Corner, 25, Tramshed Centre, cnr Schoeman & Van der Walt Streets. Tel: (27)(12) 320-4062.
"Tobacco Corner" shops owned by Pieter Krogh.

PRETORIA, MENLYN PARK

Tobacco Corner, No 1 Menlo Park Centre, Atterbury Rd. Tel: (27)(12) 348-3353.
Small but good range cigars, accessories.

PRETORIA, MUCKLENEUK

Tabak L'Art, 109 Brooklyn Mall. Tel: (27)(12) 46-7781. Owner: Willem Hoogenboezoem.

PRETORIA, SUNNYSIDE

Tobacco Corner, 37A Sunnypark Centre, Cnr Beatrix and Esselen Strs. Tel: (27)(12) 341-5290.

RANDBURG

*Wesley's, 124 Sanlam Centre. Tel: (27)(11) 787-6358. Owner: Carol Minnaar.

RICHARDS BAY

*Wesley's, Shop 9A, The Boardwalk. Tel: (27)(351) 98-7271. Owners: Dave and Mary Ash.

WESTVILLE

*Wesley's, Shop 234, The Pavillion. Tel: (27)(31) 265-0735. Owners: Tony and Alexia Zografos.

* Wesley's is franchised chain of cigar shops.

S P A I N

BARCELONA

Gimeno Paseo de Gracia, 101. Tel: (34)(3) 217-9271. Does not sell tobacco of any kind, but carries extensive range of accessories for smokers.

Gimeno, Rambla de les Flors 100. Tel: (34)(3) 302-0983. Exceptional range. Some bargains. Wonderful atmosphere. Owner: Pere Canals Gramunt.

MADRID

Casa Central del Tobaco, Calle Alcalá 44. Tel: (34)(1) 521-0420. Good range Havanas. Owned by giant tobacco monopoly, Tabacalera. Manager: Jesús Fernández-Montes.

SWEDEN

GÖTEBORG

Brobergs, Arkaden. Tel: (46)(31) 15-1260.

SWITZERLAND

GENEVA

Davidoff, 2 rue de Rive. Tel: (41)(22) 728-9041.
Perhaps world's greatest, certainly most famous, cigar shop. A must for every aficionado. Wide selection, superb cigars, impressively stored.

Gerard Pere et Fils, Noga Hilton Hotel, 19 Quai du Mont-Blanc. Tel: (41)(22) 732-6511.
Another great cigar shop, "father-and-son" enterprise. Most recent addition to ranks of master cigar dealers. Impressive cedar-lined shop. Carries enormous stock of Havanas in superb condition. Connoisseurs should look out the "Selection Gerrand". Unusual range accessories. Written beautifully produced book — "The Connoisseurs Guide to Havana Cigars".

Gresel Cigars. 2-4 Place Longemalle. Tel: (41)(22) 21-9740. In addition to Havanas, has excellent range of non-Cuban cigars. Carries lonsdale, corona and panatella especially made for them by Hoyo de Monterrey in Honduras.

Rhein, 1 Rue du Mont-Blanc. Tel: (41)(22) 32-9764.
One of oldest cigar shops in Switzerland. Knowledgeable, family-run business. Exceptional range Havanas.

ZÜRICH

Durr, Bahnhofplatz 6. Tel: (41)(1) 211-6323.
Old-world atmosphere. Good range.

UNITED KINGDOM

BATH

Frederick Tranner, 5 Church Str., Abbey Green. Tel: (44)(225) 46-6197. Fax: 46-6197.
Small organised shop. Selected range excellently stored. Advice freely available.

BEDFORD

Harrison & Simmonds, 80 High Str. Tel: (44)(234) 26-6711. Traditional high street tobacconist.

BIRMINGHAM

John Hollingsworth & Son Ltd., 5 Temple Row. Tel: (44)(21) 236-7768. Fax: 236-3696.
Good range cigars, accessories. Downstair humidor. Helpful staff.

BLACKPOOL

Birchalls of Blackpool Ltd., 14 Talbot Rd. Tel: (44)(253) 24-218. Fax: 29-1659.

BOLTON

Arthur Morris Ltd, 71 Bradshawgate. Tel: (44)(204) 21-340. Fax: 52-1340.

BRISTOL

Clive Wrigley, 35 Baldwin Str. Tel: (44)(272) 27-3676.

CAMBRIDGE

Harrison & Simmonds of Cambridge, 17 St. John's Str. Tel: (44)(223) 32-4515. Fax: 32-4515.

CARDIFF

Lewis Darbey & Co. 28-32 Wyndham Arcade, Mill Lane. Tel: (44)(222) 23-3443.

CHELTENHAM

Tobacco World, Unit F7, Regent Arcade. Tel: (44)(242) 22-2037.

CHESTER

Tobacco World, 78 Northgate Str. Tel: (44)(244) 34-8821. Fax: 34-8821. Large range quality Havanas. Good walk-in humidor. Owners: Peter Lloyd and Pat Burt.

EDINBURGH

Herbert Love Tobacconists, 31 Queensferry Str. Tel: (44)(31) 225-8082, Fax: 225-8082.
Good selection. Pleasant service.

EXETER

McGahey, The Tobacconist, 245 High Str. Tel: (44)(392) 73-625. Fax: 49-6113.

GLASGOW

Robert Graham & Co, 71 St. Vincent Str. Tel: (44)(41) 221-6588. Fax: 221-6588.

Tobacco House, 9 St Vincent Place. Tel: (44)(41) 226-4586. Fax: 226-4586. Large selection, particularly Havanas. Has unique humidified room using shop window as one wall of the room. Manager: Jim Wikinson.

LEEDS

Aston Tobacconits, 17 Thorntons Arcade. Tel: (44)(532) 34-7435.

LONDON

Alfred Dunhill, 30 Duke Str. Tel: (44)(171) 499-9566. Fax: 499-6471. Controlled by giant Rembrandt Group of South Africa. Specialist cigar shop. Large selection Havanas. Wide range humidors, accessories. Offers laying-down service to clients. Old world atmosphere. Plush leather armchairs available for clients wishing to smoke. Manager: Philip Watts.

Davidoff of London, 35, St James's Str., SW1. Tel: (44)(171) 930-3079. Fax: 930-5887.
Specialist cigar shop. Wide selection. Large well-stocked humidor. Clients welcome to smoke in comfortable chairs. Wide range accessories, humidors. Offers laying down service to regular clients. Efficient service from smartly dressed staff. Friendliness feature of this shop. Owner: Edward Sahakian.

Havana Club, 164 Sloan Str., SW1. Tel: (44)(171) 245-0890, Fax: 245-0895. Beautifully appointed shop and smoking room reminiscent of the great divans of Victorian era. Customers encouraged to sit and smoke in sumptuous surroundings. Mahogany walls, deep leather chairs and Persian rugs exude quality in a relaxed, air conditioned atmosphere. Splendid humidified room, with its floor to ceiling panelling and glass doors, holds more than 26 000 of the world's finest cigars. Smoker's paradise boasting many antique accessories. Situated next door to Monte's, private members-only club, gracing four floors. Both owned by Mohi Binhendi, proprietor of one of Dubai's leading hotels. Shop manager: Neil Millington. Assistant: Michael Whittingham.

Harrods Cigar Room, Knightsbridge, SW1. Tel: (44)(171) 730 1234. Fax: 581-9590.
Specialist cigar shop. Large well-stocked humidor. Wide range of humidors, accessories. Knowledgeable, helpful staff. Friendly, attentive service. Manager: Jean Clark.

James J. Fox and Robert Lewis, 19 St James's Str. SW1. Tel: (44)(171) 930-3787. Fax: 495-0097.
Specialist cigar shop. Large, well-stocked humidor. Wide range humidors, accessories. Merger of two of oldest cigar shops. James J. Fox (who started in Dublin, Ireland in 1881 and opened in London in 1947) taking over 207-year-old Robert Lewis shop in St. James. Visitors welcome to view outstanding cigar museum. Collection includes ledger page detailing first purchase of young, recently elected member of Parliament for Oldham, Mr. Winston Churchill from Robert Lewis on August 9 1900. Huge stocks reserved for clients. Third generation Michael Crowley delivers attentative and knowledgeable service. Managing director: Robert Emery.

Jayems, 125 Victoria Str., SW1. Tel: (44)(171) 828-1472.
General tobacconist.

Sautter of Mayfair, 106, Mount Str, W1. Tel: (44)(171) 499-4866, Fax: 499-4866. Specialist cigar shop. Opposite Connaught Hotel. Well-stocked humidor. Selling off their pipes and tobaccos to concentrate only on cigar-related products. Specialises in tobacco-related antiques. Owner: Desmond Sautter. Manager: Geoffrey Mairis.

Selfridges. Oxford Street, W1. Tel: (44)(171) 629-1234, Fax: 491-1880.
Small section specialising in cigars, near wonderfully stocked wine dept. Attentive service.

Shervingtons Ltd., 337, High Holborn, WC1. Tel:

(44)(171) 405-2929, Fax: 803-8887. Half-timbered Elizabeth building in legal area. Cigars kept in top condition.

G. Smith & Son, 74, Charing Cross Rd., WC2. Tel: (44)(171) 836-7422. Typical high-street general tobacconist. Good selection Havanas in walk-in humidor. Manager: Barry Monahan.

Walter Thurgood, Salisbury House, 161-162 London Wall, EC2. Tel: (44)(171) 628-5437, Fax: 930-5887. City's only specialist cigar shop. Owned by Edward Sahakian of Davidoff of London. Managed by Barry Coughlan.

G. Ward (Tobacconists) Ltd., 60, Gresham Street, EC2. Tel: (44)(171) 606-4318, Fax: 606-4318. General tobacconist.

MANCHESTER

Aston Tobacconists, Exchange Str., Royal Exchange Shopping Centre. Tel: (44)(61) 832-7895.

NOTTINGHAM

T.F. Gauntley Ltd., 4 High Str. Tel: (44)(159) 41-7973. Fax: 50-9519.

OTLEY

James Barber, 33 Kirkgate. Tel: (44)(943) 46-2603.

STRATFORD-ON-AVON

Lands (Tobacconists) Ltd., 29 Central Chambers, Henley Str. Tel: (44)(789) 29-2508.
Cigars kept in good humidor. Where else but to buy a Romeo y Jullieta Shakespeare?

UNITED STATES

ATLANTA (Georgia)

*Tinder Box, 3393 Peachtree Rd. Tel: (1)(404) 231-9853. Managers: Bob and Sherrin Willis.

ALBANY (California)

Drucquer & Son. 1481 Solano Ave. Tel: (1)(510) 525-5682. Owner: Ron Richards.

ANNAPOLIS (Maryland)

Fader's Tobacconists, 150F Jennifer Rd. Tel: (1)(410) 841-5155.

BALTIMORE (Maryland)

Fader & Sons, 107E Baltimore Str. Tel: (1)(410) 685-5511. Established 1891. One of six traditional tobacco shops in the area, owned by same family. Carries good range cigars, pipes and tobacco. Owner: Bill Fader, grandson of founder.

Fader's Tobacconists, 5872 Westview Mall. Tel: (1)(410) 744-9099.

Fader's Tobacconists, 7808 Eastpoint Mall. Tel: (1)(410) 282-6622.

BELLEVUE (Washington)

*Tinder Box-Bellevue, 10150 Main Str. Tel: (1)(206) 451-8544. Owner: Gene Del Giudice.

BETHESDA (Maryland)

J.B. Simms Fine Tobacco, 4914 St. Elmo Ave. Tel: (301) 656-7123. Good collection antiques. Large walk-in humidor. Good collection cigars. Upstairs is private "members only" club. Owner: J. Bart Sims.

BEVERLY HILLS (California)

Alfred Dunhill Ltd., 201 Rodeo Dr. Tel: (310) 274-5351. Wide range of accessories and cigars in excellent condition. Humidor upstairs. Contains lockers available to those who maintain stock of 10 or more of store-purchased cigars. Comfortable chairs in humidor where cigars may be smoked. Manager: Todd Thoman.

Beverley Hills Pipe & Tobacco Co., 218 N. Beverley Dr. Tel: (310) 276-3200. About 80 different cigar brands. Formerly Tinder Box Store. Owner: Todd Kornguth.

Kramer's Pipe & Tobacco, 9531 Santa Monica Blvd. Tel: (310) 273-9777. Established 1949. Oldest cigar shop in Beverley Hills. Nostalgic atmosphere. Owner: Tina Kramer.

Nazareth's, 350 N. Cannon Dr. Tel: (310) 271-5863. Good range cigars. Private-blend Romeo y Julieta cigars exclusive from this shop. Across courtyard is Nazareth's private club — first in Beverley Hills. Both closed Sundays. Owner: Nazareth Guluzian.

Thomas Hinds Tobacconist, 9632 S. Santa Monica Blvd. Tel: (310) 275-9702. Wide range cigars. Area for smoking with TV. Open Sun. Owner: David Peck.

Manager: Creighton Anderson.

Davidoff of Geneva Inc., 232, North Rodeo Drive. Tel: (1)(310) 278-4888. Wide selection cigars, accessories and humidors. Full range of Davidoff, Zino, Griffin's and Avo cigars. Upstairs is Private Keep Club, containing members' lockers and comfortable area to smoke. Manager: Lisa Staford.

BIRMINGHAM (Michigan)

Churchills, 142 S. Woodward. Tel: (1)(313) 647-4555.

BOCA RATON (Florida)

Bennington Tobacco, 80 Royal Palm Plaza, 501, S.E. Mizner Blvd. Tel: (1)(470) 391-1372.

BOSTON (Massachusetts)

David P. Ehrich & Co., 32, Tremont Str. Tel: (1)(617) 227-1720.
Established 1868 by Fanny Abrahams. Had been, predominantly, pipe shop with pipe maker on premises. Now specialises in cigars, with large range, including accessories and humidors. Also sells wine. Comfortable chairs for smokers. Owner: Paul Macdonald.

L.J. Peretti Co., Inc., 2 1/2 Park Square. Tel: (617) 482-0218. Founded on Haruard Square in 1886. Past customers include F.D. Roosevelt and Winston Churchill. Large display of Harvard memorabilia. Sells Harvard associated products. Good range cigars, pipes, tobacco, accessories and humidors. Attentative service. Manager: Paul Macdonald. Jr.

CHICAGO (Illinois)

Iwan Ries Tobacco, 19 S. Wabash Ave. Tel: (1)(312) 372-1306. Owner: Chuck Levi. Upstairs on second floor. Established 1857, been in one family ever since. In store one walk-in humidor, at back, two humidified rooms — one refrigerated. Carries over 90 brands. Large collection of antique pipes. Special item is only complete tobacco money found in steel trunk belonging to George Washington. Huge selection of pipes and pipe accessories. Pipes cleaned on premises. Claims largest selection of pipe tobacco. Loose cigars offered in unique two-ply, sealable foil/poly bag. These bags less permeable than normal zip-lock bags, as cigars not only stay moist, but also do not absorb food odours. Store owned by fourth generation (grandson of founder), Chuck Levi. Manager: Tony Palacios.

Rubovits Cigars, 320 S. Lasalle Str. Tel: (1)(312) 939-3780. Established 1894. Do not let dust and, sometimes, untidy stock put you off. Big selection. Many super premium cigars not widely available. Has separate lounge for customers to smoke their cigars. Owner, eccentric, bearded David Mohr, easily distinguishable by his height and always with large cigar in mouth. Although sometimes brusque in attitude, is knowledgeable. Over 30 years experience in cigar retail trade.

Jack Swartz Cigars. 175 W. Jackson. Tel: (1)(312) 782-7898. Situated in arcade in building which is No 175. Entrance actually off Wells Str. Large selection. Has chair for smokers in humidor. Stores cigars for selected customers.

Up Down Tobacco Shop, 1550 N. Wells. Tel: (1)(312) 337-8505. Owner: Diana Silvius-Gits. Original shop was on two levels, hence name. Wide range of cigars and accessories. Stock stored in large glass-fronted humidors. Has own brand, named after charasmatic owner, Diana Silvius. Manager: Dave Lux.

CINCINNATI (Ohio)

Straus Tobacconist, 410-412 Walnut Str. Tel: (1)(513) 621-3388. Established 1880. Large display of tobacco artifacts. Range of nearly 100 brands. Good range of accessories. Owner: James Clark.

CLAYTON (Missouri)

J.R. Tobacco, 4 North Central Ave. Tel: (1)(314) 727-5667.

CLEVELAND (Ohio)

Cousin's Cigar Co., 1828 Euclid Ave. Tel: (1)(216) 781-9390. Established 1950. Has probably largest range in Mid West. Five walk-in humidors. Mail Order catalague: Seven knowledgeable staff. Owner: likable Danny Kolod, owned shop for 19 years.

DALLAS (Texas)

Up in Smoke, 2315 Galleria Mall. Tel: (1)(214) 458-7501.

EVANSVILLE (Indiana)

Briar and Bean, 800 N. Green River Rd. Tel: (1)(812) 479-8736. Owners: Ted and Debby Clark.

FAIRFIELD (New Jersey)

J.R. Tobacco Outlet, 277 Rte. 46 West. Tel: (1)(201) 882-6446.

FALLS CHURCH (Virginia)

Tobacco Barn, 6201 Arlington Blvd., 7 Corners Centre. Tel: (1)(703) 536-5588.

FAYETTEVILLE (North Carolina)

Anstead's Tobacco, 337 Cross Creek Mall. Tel: (1)(910) 864-5707.

FORT LAUDERDALE (Florida)

Smoker's Gallery, Galleria Mall, 2366 E. Sunrise Blvd. Tel: (1)(305) 561-0002. Owner: Joel Wolk.

FORT WAYNE (Indiana)

Riegels Pipe and Tobacco. Large range of cigars in walk-in humidor. Carries stock of up to 150 000 cigars. Also sells magazines and maps. Owner: Bill Bougher with over 40 years experience. Manager: John Minnich.

GATLINBURG (Tennessee)

Gatlin-Burlier, 603 Skyline Drive. Tel: (1)(615) 436-4412. Owners: Ira and Jan Lapides.

GREENWICH (Connecticut)

Greenwich Tobacconist, 8 Havemeyer Place. Tel: (1)(203) 8695401.

HARTFORD (Connecticut)

De La Concha Tobacconists. One Civic Center Plaza. Tel: (1)(203) 527-4291. Owner: Joseph Melendi. One of two brothers, both in cigar retailers, descended from old Cuban cigar family. Wide selection of cigars, pipes and accessories. Has mail-order catalogue.

HASBROUCK HEIGHTS (New Jersey)

J.R. Tobacco, 65 Rte. 17 South. Tel: (1)(201) 288-7676. Owner: Lew Rothman.

HOUSTON (Texas)

Jeffrey Stone Ltd., 9694 Westheimer. Tel: (1)(713) 783-3555. Owner: Jeff Stone.

Lone Star Tobacco, 3741 FM 1960 W. Tel: (1)(713) 444-2464. Owner: Ben Henderson.

KANSAS CITY (Missouri)

Fred Diebel Inc., 426, Ward Parkway.

KEY LARGO (Florida)

Caribbean Cigar Factory. 103400 Overseas Highway. MM103. Tel: (1)(305) 453-0448. Has eight rollers. Manager: Chris Stanford.

LANCASTER (Pennsylvania)

Demuth's Tobacco Shop, 114 East King Str. Tel: (1)(717) 397-6613. Oldest tobacco shop in USA, established 1770. Former customers include Gen Edward Hand, one of George Washington's right-hand men; Jasper Yeates, leading American patriot; and President James Buchanan. Shop museum-like with large collection of smoking artifacts. Large range of hand-made and machine-made cigars. Owned by Demuth Foundation.

LOS ANGELES (California)

Century City Tobacco Shoppe, 10250 Santa Monica Blvd. Tel: (1)(310) 277-0760. Owner: Hugh Getzenberg.

LYNNWOOD (Washington)

*Tinder Box-Lynnwood. 3000–184th Str. SW., Space No. 222. Tel: (1)(206) 771-8418.

MIAMI (Florida) *Mikes 1 800 962-4427*

Caribbean Cigar Factory. (Little Havana). 6265 SW 8th Str. Tel: (1)(305) 267-3911. Shop in front of 30 roller, modern factory. President: Kevin Doyle.

Caribbean Cigar Factory. (South Beach). 760 Ocean Drive, S Miami Beach. Tel: (1)(305) 538-6062. Good. One roller in shop. Manager: Gayle Ritt.

El Credito. (Little Havana). 8th Str. Tel: (1)(305). Tiny sales area in compact, haphazard-looking factory that makes three brands, one of which is famed La Gloria Cubana. Owner: Ernesto Carillo. Manager: Elena Carillo. *I 95- 125'd go East*

Miker 1030 kHwe Con Course Mi Ami

King's Treasure Tobacco Co., Bayside Market Place, 401 Biscayne Blvd. Tel: (1)(305) 374-5593. Owner: Manuel Hernandez.

Smoke Shop II, Omni International Mall, 1601 Biscayne Blvd., 6–8. Tel: (1)(305) 358-1886. Small shop, but good range of cigars and accessories. Offers mail-order service. Open seven days a week. Knowledgeable owner: William Singer.

MIDDLETOWN (New York)

Golden Embers Tobacconists, Orange Plaza Mall, Rt. 211 East. Tel: (1)(914) 343-3373. Owners: Mike and Kathleen Rosenberg.

NAPA (California)

Baker Street Tobacco, 3053 Jefferson Str. Tel: (1)(707) 252-2766. Owner: Brenda Roberts.

NEWHAVEN (Connecticut)

The Owl Shop, 268 College Str. Tel: (1)(203) 624-3250. Yale's local tobacconist. Quality stock, good condition.

NEW YORK (New York)

Alfred Dunhill of London Inc., 450 Park Ave. Tel: (1)(212) 888-4000.
Prestigious store with wide range of cigars in excellent condition. Many cigar accessories also men and women's jewellery, clothing and writing implements. Offers laying-down service for regular customers. Comfortable leather chairs in humidor, where cigars can be smoked. Has private club with lockers for members and business facilities. Manager: Peter J. Katz.

Arnold's Tobacco Shop, 323 Madison Ave. Tel: (1)(212) 697-1477.
Small shop, but a real treasure. Carries over 36 brands. Comprehensive range for each brand. Aim of owner, Bruce Goldstein, to offer good selection of super premium cigars not widely available. House Brand, without a band, is a particularly good buy. Wide range of top quality accessories, pipes and tobacco. Regular customers include Rush Limbaugh and Gregory Hines.

Barclay Rex Pipe Shop, 7 Maiden Lane. Tel: (1)(212) 962-3355. Owner: Vincent Nastri.

Davidoff of Geneva Inc., 535 Madison Ave. Tel: (1)(212) 751-9060.

Wide selection cigars, accessories and humidors. Place to be seen buying cigars. Knowledgeable staff. Good service. Full range of Davidoff, Zino, Griffin's and Avo cigars. Manager: Diana Wagner.

De La Concha, 1390 Avenue of the Americas. Tel: (1)(212) 757-3167. Owner: Lionel Melendi. One of two brothers, both cigar retailers, descended from old Cuban cigar family. Wide selection of cigars, pipes and accessories. Has mail-order catalogue.

Nat Sherman International, 500 Fifth Ave. Tel: (1)(212) 246-8639. FAX 2/2) 764-5000/764-4175

One of world's most luxurious cigar shops. Carries large range of Nat Sherman cigars and small, but select range of Macanudo and Partagas brands. Nat Sherman cigar bands are colour coded to denote type of wrapper. Good range accessories and humidors. Pride of range is electronic control 500 cigar hand-made mahogany chest. Shop spread over two floors. Street level area for mainly loose cigars. Be sure to go upstairs where spacious, luxurious area houses large humidor. Facilities available to smoke. Furniture includes baby grand piano. Here cigar, cognac, wine, etc. tasting are held with background piano music. Regular customers include Harry Connick Jnr, Tom Selleck, Lou Gossert Jnr, Milton Berle and Rush Limbaugh. Has beautifully presented mail-order catalogue. Company is 65 years old. Run by second generation Joel Sherman and wife Myrna, assisted by third generation sons, William, Lawrence and daughter Michelle.

J.R. Tobacco, 219 Broadway. Tel: (1)(212) 233-6620.

J.R. Tobacco. 11E 45th Str. Tel: (1)(212) 983-4160.

OWINGS (Maryland)

Fader's Tobacconists, Valley Village, 9175 Reistertown Rd. Tel: (1)(410) 363-7799.

PHILADELPHIA (Philadelphia)

Holt's Cigar, 114 S16th Str. Tel: (1)(215) 563-0763.

PHOENIX (Arizona)

Stag Tobacconist, 9627A Metro Parkway West. Tel: (1)(602) 943-7517. Owner: Eugene Duhon.

PORTLAND (Oregon)

Rich's Cigar Store, 801 SW. Alder. Tel: (1)(800) 669-1527.
Established 1894. Largest selection of cigars on West Coast. Glass-enclosed humidors. Wide selection antiques. Friendly service. Customers include Walter Cronkite and Clint Eastwood. Owner: Tom Moran.

SALT LAKE CITY (Utah)

*Tinder Box-Salt Lake City, 505 Main, Crossroads Plaza No. A26. Tel: (1)(801) 355-7336. Owners: Fred and Joan Cvar.

SAN DIEGO (California)

*Tinder Box-San Diego. 642 Fashion Valley Rd. No. 538. Tel: (1)(619) 291-7337. Owner: John Cameron.

SANTA MONICA (California)

*Tinder Box, 2729 Wilshire Blvd. Tel: (1)(213) 828-2313. Owner: Ed Koplin.

SANTA ROSA (California)

The Pipe Square, 346 Coddington Centre. Tel: (1)(707) 573-8544.

SCOTTSDALE (Arizona)

Ford and Haig, 7076 Fifth Ave. Tel: (1)(602) 946-0608.

SELMA (North Carolina)

J.R. Tobacco, 67 JR Rd. Tel: (1)(919) 965-5055.

SHERMAN OAKS (California)

Gus' Smoke Shop, Ventura Blvd. Tel: (1)(818) 789-1401. Established 1927. Specialises in supplying smoking accessories to movie industry.Good range of cigars, pipes, tobacco and accessories. Sometimes Bill Cosby can be seen buying cigars. Next door is The Back Room, smoking club with comfortable couches, card tables, pool table and TVs. Owner: Jim Hurwitz.

SOUTHFIELD (Michigan)

J.R. Tobacco Detroit, 28815 Northwestern Highway. Tel: (1)(810) 357-2340.

STATESVILLE (North Carolina)

J.R. Tobacco of America, 1515E Broad Str., Newtowne Plaza. Tel: (1)(704) 872-5300.

ST. LOUIS (Missouri)

J.R. Tobacco, 710 Olive Str. Tel: (1)(314) 234-4434.

STUART (Florida)

Coffman's Tobacco Shop, 4336 S.E. Federal Highway. Tel: (1)(407) 287-5060. Owners: Susan and Robert Griggs.

TAMPA (Florida)

Edward's Pipe and Tobacco, 3235 Henderson Blvd. Tel: (1)(813) 872-0723.

TOWSON (Maryland)

Fader's Tobacconists, 25 Alleghany Ave., Tel: (1)(410) 828-4555.

TUCSON (Arizona)

Smoker's Haven Inc., 5870 E. Broadway. Tel: (1)(602) 747-8989. Owner: Carl Curtis.

SAN FRANCISCO (California)

Sherlock's Haven, 1 Embarcadero Centre. Tel: (1)(415) 1405. Owner: Martin Pulvers.

WASHINGTON DC

Georgetown Tobacco, 3144 M-str. Tel: (1)(202) 338-5100.

J.R. Washington, 1667 K Str. Tel: (1)(202) 296-3872. Only store in the J.R. Group that ships out of the USA.

W. Curtis Draper Tobacconist, 640 14th Str. NW. Tel: (1)(202) 638-2555. Established 1887. Past customers include Calvin Coolidge, Richard Nixon and Gerald Ford. Large range of cigars, accessories and humidors. Owners: John "Duke" Cox and Frances Martin.

WILMINGTON (North Carolina)

Davis & Son Tobacconists, Long Leaf Mall. Tel: (1)(919) 791-6688. Owner: Tim Davis.

* All Tinder Box stores are franchises to Tinder Box International. Principal owner is Daniel Blummenthall, one of major share or stock holders of Villazon & Company Inc. Franchising began in 1965.

GUIDE TO WRAPPER COLOURS

(See a full description of each colour on page 36)

Claro Claro or Candela

Claro

Colorado Claro

Colorado or English Market Selection

Colorado Maduro

Maduro or Spanish Market Selection

Oscuro

Picture by Al Todd, Cape Town.

CUBAN TOBACCO PLANT

Coronas
(top)

Centre Gordo
(thick centre)

Centro Fino
(thin centre)

Centro Ligero
(light centre)

Uno Y Medio
(one and a half)

Libre De Pie
(base)

Picture by Hunters and Frankau, London.

Tending seed beds in the Vuelta Abajo.

Picture supplied by Hunters and Frankau, London.

Fernando Piñá, a quality control agricultural engineer for Habanos SA, inspecting tobacco seeds near the town of San Juan y Martinez in the heart of the famed Vuelta Abajo, Cuba. Seeds are harvested in March and April.

Angel Ramos, an agricultural engineer and assistant director on El Corojo Tobacco Plantation, in the Vuelta Abajo, Cuba, where some of the finest wrapper tobacco in the world is grown, stands under the enormous muslin cloth tents, known as topado, that protect the wrapper leaves from direct sunlight.

Tobacco curing barn, known as casas de tabaco, *near San Juan y Martinez in the Vuelta Abajo, Cuba.*

Francisco Milian, owner of the farm, Finca la Cova-dondo Panch Perez, near San Juan y Martinez, in the prime producing Vuelta Abajo, Cuba, examining some of his top quality wrapper leaves in the curing barn. He produces 12 500 kg of tobacco from seven hectares and is considered the best grower in the area.

Wrappers undergoing their first fermentation under the supervision of a reguero.

Picture supplied by Hunters and Frankau, London.

Stacked in larger bulks, called burros, *for the second fermentation. The temperature of the leaves is constantly supervised.*

Picture supplied by Hunters and Frankau, London.

Grading wrapper leaves (rezagado) *in the La Corona Factory, Havana.*

Bernado González from the marketing department of Habanos SA, examining hands of tobacco (gavilla) *unpacked from bales known as tercios, traditionally made from the bark of the royal palm tree, in the La Corona Factory, Havana.*

The actual rolling is done by skilled workers called torcedores *who sit in rows at long, narrow work benches. They are given batches of leaves that have been expertly prepared and graded. Each batch represents the correct blend of tobacco to produce one day's production. A good Cuban* torcedor *can roll between 100 and 150 cigars a day, depending on the size.* Torcedores *are able to make a variety of sizes and shapes, but usually specialise, for long periods, in one type of cigar. Since the 1960s many women have taken their place in Havana's great factories.*

Cigars being made for the local market in a wooden, palm-covered shack at the rural village of Las Barrigonas in the province of Pinar Del Rio, Cuba.

Machine-made cigars being placed in cellophane tubes in the La Corona Factory, Havana.

CIGAR MAKING PROCESS

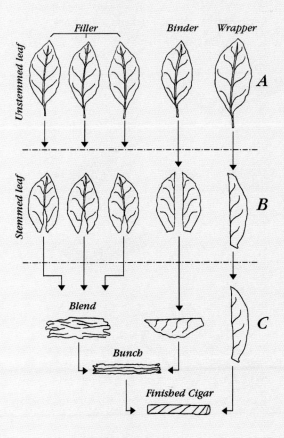

A. Leaf after fermentation
B. Leaf after ageing and curing
C. The rolling process

© Theo Rudman

CIGAR MAKING

The ligero, seco and volado leaves are blended to form the filler.

The filler is rolled into the binder to form a "bunch".

The wrapper is trimmed to size with the chaveta.

The fragile wrapper is gently stretched onto the bunch.

A separate piece of the wrapper is used to form the cap.

The cigar is cut to length in a guillotine.

The torcedor checks the girth of the finished cigar with a ring gauge.

The finished cigar is now checked for the correct length.

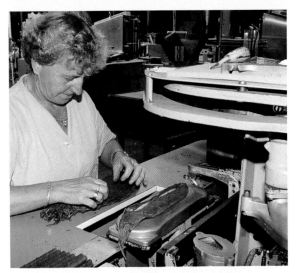

An Arenco MTR-01 complete cigar making machine, in the huge Austria Tabak Factory, Vienna, used for most cigar shapes with natural binder and wrapper leaves. Daily output is about 4 200 cigars.

Picture by Austria Tabak, Vienna.

A PMB bobbin unwinding maching (BUD) in operation in the Ritmeester Factory, Holland. Wrappers from Sumatra, Java and Brazil are die cut and accurately placed on large rolls of fabric, mainly in Sri Lanka and Gibralta, where there is plentiful low-cost labour. The completed bobbins are then shipped to various manufacturers in Holland. A conventional cigar machine with a BUD runs at 20 to 30 single or double length cigars per minute.

Managers Dick Nooy (left) and Pim Bakker behind counter in P.G.C. Hajenius shop in the Rokin, Amsterdam. It was built in 1914, based on original Dutch tobacco house and is, today, a national monument. Lavish use of carved wood, marble, crystal chandeliers. Has extensive museum.

Nicholas Freeman, Hunters & Frankau, sole importers of Cuban cigars into the UK, receiving a presentation box of rare figurado shaped cigars from Francisco Linares, head of Habanos SA, at a function in Havana to mark the 150th anniversary of the Partagas brand.

Oscar Boruchin, owner of cigar distributor and retailer, Mike's Cigars, Miami, Florida, in front of large painting of a pre-Castro cigar factory which takes the pride of place in the company's prestigious shop in a former bank building. In that era all the rollers were men.

Cuban born, Ernesto Carillo, owner of El Credito, which makes the highly sought after La Gloria Cubana, in the conditioning room in his factory in Little Havana, Miami, USA.

Richard DiMeola (left), executive vice-president , chief operating officer, and James Colucci, senior vice-president, sales and marketing, both of Consolidated Cigar Corporation, in the company's Fort Lauderdale, USA, head office.

Kevin Doyle, president, Caribbean Cigar Co., cutting a cake in shape of a cigar, at a party to launch the company's new factory in Miami, USA.

Second generation, Joel Sherman, president of Nat Sherman International, with youngest son, Lawrence, in company's luxurious shop at 500 Fith Ave, New York. Has large humidor and facilities to smoke. Furniture includes baby grand piano. Here cigar, cognac, wine, etc tastings are held with background music.

Lionel Melendi, owner of New York shop, De La Concha. He is descended from old Cuban cigar family.

Top team at Villazon & Co., taking time out at Cigar Africionado's Big Smoke in New York on 21 November 1996. From left to right, Carol Jean, daughter of co-owner, Frank Llaneza, Sherwin Seltzer, vice-president, marketing and sales, and Daniel Blumenthal, co-owner.

Mark Goldman in front of his retail shop, Mom's Cigars, in lower Manhattan, New York. He also owns distributors, House of Oxford and claims to carry over seven million cigars in spite of current shortages. In the shop window behind him can be seen part of his extensive collection of antique cigar-store figures, considered to be the largest in the USA.

Frank Fina, senior vice-president, new business development, General Cigar, makers of Macanudo, largest selling premium cigar brand in the USA.

The author with Radha Naidoo, sales manager of wholesalers, Alpine Importers, Johannesburg, South Africa, at a recent dinner of the Van Reenen "21" Cigar Club, so called, after the name of the founder and the fact that membership is limited to 21. Over the last three years, cigar dinners and cigar clubs have become exceedingly popular in South Africa.

Cuban Cigar Directory

CUBA

The Caribbean Island of Cuba is divided into five principle tobacco producing regions: *Oriente, Remedios, Partidos, Semi Vuelta* and the famed *Vuelta Abajo*. The average temperature is 25 °C (75 °F) and the average relative humidity around 80 percent. Only two, *Partidos* and *Vuelta Abajo*, grow tobacco fine enough for export quality Havanas.

The tobacco in each of these districts has some special characteristic. *Oriente* and *Remedios* produce tobacco which is used primarily for filler. A small part is kept for the local cigar market; a larger quantity is used for the manufacture of cigarettes; the largest portion of all is exported as raw material for blending in overseas factories.

Tobacco from *Partido* is used for wrappers. *Semi-Vuelta* produces filler and cigarette leaf. Only *Vuelta Abajo*, in the extreme Western part of the Island, with its unique soil and climate, produces all the leaves needed to blend a cigar. This is "Cradle of Havanas."

The most famous tobacco fields are situated in the sub-district of *Llano*, which includes the municipalites of *San Juan Y Martinez* and *San Luis* in the Province of Pinar del Rio. Irrigation and fertiliser are not used in all the tobacco growing districts, but are employed in Pinar del Rio.

Tobacco, including finished cigars, is Cuba's fourth biggest export after sugar, nickel and fruit. Local consumption of cigars is far higher than exports. Cuba, with a population of about 14 million people, consumes around 300 million cigars annually. At its peak, in the late 1970s and early 1980s, cigar exports were between 90 and 100 million.

On October 1, 1994 a new Cuban-based private limited company, Habanos SA, assumed many of the former responsibilities and activities of the state-owned Cubatabacco. During a visit in 1995 to Cuba, Adriano Martinez, then acting marketing manager of Habanos SA, told me that they exported about 50 million cigars in 1994, down from about 57 million in 1993.

In fact total exports of both hand-made and machine-made cigars for 1996 is expected to go up between 55 and 60 million. Of this amount about 30 million will go to Spain — Cuba's biggest market. Spain also imports about 75 percent of Cuba's export leaf production, worth in excess of $70 million (£46 million).

The Cuban tobacco industry has a critical shortage of foreign currency to buy fertiliser, pesticides, muslin cloth for wrappers and other agricultural requirements due largely, to the break-up of the Soviet Union. Cuba lost, almost overnight, about six billion dollars of foreign exchange.

To overcome this problem, Tabacalera, Spain's giant tobacco monopoly, designed an aid package to finance the 1995/96 crop. Agricultural requisites to the value of about $25 million (£16.6 million) were bought by Tabacalera and shipped to Cuba. The Spaniards ensured that farmers, co-operatives and other growing concerns received these goods. This is, in effect, an advance payment, with the Spanish company paying the balance against cigars actually shipped. These plans include incentives, paid in US dollars, to farmers and workers if they surpass their target.

With this annual aid mechanism and favourable weather conditions, Cuba hopes, before the end of this century, to again export around 100 million cigars a year.

Despite savage rains in October 1995 that uprooted young seedlings causing seed beds to be replanted, resulting in a late crop, and further heavy rains in January 1996, with blue mould in some areas the Cuban authorities are adamant that this crop is the best in the past 10 years, particularly for large wrapper leaves. They, therefore, predict a more plentiful supply, in the next year or two, of big cigars.

Considerably more tabacco has been planted in the prime tobacco growing province of Pinar del Rio.

During my 1995 interview with Martinez I was told that the future marketing strategy would be to promote Cuban cigars as *Habanos*, as Havanas has become a generic word. The word *Habanos* on a box would be the consumer's guarantee that this was the real product, made and grown in Cuba, with its unique taste due to *terrior*. Hence the change in name on October 1, 1994 of the state monopoly controlling cigar exports from Cubatabacco to Habanos SA.

Martinez told me that the present government had steadily rationalised and reduced the vast number of models to about 700 in 1980 and to only 438, across 32 brands, today. He also said that over the next few years this would be reduced even further.

On January 1, 1995 Francisco Linares, former minister of labour, replaced Francisco Padron as head of Habanos SA. The latter had been director general of Cubatabacco since 1985. Padron, largely responsible for establishing the flagship, Cohiba, is now teaching economics and business strategy at the University of Havana.

Linares was born in the Pinar del Rio region and has spent a life-time in or associated with the tobacco industry. He is a qualified cigar roller or *torcedor*. He has, for many years, worked with tobacco workers' unions in the Vuelta Abajo. He declares: "We are going to recover our position in the world market and return to the historic levels we enjoyed years ago".

At the time of my visit he had already spent a great deal of time in the tobacco fields as well as in the factories in Havana emphasising, to workers and management, the need to increase production while still maintaining quality.

Cuba is still a shopping paradise for cigar lovers, despite severe price hikes during 1995 and 1996. Except for the Cohiba range that retails for between $100 (£66) and $300 (£200) depending on size per box of 25, most cigars can be bought in the official tourist shops at between $50 (£33) and $125 (£83) per box. However, there might be further increases towards the end of 1996.

It is Habanos' intention to increase price until they are close to that of the duty-free level in Spain, to discourage commercial trade in conflict with officially appointed importers, in their respective countries.

Generally, resorts in the east of the country are of a high standard and typical of what one would expect in a Caribbean paradise. They are usually run by foreign companies in a joint venture with the Cuban government or under management contracts.

In Havana there is a wide range of hotels ranging from quite awful to quite good. I can recommend the following:

Hotel Nacional, built in 1929 and renovated in 1992 to its original showpiece status. Has 480 rooms catering mainly to businessmen and affluent tourists. It has luxurious ambience and professional service, and also a good cigar shop. Fax: (53)(7) 533-5054.

Melia Cohiba, Havana's newest luxury hotel, opened

early 1995, has 462 rooms in 22-storey building. It is operated by Spanish group, Grupo Sol, which runs many hotels worldwide. It has a fully equipped gym, sauna, business centre and several restaurants. A boom to cigar lovers is the hotel's smoking bar, called El Relicario, stocked with a superb range of Havanas. This is in addition to a good cigar shop. Fax: (53)(7) 33-4555.

Hotel Victoria. Probably about three-star standard, but ideal for businessmen. Has 40 rooms and provides attentative service. Good facilities, including espresso bar. No cigar shop, but only three blocks from Hotel Nacional and not far from Melia Cohiba. Moderately priced. Good value. Fax: (53)(7) 33-3109.

Visitors to Cuba should be warned not to deal with the hundreds of street vendors or staff in hotels offering the "Grande Marques" for between $20 and $25 per box, as these were always forgeries or stolen goods.

Another word of warning. Tourists are only permitted to take only $1 000 worth of cigars out of Cuba. So be sure to keep official invoices of purchases handy while passing through the airport.

In Cuba the tourist currency is US dollars. All purchases are made in US dollars and change given in that currency. Travellers cheques can only be changed in the hotel where the tourist is staying.

THE COMPLETE GUIDE TO THE SIZES AND SHAPES OF HAVANA CIGARS

There is a total of 33 brands in 70 shapes and sizes of Havanas. Although some sizes are seldom used or made only for certain markets.

They vary in length from under 102mm/4 inches to over 230mm/9 inches and the diameter from 10.32mm/26 to 20.64mm/52. The figure after the metric measurement is the ring gauge, which is the diameter measured in 64ths of an inch. Hence a ring gauge of 26 is 26 64th of an inch.

Confusion is caused when a particular size is used for Havana marques that are not necessarily uniform. A Cohiba Coronas Especiale is 152mm/6 in long with a diameter of 15.08mm/38, while a H. Upmann Especiale is 140mm/5 1/2 in long with a diameter of 15.87mm/40. A standard Corona has a diameter of 16.67mm/42 with a length of 142mm/5 1/2 ins. However, the Montecristo Especial (not to be confused with the Montecristo

Especiale No 2) has a diameter of 15.08mm/38 with a length of 192mm/7 1/2 ins.

Often cigars of the same size are called by different names. One that has a diameter of 18.65mm/47 and a length of 178mm/7 in is known as a Churchill. However that same size can be called Esplendido, Coronas Gigantes or Prince of Wales, depending on whether it is a Cohiba, Bolivar or a Romeo y Julieta. But Romeo y Julieta also call the same size a Churchill and a Clemenceau, in addition to Prince of Wales.

However, in Cuba each size variation has a specific *Vitola de Galera* or factory name. A list of 70 sizes follows with the more popular model names or styles.

In the "Cigar Directory of Cuban Cigars" I have listed where possible the general or common name of the shape, with the Vitola de Galera, or factory name, in italics.

In this list the factory name is followed by the measurements and the general name.

VITOLA DE GALERA	SIZE	POPULAR NAME
Gran Corona	D18.65mm/47 L 235mm/9 1/2 in	diamedes (figurado)
Prominente	D19.45mm/49 L 194mm/7 5/8 in	double corona
Julieta. 2	D18.65mm/47 L 178mm/7 in	churchill
Piramide	D20.64mm/52 L 156mm/6 1/8 in	torpedo/figurado
Dalias	D17.07mm/43 L 170mm/6 3/4 in	corona grande
Cazadore	D17.46mm/44 L 162mm/6 3/8 in	corona grande
Tacos	D18.65mm/47 L 158mm/6 1/8 in	corona grande
Conservas	D17.46mm/44 L 145mm/5 11/16 in	corona grande
Franciscos	D17.46mm/44 L 143mm/5 5/8 in	corona grande
Corona Gorda	D18.26mm/46 L 143mm/5 5/8 in	corona extra
Campana	D20.64mm/52 L 140mm/5 1/2 in	figurado
Hermoso No 4	D19.05mm/48 L 127mm/5 in	robusto royal
Britanica	D18.26mm/46 L 137mm/5 3/8 in	robusto royal
Especiale	D17.86mm/45 L 134mm/5 1/4 in	figurado
Robusto	D19.84mm/50 L 124mm/4 7/8 in	robusto/rothschild
Cervante	D16.67mm/42 L 165mm/6 1/2 in	lonsdale
Corona grande	D16.67mm/42 L 155mm/6 1/8 in	lonsdale
Cristale	D16.27mm/41 L 150mm/5 7/8 in	corona
Superiore	D15.87mm/40 L 146mm/5 3/4 in	corona
Las Tres coronas	D15.87mm/40 L 142mm/5 9/16 in	corona
Corona	D16.67mm/42 L 142mm/5 9/16 in	corona
Cosaco	D16.67mm/42 L 135mm/5 5/16 in	corona
Crema/Naçionale	D15.87mm/40 L 140mm/5 1/2 in	petit corona
Eminente	D17.46mm/44 L 132mm/5 3/16 in	petit corona
Almuerzo	D15.87mm/40 L 130mm/5 1/8 in	petit corona
Mareva/petit corona	D16.67mm/42 L 129mm/5 1/16 in	petit corona
Perfecto	D17.46mm/44 L 127mm/5 in	petit corona/ figurado
Petit cetros	D15.87mm/40 L 129mm/5 1/16 in	petit corona

Londres	D15.87mm/40 L 126mm/5 in	petit corona
Standard	D15.87mm/40 L 123mm/4 7/8 in	petit corona
Minuto	D16.67mm/42 L 110mm/4 5/16 in	petit corona
Franciscano	D15.87mm/40 L 116mm/4 9/16 in	petit corona
Coronita	D15.87mm/40 L 117mm/4 5/8 in	petit corona
Perla	D15.87mm/40 L 102mm/4 in	petit corona
Laguito No 1/		
Delicado	D15.08mm/38 L 192mm/7 9/16 in	gran/long panetela
Delicados extra	D14.29mm/36 L 185mm/7 5/16 in	long panetela
Ninfas	D13.10mm/33 L 178mm/7 in	panetela
Parejos	D15.08mm/38 L 166mm/6 9/16 in	panetela
Topper	D15.48mm/39 L 160mm/6 5/16 in	panetela
Delicioso	D13.89mm/35 L 159mm/6 1/4 in	panetela
Naturale	D14.68mm/37 L 155mm/6 1/16 in	panetela
Laguito No 2	D15.08mm/38 L 152mm/6 in	panetela
Carlota	D13.89mm/35 L 143mm/5 5/8 in	panetela
Palma	D13.10mm/33 L 170mm/6 3/4 in	slim panetela
Palmitas	D12.70mm/32 L 152mm/6 in	slim panetela
Panetela larga	D11.11mm/28 L 175mm/6 7/8 in	slim panetela
Culebras	D15.48mm/39 L 146mm/5 3/4 in	culebras
Universales	D15.08mm/38 L 134mm/5 1/4 in	short panetela
Preferido	D15.08mm/38 L 127mm/5 in	short panetela
Veguerito	D14.29mm/36 L 127mm/5 in	short panetela
Trabuco	D15.08mm/38 L 110mm/4 5/16 in	short panetela
Cadete	D14.29mm/36 L 115mm/4 9/16 in	short panetela
Infante	D14.68mm/37 L 98mm/3 7/8 in	short panetela
Sport	D13.89mm/35 L 117mm/4 9/16 in	short panetela
Epicure	D13.89mm/35 L 110mm/4 5/16 in	short panetela
Belvedere	D15.48mm/39 L 125mm/4 15/16 in	belvedere
Seoane	D14.30mm/36 L 125mm/4 15/16 in	belvedere
Conchita	D13.89mm/35 L 127mm/5 in	panetela
Placera	D13.49mm/34 L 125mm/4 15/16 in	small panetela
Demi tip	D11.51mm/29 L 126mm/5 in	small panetela
Panetela	D13.49mm/34 L 117mm/4 9/16 in	small panetela
Demi tasse	D12.70mm/32 L 100mm/3 15/16 in	small panetela
Petit	D12.30mm/31 L 108mm/4 1/4 in	small panetela
Entreacto	D11.90mm/30 L 100mm/3 15/16 in	small panetela
Carolina	D10.32mm/26 L 121mm/4 3/4 in	panetela/cigarillo
Laguito No 3	D10.32mm/26 L 115mm/4 1/2 in	cigarillo
Chico	D11.51mm/29 L 106mm/4 3/16 in	cigarillo

Further confusion is caused by the large-scale manufacture of machine-bunched and hand-finished cigars. During research for this book I discovered that no fewer than 132 Havanas are made in this way.

Of the 447 styles or models listed in this directory, 295 are hand-made, 156 machine-made and 132 machine-bunched & hand-finished. That means 447 styles come in a total of 583 different finishes.

Frequently I found that a particular style was hand-made, machine-made and machine-bunched & hand-finished.

STAR RATING

The author's subject ratings for cigars take into account

the following: appearance, construction, quality of wrapper and colour; smoking characteristics and texture of the smoke; flavour and aroma; overall impression including enjoyment of the cigar.

★★★★★   Outstanding. A classic.
★★★★   Excellent.
★★★   Good.
★★   Fair, ordinary.
★   Poor or faulty.

No Star: Not evaluated.

BELINDA

Four models — all machine-made and machine-bunched & hand-finished.
Quality: fair.

A lower priced range. Same name brand now made in Honduras.

BELVEDERES (belvedere — *belvedere* — machine-made — machine-bunched & hand-finished)
Diameter: 15.48mm/39 Length: 125mm/4 15/16 in

PETIT CORONAS (petit corona — *petit corona* — machine-made — machine-bunched & hand-finished)
Diameter: 16.67mm/42 Length: 129mm/5 1/16 in
PANETELAS (demi tasse — *sport* — machine-made — machine-bunched & hand-finished)
Diameter: 13.89mm/35 Length: 117mm/4 9/16 in

PRINCESS (demi tasse — *epicure* — machine-made — machine-bunched & hand-finished)
Diameter: 13.89mm/35 Length: 110mm/4 5/16 in

BOLIVAR

27 styles — 22 hand-made — five machine-made — five machine-bunched & hand-finished.
Quality: superior

Distinctive label features 19th century Venezuelan revolutionary hero Simon Bolivar, who led revolt against Spain. Bolivar brand, founded in 1901, taken over by Ramon and Rafael Cifuentes in early 1950s, when they promoted brand to present prominence.
　These cigars well-constructed, wonderfully rich, full-bodied, with consistent high quality in aroma and taste, definitely not for beginners.

The 22 hand-made models among the cheapest of hand-made Cuban cigars. Even machine-made ones represent good buy.

Connoisseurs attracted by characteristic dark wrappers, their ability to age well, their good draw and their even burn.

Smaller, machine-made shapes not as rich and robust as larger, hand-made Bolivars but good place to start initiation to this range of heavyweights.

CORONAS GIGANTES (churchill — *julieta 2* — hand-made)★★★★★
Diameter: 18.65mm/47 Length: 178mm/7 in
Comment: Excellent after heavy, rich or spicy meal. Aromatic. Age well. Top Churchill cigar. One of Bolivar's best. Recommended for experienced smokers able to cope with rich, full-flavoured, spicy, strong cigars.

SUPREMAS CHURCHILL (churchill — *julieta 2* — hand-made)
Diameter: 18.65mm/47 Length: 178mm/8 in

INMENSAS (*corona grande* — *dalias* — hand-made)★★★★
Diameter: 17.07mm/43 Length: 170mm/6 3/4 in
Comment: Powerful, spicy and earthy aromas. Dominating cigar not for timid. Definitely not for smoking in confined spaces.

ESPECIALES (gran or long panetela — *laguito No 1* — hand-made)
Diameter: 15.08mm/38 Length: 192/7 9/16 in

PALMAS (long panetela — *ninfas* — hand-made)★★★
Diameter: 13.10mm/33 Length: 178mm/7 in
Comment: Aggressive, but still full-flavoured. Not easiest of smokes. Small production.

PANETELA (small panetela — *conchita* — machine-made — machine-bunched & hand-finished)
Diameter: 13.89mm/35 Length: 127mm/5 in

GOLD MEDAL LONSDALE (lonsdale — *cervante* — handmade)★★★
Diameter: 16.67mm/42 Length: 165/6 1/2 in
Comment: Full spicy aroma with earthly tones. Lacks subtlety. Has selective following.

AMADO SELECCION C (grand corona — *franciscos* — hand-made)
Diameter: 17.46mm/44 Length: 143mm/5 5/8 in

AMADO SELECCION E (robusto — *robusto* — hand-made)
Diameter: 19.84mm/50 Length: 124mm/4 7/8 in

AMADO SELECCION G (half corona — *minuto* — hand-made)
Diameter: 16.67mm/42 Length: 110mm/4 3/8 in

BOLIVAR TUBOS No. 1 (corona — *corona* — hand-made
Diameter: 16.67mm/42 Length: 142mm/4 5/8 in

BOLIVAR TUBOS No. 2 (petit corona — *mareva* — hand-made)
Diameter: 16.67mm/42 Length: 129mm/5 1/16 in

BOLIVAR TUBOS No. 3 (small panetela — *placera* — hand-made)
Diameter: 13.49mm/34 Length: 125mm/4 15/16 in

BELICOSOS FINOS (figurado — *campana* — hand-made)★★★★★
Diameter: 20.64mm/52 Length: 140mm/5 1/2 in
Comment: Outstanding torpedo-shaped cigar. Characteristic spicy aroma not quite as prominent as others in Bolivar range.

BELEVEDERES (belvedere — *belvedere* — machine-made — machine-bunched & hand-finished)
Diameter: 15.48mm/39 Length: 125mm/4 15/16 in

BONITAS (petit corona — *londres* — hand-made)
Diameter: 15.87mm/40 Length: 126mm/5 in

CHAMPIONS (petit corona — *cremas* — machine-made — machine-bunched & hand-finished)
Diameter: 15.87mm/40 Length: 140mm/5 1/2 in

CORONAS (corona — *corona* — hand-made)★★★★★
Diameter: 16.67mm/42 Length: 142mm/5 9/16 in
Comment: Typical dark oily wrappers. Rich, well balanced. Ideal to follow meal.

LAS TRES CORONAS (corona — *tres corona* — hand-made)
Diameter: 15.87mm/40 Length: 142mm/5 9/16 in

CORONAS EXTRA (grand corona — *franciscos* — hand-made)★★★★
Diameter: 17.46mm/44 Length: 143mm/5 9/16 in
Comment: Thicker than most coronas and among most full-bodied. Has exotically spicy aromas. Well worth

ageing and properly maturing.

ROYAL CORONAS (robusto — *robusto* — hand-made)★★★★★
Diameter: 19.84mm/50 Length: 124mm/4 7/8 in
Comment: Good daytime cigar, suitable for break during work or after meal. Has dark wrappers, eminently suitable for ageing. Rich, well balanced, with subtle spicy aromas that do not linger. One of my favourite robusto size cigars.

CORONAS JUNIOR (half corona — *minuto* — hand-made)
Diameter: 16.67mm/42 Length: 110mm/4 5/16 in

PETIT CORONAS (petit corona — *mareva* — hand-made)★★★★
Diameter: 16.67mm/42 Length: 129mm/5 1/8 in
Comment: Robust petit corona with plenty of spicy aromas. Quick smoke for one liking full-bodied cigars.

PETIT CORONAS ESPECIALES (petit corona — *eminente* — machine-made — machine-bunched & hand-finished)
Diameter: 17.46mm/44 Length: 132mm/5 1/8 in

REGENTES (small panetela — *placera* — hand-made)
Diameter: 13.49mm/34 Length: 125mm/4 15/16 in

DEMI TASSE (cigarillo — *entreacto* — hand-made)
Diameter: 11.91mm/30 Length: 100mm/3 15/16 in

CHICOS (cigarillo — *chico* — machine-made — machine-bunched & hand-finished)
Diameter: 11.51mm/29 Length: 106mm/4 3/16 in

CANEY

Seven styles — seven machine-made; six machine-bunched & hand-finished — short filler
Quality: medium
Comment: Good buy considering low cost compared to hand-made cigars. Medium body. Ideal for beginners to Havanas.

SELECTOS (corona — *naçionale* — machine-made — machine-bunched & hand-finished)
Diameter: 15.87mm/40 Length: 140mm/5 1/2 in

VEGUEROS (demi tasse — *preferido* — machine-made — machine-bunched & hand-finished)
Diameter: 15.08mm/38 Length: 127mm/5 in

PREDILECTOS (petit corona — *standard* — machine-made — machine-bunched & hand-finished)
Diameter: 15.87mm/40 Length: 123mm/4 7/8 in

BOUQUETS FINOS (demi tasse — *veguerito* — machine-made — machine-bunched & hand-finished)
Diameter: 14.29mm/37 Length: 127mm/5 in

ESPECIALES (culebras — *culebras* — machine-made)
Diameter: 15.48mm/39 Length: 146mm/5 3/4 in

DELGADOS (demi tasse — *veguerito* — machine-made — machine-bunched & hand-finished)
Diameter: 14.29mm/37 Length: 127mm/5 in

CANAPE (cigarillo — *chico* — machine-made — machine-bunched & hand-finished)
Diameter: 11.51mm/29 Length: 106mm/4 3/16 in

CIFUENTES

Seven styles — six machine-made — six machine-bunched & hand-finished — one hand-made
Quality: medium

A range of mostly machine-made cigars. Huge quantity exported to Spain and former Eastern bloc. Named after pre-revolutionary Cuban cigar-making family. Ramon Cifuentes today in charge of production of range of cigars in Dominican Republic.

SUPER ESTUPENDOS (diamedes — *gran corona* — hand-made)
Diameter: 18.65mm/47 Length: 235mm/9 1/2

CRISTAL TUBO (glass tubes) (corona grande — *conserva* — machine-made — machine-bunched & hand-finished)
Diameter: 17.46mm/44 Length: 145mm/5 11/16 in

VEGUERITOS (demi tasse — *veguerito* — machine-made — machine-bunched & hand-finished)
Diameter: 14.29mm/37 Length: 127mm/5 in

EMBOQUILLADOS No 5 (small panetela — *demi-tip* — machine-made — machine-bunched & hand-finished)
Diameter: 11.51mm/29 Length: 126mm/5 in

CUBANITOS (cigarillo — *chico* — machine-made — machine-bunched & hand-finished)
Diameter: 11.51mm/29 Length: 106mm/4 3/16 in

HABANITOS (cigarillo — *chico* — machine-made — machine-bunched & hand-finished)
Diameter: 11.51mm/29 Length: 106mm/4 3/16 in

PETIT BOUQUETS (demi tasse — *infante* — machine-made — machine-bunched & hand-finished)
Diameter: 14.68mm/37 Length: 98mm/3 7/8 in

COHIBA

12 styles — 11 hand-made — one machine-made
Quality — finest available

Considered pride of Havanas. Named after what ancient Tairo Indians of Cuba called tobacco. Cohiba are some of the finest cigars available.

Created in 1968 for personal use of Cuban President, Fidel Castro, and for diplomatic gifts. In 1982 production increased to serve world cognoscenti. Unique bright, white and black band recognised symbol of success.

Majority of range made in El Laquito factory, former private home of the Prince of Pinar del Rio, on outskirts of Havana. Only women roll Cohiba cigars. Robusto and Esplendido sizes also produced by Partagas and H. Upmann factories in Old Havana, under strict control, using leaves blended at El Laguito. Factory also produces some Montecristo sizes. Boxes could follow manufacturing codes: "EL" (El Laguito), "EPG" (Francisco Perez German Factory, formerly Partagas) and "JM" (Jose Marti Factory, formerly H. Upmann).

To ensure Cohiba range is supreme in quality, only finest leaves chosen from best *vegas* (farms) in Vuelta Abajo region.

Only 10 *vegas* can supply leaf and total 700 acres out of about 98 000 usually planted for tobacco in Pinar del Rio district. Two famous vegas, Hoyo del Monterrey, and El Corojo consistently send leaf to El Laguito but on average, tobacco from only five *vegas* is supplied in any given year.

Fermentation is unique factor in Cohiba cigars. While tobacco from other cigars undergoes two thorough fermentations, leaves for Cohiba go through third fermentation at El Laguito. Some leaves aged for 18 months during processes. While this is costly it gives Cohiba cigars their finesse and refinement.

These three fermentation greatly reduce nicotine and tars.

Only best *torcedores* (cigar rollers) in Cuba employed at El Laguita. They are mostly women.

According to Francisco Padron, former president of Habanos SA, Cuba's export sales monopoly, in 1993 total Cohiba production was little more than two million cigars.

This small production, across 12 sizes, plus additional cost of third fermentation and of packaging (superior varnished box stamped with head of Cuban Indian) justifies high cost of Cohibas, most expensive of Havanas (up to 50 percent more than equivalent sizes). This price deliberately designed to maintain Cohiba's position at top of market.

ESPLENDIDO (churchill — *julieta 2* — hand-made)★★★★★
Diameter: 18.65mm/47 Length: 178mm/7 in
Comment: Probably best of all Churchill-size cigars. A really great Havana, rich in flavour, a retaining certain roundness throughout smoke. Should be focal point of smoker's concentration. Too good to be wasted while pursuing other activity.

LANCEROS (granllong panetela — *laguito No 1* — hand-made) (cellophaned)★★★
Diameter: 15.08mm/38 Length: 192mm/7 9/16 in
Comment: Top-quality, easy-burning, gran panetela. Cellophane should be removed as soon as possible to enhance maturing process. Excellent after-dinner cigar. Rich, consistent, fruity aroma. Well worth high price. Good alternative for those usually enjoying double corona size cigars.

CORONAS ESPECIALES (panetela — *laguito No 2* — hand-made)★★★★
Diameter: 15.08mm/38 Length: 152mm/6 in
Comment: Has curly head (flaged). Smooth, mellow, easy-burning. Small boxes of five. Individually wrapped in cellophane. This should be removed as soon as possible to enhance maturation. Elegant corona style cigar. Appreciated by beginner and aficionado. Finished with curly head.

ROBUSTOS (robusto — *robusto* — hand-made)★★★★★
Diameter: 19.84mm/50 Length: 124mm/4 7/8 in
Comment: Probably best of this size. Excellent after luncheon cigar for smoker capable of appreciating great deal of flavour. Good cigar to share in company of others, easy to smoke, almost too rich, doesn't leave lasting aroma. Woody, spicy opulent coffee and hon-

eyed flavours.

EXQUISITOS (belvedere — *seoane* — hand-made)
(cellophaned)★★★
Diameter: 14.30mm/36 Length: 125mm/4 15/16 in
Comment: Not as subtle as other Cohibas, burning
faster at fairly high temperatures. Aroma spicy, slightly
honeyed. Good after-lunch cigar. Remove cellophane
as soon as possible.

PANETELAS (small panetela — *laguito No 3* —
hand-made)★★★★
Diameter: 10.32mm/26 Length: 115mm/4 1/2 in
Comment: Small boxes of five. Individually cellophoned
wrapped. Remove wrapping as soon as possible to
enhance maturing process. Spicy, farmyard aromas.
Slightly aggressive smoke, but fairly quick, ideal to
accompany espresso coffee.

MINI   CIGARILLOS   (mini-cigarillo   —   machine-
made)★★★
Diameter: 8.73mm/20 Length: 83mm/3 1/4 in
Comment: Made in France with 100 percent Cuban
tobacco, under licence to Habanos SA. Launched
November 1994. Available in France, Spain and Belgium. Unofficial sales for first six months in France
estimated at about 1,5 to 2 million units. Full bodied.
Hint of rich coffee undertones. Slightly harsh finish.

COHIBA LINEA 1492 RANGE

Launched mid 1993 to celebrate 500th anniversary of
Columbus discovering Cuba and tobacco. Five cigars
in range called Siglo I to V. Siglo means "century" in
Spanish; each cigar represents one century since
Columbus's discovery. Siglo I to IV same size as old
Davidoff range; discontinued in Cuba in 1990.

Before launch, Cubatabaco (Cuba's state-owned
authority responsible for all cigar exports) planned to
make and sell one million cigars in this range (200 000
per cigar). According to former director general, Francisco Padron, only about 500 000 produced, due to
shortages of raw materials such as fertilisers, shade
cloth, oil, gasoline and diesel, as well as serious
hurricane damage in 1993.

SIGLO I (half corona — *perla* — hand-made)★★★★★
Diameter: 15.87mm/40 Length: 102mm/4 in
Comment: Rich chocolate, spicy aromas. Beautifully-

made short cigar. Wonderful quick smoke.

SIGLO II (petit corona — *mareva* — hand-made)★★★★★
Diameter: 16.67mm/42 Length: 129mm/5 1/16 in
Comment: Full-bodied with earthy, spicy aromas.

SIGLO III (lonsdale — *corona grande* — hand-made)★★★★★
Diameter: 16.67mm/42 Length: 155mm/6 1/8 in
Comment: Has finesse and style.

SIGLO IV (corona extra — *corona gorda* — hand-made)★★★★
Diameter: 18.26 mm/46 Length: 143mm/5 5/8 in
Comment: Rich, opulent cinnamon aromas. Ideal after rich, spicy meal.

SIGLO V (corona grande — *dalias* — hand-made)★★★★★
Diameter: 17.07mm/43 Length: 170mm/6 3/4 in
Comment: Full-bodied, well-balanced cigar ideal for connoisseur.

CUABA

4 styles — all hand-made
Quality: superior

New brand. First launched on UK market end of 1996. Smallest size 101.6mm/4 in long x 15.9mm/40. — Largest over 12.7mm/5 in with heavier girth. All are *perfecto* shapes, based on old style of Havanas popular in 19th Century and, all but disappeared during 1930's. Similar short cigars were popular in Britain.

Although world trend is for big cigars, which are scarce, due to shortage of large wrapper leaves, Habanos SA intends, through this brand, to popularise small cigars. Cuaba, like Caliba, is another old Taino indian word. It describes a particularly flammable bush, which was used to make flaming torches. It's still used in country areas for lighting fires.

DAVIDOFF

15 styles — all hand-made (not made in Cuba since 1992)
Quality: superior

Range now owned by Max Oettinger Company of Basel, Switzerland and made in Dominican Republic.

DIPLOMATICAS

Seven styles — all hand-made
Quality: good to superior

Created in 1966 as lower-priced range than
Montecristo for French Market. Difficult to obtain but
good value considering quality and construction. Sizes
and numbering accord to those of the Montecristo
range.

DIPLOMATICAS No 1 (lonsdale — *cervante* — hand-made)★★★★
Diameter: 16.67mm/42 Length: 165mm/6 1/2 in
Comment: Medium flavour and strength. Good burning
qualities.

DIPLOMATICAS No 2 (torpedo — *piramide* — hand-made)★★★
Diameter: 20.64mm/52 Length: 156mm/6 1/8 in
Comment: Full-bodied. Pronounced aroma. Not for
beginners.

DIPLOMATICAS No 3 (corona — *corona* — hand-made)★★★
Diameter: 16.67mm/42 Length: 142mm/5 9/16 in
Comment: Medium strength flavour and aroma.

DIPLOMATICAS No 4 (petit corona — *mareva* —
hand-made)★★★
Diameter: 16.67mm/42 Length: 129mm/5 in
Comment: Medium strength flavour and aroma.

DIPLOMATICAS No 5 (half corona — *perla* — hand-made)★★★★
Diameter: 15.87mm/40 Length: 102mm/4 in
Comment: Ideal quick smoke. Medium strength flavour
and aroma.

DIPLOMATICAS No 6 (gran panetela — *laguito No 1* —
hand-made)★★★
Diameter: 15.08mm/38 Length: 192mm/7 9/16 in
Comment: Same size as Montecristo Especial No 1.
Medium strength flavour and aroma. Tends to burn fast.

DIPLOMATICAS No 7 (panetela — *laguito No 2* —
hand-made)★★★
Diameter: 15.08mm/38 Length: 152mm/6 in
Comment: Same size as Montecristo Especial No 2.
Also has curly head. Medium strength flavour and
aroma, also tends to burn fast. Might be too hard a draw

for a beginner. Good value for money.

EL REY DEL MUNDO

19 models — 17 hand-made — 2 machine-made and one machine-bunched & hand-finished.
Quality: medium

Brand established in 1848. Means "King of the World". Subtle aroma. Large range of wrappers. Daytime range has even larger sizes suitable after heavy meal.
Made in same factory (Briones Monoto) as Romeo y Julieta. Boxes may carry code "BM".

Same name brand also made in Honduras. These very full bodied.

TAINOS (churchill — *julieta 2* — hand-made)★★★★
Diameter: 18.65mm/47 Length: 178mm/7 in
Comment: Could do with more body. Easy burning.

GRAN CORONA (corona extra — *corona gorda* — hand-made)★★★
Diameter: 18.26mm/46 Length: 143mm/5 5/8 in
Comment: Enjoyable light cigar but lacks character. Usually with oily, smooth wrapper. Daytime smoke.

CHOIX SUPREME (robusto royal — *hermoso No 4* — hand-made)★★★
Diameter: 19.05mm/48 Length: 127mm/5 in
Comment: Accessible, light, suitable for daytime.

FOX SELECTION No 47 (robusto royal — *hermoso No 4* — hand-made)
Diameter: 19.05mm/48 Length: 127mm/5 in

LONSDALE (lonsdale — *cervante* — hand-made)★★★★
Diameter: 16.67mm/42 Length: 165mm/6 1/2 in
Comment: Attractive aroma. Soft, gentle smoke.

CORONAS DE LUXE (corona — *corona* — hand-made)★★★
Diameter: 16.67mm/42 Length: 142mm/5 9/16 in
Comment: Needs more subtlety and complexity. Beginners' cigar.

GRANDES DE ESPANA (gran or long panetela — *delicado* — hand-made)★★★★
Diameter: 15.08mm/38 Length: 192mm/7 9/16 in
Comment: Pleasant, elegant daytime cigar. Attractive woody aroma.

PANETELAS LARGAS (slim panetela — *panetela*

larga — hand-made)★★★
Diameter: 11.11mm/28 Length: 175mm/6 7/8 in
Comment: Easy smoke. Discreet aroma. Bland taste.

ELEGANTES (slim panetela — *panetela larga* — hand-made)★★★
Diameter: 11.11mm/28 Length: 175mm/6 7/8 in
Comment: Light aroma, bland flavour.

ISABEL (panetela — *carlota* — hand-made)★★★
Diameter: 13.89mm/35 Length: 143mm/5 9/16 in
Comment: Light, pleasant daytime cigar for beginner.

TUBO No 1 (corona — *corona* — machine-made)★★★
Diameter: 16.67mm/42 Length: 142mm/5 9/16 in
Comment: Pleasant woody aroma.

TUBO No 2 (petit corona — *mareva* — hand-made)
Diameter: 16.67mm/42 Length: 129mm/5 1/16 in

TUBO No 3 (half corona — *franciscano* — hand-made)
Diameter: 15.87mm/40 Length: 116mm/4 9/16 in

PETIT CORONAS (petit corona — *mareva* — hand-made)
Diameter: 16.67mm/42 Length: 129mm/5 1/16 in

PETIT LONSDALE (petit corona — *mareva* — hand-made)
Diameter: 16.67mm/42 Length: 129mm/5 1/16 in

LUNCH CLUB (half corona — *franciscano* — hand-made)
Diameter: 15.87mm/40 Length: 116mm/4 9/16 in

VARIEDADES (demi tasse — *chico* — machine-made — machine-bunched & hand-finished)
Diameter: 11.51mm/29 Length: 106mm/4 3/16 in

SENORITAS (cigarillo — *laguito No 3* — hand-made)
Diameter: 10.32mm/26 Length: 115mm/4 1/2 in

DEMI TASSE (demi tasse — *entreacto* — hand-made)★★★
Diameter: 11.91mm/30 Length: 100mm/3 15/16 in
Comment: Burns easily. Ideal for quick smoke.

FONSECA

Five sizes — four hand-made — one machine-made and one machine-bunched & hand-finished
Quality: medium

Relatively unknown brand wrapped in manner not often seen. In white tissue paper. This accentuates characteristic lightness or softness. Brand accessible and ideal for beginners. Not expensive. Available in Switzerland and Spain, where it is the second most popular brand.

INVICTOS (figurado — *especiale* — hand-made)★★★★
Diameter: 17.86mm/45 Length: 134mm/5 1/4 in
Comment: Light cigar with character.

FONSECA No 1 (corona grande — *cazadore* — hand-made)★★★
Diameter: 17.46mm/44 Length: 162mm/6 3/8 in
Comment: Probably lightest of all Havana Lonsdales. Burns extremely well. Smooth. Good balance between strenght and flavour, touch of honey. Good introduction for the beginner to Lonsdale size.

COSACOS (corona — *cosaco* — hand-made)★★★
Diameter: 16.67mm/42 Length: 135mm/5 1/16 in
Comment: Could be lightest of all Havana coronas. Could do with subtlety.

DELICIAS (petit corona — *standard* — machine-made — machine-bunched & hand-finished)★★★
Diameter: 15.87mm/40 Length: 123mm/4 7/8 in
Comment: Slightly more full bodied than hand-made shapes. Even less subtle.

KDT CADETES (demi tasse — *cadete* — hand-made)
Diameter: 14.29mm/36 Length: 115mm/4 9/16 in

GISPERT

Three models — two hand-made — one machine-made and one machine-bunched & hand-finished

Old Havana brand which has dwindled to only three sizes. Until early 1994, hand-made. Now machine-made and hand-finished. Mild, good quality.

CORONAS (corona — *corona* — hand-made)★★★
Diameter: 16.67mm/42 Length: 142mm/5 9/16 in
Comment: Almost bland, lacking in body. Pleasant cigar for beginners.

PETIT CORONAS DE LUXE (petit corona — *mareva* — hand-made)★★★
Diameter: 16.67mm/42 Length: 129mm/5 1/16 in
Comment: Acceptable cigar between meals.

HABANERAS No 2 (petit corona — *standard* —

machine-made — machine-bunched & hand-finished)★★★
Diameter: 15.87mm/40 Length: 123mm/4 7/8 in
Comment: Little dull. Suitable for beginners.

H. UPMANN

42 styles — 28 hand-made — 18 machine-made — 18 machine-bunched & hand-finished

Quality: Superior for the hand-made and medium to below medium for machine-made.

Brand established in 1844 by German, Herman Upmann, who three years earlier, with brother, Alfonso, set up, in Havana, a branch of family bank.
  The Havanas Herman sent to his European clients as gifts in boxes stamped with the bank's emblem proved so popular he decided to invest in a cigar factory.
  Within a few years care of the H. Upmann brand on the British market was put in the hands of J. Frankau & Co where it remains to this day as part of the Hunters and Frankau Group.
  Obsessed with the quality of his cigars, Herman decided to put his signature on each box when labels were introduced during the 1860s, a tradition maintained until this day.
  The Upmann bank went into liquidation and was folllowed by the cigar company in 1922. J. Frankau & Co, under new owners, bought the factory and brand, creating a local Cuban company called J. Frankau S.A.
  In 1935 H. Upmann bought by company Menendez y Garcia for $250 000 (£100 000). Brand's production reorganised and almost immediately a new brand — Montecristo — added to the range of cigars produced at the H. Upmann factory.
  Company also responsible for introduction of cedar-lined aluminium tubes.
  Big difference in quality and flavour of hand-made and machine-made Upmanns. Hand-made are generally smooth, medium-flavoured, subtle. Sometimes fault in construction can cause over-heating with resultant bitter after-taste.
  Considerable number of machine-made and machine-bunched & hand-finished sizes sold in aluminium tubes. Only hand-made Havanas, including Upmanns, imported into Britain.
  Hand-made Upmanns with Cameroun wrappers and

South American fillers produced by Consolidated Cigar Corporation in Dominican Republic. (Detailed in Dominican Republic section.)

MONARCH (churchill — *julieta 2* — hand-made)★★★★★
Diameter: 18.65mm/47 Length: 178mm/7 in
Comment: Packed in both aluminium tubes and boxes of 25. Heavy robust cigar with lots of complexity. Good balance between strength and flavour. Have personal preference for box pressed Monarchs. A wonderful end to a wonderful meal.

SIR WINSTON (churchill — *julieta 2* — hand-made)★★★★
Diameter: 18.65mm/47 Length: 178mm/7 in
Comment: Powerful cigar for experienced smoker. Popular in Britain. Full flavour. Ideal for after a heavy spicy meal.

SUPER CORONA (corona grande — *corona gorda* — hand-made)★★★★
Diameter: 18.26mm/46 Length: 143mm/5 1/2 in
Comment: Wonderfully rich honey aromas and flavours. Full flavour. Appreciated by connoisseurs. Is slightly thicker than normal corona.

MAGNUM 46 (corona extra — *corona gorda* — hand-made)
Diameter: 18.26mm/46 Length: 143mm/5 1/2 in

CULEBRAS (culebras — *culebras* — hand-made)
Diameter: 15.48mm/39 Length: 146mm/5 3/4 in
Comment: Three cigars twisted into a rope-like shape.

ROYAL CORONA (corona grande — *conserva* — hand-made — machine-made — machine-bunched & hand-finished)
Diameter: 17.46mm/44 Length: 145mm/5 11/16 in

CORONAS MAJOR (petit corona — *mareva* — hand-made — machine-made — machine-bunched & hand-finished)
Diameter: 17.46mm/44 Length: 129mm/5 1/16 in

MEDIAS CORONA (petit corona — *mareva* — hand-made — machine-made — machine-bunched & hand-finished)
Diameter: 17.46mm/44 Length: 129mm/5 1/16 in

CRISTALES (corona — *cosaco* — hand-made)★★★★
Diameter: 16.67mm/42 Length: 135mm/5 5/16 in

Comment: Only Havana currently sold in glass jars. Soft. Absence of characteristic earthy flavour. Good value for money. Very small production. Constant quality. Ideal for a beginner or after light lunch.

EXCEPTIONALES ROTHSCHILD (petit corona — *perfecto* — machine-bunched & hand-finished)
Diameter: 17.46mm/44 Length: 127mm/5 in

CONNOISSEUR No 1 (robusto royal — *hermoso No 4* — hand-made)★★★★
Diameter: 19.05mm/48 Length: 137mm/5 7/16 in
Comment: Spicy, earthy. Good balance. After dinner cigar.

CORONA (corona — *corona* — hand-made)★★★★
Diameter: 16.67mm/42 Length: 142mm/5 9/16 in
Comment: Woody, discreet aroma. Smooth. Daytime smoke for experienced smoker. Suitable for beginners.

CINCO BOCAS (lonsdale — *cervante* — hand-made)
Diameter: 16.67mm/42 Length: 165mm/6 1/2 in

CRISTALES (corona — *cosaco* — hand-made)
Diameter: 16.67mm/42 Length: 135mm/5 5/16 in

LONSDALES (lonsdale — *cervante* — hand-made)★★★★★
Diameter: 16.67mm/42 Length: 165mm/6 1/2 in
Comment: Subtle, elegant, smooth. Well made. Small production.

NOELLAS (corona — *cosaco* — hand-made)
Diameter: 16.67mm/42 Length: 135mm/5 5/16 in

EXQUISITOS (petit corona — *mareva* — machine-made — machine-bunched & hand-finished)
Diameter: 16.67mm/42 Length: 129mm/5 1/8 in

KINGS (petit corona — *mareva* — machine-made — machine-bunched & hand-finished)
Diameter: 16.67mm/42 Length: 129mm/5 1/16 in

PETIT CORONA (petit corona — *mareva* — hand-made
Diameter: 16.67mm/42 Length: 129mm/5 1/8 in

REGALIA (petit corona — *mareva* — machine-made — machine-bunched & hand-finished)
Diameter: 16.67mm/42 Length: 129mm/5 1/16 in

AMATISTAS (corona — *superiore* — hand-made)
Diameter: 15.87mm/40 Length: 146mm/5 3/4 in

ESPECIALES (petit corona — *crema* — machine-made — machine-bunched & hand-finished)
Diameter: 15.87mm/40 Length: 140mm/5 1/2 in

MAJESTIC (corona — *crema* — machine-made — machine-bunched & hand-finished)
Diameter: 13.87mm/40 Length: 140mm/5 1/2 in

SELECCION SUPREMA 23 (long panetela — *ninfas* — hand-made)
Diameter: 13.10mm/33 Length: 178mm/7 in

EL PRADO (panetela — *delicioso* — machine-made — machine-bunched & hand-finished)
Diameter: 13.89mm/35 Length: 159mm/6 1/4 in

NATURALS (panetela — *naturale* — machine-made — machine-bunched & hand-finished)
Diameter: 14.68mm/37 Length: 155mm/6 1/16 in

SHORT CORONA (corona — *cosaco* — hand-made)
Diameter: 16.67mm/42 Length: 135mm/5 5/16 in

BELVEDERE (belvedere — *belvedere* — machine-made — machine-bunched & hand-finished)
Diameter: 15.48mm/39 Length: 125mm/4 15/16 in

SINGULARE (half corona — *coronita* — machine-made — machine-bunched & hand-finished)****
Diameter: 15.87mm/40 Length: 117mm/4 5/8 in
Comment: Smooth, full flavour. Elegant. Good daytime smoke.

PETIT PALATINOS (demi tasse — *cadete* — hand-made)
Diameter: 14.29mm/36 Length: 115mm/4 9/16 in

EPICURES (demi tasse — *epicure* — machine-made — machine-bunched & hand-finished)
Diameter: 13.89mm/35 Length: 110mm/4 5/16 in

GLORIAS (demi tasse — *epicure* — machine-made — machine-bunched & hand-finished)
Diameter: 13.89mm/35 Length: 110mm/4 5/16 in

PETIT UPMANN (demi tasse — *cadete* — hand-made — machine-made — machine-bunched & hand-finished)***
Diameter: 14.29mm/36 Length: 115mm/4 9/16 in
Comment: Surprisingly big smoke for small cigar. Tends to burn fast causing some harshness.

UPMANN No 1 (lonsdale — *cervante* — hand-made)

Diameter: 16.67mm/42 Length: 165mm/6 1/2 in

UPMANN No 2 (torpedo — *piramide* — hand-made)★★★★★
Diameter: 20.64mm/52 Length: 156mm/6 1/8 in
Comment: Powerful, but refined. For the true lover of a torpedo shape. Has punch no longer found in Montecristo No 2. Not for the beginner.

UPMANN No 3 (corona — *corona* — hand-made)
Diameter: 16.67mm/42 Length: 142mm/5 9/16 in

UPMANN No 4 (petit corona — *mareva* — hand-made)
Diameter: 16.67mm/42 Length: 129mm/5 1/8 in

UPMANN No 5 (half corona — *perla* — hand-made)
Diameter: 15.87mm/40 Length: 102mm/4 in

AROMATICOS (half corona — *coronita* — machine-made — machine-bunched & hand-finished)
Diameter: 15.87mm/40 Length: 116mm/4 5/8 in

CORONAS MINOR (half corona — *coronita* — hand-made — machine-made — machine-bunched & hand-finished)
Diameter: 15.87mm/40 Length: 117mm/4 5/8 in

CORONA JUNIORS (demi tasse — *cadette* — hand-made)
Diameter: 14.29mm/36 Length: 115mm/4 9/16 in

PRECIOSAS (cigarillo — *demi tasse* — machine-made — machine-bunched & hand-finished)
Diameter: 12.70mm/32 Length: 100mm/3 15/16 in

HOYO DE MONTERREY

29 models — 24 hand-made, seven machine-made, seven machine-bunched & hand-finished
Quality: superior

One of oldest brands of Havanas. Introduced in 1867 by José Gener who also founded La Escepcion brand.

In 1960s range of mainly small and medium sizes introduced by Le Hoyo. Today consist of seven models. More full bodied than Hoya de Monterrey range proper.

Hoyo de Monterrey range of hand-made cigars most attractive, Smooth, mild accessible for beginner or occasional smoker.

Larger sizes including double corona, Churchill and Epicure No 2, robusto size, much more full-bodied, spicier and, perhaps, due to consistent good construction have loyal and devoted following. Epicures, No 1 and No 2, come unbanded in cabinet selection bundles.

Has separate range called Le Hoyo.

Some wonderful cigars found in these two ranges and, although some believe they do not age particularly well, I have had considerable success in ageing Epicure No 2s.

Hoyo de Monterrey also hand-made in Honduras by Villazon, based in Honduras and the USA. Surprisingly these more full bodied than Cuban range.

PARTICULARES (diamedes — *gran corona* — hand-made)★★★
Diameter: 18.65mm/47 Length: 235mm/9 1/2 in
Comment: Could be more balanced and subtle. Ideal giant cigar for casual smoker or beginner.

DOUBLE CORONA (double corona — *prominente* — hand-made)★★★★
Diameter: 19.45mm/49 Length: 194mm/7 5/8 in
Comment: One of lightest and most mellow double coronas. Despite size, not recommended after rich meal.

CHURCHILL (churchill — *julieta 2* — hand-made)★★★★
Diameter: 18.65mm/47 Length: 178mm/7 in
Comment: Good churchill. Accessible and mild. Integrated flavours. Good balance between strength and flavour. Spicy, hint of chocolate aroma. Only small quantity offered each year but all consistently well made.

CONCORDE (churchill — *julieta 2* — hand-made)★★★
Diameter: 18.65mm/47 Length: 178mm/7 in
Comment: Do not expect same from this cigar as from its sister.

HUMIDOR No 1 (corona grande — *conserva* — machine-made — machine-bunched & hand-finished)★★★
Diameter: 17.46mm/44 Length: 145mm/5 11/16 in
Comment: Lacks subtlety.
SUPER SELECTION No 1 (lonsdale — *corona grande* — hand-made)
Diameter: 16.67mm/42 Length: 155mm/6 1/8 in

HOYO CORONA (corona — *corona* — hand-made)
Diameter: 16.67mm/42 Length: 142mm/5 9/16 in

OPERA (corona — *corona* — hand-made)
Diameter: 16.67mm/42 Length: 142mm/5 9/16 in

ROYAL CORONATION (corona — *conserva* — hand-made — machine-made — machine-bunched & hand-finished)
Diameter: 17.46mm/44 Length: 145mm/5 11/16 in
Comment: Originally made exclusively for Joseph Samuel and Son for UK market.

SOUVENIR DE LUXE (petit corona — *mareva* — machine-made — machine-bunched & hand-finished)
Diameter: 16.67mm/42 Length: 129mm/5 1/8 in

EPICURE No 2 (robusto — *robusto* — hand-made)*****
Diameter: 19.84mm/50 Length: 124mm/4 7/8 in
Comment: Spicy with floral undertone. Good balance between strength and flavour. Flavour develops. Popular for this size. Can be enjoyed by connoisseur and beginner alike. Although the experienced smoker would want to alternate this with other brands.

CORONATION (petit corona — *mareva* — hand-made — machine-made — machine-bunched & hand-finished)
Diameter: 16.67mm/42 Length: 129mm/5 1/8 in
Comment: Again originally made exclusively for Joseph Samuel and Son for UK market.

PETIT CORONATION (half corona — *coronita* — hand-made — machine-made — machine-bunched & hand-finished)
Diameter: 15.87mm/40 Length: 117mm/4 9/16 in
Comment: Made for Joseph Samuel and Son for UK market.

EPICURE No 1 (corona extra — *corona gorda* — hand-made)*****
Diameter: 18.26mm/46 Length: 143mm/5 5/8 in
Comment: One of most popular models of this size. Has loyal following. Wonderful kaleidoscope of flavours and aromas.

PALMAS EXTRA (corona — *crema* — machine-made — machine-bunched & hand-finished)
Diameter: 15.87mm/40 Length: 140mm/5 1/2 in

EXQUISITOS (petit corona — *petit cetros* — machine-made — machine-bunched & hand-finished)
Diameter: 14.87mm/40 Length: 129mm/5 1/16 in

SHORT HOYO CORONA (corona grande — *conserva* — hand-made)

Diameter: 17.46mm/44 Length: 145mm/5 11/16 in

ODEON (panetela — *laguito No 2* — hand-made)
Diameter: 15.08mm/38 Length: 152mm/5 15/16 in

LONGOS (long panetela — *ninfas* — hand-made)
Diameter: 13.10mm/33 Length: 178mm/7 in

VERSAILLE (slim panetela — *palma* — hand-made)
Diameter: 13.10mm/33 Length: 170mm/6 3/4 in

JEANNE D 'ARC (panetela — *carloto* — hand-made)
Diameter: 13.89mm/35 Length: 143mm/5 5/8 in

MAGARITAS (cigarillo — *carolina* — hand-made)
Diameter: 10.82mm/27 Length: 121mm/4 3/4 in

LE HOYO DU ROI (corona — *corona* — hand-made)★★★
Diameter: 16.67mm/42 Length: 142mm/5 9/16 in
Comment: Tough and not subtle. Burns evenly and slowly. Suitable after meal.

LE HOYO DU PRINCE (petit corona — *almuerzo* — hand-made)★★★
Diameter: 16.67mm/42 Length: 130mm/5 1/8 in
Comment: Small lively cigar for experienced smoker. Difficult burning. Tends to become slightly harsh towards end.

LE HOYO DU MAIRE (cigarillo — *entreacto* — hand-made)★★★
Diameter: 11.91mm/30 Length: 100mm/3 15/16 in
Comment: Bit harsh for small cigar. Tiresome if smoked regularly.

LE HOYO DES DIEUX (lonsdale — *corona grande* — hand-made)★★★★
Diameter: 16.67mm/42 Length: 155mm/6 1/8 in
Comment: Slow burning, well constructed. Best in Le Hoyo range. Smooth.

LE HOYO DU GOURMET (slim panetela — *palma* — hand-made)★★★
Diameter: 13.10mm/33 Length: 170mm/6 3/4 in
Comment: Elegant shape camouflages strength. Difficult burning. Smoke this one slowly.

LE HOYO DU DAUPHIN (panetela — *laguito No 2* — hand-made)★★★
Diameter: 15.08mm/38 Length: 152mm/6 in
Comment: Last made 1990. Felt did not fit into Hoyo de Monterrey style. Harsh.

LE HOYO DU DEPUTÉ (demi tasse — *trabuco* — hand-made)★★★
Diameter: 15.08mm/38 Length: 110mm/4 5/16 in
Comment: Too robust for beginner. Harsh. Difficult burning. Ideal quick cigar to accompany cup espresso coffee.

JOSE L. PIEDRA

Seven models, but in only two sizes — one hand-made, six machine-bunched & hand-finished.

Little known brand, rarely seen.

SUPERIORES (corona — *superiore* — hand-made)
Diameter: 15.87mm/40 Length: 146mm/5 3/4 in

BREVAS (petit corona — *perfecto* — machine-bunched & hand-finished)
Diameter: 17.46mm/44 Length: 127mm/5 in
CAZADORES (petit corona — *perfecto* — machine-bunched & hand-finished)
Diameter: 17.46mm/44 Length: 127mm/5 in

CONSERVAS (petit corona — *perfecto* — machine-bunched & hand-finished)
Diameter: 17.46mm/44 Length: 127mm/5 in

PETIT CETROS (petit corona — *perfecto* — machine-bunched & hand-finished)
Diameter: 17.46mm/44 Length: 127mm/5 in

NACIONALES (petit corona — *perfecto* — machine-bunched & hand-finished)
Diameter: 17.46mm/44 Length: 127mm/5 in

CREMAS (petit corona — *perfecto* — machine-bunched & hand-finished)
Diameter: 17.46mm/44 Length: 127mm/5 in

JUAN LOPEZ

(FLOR DE JUAN LOPEZ)
Six models — all hand-made
Quality: superior

Old Havana brand presently enjoying revival, particularly in Switzerland and Spain. Range light and accessible. Consistent good quality reason why often unavailable. Daytime cigar for experienced smoker comfortable introduction for beginner.

CORONA (corona — *corona* — hand-made)★★★★
Diameter: 16.67mm/42 Length: 142mm/5 5/8
Comment: Pleasant, slow-burning, daytime cigar with some character. Consistent and reliable. Ideal for beginner or occasional smoker.

SELECTION No 1 (corona extra — *corona gorda* — hand-made)★★★
Diameter: 18.26mm/46 Length: 143mm/5 5/8 in
Comment: Light cigar, can tire if smoked too often. A day-time smoke.

SELECTION No 2 (robusto — *robusto* — hand-made)★★★★
Diameter: 19.84mm/50 Length: 124mm/4 7/8 in
Comment: Worth trying even by experience smokers. This cigar synonymous with good living. Daytime smoke.

PANETELA SUPERBA, recently replaced by SLIMARANAS (small panetela — *placera* — hand-made)★★★★
Diameter: 13.49mm/34 Length: 125mm/4 15/16 in
Comment: Elegant. Smooth.

PETIT CORONAS (petit corona — *mareva* — hand-made)★★★★
Diameter: 16.67mm/42 Length: 129mm/5 1/8 in
Comment: Most enjoyable petit corona. Deserves to be better known. Ideal after light lunch.

PATRICIAS (half corona — *coronita* — hand-made)★★★★
Diameter: 15.87mm/40 Length: 117mm/4 5/8 in
Comment: Morning cigar for experienced smoker. Has discreet aroma and flavour. Not overpowering.

LA CORONA

Nine models — nine machine-made — eight machine-bunched & hand-finished
Quality: fair

An old Cuban brand. Founded in 1844. Has almost disappeared. Made only in small quantities. Cigar of same name formerly made in USA, now made in Dominican Republic.

CORONAS (petit corona — *crema* — machine-made — machine-bunched & hand-finished)
Diameter: 15.87mm/40 Length: 140mm/5 1/2 in

PERFECTOS (petit corona — *perfecto* — machine-made — machine-bunched & hand-finished)
Diameter: 17.46mm/44 Length: 127mm/5 in

PETIT CORONA (petit corona — *petit corona* — machine-made)
Diameter: 16.67mm/42 Length: 129mm/5 1/16 in

BELVEDERES (belvedere — *belvedere* — machine-made — machine-bunched & hand-finished)★★★
Diameter: 15.48mm/39 Length: 125mm/4 15/16 in
Comment: Quick burning causes harshness.

CORONITAS (cigarillo — *chico* — machine-made — machine-bunched & hand-finished)
Diameter: 11.51mm/29 Length: 106mm/4 3/16 in

PANETELAS (small panetela — *conchita* — machine-made — machine-bunched & hand-finished)
Diameter: 13.89mm/35 Length: 127mm/5 in

PETIT CETROS (petit corona — *petit cetros* — machine-made — machine-bunched & hand-finished)
Diameter: 15.87mm/40 Length: 129mm/5 1/16 in

PETIT (cigarillo — *petit* — machine-made — machine-bunched & hand-finished)
Diameter: 12.30mm/31 Length: 108mm/4 1/4 in

DEMI TASSE (cigarillo — *demi tasse* — machine-made — machine-bunched & hand-finished)
Diameter: 12.70mm/32 Length: 100mm/3 15/16 in

LA ESCEPCION

Six models — two hand-made, four machine-made, three machine-bunched & hand-finished
Quality: medium

Old brand registered by José Gener, who started Hoyo de Monterrey. Has declined in popularity. Robust, slow burning and richly flavoured for experienced smoker.

CAZADORES (corona grande — *cazadore* — hand-made)★★★★
Diameter: 17.46mm/44 Length: 162mm/6 3/8 in
Comment: Rich honeyed flavours. Ideal to follow meal.

PERFECTOS (petit corona — *perfecto* — machine-made — machine-bunched & hand-finished)
Diameter: 17.46mm/44 Length: 127mm/5 in

EXCEPTIONALES (petit corona — *standard* — ma-

chine-made — machine-bunched & hand-finished)★★★★
Diameter: 15.87mm/40 Length: 123mm/4 7/8 in
Comment: Full flavoured. Ideal to follow a meal.

BELVEDERES (belvedere — *belvedere* — machine-made — machine-bunched & hand-finished)
Diameter: 15.48mm/39 Length: 125mm/4 15/16 in

SUPERFINOS (half corona — *coronita* — machine-made)★★★
Diameter: 15.87mm/40 Length: 117mm/4 5/8 in
Comment: A quick daytime smoke. Ideal for casual smoker.

LONGOS (panatela — *ninfas* — hand-made)
Diameter: 13.10mm/33 Length: 178mm/7 in
Comment: Rewarding experience. Good example of this size. Daytime smoke or after lunch.

LA FLOR DE CANO

Nine models — five hand-made — four machine-made — four machine-bunched & hand-finished
Quality: superior

Small, well-made range. Not widely available. Not too robust or full bodied. Accessible. Good cigar for experienced smoker.

DIADEMAS (churchill — *julieta 2* — hand-made)★★★★★
Diameter: 18.65mm/47 Length: 178mm/7 in
Comment: Good smoke. Accessible churchill for beginner as unlikely to overpower. Experienced smokers will soon tire if smoked too frequently. Suitable for afternoon or after lunch.

GRAN CORONAS (corona extra — *corona gorda* — hand-made)★★★★
Diameter: 18.26mm/47 Length: 143mm/5 5/8 in
Comment: Burns evenly, easily. Subtle. Suitable for after lunch. Exotic flavour.

SELECTOS (corona — *cristale* — machine-made — machine-bunched & hand-finished)
Diameter: 16.27mm/41 Length: 150mm/5 7/8 in

SHORT CHURCHILL (robusto — *robusto* — hand-made)★★★★★

Diameter: 19.84mm/50 Length: 124mm/4 7/8 in
Comment: Wonderful aromas. Ideal for new devotee of Havanas. Natural successor to Hoyo de Monterrey Epicure No 2. Soft cigar with rich flavour right from first puff. Really good cigar. Worth looking for. Daytime or after lunch smoke.

CORONAS (petit corona — *mareva* — hand-made)★★★★
Diameter: 16.67mm/42 Length: 129mm/5 1/8 in
Comment: Particularly pleasant corona for both experienced smoker and beginner. Connoisseur may tire of it if smoked too often.

PREFERIDOS (demi tasse — *veguerito* — machine-made — machine-bunched & hand-finished)★★★
Diameter: 14.29mm/37 Length: 127mm/5 in
Comment: Soft smoke. Good quality and flavour for machine-made cigar. Ideal for beginner. Good value.

PETIT CORONA (petit corona — *standard*— machine-made — machine-bunched & hand-finished)★★★
Diameter: 15.87mm/40 Length: 123mm/4 7/8 in
Comment: Good flavourful small cigar. Burns evenly and fairly slowly for machine-made product. Mild. Packed in cedar tubes.

PREDILECTOS TUBULARES (petit corona — *standard* — machine-made — machine-bunched & hand-finished)★★★
Diameter: 15.87mm/40 Length: 123mm/4 7/8 in
Comment: Same as Petit Corona, but packed in aluminium tubes. Wrappers not as consistently uniform as for Petit Corona.

LA GLORIA CUBANA

Nine models — all hand-made
Quality: Good

Old Havana brand. Re-introduced about 20 years ago by Partagas factory to extend range of full bodied cigars by introducing smooth, easy smoking ones.
   Range comes in 8-9-8 varnished boxes recently marketed UK. Also available in Switzerland.
   La Gloria Cubana also hand-made in Miami, USA.

TAINOS (churchill — *julieta 2* — hand-made)★★★★★
Diameter: 18.65mm/47 Length: 178mm/7 in

Comment: Subtle. Smooth. Ideal after dinner smoke.

CETROS (lonsdale — *cervante* — hand-made)★★★★
Diameter: 16.67mm/42 Length: 165mm/6 1/2 in
Comment: Burns well. Lighter than other cigars from this brand. When first lit rather strung, after about 20 percent develops good balance between strength and flavour. Not for the beginner. Good after-lunch Havana.

SABROSOS (lonsdale — *corona grande* — hand-made)
Diameter: 16.67mm/42 Length: 155mm/6 1/8 in

TAPADOS (corona — *cosaco* — hand-made)★★★
Diameter: 16.67mm/42 Length: 135mm/5 5/16 in
Comment: Attractive day-time cigar.

MINUTOS (half corona — *franciscano* — hand-made)
Diameter: 15.87mm/40 Length: 116mm/4 9/16 in
MEDAILLE D'OR No 1 (long panetela — *delicado extra* — hand-made)★★★★
Diameter: 14.29mm/36 Length: 185mm/7 5/16 in
Comment: Cigar for experienced smokers at end of evening. Elegant in appearance. Burns more easily than other cigars in this format.

MEDAILLE D'OR No 2 (corona grande — *dalias* — hand-made)★★★
Diameter: 17.07mm/43 Length: 170mm/6 3/4 in
Comment: Produced in small quantities. Full bodied. Spicy aroma, slightly peppery flavour. Not easy to smoke as frequently goes out becoming harsh.

MEDAILLE D'OR No 3 (slim panetela — *panetela larga* — hand-made)★★★
Diameter: 11.11mm/28 Length: 175mm/6 7/8 in
Comment: Burns easily for panetela. Fairly strong flavour. Little harsh for beginner.

MEDAILLE D'OR No 4 (slim panetela — *palmitas* — hand-made)★★★★
Diameter: 12.70mm/32 Length: 152mm/6 7/8 in
Comment: Good daytime cigar for beginner. Soft, floral aroma and flavour.

MONTECRISTO

13 models — all hand-made
Quality: superior

Montecristo marque created in 1934 by Menendez and

Garcia families. In 1844, they registered H. Upmann brand. Menendez family moved to Canary Islands after Castro revolution.

When launched, H. Upmann's Montecristo was only available in five sizes and in limited quantities. In 1935 Menendez y Garcia approached importers, John Hunter Morris and Elkan Ltd (later to become Hunters and Frankau), to take the brand in the UK. This agreed on condition it be known only as "Montecristo", as H. Upmann name in hands of competitors, J. Frankau & Co.

Jack Benham, director of Hunters, designed a livery for brand, developing theme of Alexander Duma's legandary, "Count of Montecristo" with emblem of crossed epees surrounding fleur de lys. Finished design in red and gold on bright yellow background surrounded by chequered strip must have shocked traditionalists as it resembled no other Havana cigar packaging.

Brand received boost when Alfred Dunhill's shop in New York started to carry large stocks and, because of this, became one of few brands available to British during and shortly after World War II.

Until Cohiba range released for public sale in 1982 Montecristo was Cuba's premium brand. It is still biggest Havana seller. In the 1980s it was equal in size to all other Havana brands put together. Current annual sales, 30 to 35 million cigars.

Spain alone accounts for more than 50 percent of the Cuban cigar market in that country. Of this, the No 4, which is a petit corona, accounts for about 50 percent, followed by the No 2 (torpedo). In 1991 the French market consumed six million cigars or 50 percent of that market, while British smoked two million and Swiss one million.

However, quality tended to suffer. Range available in Spain can be of lower quality to those found in UK.

Larger sizes remain of consistently high quality.

There is dispute over ownership of this brand between Partagus with Consolidated Cigar Corporation and Spain's tobacco monopoly, Tabacalera on the one hand and Cuba's export organisation, Habanos on the other. Similar dispute occurred in France, involving French tobacco monopoly, SEITA. In 1994 verdict of in French courts went against Habanos (then Cubatobaco), but case now pending appeal. Rumoured that damages of more US $10 million are involved.

For a while, because of the court case, Montecristo, Partagas, Ramone Allones, La Gloria Cubana, Por Larranaga were taken off French market.

Montecristos made in H. Upmann factory, now re-named José Marti (JM) factory as well as in Cohiba factory, El Laquido (EL) and Partagas factory, now called Francisco Perez German (EPG). Codes at back of the boxes indicate factory of manufacture.

Alexander Dumas' novel "The count of Monte Cristo" was favourite with 19th century and early 20th century lector de tabaquerias (readers) who read aloud to workers while they made cigars thus, inspiring name for this brand.

Brand's success has lot to do with unique, tangy flavour. This partly created by storing ligero leaves for filler in special type of cedar wood boxes, and partly because of unique technique of arranging filler leaf. This process attributed to great cigar roller, José Manuel Gongalez, nicknamed "Masinguilla" — "the masseur" — for his enormous skill.

Montecristos are, generally, slightly milder than Cohibas with less *ligero* in their blend. They have characteristic dark, slightly oily wrappers with a district aromatic flavour.

MONTECRISTO "A" (diamedes — *gran corona* — hand-made)★★★★★
Diameter: 18.65mm/47 Length: 235mm/9 1/2 in
Comment: Probably greatest of all Havanas. Treat for connoisseur. Difficult to produce because it requires exceptionally long and perfect leaves. Not a cigar to rush. If stored in varnished box, ensure that the lid is open to allow the cigars to breathe easily and mature.

MONTECRISTO "B" (corona — *cosaco* — hand-made)★★★★
Diameter: 16.67mm/42 Length: 135mm/5 5/16 in
Comment: Subtle, elegant. Smooth, slow burning. Well made.

MONTECRISTO TUBOS (lonsdale — *coronas grande* — hand-made)★★★
Diameter: 16.67mm/42 Length: 155mm/6 1/8 in
Comment: Not as impressive as Montecristo No 1. Offered in aluminium tubes, but still big seller.

MONTECRISTO ESPECIAL No 1 (long panetela — *laguito No 1* — hand-made)★★★★★
Diameter: 15.08mm/38 Length: 192mm/7 9/16 in

Comment: Expensive cigar due, largely, to extreme dexterity required by *torcedor* (roller). Fast-burning. Wrappers tend to be light claro colour, not ideal for ageing.

MONTECRISTO ESPECIAL No 2 (panetela — *laguito No 2* — hand-made)★★★★
Diameter: 15.08mm/38 Length: 152mm/6 in
Comment: Milder than what one expects from Montecristo range, but can be hot smoke. Has curly head.

MONTECRISTO No 1 (lonsdale — *cervante* — hand-made)★★★
Diameter: 16.67mm/42 Length: 165mm/6 1/2 in
Comment: Can also be hot smoke. Not best lonsdale available. Pleasant, aromatic aroma. One of most popular Havana lonsdales in Europe.

MONTECRISTO No 2 (torpedo — *piramide* — hand-made)★★★★★
Diameter: 20.64mm/52 Length: 156mm/6 1/8 in
Comment: Great cigar. Very full bodied and easy to smoke, because of its large girth. Definitely not for beginner.

MONTECRISTO No 3 (corona — *corona* — hand-made)★★★
Diameter: 16.67mm/42 Length: 142mm/5 9/16 in
Comment: Is a consistent cigar of medium strength, taste and aroma. Spicy.

MONTECRISTO No 4 (petit corona — *mareva* — hand-made)★★★★★
Diameter: 16.67mm/42 Length: 129mm/5 1/16 in
Comment: Consistent cigar with medium strength and aroma. Spicy.

MONTECRISTO No 5 (half corona — *perla* — hand-made)★★★★
Diameter: 16.67mm/42 Length: 102mm/4 in
Comment: The shortest of the regular Montecristo series, but with a ring gauge of 42 is the same as that of the Montecristo No 1, No 3 and No 4. Has the same strength and aromas as those cigars, but is an ideal quick smoke in a restaurant after lunch or dinner when there is a shortage of time to enjoy a cigar.

MONTECRISTO No 6 (belvedere — *seone* — hand-made)
Diameter: 14.29mm/36 Length: 125mm/4 15/16 in

Comment: This size was discontinued in the early 1990s and has been, largely, replaced by the Montecristo Joyita.

MONTECRISTO No 7 (long panetela — *panetela larga* — hand-made)
Diameter: 11.11mm/28 Length: 175mm/6 7/8 in
Comment: This size was discontinued in the early 1990s.

MONTECRISTO JOYITAS (demi tasse — *laguito No 3* — hand-made)★★★
Diameter: 10.32mm/26 Length: 115mm/5 7/8 in
Comment: Has rich taste with subtle, fragrant aroma. Usually has slightly darker wrapper than rest of range.

MINI CIGARILLOS (mini — cigarillo — machine-made)★★★
Diameter: 8.73mm/20 Length: 83mm/3 1/4 in
Comment: Made in Spain by Tabacalera with 100 percent Cuban tobacco. Pleasant quick smoke.

PARTAGAS

58 models — 28 hand-made — 30 machine-made — 25 machine-bunched & hand-finished.
Quality: hand-made is superior — machine-made poor to medium.

Second oldest Cuban brand, established in 1845 by Dom Jaime Partagas, who founded La Flor de Tabacos Partagas in 1827. In September 1995, 150th anniversary dinner in Havana attended by industry's leading personalities and aficionadoa from all over the world.

At the same time as establishing his factory, Don Jaime ensured continuity of supply of best Cuban tobacco by cultivating farms in Vuelta and Semi Vuelta areas where rich red soils produce some of Cuba's finest leaves.

Factory in downtown Havana, renamed Francisco Perez German, uses FPG initials on bottom of boxes. Today some 400 operatives make more than 12 million cigars each year in 30 standard measurements so that those seeking Partagas can always find suitable size for the occasion — from impressive Lusitania to utilitarian Chico.

Quality, however, can vary, larger sizes being excellent but smaller ones tending to be badly made, which do not draw well and lack flavour.

Brand also made in Dominican Republic by General Cigar with Cameroon wrapper. Cuban offerings carry the word "Habana", while Dominican Republic ones show year 1845.

LUSITANIA (double corona — *prominente* — hand-made)★★★★★
Diameter: 19.45mm/49 Length: 194mm/7 5/8 in
Comment: Excellent cigar for true connoisseurs. Beautifully made. Strong yet tempered. Unusual flavour.

CHURCHILL DE LUXE (churchill — *julieta 2* — hand-made)★★★
Diameter: 18.65mm/47 Length: 178mm/7 in
Comment : Not best of churchills. Has strength but lacks subtlety and mellowness.

PRESIDENTE (corona grande — *tacos* — hand-made)★★★★
Diameter: 18.65mm/47 Length: 158mm/6 1/8 in
Comment: High quality. For the experienced smoker after spicy meal.

PARTAGAS DE PARTAGAS No 1 (corona grande — *dalia* — hand-made)★★★★
Diameter: 17.07mm/43 Length: 170mm/6 3/4 in
Comment: Certain cigar lovers attracted by coarse, matt finish. Robust cigar with little subtlety.

LONSDALE (lonsdale — *Cervante* — hand-made)★★★★★
Diameter: 16.67mm/42 Length: 165mm/6 1/2 in
Comment: One of best lonsdales available. Treat for experienced smokers, particularly after lunch. Rich unique aroma.

SELECCION PRIVADA No 1 (corona grande — *dalias* — hand-made)★★★★
Diameter: 17.07mm/43 Length: 170mm/6 3/4 in
Comment: This is an aggressive and powerful cigar. Because of its heavy smoke it is probably better to smoke outside.

8-9-8 CABINET SELECTION (varnished) (corona grande — *Dalias* — hand-made)★★★★
Diameter: 17.07mm/43 Length: 170mm/6 3/4
Comment: This cigar is named after the manner in which they are layered in their boxes — a row of 8, followed by a row of 9 and then one of 8. Requires time to age and mature. This is a rich, robust cigar, ideal after

a good meal.

PARTAGAS 8-9-8 (unvarnished) (lonsdale — *corona grande* — hand-made)★★★
Diameter: 16.67mm/42 Length: 155mm/6 1/8 in
Comment: This cigar is also named after the manner in which they are layered in their boxes — a row of 8, followed by a row of 9 and then one of 8. Attractive flavour and aroma.

CORONAS GRANDE (lonsdale — *corona grande* — hand-made)★★★
Diameter: 16.67mm/42 Length: 155mm/6 1/8 in
Comment: A light cigar with no harshness. Burns well. An obvious cigar for beginners.

CORONAS (corona — *corona* — hand-made)★★★★
Diameter: 16.67mm/42 Length: 142mm/5 9/16 in
Comment: Consistently good cigar. It is fairly strong for a corona. Has plenty of flavour and an attractive aroma. Burns slowly and evenly.

CORONAS "A" MEJORADO (corona — *corona* — hand-made)
Diameter: 16.67mm/42 Length: 142mm/5 9/16 in

PRIVADOS (corona — *corona* — machine-made)
Diameter: 16.67mm/42 Length: 142mm/5 9/16 in

PALMAS GRANDES (long panetela — *ninfas* — machine-made)
Diameter: 13.10mm/33 Length: 178mm/7 in

SERIE DU CONNAISSEUR No 1 (long panetela — *delicado* — hand-made)★★★★
Diameter: 14.00mm/36 Length: 192mm/7 9/16 in
Comment: An attractive looking cigar that burns well for this shape. This is a powerful cigar with spicy aroma. A good daytime cigar.

SERIE DU CONNAISSEUR No 2 (long panetela — *parejos* — hand-made)★★★★
Diameter: 15.08mm/38 Length: 166mm/6 9/16 in
Comment: Well-made cigar with spicy aroma. A good daytime cigar.

SERIE DU CONNAISSEUR No 3 (panetela — *carlota* — hand-made)★★★
Diameter: 13.89mm/35 Length: 143mm/5 5/8 in
Comment: Good beginner's cigar. Light with a good range of flavours and aromas.

SERIE DU CONNAISSEUR No 4 (robusto — *robusto* — hand-made)★★★★★
Diameter: 19.84mm/50 Length: 124mm/4 7/8 in
Comment: Rich, full flavour, spicy aroma. For connoisseur. One of better Partagas's. Ideal to follow a meal.

PETIT CORONAS (petit corona — *mareva* — hand-made)★★★★
Diameter: 16.67mm/42 Length: 129mm/5 1/16 in
Comment: Full bodied cigar with spicy aromas for the experienced smoker.

ASTORIAS (corona — *cosaco* — hand-made)
Diameter: 16.67mm/42 Length: 135mm/5 5/16 in

PETIT PRIVADOS (petit corona — *mareva* — hand-made)
Diameter: 16.67mm/42 Length: 129mm/5 1/16 in

PETIT CORONAS ESPECIALES (petit corona — *eminente* — machine-made — machine-bunched & hand-finished)
Diameter: 17.46mm/44 Length: 132mm/ 5 3/16 in

PETIT CORONAS TUBOS (petit corona — *eminente* — machine-made — machine-bunched & hand-finished)
Diameter: 17.46mm/44 Length: 132mm/5 3/16 in

CORONAS SENIOR (petit corona — *eminente* — machine-made — machine-bunched & hand-finished)
Diameter: 17.46mm/44 Length: 132mm/5 3/16 in

CORONAS JUNIOR (half corona — *coronita* — machine-made — machine-bunched & hand-finished)
Diameter: 15.87mm/40 Length: 117mm/4 5/8 in

PARTAGAS DE LUXE (petit corona — *crema* — machine-made — machine-bunched & hand-finished)
Diameter: 15.87mm/40 Length: 140mm/5 1/2 in

PETIT PARTAGAS (petit corona — *petit cetros* — machine-made — machine-bunched & hand-finished)
Diameter: 15.87mm/40 Length: 129mm/5 1/16 in

PARISANOS (petit corona — *petit cetros* — machine-made — machine-bunched & hand-finished)
Diameter: 15.87mm/40 Length: 129mm/5 1/16 in

LONDRES EXTRA (petit corona — *petit cetros* — machine-made — machine-bunched & hand-finished)
Diameter: 15.87mm/40 Length: 129mm/5 1/16 in

LONDRES FINOS (petit corona — *petit cetros* — machine-made — machine-bunched & hand-finished)
Diameter: 15.87mm/40 Length: 129mm/5 1/16 in

PERSONALES (petit corona — *petit cetros* — machine-made — machine-bunched & hand-finished)
Diameter: 15.87mm/40 Length: 129mm/5 1/16 in

ARISTOCRATS (petit corona — *petit cetros* — machine-made — machine-bunched & hand-finished)★★★★
Diameter: 15.87mm/40 Length: 129mm/5 1/16 in
Comment: Slightly honeyed aroma before lit. Good balance between strength and flavour.

PERFECTOS (petit corona — *perfecto* — machine-made)
Diameter: 17.46mm/44 Length: 127mm/5 in

EMINENTES (petit corona — *eminente* — machine-made — machine-bunched & hand-finished)
Diameter: 17.46mm/44 Length: 132mm/5 3/16 in

MILLE FLEURS (petit corona — *mareva* — machine-made — machine-bunched & hand-finished)
Diameter: 16.67mm/42 Length: 129mm/5 1/16 in

HALF CORONA (half corona — *minuto* — machine-made)
Diameter: 16.67mm/42 Length: 110mm/4 15/16 in

PARTAGAS PRIDE (half corona — *minuto* — hand-made)
Diameter: 16.67mm/42 Length: 110mm/4 15/16 in

SELECCION Fox No 7 (half corona — *minuto* — hand-made)
Diameter: 16.67mm/42 Length: 110mm/4 5/16 in

SHORTS (half corona — *minuto* — hand-made)★★★★
Diameter: 16.67mm/42 Length: 110mm/4 5/16 in
Comment: One of best small coronas, especially those sold in cabinets. Good morning cigar, perhaps with coffee. Ideal for beginner.

CAPITOL (petit corona — *petit cetros* — machine-made — machine-bunched & hand-finished)
Diameter: 15.87mm/40 Length: 129mm/5 1/16 in

ROYALES (petit corona — *londres* — hand-made)
Diameter: 15.87mm/40 Length: 126mm/5in

REGALIAS DE LA REINA BUENO (half corona —

coronita — machine-made — machine-bunched & hand-finished)
Diameter: 15.87mm/40 Length: 117mm/4 5/8 in

LONDRES EN CEDRO (petit corona — *petit cetros* — machine-made — machine-bunched & hand-finished)
Diameter: 15.87mm/40 Length: 129mm/5 1/16 in

TRES PETIT CORONAS (half corona — *franciscano* — hand-made)★★★★
Diameter: 15.87mm/40 Length: 116mm/4 9/16 in
Comment: Ideal for beginners. Originally made exclusively for Joseph Samuel and Son Ltd in U.K.

SUPER PARTAGAS (petit corona — *cremas* — machine-made — machine-bunched & hand-finished)
Diameter: 15.87mm/40 Length: 140mm/5 1/2 in

CULEBRAS (culebras — *culebras* — machine-made — machine-bunched & hand-finished)★★★
Diameter: 15.58mm/39 Length: 146mm/5 3/4 in
Comment: Partagas only remaining brand regularly producing a culebras. Good conservation piece. Very mild.

TOPPERS (panetela — *topper* — machine-made)
Diameter: 15.48mm/39 Length: 160mm/6 5/16 in

HABANEROS (short panetela — *belvedere* — machine-made — machine-bunched & hand-finished)
Diameter: 15.48mm/39 Length: 125mm/4 15/16 in

PANETELAS (small panetela — *conchita* — machine-made — machine-bunched & hand-finished)
Diameter: 13.89mm/35 Length: 127mm/5 in

PRINCESS (small panetela — *conchita* — machine-made — machine-bunched & hand-finished)
Diameter: 13.89mm/35 Length: 127mm/5 in

BELVEDERES (belvedere — *belvedere* — machine-made — machine-bunched & hand-finished)
Diameter: 15.48mm/39 Length: 125mm/4 15/16 in

CHARLOTTES (panetela — *carloto* — hand-made)
Diameter: 13.89mm/35 Length: 143mm/5 5/8 in

DEMI-TIP (small panetela — *demi-tip* — machine-made — machine-bunched & hand-finished)
Diameter: 11.51mm/29 Length: 126mm/5 in
Comment: Has a plastic mouth-piece on tip of cigar.

FILIPOS (small panetela — *placera* — hand-made)

Diameter: 13.49mm/34 Length: 125mm/4 15/16 in

SELECCION FOX No 11 (small panetela — *placeras* — hand-made)
Diameter: 13.49mm/34 Length: 125mm/4 15/16 in

CUBANOS (small panetela — *placera* — hand-made)
Diameter: 13.49mm/34 Length: 125mm/4 15/16 in

CHICOS (cigarillo — *chicos* — machine-made — machine-bunched & hand-finished)★
Diameter: 11.51mm/29 Length: 106mm/4 3/16 in
Comment: Rough wrapper. Difficult burning. Hard draw. Not best cigarillo.

RAMONITAS (small panetela/cigarillo — *carolina* — hand-made)
Diameter: 10.32mm/26 Length: 121mm/4 3/4 in

PETIT BOUQUET (demi tasse — *infante* — machine-made — machine-bunched & hand-finished)
Diameter: 14.68mm/37 Length: 98mm/3 7/8 in

POR LARRAÑAGA

15 models — seven hand-made — eight machine-made — six machine-bunched & hand-finished
Quality: superior

Oldest brand still in production. Established 1834. Production limited, not widely distributed. Early in 1994 hand-made models of Por Larrañaga withdrawn due to trademark dispute. Keen following among Havana connoisseurs. Medium to full bodied in flavour. First brand to introduce machines. Hand-made and machine-made versions exist in same size.

Rich, smooth, very aromatic. Have touch of sweetness in flavour. Fine cigars using same brand name made in Dominican Republic, using Connecticut shade wrappers. Bands of Cuban versions contain word "Habana", those from Dominican Republic show "La Romana".

LONSDALE (lonsdale — *cervante* — hand-made)★★★★★
Diameter: 16.67mm/42 Length: 165mm/6 1/2 in
Comment: Well-made cigar. Unique rich, sweetish flavour. Slow burning, aromatic.

LANCERO (corona — *corona* — hand-made)
Diameter: 16.67mm/42 Length: 142mm/5 9/16 in

CORONAS (petit corona — *corona* — hand-made)★★★★
Diameter: 16.67mm/42 Length: 142mm/5 5/8 in
Comment: Rich cigar. Not assertive. Ideal for after dinner. Not for beginners.

LOLOS EN CEDRO (petit corona — *petit corona* — machine-made)
Diameter: 16.67mm/42 Length: 129mm/5 1/16 in

PETIT CORONAS (petit corona — *mareva* — hand-made)
Diameter: 16.67mm/42 Length: 129mm/5 1/16 in

PETIT LANCEROS (petit corona — *mareva* — hand-made)
Diameter: 16.67mm/42 Length: 129mm/5 1/16 in

BELVEDERES (belvedere — *belvedere* — machine-made)
Diameter: 15.48mm/39 Length: 125mm/4 15/16 in

SUPER CEDROS (petit corona — *standard* — machine-made — machine-bunched & hand-finished)
Diameter: 15.87mm/40 Length: 123mm/4 7/8 in

SMALL CORONA (half corona — *franciscano* — hand-made)
Diameter: 15.87mm/42 Length: 116mm/4 9/16 in

LARGOS DE LARRAÑAGA (panetela — *delicioso* — machine-made — machine-bunched & hand-finished)
Diameter: 13.89mm/35 Length: 159mm/6 1/4 in

MONTECARLOS (panetela — *delicioso* — machine-made — machine-bunched & hand-finished)
Diameter: 13.89mm/35 Length: 159mm/6 1/4 in

PANETELA (demi tasse — *veguerito* — machine-made — machine-bunched & hand-finished)
Diameter: 14.29mm/37 Length: 127mm/5 in

CORONITA (small panetela — *panetela* — hand-made)
Diameter: 13.49mm/34 Length: 117mm/4 9/16 in

CURRITOS (cigarillo — *chico* — machine-made — machine-bunched & hand-finished)
Diameter: 11.51mm/29 Length: 106mm/4 3/16 in

JUANITOS (cigarillo — *chico* — machine-made — machine-bunched & hand-finished)
Diameter: 11.51mm/29 Length: 106mm/4 3/16 in

PUNCH

39 models — 32 hand-made — 10 machine-made —
seven machine-bunched & hand-finished
Quality: superior

One of oldest brands still being made. Established by
Manuel Lopez, but more associated with Fernando
Paticio, last private owner before Castro revolution.

Punch has noticeably tangy flavour with woody
aroma.

Because popular, moderately priced brand, is
avoided without justification by cigar snobs. Large
range mainly machine-made in Fernando Roig Factory,
formerly La Corona factory. Boxes may carry "FR"
mark.

Full-bodied Honduran Punch brand also made with
Havana seed wrappers. Names of Honduran cigars
are, with one or two exceptions, not similar to the
Cuban ones. Cuban products carry the word "Habana"
on band.

DIADEMAS EXTRA (diamedes — *gran corona* —
hand-made)★★★★
Diameter: 180mm/47 Length: 235mm/9 1/2 in
Comment: Surprisingly light Havana for cigar of its size.
Burns well. Pronounced woody flavour and aroma.
Ideal for rounding off good lunch or dinner.

DOUBLE CORONAS (double corona — *prominente* —
hand-made)★★★★★
Diameter: 190mm/49 Length: 194mm/7 5/8 in
Comment: Great double corona. Pleasantly control-
lable cigar for keen smoker. Good after lunch or dinner.
Lovers of double coronas may equally enjoy this cigar
during daytime.

CHURCHILL (churchill — *julieta 2* — hand-made)★★★
Diameter: 18.65mm/47 Length: 178mm/7 in
Comment: Easy smoking, mild cigar. Could do with
some more "punch" in flavour and aroma.

MONARCAS (churchill — *julieta 2* — hand-
made)★★★★★
Diameter: 18.65mm/47 Length: 178mm/7 in
Comment: Only hand-made Punch sold in tubes. Well-
made. Full bodied, subtle cigar with earth and honeyed
flavours to follow good meal. A smoke for the connoisseur.

PUNCH PUNCH (corona extra — *corona gorda* —

hand-made)★★★★★
Diameter: 18.26mm/46 Length: 143mm/5 5/8 in
Comment: One of great cigars in this size. Elegant, with a touch of honey. Good after meal cigar. Not for beginners.

BLACK PRINCE (corona extra — *corona gorda* — hand-made)★★★★
Diameter: 18.26mm/46 Length: 143mm/5 5/8 in
Comment: Freshness and lightness make this a lovely cigar. Could do with more flavour concentration. Would become boring if smoked too often. Accessibility makes it ideal for beginner or casual smoker.

SUPER SELECTION No 2 (corona extra — *corona gorda* — hand-made)★★★★★
Diameter: 18.26mm/46 Length: 143mm/5 5/8 in
Comment: Extremely good corona extra. Needs long time to reach maturity. Magnificent if well-kept. Daytime cigar for experienced smoker. Even burning, with rich flavours, quite hard on palate.

SELECCION DE LUXE No 1 (corona extra — *corona gorda* — hand-made)★★★★
Diameter: 18.26mm/46 Length: 143mm/5 5/8 in
Comment: Excellent cigar. Darker the wrapper, more pronounced are flavour and aroma.

ROYAL SELECTION No 11 (corona extra — *corona gorda* — hand-made)★★★★
Diameter: 18.26mm/46 Length: 143mm/5 5/8 in
Comment: Varies in quality from good to excellent. Has rich flavour and aroma. Recommended for experienced smoker as has "punch" in finish.

ROYAL SELECTION No 12 (petit corona — *mareva* — hand-made)
Diameter: 16.67mm/42 Length: 129mm/5 1/16 in
Comment: More subtle than other petit coronas from Punch.

NECTARES No 2 (corona extra — *corona gorda* — hand-made)
Diameter: 18.26mm/46 Length: 143mm/5 5/8 in

NECTARES No 4 (half corona — *Franciscano* — hand-made)
Diameter: 15.87mm/40 Length: 116mm/4 9/16 in

NECTARES No 5 (long panetela — *ninfas* — machine-made)
Diameter: 13.10mm/33 Length: 178mm/7 in

ROYAL CORONATIONS (corona grande — *conserva* — hand-made — machine-made — machine-bunched & hand-finished)
Diameter: 17.46mm/44 Length: 145mm/5 11/16 in

SUPER SELECTION No 1 (lonsdale — *corona grande* — hand-made)★★★★
Diameter: 16.67mm/42 Length: 155mm/6 1/8 in
Comment: Not for beginner. Assertive with rich pronounced flavour. Not subtle. Good cigar to follow lunch or dinner.

CORONAS (corona — *corona* — hand-made)★★★
Diameter: 16.67mm/42 Length: 142mm/5 9/16 in
Comment: Burns well but little aroma. Lacks finesse and charm, but still reasonable.

NACIONALES (corona — *cosaco* — hand-made)
Diameter: 16.67mm/42 Length: 135mm/5 5/16 in

CORONATIONS (petit corona — *mareva* — hand-made — machine-made — machine-bunched & hand-finished)
Diameter: 16.67mm/42 Length: 129mm/5 1/16 in

SELECCION DE LUXE No 2 (petit corona — *mareva* — hand-made)★★★★
Diameter: 16.67mm/42 Length: 129mm/5 1/16 in
Comment: Pleasant cigar. More subtle than many other petit coronas from Punch.

SOUVENIR DE LUXE (petit coronas — *mareva* — hand-made — machine-made — machine-bunched & hand-finished)
Diameter: 16.67mm/42 Length: 129mm/5 1/16 in

PETIT CORONAS DEL PUNCH (petit coronas — *mareva* — hand-made)★★★★
Diameter: 16.67mm/42 Length: 129mm/5 1/16 in
Comment: Well-made good quality cigar.

PETIT CORONAS DEL ONES (petit corona — *mareva* — hand-made)★★★
Diameter: 16.67mm/42 Length: 129mm/5 1/16 in
Comment: Presented in semi-plain boxes of 25. Each cigar wrapped in cellophane then individual cardboard boxes. Similar to Coronas in flavour.

PRESIDENTES (petit corona — *mareva* — hand-made)
Diameter: 16.67mm/42 Length: 129mm/5 1/16 in

CORONAS DEL PUNCH (petit corona — *mareva* — hand-made)
Diameter: 16.67mm/42 Length: 129mm/5 1/16 in

TRES PETIT CORONAS (petit coronas — *minuto* — hand-made)
Diameter: 16.67mm/42 Length: 110mm/4 5/16 in

GRAN CORONA (corona — *superiore* — hand-made)
Diameter: 15.87mm/40 Length: 146mm/5 3/4 in

PALMAS REALES (petit corona — *crema* — machine-made — machine-bunched & hand-finished)
Diameter: 15.87mm/40 Length: 140mm/5 1/2 in

BELVEDERE (petit corona — *belvedere* — machine-made — machine-bunched & hand-finished)
Diameter: 15.48mm/39 Length: 125mm/4 15/16 in
PETIT CORONATIONS (half corona — *coronita* — hand-made — machine-made — machine-bunched & hand-finished)
Diameter: 15.87mm/40 Length: 117mm/4 5/8 in

EXQUISTOS (petit corona — *petit cetros* — machine-made — machine-bunched & hand-finished)
Diameter: 15.87mm/40 Length: 129mm/5 1/16 in

PETIT PUNCH (half corona — *perla* — hand-made)
Diameter: 15.87mm/40 Length: 102mm/4 in
Comment: Good cigar for this size. Accessible daytime smoke. Ideal Havana for beginner.

PETIT PUNCH DE LUXE (half corona — *perla* — hand-made)★★★★
Diameter: 15.87mm/40 Length: 102mm/4 in
Comment: Well made cigar. Daytime smoke.

CORONETS (small panetela — *panetela* — hand-made)
Diameter: 13.49mm/34 Length: 117mm/4 9/16 in

PUNCHINELLO (small panetela — *panetela* — hand-made)
Diameter: 13.49mm/34 Length: 117mm/4 9/16 in

PANETELAS (small panatela — *panetela* — hand-made)
Diameter: 13.49mm/34 Length: 117mm/4 9/16 in

NINFAS (long panetela — *ninfas* — hand-made)★★★
Diameter: 13.10mm/33 Length: 178mm/7 in
Comment: Could do with little more flavour. Burns evenly, accessible, elegant, daytime panetela.

PANETELAS GRANDES (long panetela — *ninfas* — hand-made)★★★
Diameter: 13.10mm/33 Length: 178mm/7 in
Comment: Rapid burning cigar for experienced smokers. Robust. Strong enough to end heavy meal.

MARGARITAS (small panetela/cigarillo — *carolina* — machine-made)
Diameter: 10.32mm/26 Length: 121mm/4 3/4 in

CIGARILLOS (cigarillo — *chico* — machine-made)
Diameter: 11.51mm/29 Length: 106mm/4 3/16

QUAI D'ORSAY

Four models — all hand-made
Quality: Good.

This brand created in 1970s for the French tobacco monopoly, SEITA. Only distributed in France. Well made quality range with characteristic spicy flavour.

IMPERIALES (churchill — *julieta 2* — hand-made)
Diameter: 18.65mm/47 Length: 178mm/7 in
Comment: well constructed medium body. Easy smoking.

GRAN CORONA (lonsdale — *corona grande* — hand-made)★★★★
Diameter: 16.67mm/42 Length: 155mm/6 1/8 in
Comment: Easy burning cigar, earthy integrated well balanced flavours. Ideal after lunch or after dinner.

CORONAS (corona — *corona* — hand-made)★★★★
Diameter: 16.67mm/42 Length: 142mm/5 9/16 in
Comment: Produced to sell alongside Montecristo No 3 in France. Charming after dinner cigar for experienced smoker.

PANETELAS (long panetela — *ninfas* — hand-made)★★★
Diameter: 13.10mm/33 Length: 178mm/7 in
Comment: Well-made panetela. Not subtle. Good for daytime.

QUINTERO Y HERMANO

10 models — five hand-made — five machine-made — five machine-bunched & hand-finished
Quality: medium

Old brand. Robust range not for beginners. One of top

selling Havana in Germany.

CHURCHILL (lonsdale — *cervante* — hand-made)★★★
Diameter: 16.67mm/42 Length: 165mm/6 1/2 in
Comment: Has unique, raw, robust aroma. Definitely not for beginner.

CORONAS (corona — *corona* — hand-made)
Diameter: 16.67mm/42 Length: 142mm/5 9/16 in

CORONAS SELECTAS (corona — *corona* — hand-made)
Diameter: 16.67mm/42 Length: 142mm/5 9/16 in

BREVAS (petit corona — *nacionale* — hand-made)★★★★
Diameter: 15.87mm/40 Length: 140mm/5 1/2 in
Comment: One of Quinteros' best cigars. Not easily available. Robust right to follow rich meal by experienced smoker.

NACIONALES (corona — *nacionale* — machine-made — machine-bunched & hand-finished)★★★
Diameter: 15.87mm/40 Length: 140mm/5 1/2 in
Comment: Robust, lacks subtlety. One dimensional. Good value for money.

MEDIAS CORONAS (petit corona — *londres* — hand-made)
Diameter: 15.87mm/40 Length: 126mm/5 in

LONDRES (petit corona — *standard* — machine-made — machine-bunched & hand-finished)
Diameter: 15.87mm/40 Length: 123mm/4 7/8 in

LONDRES EXTRA (petit corona — *standard* — machine-made — machine-bunched & hand-finished)
Diameter: 15.87mm/40 Length: 123mm/4 7/8 in

PANETELAS (demi tasse — *veguerito* — machine-made — machine-bunched & hand-finished)
Diameter: 14.29mm/37 Length: 127mm/5 in

PURITOS (cigarillo — *chico* — machine-made — machine-bunched & hand-finished)
Diameter: 11.51mm/29 Length: 106mm/4 3/16 in

RAFAEL GONZALEZ

Nine models — all hand-made
Quality: superior

Old Cuban brand. Originally created for English market by George Samuel and Frank Warwick. Unique label states:

"These cigars have been manufactured from a secret blend of pure Vuelta Abajo tobaccos selected by the Marquez Rafael Gonzalez, Grandee of Spain. For more than 20 years this brand existed. In order that the connoisseur may fully appreciate the perfect fragrance they should be smoked either within one month of the date of shipment from Havana or should be carefully matured for about one year."

Brand created for Lord Lonsdale. Made in Biones Montoto factory, formerly Romeo y Julieta factory. Boxes may carry BM stamp.

High quality tobacco, with distinctive honey flavours. Rafael Gonzalez can be compared to early Montecristos. Band similar to Montecristo in colour/design.

Elegant, mild range.

LONSDALE (lonsdale — *cervante* — hand-made)*****
Diameter: 16.67mm/42 Length: 165mm/6 1/2 in
Comment: Good quality reminiscent of Montecristo No 1 of few decades ago. Slow-burning with rich, unaggressive aroma. Not easy to smoke, but still a great cigar. Difficult to find but worth effort.

CORONAS EXTRA (corona extra — *corona gorda* — hand-made)****
Diameter: 18.26mm/46 Length: 143mm/5 5/8 in
Comment: Probably best Rafael Gonzalez. Strong following among connoisseurs. Smoke after good lunch. But not too often so as not to tire of it.

PETIT LONSDALES (petit corona — *mareva* — hand-made)****
Diameter: 16.67mm/42 Length: 129mm/5 1/16 in
Comment: Aromatic, flavoursome. Assertive cigar that can take over smoker. After-lunch treat for experienced smokers wanting pronounced flavour.

PETIT CORONAS (petit corona — *mareva* — hand-made)****
Diameter: 16.67mm/42 Length: 129mm/5 1/16 in
Comment: Light cigar with pronounced woody-vegetal flavours more traditionally associated with Havana. Daytime cigar.

TRES PETIT LONSDALE (half corona — *franciscano* — hand-made)****
Diameter: 15.87mm/40 Length: 116mm/4 9/16 in
Comment: Easily accessible to beginner. Not too much

flavour. Reminiscent of what Havanas used to be. Good daytime cigar.

PANETELAS (small panetela — *panetela* — hand-made)★★★
Diameter: 13.49mm/34 Length: 117mm/4 9/16 in
Comment: Easy to smoke but lacks flavour. Acceptable daytime cigar.

SLENDERELLALS (slim panetela — *panetela larga* — hand-made)★★★★
Diameter: 11.11mm/28 Length: 175mm/6 7/8 in
Comment: One of few panetelas that burns well. Easily accessible to beginner. Ideal to follow morning coffee.

DEMI TASSE (cigarillo — *entreacto* — hand-made)★★★★
Diameter: 11.91mm/30 Length: 100mm/3 15/16 in
Comment: Do not be fooled by size. Is classy small cigar. Ideal quick daytime cigar.

CIGARRITOS (demi tasse — *laguito No 3* — hand-made)★★★★
Diameter: 10.32mm/26 Length: 115mm/4 1/2 in
Comment: Excellent cigarillo. One of best examples of size often considered unsatisfactory. Ideal for women, but stronger than expected. Treat as cigar, not cigarette. Don't inhale.

RAMON ALLONES

16 models — nine hand-made — seven machine-made — five machine-bunched & hand-finished
Quality: superior

Established in 1839 by Ramon Allones, immigrant from Galacia, Spain. First person to put colourful printed labels on boxes. Favourite among connoisseurs of full bodied cigars.

Usually, larger sizes with darker wrappers. Stronger than smaller variety. Generally, not for beginner. Nearly as full bodied as Bolivar. Both made in same factory as Partagas.

Boxes may be marked "FPG", abbreviation for Francisco Perez German, post-revolutionary name for Partagas.

First brand to use 8-9-8 configuration for packing boxes of 25s.

Good range of Ramon Allones are produced in Dominican Republic, with medium to dark Cameroon wrappers. Cuban product has "Habana" on label.

GIGANTES (double corona — *prominente* — hand-made)★★★★
Diameter: 19.45mm/49 Length: 194mm/7 5/8 in
Comment: Needs maturing. Good after dinner cigar for connoisseur. Full yet subtle and complex.

CHURCHILL 8-9-8 (corona grande — *dalias* — hand-made)★★★★
Diameter: 17.07mm/43 Length: 170mm/6 3/4 in
Comment: Full floral flavour. Good after lunch smoke.

CORONAS 8-9-8 (corona — *corona* — hand-made)★★★★
Diameter: 16.67mm/42 Length: 142mm/5 9/16 in
Comment: Good after-lunch cigar.

CORONAS (corona — *corona* — hand-made)★★★
Diameter: 16.67mm/42 Length: 142mm/5 9/16 in
Comment: Pleasant, easy cigar for daytime smoking. Rather one-dimensional.

PETIT CORONAS (petit corona — *mareva* — hand-made)★★★★
Diameter: 16.67mm/42 Length: 129mm/5 1/16 in
Comment: Ideal for experienced smoker needing cigar with pronounced flavour. Daytime smoke.

MILLE FLEURS (petit corona — *mareva* — machine-made — machine-bunched & hand-finished)
Diameter: 16.67mm/42 Length: 129mm/5 1/16 in

DELGADOS (panatela — *topper* — machine-made — machine-bunched & hand-finished)
Diameter: 15.48mm/39 Length: 160mm/6 5/16 in

TOPPERS (panatela — *topper* — machine-made — machine-bunched & hand-finished)
Diameter: 15.48mm/39 Length: 160mm/6 5/16 in

RAMONDOS (petit corona — *crema* — machine-made)
Diameter: 15.87mm/40 Length: 140mm/5 1/2 in

BELVEDERES (belvedere — *belvedere* — machine-made)
Diameter: 15.48mm/39 Length: 125mm/4 15/16 in

ALLONES SPECIALLY SELECTED (robusto — *robusto* — hand-made)★★★★★
Diameter: 19.84mm/50 Length: 124mm/4 7/8 in
Comment: Made originally for Hunters and Frankau, UK importers of Havanas. Earthly robusto for experienced smoker. Rich flavour, ideal end to lunch or

dinner.

PALMITAS (panatela — *palmitas* — hand-made)
Diameter: 12.70mm/32 Length: 152mm/6 in

PANETELAS (small panetela — *conchita* — machine-made — machine-bunched & hand-finished)
Diameter: 13.89mm/35 Length: 127mm/5 in

RAMONITAS (small panetela — *carolina* — hand-made)★★★
Diameter: 10.32mm/26 Length: 121mm/4 3/4 in
Comment: Rough, earthy flavour.

SMALL CLUB CORONAS (half corona — *minuto* — hand-made)
Diameter: 16.67mm/42 Length: 110mm/4 5/16 in

BITS OF HAVANA (cigarillo — *chico* — machine-made — machine-bunched & hand-finished)
Diameter: 11.51mm/29 Length: 106mm/4 3/16 in

ROMEO Y JULIETA

46 models — 27 hand-made — 20 machine-made — 12 machine-bunched & hand finished
Quality: superior

Probably best known Havana brand. Established 1875. Huge range many shapes and sizes with many hand-made and machine-made models. Because of huge range not all sizes of equal quality. However some regarded as finest available.

In 1903 "Pepin" Rodriguez Fernandez, manager of Cabanas factory in Havana bought out the business and promoted Romeo y Julieta into one of the world's leading cigar boards.

Factory now called Briones Monoto and boxes can carry "BM" code.

Pepin specialised in providing personalised cigar bands to heads of state and other important people, producing many thousands of different bands.

Romeo y Julieta was creator of churchill size and appellation, in honour of Sir Winston Churchill. This undoubtedly contributed to its huge success in Great Britain.

Three churchill sizes and De Luxe series have distinctive gold bands. Others have red bands.

Range made for experienced aficionados who like rich, complex cigars.

Some of best cigars of their size found in this range.

In Britain all Romeo y Julietas in tubes are hand-made.

Cigars called Romeo y Julieta are made both in Dominican Republic and Honduras.

FABULOSOS (diamedes — *gran corona* — hand-made)★★★★★
Diameter: 18.65mm/47 Length: 235mm/9 1/2 in
Comment: Same size as Montecristo "A". Superb cigar. Burns well. Subtle although powerful. Ideal for connoisseur to enjoy after dinner.

CHURCHILL (churchill — *julieta 2* — hand-made)★★★★
Diameter: 18.65mm/47 Length: 178mm/7 in
Comment: Quality can vary because of large production. Good cigar. Enjoys enthusiastic following among experienced smokers.
Wonderful ending to good meal.

PRINCE OF WALES (churchill — *julieta 2* — hand-made)★★★★
Diameter: 18.65mm/47 Length: 178mm/7 in
Comment: Lightest of three Romeo y Julieta churchills. Has subtle woody aroma. Ideal to follow heavy meal.

CLEMENCEAUS (churchill — *julieta 2* — hand-made)★★★★★
Diameter: 18.65mm/47 Length: 178mm/7 in
Comment: Produced in small quantities with resultant consistent quality. Soft and accessible. Complex range of aromas. Rich and robust. Worth experiencing after good meal.

CEDROS DE LUXE No 1 (lonsdale — *cervante* — hand-made)★★★
Diameter: 16.67mm/42 Length: 165mm/6 1/2 in
Comment: Pleasant cigar. Could do with more aroma.

CEDROS DE LUXE No 2 (corona — *corona* — hand-made)★★★★
Diameter: 16.67mm/42 Length: 142mm/5 9/16
Comment: Probably lightest corona available. Ideal for beginner. Excellent corona.

CEDROS DE LUXE No 3 (petit corona — *mareva* — hand-made)★★★★
Diameter: 16.67mm/42 Length: 129mm/5 1/16 in
Comment: Mild, easy-to-smoke. Accessible.

BELICOSOS (figurado — *campana* — hand-made)★★★★★

Diameter: 20.64mm/52 Length: 140mm/5 1/2 in
Usually has dark oily wrappers. Ideal for ageing. Rich smoke after a heavy meal. Favourite of many connoisseurs.

CAZADORES (corona grande — *cazadore* — hand-made)★★★★★
Diameter: 17.46mm/44 Length: 162mm/6 3/8 in
Comment: Pronounced aroma. Probably best to smoke outdoors. Most powerful in Romeo y Julieta range. Suitable for experienced smoker who can appreciate strength. One of lowest-priced cigars in range.

CELESTIALES FINOS (corona extra — *britanica* — hand-made)★★★★
Diameter: 18.26mm/46 Length: 137mm/5 3/8
Comment: Elegant, burning extremely well. Pleasant aroma. Ideal to follow good meal.

ROMEO No 1 (petit corona — *crema* — machine-made — machine-bunched & hand-finished)
Diameter: 15.87mm/40 Length: 140mm/5 1/2 in

ROMEO No 1 DE LUXE (corona — *corona* — hand-made)
Diameter: 16.67mm/42 Length: 142mm/5 9/16 in

ROMEO No 2 (petit corona — *mareva* — machine-made — machine-bunched & hand-finished)
Diameter: 16.67mm/42 Length: 129mm/5 1/16 in
ROMEO No 2 DE LUXE (petit corona — *mareva* — hand-made)★★★
Diameter: 16.67mm/42 Length: 129mm/5 1/16 in
Comment: Light cigar compared to rest of Romeo y Julieta range. Mostly sold in aluminium tubes.

ROMEO No 3 (half corona — *coronita* — machine-made — machine-bunched & hand-finished)
Diameter: 15.87mm/40 Length: 117mm/4 5/8 in

ROMEO No 3 DE LUXE (half corona — *franciscano* — hand-made)
Diameter: 15.87mm/40 Length: 116mm/4 9/16 in

ROMEO No 4 DE LUXE (small panetela — *panetela* — hand-made)
Diameter: 13.49mm/34 Length: 117mm/4 9/16 in

CORONITAS (half corona — *petit cetros* — machine-made — machine-bunched & hand finished)★★★★
Diameter: 15.87mm/40 Length: 129mm/5 1/16 in.

Comment: Medium bodied. A surprisingly good cigar for its size. Extremely good value.

PERFECTOS (perfecto/figurado — *perfecto* — machine-made — machine-bunched & hand-finished)
Diameter: 17.46mm/44 Length: 127mm/5 in

PLATEADOS DE ROMEO (petit corona — *petit cetros* — hand-made — machine-made — machine-bunched & hand-finished)
Diameter: 15.87mm/40 Length: 129mm/5 1/16 in

PETIT CORONAS (petit corona — *mareva* — hand-made)
Diameter: 16.67mm/42 Length: 129mm/5 1/16 in

REGALIAS DE LA HABANA (belvedere — *belvedere* — machine-made — machine-bunched & hand-finished)
Diameter: 15.48mm/39 Length: 125mm/4 15/16 in

BELVEDERES (belvedere — *belvedere* — machine-made — machine-bunched & hand-finished)★★
Diameter: 15.48mm/39 Length: 125mm/4 15/16 in
Comment: Difficult burning. A bit harsh.

FAVORITAS (belvedere — *belvedere* — machine-made)
Diameter: 15.48mm/39 Length: 125mm/4 15/16 in

REGALIAS DE LONDRES (half corona — *coronita* — machine-made — machine-bunched & hand-finished)
Diameter: 15.87mm/40 Length: 117mm/4 5/8 in

SHAKESPEARES (slim panetela — *panetela larga* — hand-made)
Diameter: 11.11mm/28 Length: 175mm/6 7/8 in

TRES PETIT CORONAS (half corona — *franciscano* — hand-made)
Diameter: 15.87mm/40 Length: 116mm/4 9/16 in

SPORT LARGOS (demi tasse — *sport* — machine-made — machine-bunched & hand-finished)
Diameter: 13.89mm/35 Length: 117mm/4 9/16 in

MONTAGUES (panetela — *topper* — machine-made — machine-bunched & hand-finished)
Diameter: 15.48mm/39 Length: 160mm/6 5/16 in

CORONAS GRANDES (lonsdale — *corona grande* — hand-made)
Diameter: 16.67mm/42 Length: 155mm/6 1/8 in

EXHIBICION No 3 (corona extra — *corona gorda* — hand-made)****
Diameter: 18.26mm/46 Length: 143mm/5 5/8 in
Comment: Earthy, and spicy aroma. Powerful but lacks subtlety. Ideal cigar for experienced smoker appreciating a powerful, earthy Havana.

EXHIBICION No 4 (robusto royal — *hermoso 4* — hand-made)*****
Diameter: 19.05mm/48 Length: 127mm/5 in
Comment: Well made elegant cigar. Has unusual tropical fruit aroma. Rich and subtle. Difficult to obtain but worth effort. Also available in Cabinet boxes.

CULEBRAS (culebras — *culebras* — hand-made)
Diameter: 15.48mm/39 Length: 146mm/5 3/4 in

CORONAS (corona — *corona* — hand-made)
Diameter: 16.67mm/42 Length: 142mm/5 9/16 in

NACIONALES (corona — *cosaco* — hand-made)
Diameter: 16.67mm/42 Length: 135mm/5 5/16 in

CLUB KING (petit corona — *mareva* — machine-made)
Diameter: 16.67mm/42 Length: 129mm/5 1/16 in

CORONITAS (petit corona — *petit cetros* — machine-made)
Diameter: 15.87mm/40 Length: 129mm/5 1/16 in
CORONITAS EN CEDRO (petit corona — *petit cetros* — machine-made — machine-bunched & hand-finished)
Diameter: 15.87mm/40 Length: 129mm/5 1/16 in

EXCEPCIONALES (petit corona — *mareva* — machine-made — machine-bunched & hand-finished)
Diameter: 16.67mm/42 Length: 129mm/5 1/16 in

MILLE FLEURS (petit corona — *mareva* — machine-made)
Diameter: 16.67mm/42 Length: 129mm/5 1/16 in

PALMAS REALES (long panetela — *ninfas* — machine-made)
Diameter: 13.10mm/33 Length: 178mm/7 in

EXQUISTOS (petit corona — *petit cetros* — machine-made)
Diameter: 15.87mm/40 Length: 129mm/5 1/16 in

JULIETAS (half corona — *franciscano* — hand-made)
Diameter: 15.87mm/40 Length: 116mm/4 9/16 in

CLARINES (half corona — *coronita* — machine-made)
Diameter: 15.87mm/40 Length: 117mm/4 5/8 in

PANETELAS (demi tasse — *sport* — machine-made)
Diameter: 13.89mm/35 Length: 117mm/4 9/16 in

PETIT PRINCESS (half corona — *perla* — hand-made)
Diameter: 16.67mm/42 Length: 102mm/4 in

PETIT JULIETAS (cigarillo — *entreacto* — hand-made)
Diameter: 11.91mm/30 Length: 100mm/3 15/16 in
Comment: Full flavoured. Probably best made cigar of
this size.

SAINT LUIS REY

Seven models — all hand-made
Quality: superior

Created more than 50 years ago for British market.
Comes in white box with gold edging. Has a red label.
Bands of red and gold. Should not be confused with
San Luis Rey, made in Cuba for the German market
with green and gold label and the same emblem.

Generally, this small range full bodied and of excellent quality. It is rated among best Havanas. Wrappers
usually dark, smooth and oily with refined flavour and
aroma. Made in Romeo y Julieta factory and usually
have "BM" stamped under box.

Difficult to find, but worth looking for.

Frank Sinatra and actor James Coburn are among
devotees of this cigar which aimed at connoisseurs.

DOUBLE CORONA (double corona — *prominente* —
hand-made)★★★★★
Diameter: 19.45mm/49 Length: 194mm/7 5/8 in
Comment: Full flavour, ideal after good meal.

CHURCHILL (churchill — *julieta 2* — hand-
made)★★★★★
Diameter: 18.65mm/47 Length: 178mm/7 in
Comment: Medium bodied pleasant aroma of flavours.
Ideal cigar to follow good meal. A wonderful smoke if
properly humidified.

LONSDALE (lonsdale — *cervante* — hand-made)★★★★
Diameter: 16.67mm/42 Length: 165mm/6 1/2 in
Comment: Not as rich as other lonsdales. Still has
plenty of flavour. Ideal ending to good dinner. Machine-
made version quite different.

SERIE A (corona extra — *corona gorda* — hand-made)★★★★
Diameter: 18.26mm/46 Length: 143mm/5 5/8 in
Comment: Subtle, easy burning, enjoyable cigar. Suitable after lunch or a daytime cigar. Machine-made version different.

REGIOS (robusto royal — *hermoso 4* — hand-made)★★★★
Diameter: 19.05mm/48 Length: 127mm/5 in
Comment: Excellent robusto. Limited production ensures reliable quality. Enjoyable cigar outside of mealtimes. Machine-made version varies.

CORONAS (corona — *corona* — hand-made)★★★★★
Diameter: 16.67mm/42 Length: 142mm/5 9/16 in
Comment: Worth smoking. Exellent example for its size.
PETIT CORONA (petit corona — *mareva* — hand-made)★★★★★
Diameter: 16.67mm/42 Length: 129mm/5 1/16 in
Comment: One of best cigars of its size. Despite smallness, rich in flavour. Could complete good meal.

SANCHA PANZA

Nine models — all hand-made
Quality: superior

Good range for beginners and as daytime cigar for experienced smokers. Brand only appears in Britain occasionally, but is popular in Spain and, to lesser extent, Switzerland.

Only some of sizes are well constructed. Cigars with same brand name to be made in Honduras during 1995.

SANCHOS (diamedes — *gran corona* — hand-made)★★★★★
Diameter: 18.65mm/47 Length: 235mm/9 1/2 in
Comment: Slow burning cigar. Lovely woody aroma. Lot of presence but smooth. Requires nearly two hours to smoke.

CORONAS CIGANTES (churchill — *julieta 2* — hand-made)★★★★★
Diameter: 18.67mm/47 Length: 178mm/7 in
Comment: Fantastic finesse, softness and woody aroma. Very subtle. Great pleasure to experience after lunch or dinner.

MOLINOS (lonsdale — *cervante* — hand-made)★★★★★
Diameter: 16.67mm/42 Length: 165mm/6 1/2 in
Comment: Refined. For both experienced or occasional smoker. Sweet finish, and slightly caramelised aroma. Great cigar providing enchanting experience.

DORADOS (lonsdale — *cervante* — hand-made)★★★★
Diameter: 16.67mm/42 Length: 165mm/6 1/2 in
Comment: Half wrapped in gold foil. Similar to Molinos with sweet finish, and slightly caramelised aroma. Great cigar.

BELICOSOS (figurado — *campana* — hand-made)★★★★
Diameter: 20.64mm/52 Length: 140mm/5 1/2 in
Comment: Soft, fragrant torpedo cigar. Not for beginner or occasional smoker. Excellent to end light lunch.

CORONAS (corona — *corona* — hand-made)
Diameter: 16.67mm/42 Length: 142mm/5 9/16 in

TRONQUITOS (corona — *corona* — hand-made)
Diameter: 16.67mm/42 Length: 142mm/5 9/16 in

NON PLUS (petit corona — *mareva* — hand-made)
Diameter: 16.67mm/42 Length: 129mm/5 1/16 in

BACHILLERS (half corona — *franciscano* — hand-made)★★★
Diameter: 15.87mm/40 Length: 116mm/4 9/16 in
Comment: Light cigar. Ideal for beginners.

SIBONEY

One model — hand-made
Quality: superior

This brand consisting of one shape, made exclusively for Austria Tabak, which has monopoly on all tobacco products in Austria. Austria Tabak one of oldest cigar factories in Europe.

ESPECIALE (panetela — *laquito No 2* — hand-made)
Diameter: 15.08mm/38 Length: 152mm/6 in
Comment: Finished with curly head.

STRATOS DE LUXE

Five models — all machine-made — and all machine-bunched & hand-finished as well.
Quality: fair

All models available entirely machine-made and machine-bunched and hand-finished. Represents value, particularly for beginner. Good range of sizes at affordable prices. Packed in cellophaned cartons. Produced mainly for Spanish market, which is biggest single consumer of Havanas outside of Cuba.

BREVAS (corona — *crema* — machine-made — machine-bunched & hand-finished)
Diameter: 15.87mm/40 Length: 140mm/5 1/2

CREMAS (corona — *crema* — machine-made — machine-bunched & hand-finished)
Diameter: 15.87mm/40 Length: 140mm/5 1/2 in

SELECTOS (corona — *crema* — machine-made — machine-bunched & hand-finished)
Diameter: 15.87mm/40 Length: 140mm/5 1/2 in

DELIRIOS (petit corona — *standard* — machine-made — machine-bunched & hand-finished)
Diameter: 15.87mm/40 Length: 123mm/4 7/8 in
DOBLES (petit corona — *standard* — machine-made — machine-bunched & hand-finished)
Diameter: 15.87mm/40 Length: 123mm/4 7/8 in

TRINIDAD

One model.
Quality: very best
(gran/long panetela — *laguito No1* — hand-made)
Diameter: 15.08mm/38 Length: 178mm/7 in

Named after one of Cuba's most beautiful historical cities. Not available for public distribution. Packed in simple cedar box of 100 cigars. Created specially for President Fidel Castro to give as gifts to important visitors. Other top Cuban officials give Cohiba; only Fidel Castro can present Trinidads.
   Three top rollers in El Laguito Factory (where Cohiba is made) produce an average of 20 boxes of Trinidad a month.
   Cigar has simple, but elegant, gold band with "Trinidad" printed in black letters. Similar to Cohiba Lancero in size. Finished with curly head.
   First public tasting of Trinidad cigar was "The Dinner of the century" staged by "Cigar Aficionado" magazine at the Laurent Restaurant in Paris on October 22, 1994. One Trinidad was presented to each guest.
   Nine special boxes of cigars were auctioned raising a staggering US$344 000 for medical aid to Cuba.

TROYA

Two models — all machine-made and machine-made & hand-finished as well. Short filler.
Quality: fair

Both models available entirely machine-made and machine-made and hand-finished. Considering low costs, compared to hand-made cigars range represents good value. Cigars packed mainly in cellophaned carton packs and are generally small sizes. Produced mainly for Spanish market.

UNIVERSALES (demi tasse — *universales* — machine-made — machine-bunched & hand-finished)
Diameter: 15.08mm/38 Length: 134mm/5 1/4 in

CORONAS CLUB TUBULARES (petit corona — *standard* — machine-made — machine-bunched & hand-finished)★★
Diameter: 15.87mm/40 Length: 123mm/4 7/8 in
Comment: Sold in aluminium tubes. Ordinary. One dimensional.

Cuban Cigar Imports into the USA

US Treasury has advised the Retail Tobacco Dealers of America of the following definitive position vis-à-vis the importation of Cuban cigars:

1) US residents returning from a licensed visit to Cuba may bring back Cuban cigars provided their value does not exceed $100.
2) Cuban cigars bought in any other country (say Canada or the UK) may not be so imported by US residents or anyone else.
3) It is illegal to buy, sell, donate or trade in any illegally imported Cuban cigars, the penalty for infringement being a fine of up to $50 000 and/or criminal prosecution leading to imprisonment.

Cuban Cigars Listed by Sizes

If you wish to see what models and sizes are made under a particular brand, then use the CUBAN CIGAR DIRECTORY. If you have a favourite size and wish to see what brands made that size then use this directory.

The popular name or size is listed first with the *Vitola de Galera*, or factory name, next to it with the exact dimensions.

When you have the brand and model name for that particular size, then refer to the appropriate listing in the CUBAN CIGAR DIRECTORY for full available details of that cigar.

DIAMEDES (FIGURADO) (GRAN CORONA)
D18.65MM/47 L235MM/9 1/2 IN
CIFUENTES—Super Estupendos
HOYO DE MONTERREY—Particulares★★★
MONTECRISTO—Montecristo A★★★★★
PUNCH—Diademas Extra★★★★
ROMEO Y JULIETA—Fabulosos★★★★★
SANCHO PANZA—Sanchos★★★★★

DOUBLE CORONA (PROMINENTE)
D19.45MM/49 L194MM/7 5/8 IN
HOYO DE MONTERREY—Double Corona★★★★
PARTAGAS—Lusitanias★★★★★
PUNCH—Double Coronas★★★★★
RAMON ALLONES—Gigantes★★★★
SAINT LUIS REY—Double Corona★★★★★

CHURCHILL (JULIETA 2)
D18.65MM/47 L178MM/7 IN
BOLIVAR—Supremas Churchills, Corona Gigantes★★★★★
COHIBA—Esplendidos★★★★★
EL REY DEL MUNDO—Tainos
HOYO DE MONTERREY—Concorde★★★, Churchill★★★★
H. UPMANN—Monarchs★★★★★, Sir Winston★★★★
LA FLOR DE CANO—Diedemas★★★★★
LA GLORIA CUBANA—Tainos★★★★★
PARTAGAS—Churchill De Luxe★★★★★
PUNCH—Monarcas★★★★★, Churchills★★★

QUAI D'ORSAY—Imperiales
ROMEO Y JULIETA—Churchill★★★★,
Clemenceaus★★★★★, Prince of Wales★★★★★
SANCHO PANZA—Coronas Gigantes★★★★★
SAINT LUIS REY—Churchill★★★

TORPEDO (PIRAMIDE)
D20.64MM/52 L156MM/6 1/8 IN
DIPLOMATICOS—Diplomaticos No 2★★★
H. UPMANN—Upmann No 2★★★★★
MONTECRISTO—Montecristo No 2★★★★★

CORONA GRANDE (DALIAS)
D17.07MM/43 L170MM/6 3/4 IN
BOLIVAR—Inmensas★★★★
COHIBA—Siglo V★★★★★
LA GLORIA CUBANA—Medaille D'Or No 2★★★
PARTAGAS—8-9-8★★★★★, Partagas De Partagas No
1★★★★, Seleccion Privada No 1★★★★
RAMON ALLONES—Churchill 8-9-8★★★★

CORONA GRANDE (CAZADORE)
D17.46MM/44 L162MM/6 3/8 IN
FONSECA—Fonseca No 1★★★
LA ESCEPCION—Cazadores
ROMEO Y JULIETA—Cazadores★★★★★

CORONA GRANDE (TACOS)
D18.65MM/47 L158MM/6 1/8 IN
PARTAGAS—Presidentes★★★★

CORONA GRANDE (CONSERVAS)
D17.46MM/44 L145MM/5 11/16 IN
CIFUENTES—Cristal Tubo
HOYO DE MONTERREY—Humidor No 1★★★, Royal
Coronation
H. UPMANN—Royal Corona
PUNCH—Royal Coronation

GRAN CORONA (FRANCISCOS)
D17.46MM/44 L143MM/5 5/8 IN
BOLIVAR—Coronas Extra★★★★, Amodo Seleccion C

CORONA EXTRA (CORONA GORDA)
D18.26MM/46 L143MM/5 5/8 IN
COHIBA—Siglo IV★★★★
EL REY DEL MUNDO—Gran Corona★★★

HOYO DE MONTERREY—Epicure No 1★★★★★
H. UPMANN—Super Coronas★★★★, Magnum 46
JUAN LOPEZ—Seleccion No 1★★★
LA FLOR DE CANO—Gran Corona★★★★
PUNCH—Black Prince★★★★, Punch Punch★★★★, Royal
Selection No 11★★★★, Super Selection No 2★★★★★,
Seleccion De Luxe No 1★★★★, Nectares No 2
RAFAEL GONZALEZ—Coronas Extra★★★★
ROMEO Y JULIETA—Exhibition No 3
SAINT LUIS REY—Serie A★★★★

FIGURADO (CAMPANA)
20.64MM/52 L140MM/5 1/2 IN
BOLIVAR—Belicosos Finos★★★★★
ROMEO Y JULIETA—Belicosos★★★★★
SANCHO PANZA—Belicosos★★★★

ROBUSTO ROYAL (HERMOSO NO 4)
D19.05MM/48 L127MM/5 IN
H. UPMANN—Connoisseurs No 1★★★★
EL REY DEL MUNDO—Choix Supreme★★★, Fox Selection No 47
ROMEO Y JULIETA—Exhibicion No 4★★★★★
SAINT LUIS REY—Regios★★★★

ROBUSTO ROYAL (BRITANICA)
D18.26MM/46 L137MM/5 3/8 IN
ROMEO Y JULIETA—Celestiales Fino★★★★

FIGURADO (ESPECIALE)
D17.86MM/45 L134MM/5 1/4 IN
FONSECA—Invictos★★★★

ROBUSTO/ROTHSCHILD (ROBUSTO)
D19.84MM/50 L124MM/4 7/8 IN
BOLIVAR—Royal Coronas★★★★★, Amado Seleccion E
COHIBA—Robustos★★★★★
HOYO DE MONTERREY—Epicure No 2★★★★★
JUAN LOPEZ—Seleccion No 2★★★★
LA FLOR DE CANO—Short Churchill★★★★
PARTAGAS—Serie D No 4★★★★★
RAMON ALLONES—Allones Specially
Selected★★★★★

LONSDALE (CERVANTE)
D16.67MM/42 L165MM/6 1/2 IN
BOLIVAR—Gold Medal★★★

DIPLOMATICOS—Diplomaticos No 1★★★★★
EL REY DEL MUNDO—Lonsdale
H. UPMANN—Upmann No 1, Cinco Bocas, Lonsdale★★★★★
LA GLORIA CUBANA—Cetros
MONTECRISTO—Montecristo No 1★★★★★
PARTAGAS—Lonsdales★★★★★
POR LARRANAGA—Lonsdales★★★★★
QUINTERO—Churchills★★★
RAFAEL GONZALEZ—Lonsdales★★★★★
ROMEO Y JULIETA—Cedros De Luxe No 1★★★
SANCHO PANZA—Dorados★★★★, Molinos★★★★★
SAINT LUIS REY—Coronas★★★★★, Lonsdales★★★★

LONSDALE (CORONA GRANDE)
D16.67MM/42 L155MM/6 1/8 IN
COHIBA—Siglo III★★★★★
HOYO DE MONTERREY—Le Hoyo Des Dieux★★★★,. Super Selection No 1
LA GLORIA CUBANA—Sabrasos
MONTECRISTO—Montecristo Tubos★★★
PARTAGAS—Coronas Grandes★★★, 8-9-8★★★★
PUNCH—Super Selection No 1★★★★, Quai D'Orsay★★★★, Gran Corona★★★★
ROMEO Y JULIETA—Coronas Grandes

CORONA (CRISTALE)
D16.27MM/41 L150MM/5 7/8 IN
LA FLOR DE CANO—Selectos

CORONA (SUPERIORE)
D15.87MM/40 L146MM/5 3/4 IN
H. UPMANN—Amatistas
JOSE L. PIEDRA—Superiores
PUNCH—Gran Corona

CORONA (CORONA)
D16.67MM/42 L142MM/5 9/16 IN
BOLIVAR—Coronas★★★★, Bolivar Tubos No 1
DIPLOMATICOS—Diplomaticos No 3★★★
EL REY DEL MUNDO—Corona De Luxe★★★, Tubo No 1★★★
GISPERT—Coronas★★★
HOYO DE MONTERREY—Hoyo Coronas, Le Hoyo Du Roi★★★, Opera, Royal Coronations
H. UPMANN—Coronas★★★★★, Royal Coronas, Upmann No 3

JUAN LOPEZ—Coronas★★★★★
MONTECRISTO—Montecristo No 3★★★
PARTAGAS—Coronas★★★★, Privados
POR LARRANAGA—Coronas★★★★, Lanceros
PUNCH—Coronas★★★, Royal Coronations
QUAI D'ORSAY—Coronas
QUINTERO—Coronas★★★, Coronas Selectas
RAMON ALLONES—Coronas★★★, Coronas 8-9-8★★★★
ROMEO Y JULIETA—Cedros De Luxe No 2★★★★, Coronas, Romeo No 1 De Luxe
SANCHO PANZA—Coronas, Tronquitos
SAN LUIS REY—Coronas★★★★★

CORONA GRANDE (CONSERVAS)
CIFUENTES—Cristal Tubo
HOYO DE MONTERREY—Humidor No 1★★★, Royal Coronations
H UPMANN—Royal Coronas
PUNCH—Royal Coronations

CORONA (COSACO)
D16.67MM/42 L135MM/5 5/16 IN
FONSECA—Cosacos★★★
H. UPMANN—Cristales★★★★, Noellas, Short Coronas
LA GLORIA CUBANA—Tapados★★★
MONTECRISTO—Montecristo B★★★★
PARTAGAS—Astorias
PUNCH—Nacionales
ROMEO Y JULIETA—Nacionales

CORONA (CREMA/NACIONALE)
D15.87MM/40 L140MM/5 1/2 IN
BOLIVAR—Champions
CANEY—Selectos
HOYO DE MONTERREY—Palmas Extra
H. UPMANN—Majestic, Especiales
LA CORONA—Coronas
PARTAGAS—Partagas De Luxe, Super Partagas
PUNCH—Palmas Reales
QUINTERO—Brevas★★★★, Nacionales★★★
RAMON ALLONES—Ramondos
ROMEO Y JULIETA—Romeo No 1
STATOS DE LUXE—Cremas, Brevas, Selectos

PETIT CORONA (EMINENTE)
D17.46MM/44 L132MM/5 3/16 IN
BOLIVAR—Petit Coronas Especiales

H. UPMANN—Coronas Major, Medias Coronas, Petit Coronas Especiales
PARTAGAS—Corona Senior, Eminentes, Petit Coronas Especiales, Petit Coronas Tubos

PETIT CORONA (ALMUERZO)
D15.87MM/40 L130MM/5 1/8 IN
HOYO DE MONTERREY—Le Hoyo Du Prince★★★

PETIT CORONA (MAREVA)
D16.67MM/42 L129MM/5 1/16 IN
BELINDA—Petit Coronas
BOLIVAR—Petit Coronas, Bolivar Tubos No 2
COHIBA—Siglo II★★★★
DIPLOMATICOS—Diplomaticos No 4★★★
EL REY DEL MUNDO—Petit Coronas, Petit Lonsdales, Tubo No 2
GISPERT—Petit Coronas De Luxe★★★
HOYO DE MONTERREY—Short Hoyo Coronas, Souvenir De Luxe, Coronations
H. UPMANN—Aromaticos, Exquisitos, Kings, Coronas Major, Medias Coronas, Petit Coronas, Regalias, Upmann No 4
JUAN LOPEZ—Petit Coronas★★★★
LA FLOR DE CANO—Coronas★★★★
MONTECRISTO—Montecristo No 4★★★★★
PARTAGAS—Mille Fleurs, Petit Coronas, Petit Privados
POR LARRANAGA—Lolas en Cedro, Petit Coronas
PUNCH—Coronations, Petit Coronas Del Punch★★★★, Presidentes, Royal Selection No 12, Seleccion De Luxe No 2★★★★, Souvenir De Luxe
RAFAEL GONZALEZ—Petit Coronas★★★★, Petit Lonsdales★★★★
RAMON ALLONES—Mille Fleurs, Petit Coronas★★★★
ROMEO Y JULIETA—Cedros De Luxe No 3★★★★, Club King, Excepcionales, Mille Fleurs, Petit Coronas, Plateados De Romeo, Romeo No 2 De Luxe★★★
SANCHO PANZA—Non Plus
SAN LUIS REY—Petit Corona★★★★★

PETIT CORONA/FIGURADO (PERFECTO)
D17.46MM/44 L127MM/5 IN
JOSE L. PIEDRA—Brevas, Cazadores, Conservas, Cremas, Nacionales, Petit Cetros
LA CORONA—Perfectos
LA ESCEPCION—Perfectos

PARTAGAS—Perfectos
ROMEO Y JULIETA—Perfectos

PETIT CORONA (PETIT CETROS)
D15.87MM/40 L129MM/5 1/16 IN
HOYO DE MONTERREY—Exquisitos
LA CORONA—Petit Cetros
PARTAGAS—Aristocrats★★★★, Capitols, Londres En
Cedro, Londres Extra, Londres Finos, Parisianos,
Personales, Petit Partagas
PUNCH—Exquisitos
ROMEO Y JULIETA—Coronitas, Coronitas En Cedro,
Exquisitos, Plateados De Romeo

PETIT CORONA (LONDRES)
D15.87MM/40 L126MM/5 IN
BOLIVAR—Bonitas
PARTAGAS—Royales
PUNCH—Souvenir De Luxe
QUINTERO—Medias Coronas

PETIT CORONA (STANDARD)
D15.87MM/40 L123MM/4 7/8 IN
CANEY—Predilectos
FONSECA—Delicias★★★
GISPERT—Habaneras No 2★★★
LA ESCEPCION—Excepcionales★★★★
LA FLOR DE CANO—Predilectos Tubulares★★★, Petit
Coronas★★★
POR LARRANAGA—Super Cedros
QUINTERO—Londres, Londres Extra
STATOS DE LUXE—Delirios, Dobles
TROYA—Coronas Club Tubulares★★

HALF CORONA (MINUTO)
D16.67MM/42 L110MM/4 5/16 IN
BOLIVAR—Amado Seleccion G, Corona Junior
PARTAGAS—Shorts★★★★, Seleccion Fox No 7, Par-
tagas Pride, Half Coronas
PUNCH—Tres Petit Coronas
RAMON ALLONES—Small Club Coronas

HALF CORONA (FRANCISCANO)
D15.87MM/40 L116MM/4 9/16 IN
EL REY DEL MUNDO—Tubo No 3, Lunch Club
HOYO DE MONTERREY—Petit Coronation
LA GLORIA CUBANA—Minutos

PARTAGAS—Tres Petit Coronas★★★★
POR LARRANAGA—Small Coronas
PUNCH—Nectares No 4
RAFAEL GONZALEZ—Tres Petit Lonsdales★★★★
ROMEO Y JULIETA—Julietas, Romeo No 3 De Luxe,
Tres Petit Coronas
SANCHO PANZA—Bachilleres★★★

PETIT CORONA (CORONITA)
D15.87MM/40 L117MM/4 5/8 IN
HOYO DE MONTERREY—Petit Coronation
H. UPMANN—Coronas Minor, Singulare★★★★,
Aromaticos
JUAN LOPEZ—Patricias★★★★
LA ESCEPCION—Superfinos★★★
PARTAGAS—Coronas Junior, Regalias De La Reina
Bueno
PUNCH—Petit Coronations
ROMEO Y JULIETA—Clarines, Romeo No 3, Regalias
De Londres

PETIT CORONA (PERLA)
D15.87MM/40 L102MM/4 IN
COHIBA—Siglo I★★★★★
DIPLOMATICOS—Diplomaticos No 5★★★★
H. UPMANN—Upmann No 5
MONTECRISTO—Montecristo No 5★★★★
PUNCH—Petit Punch★★★★, Petit Punch De Luxe★★★★
ROMEO Y JULIETA—Petit Princess

GRAN/LONG PANETELA (LAGUITO NO 1/ DELICADO)
D15.08MM/38 L192MM/7 9/16 IN
BOLIVAR—Especiales
COHIBA—Lanceros★★★
DIPLOMATICOS—Diplomaticos No 6★★★
EL REY DEL MUNDO—Grandes De Espa★★★★
MONTECRISTO—Montecristo Especial No 1★★★★★
PARTAGAS—Serie Du Connaisseur No 1★★★★

TRINIDAD

LONG PANETELA (DELICADOS EXTRA)
D14.29MM/36 L185MM/5 5/16 IN
LA GLORIA CUBANA—Medaille D'Or No 1★★★★

PANETELA (NINFAS)
D13.10MM/33 L178MM/7 IN
BOLIVAR—Palmas★★★
HOYO DE MONTERREY—Longos
H. UPMANN—Seleccion Suprema 23
LA ESCEPCION—Longos
PARTAGAS—Palmas Grandes
PUNCH—Ninfas★★★,   Panetelas   Grandes★★★,
Nectares No 5
QUAI D'ORSAY—Panetelas★★★
ROMEO Y JULIETA—Palmas Reales

LONG PANETELA (PAREJOS)
D15.08MM/38 L166MM/6 9/16 IN
PARTAGAS—Serie Du Connaisseur No 2★★★★

PANETELA (TOPPER)
D15.48MM/39 L160MM/6 5/16 IN
PARTAGAS—Toppers
RAMON ALLONES—Toppers, Delgados
ROMEO Y JULIETA—Montagues

PANETELA (DELICIOSO)
D13.89MM/35 L159MM/6 1/4 IN
H. UPMANN—El Prado
POR   LARRANAGA—Largos   De   Larranaga,
Montecarlos

PANETELA (NATURALE)
D14.68MM/37 L155MM/6 1/16 IN
H. UPMANN—Naturals

PANETELA (LAGUITO NO 2)
D15.08MM/38 L152MM/6 IN
COHIBA—Corona Especiales★★★★
DIPLOMATICOS—Diplomaticos No 7★★★
HOYO DE MONTERREY—Le Hoyo Du Dauphin★★★
MONTECRISTO—Montecristo Especial No 2★★★★
SIBONEY—Especiale

PANETELA (CARLOTA)
D13.89MM/35 L143MM/5 5/8 IN
EL REY DEL MUNDO—Isabel★★★
HOYO DE MONTERREY—Jeanne D'Arc
PARTAGAS—Charlottes, Serie Du Connaisseur No
3★★★

SLIM PANETELA (PALMA)
D13.10MM/33 L170MM/6 3/4 IN
HOYO DE MONTERREY—Le Hoyo Du Gourmet★★★,
Versaille

SLIM PANETELA (PALMITAS)
D12.70MM/32 L152MM/6 IN
LA GLORIA CUBANA—Medaille D'Or No 4★★★★
RAMON ALLONES—Palmitas

SLIM PANETELA (PANETELA LARGA)
D11.11MM/28 L175MM/6 7/8 IN
EL REY DEL MUNDO—Panetelas Largas★★★,
Elegantes
LA GLORIA CUBANA—Medaille D'Or No 3★★★
MONTECRISTO—Montecristo No 7
RAFAEL GONZALEZ—Slenderellas★★★★
ROMEO Y JULIETA—Shakespeares

CULEBRAS (CULEBRAS)
D15.48MM/39 L146MM/5 3/4 IN
CANEY—Especiales
H. UPMANN—Culebras
PARTAGAS—Culebras★★★
ROMEO Y JULIETA—Culebras

SHORT PANETELA (UNIVERSALES)
D15.08MM/38 L134MM/5 1/4 IN
TROYA—Universales

SHORT PANETELA (PREFERIDO)
D15.08MM/38 L127MM/5 IN
CANEY—Vegueros

SHORT PANETELA (VEGUERITO)
D14.29MM/37 L127MM/5 IN
CANEY—Bouqets Finos, Delgados
CIFUENTES—Vegueritos
LA FLOR DE CANO—Preferidos★★★
POR LARRANAGA—Panetelas
QUINTERO Y HERMANO—Panetelas

SHORT PANETELA (TRABUCO)
D15.08MM/38 L110MM/4 5/16 IN
HOYO DE MONTERREY—Le Hoyo Du Depute★★★

SHORT PANETELA (CADETE)
D14.29MM/36 L115MM/4 9/16 IN
FONSECA—KDT Cadetes
H. UPMANN—Petit Palatinos, Corona Juniors, Petit Upmann★★★

SHORT PANETELA (INFANTE)
D14.68MM/37 L98MM/3 7/8 IN
CIFUENTES—Petit Bouquets
PARTAGAS—Petit Bouquet

SHORT PANETELA (SPORT)
D13.89MM/35 L117MM/4 9/16 IN
BELINDA—Panetelas
ROMEO Y JULIETA—Panetelas, Sport Largos

SHORT PANETELA (EPICURE)
D13.89MM/35 L110MM/4 5/16 IN
BELINDA—Princess
H. UPMANN—Epicures, Glorias

BELVEDERE (BELVEDERE)
D15.48MM/39 L125MM/4 15/16 IN
BELINDA—Belvederes
H. UPMANN—Belvederes
LA CORONA—Belvederes
LA ESCEPCION—Belvederes★★★
PARTAGAS—Belvederes, Habaneros
POR LARRANAGA—Belvederes
PUNCH—Belvederes
RAMON ALLONES—Belvederes
ROMEO Y JULIETA—Regalias De La Habana★, Belvederes★★, Favoritas

BELVEDERE (SEOANE)
D14.30MM/36 L125MM/4 15/16 IN
COHIBA—Exquisitos★★★
MONTECRISTO—Montecristo No 6

PANETELA (CONCHITA)
D13.89MM/35 L127MM/5 IN
BOLIVAR—Panetelas
LA CORONA—Panetelas
PARTAGAS—Panetelas, Princess
RAMON ALLONES—Panetelas

SMALL PANETELA (PLACERA)
D13.49MM/34 L125MM/4 15/16 IN
BOLIVAR—Regentes, Bolivar Tubos No 3
JUAN LOPEZ—Panetela Superba★★★★
PARTAGAS—Filipos, Seleccion Fox No 11, Cubanos

SMALL PANETELA (DEMI TIP)
D11.51MM/29 L126MM/5 IN
CIFUENTES—Emboquillados No 5
PARTAGAS—Demi-Tip

SMALL PANETELA (PANETELA)
D13.49MM/34 L117MM/4 9/16 IN
POR LARRANAGA—Coronitas
PUNCH—Coronets, Punchinello, Panetelas
RAFAEL GONZALEZ—Panetelas★★★
ROMEO Y JULIETA—Panetelas, Romeo No 4 De Luxe

SMALL PANETELA (DEMI TASSE)
D12.70MM/32 L100MM/3 15/16 IN
H. UPMANN—Preciosas
LA CORONA—Demi Tasse

SMALL PANETELA (PETIT)
D12.30MM/31 L108MM/4 1/4 IN
LA CORONA—Petit

SMALL PANETELA (ENTREACTO)
D11.91MM/30 L100MM/3 15/16 IN
BOLIVAR—Demi Tasse
EL REY DEL MUNDO—Demi Tasse★★★
HOYO DE MONTERREY—Le Hoyo Du Maire★★★
RAFAEL GONZALEZ—Demi Tasse★★★★
ROMEO Y JULIETA—Petit Julietas

PANETELA/CIGARILLO (CAROLINA)
D10.32MM/26 L121MM/4 3/4 IN
HOYO DE MONTERREY—Margaritas
PARTAGAS—Ramonitas
PUNCH—Margaritas
RAMON ALLONES—Ramonitas★★★

CIGARILLO/LAGUITO NO 3
D10.32MM/26 L115MM/4 1/2 IN
COHIBA—Panetelas★★★★
EL REY DEL MUNDO—Senoritas
MONTECRISTO—Joyitas★★★

RAFAEL GONZALEZ—Cigarritos★★★★

CIGARILLO (CHICO)
D11.51MM/29 L106MM/4 3/16 IN
BOLIVAR—Chicos
CANEY—Canape
CIFUENTES—Cubanitos, Habanitos
EL REY DEL MUNDO—Variedades
LA CORONA—Coronitas
PARTAGAS—Chicos
POR LARRANAGA—Curritos, Juanitos
PUNCH—Cigarrillos
QUINTERO Y HERMANO—Puritos
RAMON ALLONES—Bits of Havana

Cigar Clubs

The cigar boom has given birth to a multitude of "smoker" nights in cities throughout the world. This has led also to the establishment of many cigar clubs some with fixed premises, others offering benefits through the mail.

Just two such clubs are:

SPAIN

CLUB EPICUR, is a Havana's smoker's club founded in Barcelona in November 1994. Now holds regular dinners, occasional smoker's nights and organized visits to places with cigar interest, from both Barcelona and Madrid, and to a lesser extent elsewhere.

Annual membership is 12 000 Pts. (US $90 or £60) a year.

For further details contact:

Club Epicur, C/Bea y Mata 139 pral, 08029, Barcelona, Spain. Tel: (34) (3) 322-1199. Fax: (34)(3) 322-1203.

USA

CIGAR OF THE MONTH CLUB, founded in May 1994, is a samplers' club that provides rare and previously unavailable high-quality cigars to members. Membership throughout USA and seven foreign countries.

Primary benefits to members is early, exclusive sampling of premium cigars, a high quality monthly newsletter, staging of special events and benefit to members of expanding their cigar hobby horizons through club affiliation.

For further details contact:

Craig Nelson, President, Cigar of the Month Club, 1081 Black Oak Trail, Deerfield, WI 53531, USA. Tel: (1)(608) 764-8487. Fax: (1)(608) 764-5161.

World Directory

STAR RATING

The author's subjective ratings for cigars take into account the following: appearance, construction, quality of wrapper and colour; smoking characteristics and texture of the smoke; flavour and aroma; overall impression including enjoyment of the cigar.

★★★★★	Outstanding. A classic.
★★★★	Excellent.
★★★	Good.
★★	Fair, ordinary.
★	Poor or faulty.

No Star: Not evaluated.

AUSTRIA

AUSTRIA TABAK

This state-owned monopoly makes all cigars and cigarettes in Austria. It owns or has licence agreements with more than 200 brands and produces about 29 million cigars a year. Established in 1784 it is one of Europe's oldest cigar manufacturers mainly using tobacco imported from Sumatra, Java, Brazil, with small quantity from Cuba for cigarillos.

In 1996 plans were put in motion to privatise the group which was estimated to be worth $1.2 billion to $1.5 billion (£800 million to £1 billion).

Generally, cigarillos are particularly good quality.

Most cigars produced by Austria Tabak are machine-made with short filler.

AIRPORT★★★   142mm/4 1/2 ins × 11.11mm/28
Sumatran tobacco. Packed in aluminium foil. Full bodied. One dimentional, probably due to its thinness.
ANATOL SUMATRA   145mm/5 3/4 ins × 8.5mm/21
*ANATOL VIRGINETTE★★
                   145mm/5 3/4 ins × 8.5mm/21
HTL binder. Short filler. Rolled around a straw. Good flavour. Mild. Good conversation piece.
ARLBERG★★   100mm/3 15/16 ins × 16.00mm/40
Mild spicy aromas. Chalky smoke.
ATTACHE ROYAL   105mm/4 1/8 ins × 9.7mm/25

CABALLERO 110mm/4 3/16 ins × 10.00mm/25
CAPRIOLE BRASIL (green tin)★★★★
90mm/3 9/16 ins × 9.00mm/23
Medium bodied. Spice and coffee. Good cigarillo.
CAPRIOLE LIGHT (cream tin)★★★
90mm/3 9/16 ins × 9.00mm/23
Pleasant, mild and smooth.
CAPRIOLE SUMATRA (red tin)★★★★
90mm/3 9/16 ins × 9.00mm/23
Lots of flavour. Burns easily. Good cigarillo.
CARMEN Y JOSE★★★ 142mm/4 5/16 ins × 11.1mm/28
Rich flavour with touch of coffee. Has pierced hole.
CHIC 97mm/3 13/16 ins × 16.00mm/41
CLUBMASTER 106mm/4 3/16 ins × 11.2mm/28
CORONAS 131mm/5 1/8 ins × 15.00mm/38
FALSTAFF No 1★★★ 150mm/5 7/8 ins × 18.00mm/46
Medium to full bodied. Rich finish. Tends to become
tiresome and loses some of its complexity.
FALSTAFF No 2 131mm/5 1/8 ins × 15.00mm/38
FALSTAFF No 3★★★★
142mm/4 5/16 ins × 11.10mm/28
Easy, even burn. Herbaceous with hint of coffee. Good
daytime smoke.
FALSTAFF No 4 108mm/4 1/4 ins × 16.00mm/14
FALSTAFF No 5 110mm/4 3/16 ins × 10.00mm/25
FLIP 107mm/4 3/16 ins × 9.00mm/23
GRACIOSAS 108mm/4 1/4 ins × 16.00mm/14
GROSS GLOCKNER★★★
115mm/5 7/8 ins × 18.20mm/46
HTL binder. Torpedo shaped. Rich flavours. Good
balance.
HAVANITOS★★★★ 90mm/3 9/16 ins × 9.00mm/23
Made with tobacco imported from Cuba. Mildly aro-
matic.

IMPERIALES SUPERIORES★★★
150mm/5 7/8 ins × 18.00mm/46
Gold foil. Medium to full bodied. Spicy, honeyed
aromas.
IMPERIALES★★★ 150mm/5 7/8 ins × 18.00mm/46
Sumalian tobacco. Packed in aluminium foil. Attractive
aroma and flavour. Tends to lose its character. Daytime
smoke.
*JUBILAUMS-VIRGINIER
205mm/8 1/16 ins × 10.5mm/26
JUBILAR 200★★ 200mm/7 7/8 ins × 18.00mm/46
Mild. Little flavour.

KAVALIER★★★   110mm/4 15/16 ins × 10.00mm/25
Slightly sweet, fruity taste on palate. Pleasant cigarillo.
LEICHTE BRUNS★★★   115mm/4 9/16 ins × 10mm/25
Light bodied. Good flavour. Touch of menthol.
LIVARDE   90mm/3 9/16 ins × 9.00mm/23
MOCCA   110mm/ ins × 9.20mm/23

MOZART
Machine-made. Quality: superior. Available through
most of Europe. Full bodied, subtle range. Reminiscent
of Honduran cigar. Most satisfying, especially for
machine-made range.

Idomeneo no 1★★★★   150mm/5 1/8 ins × 18.00mm/46
Mushroom flavour. Perhaps too tightly rolled. Full
bodied.

Don Giovani no 2★★★★
                  131mm/5 1/8 ins × 15.00mm/38
Well-made, good cigar with dark Java wrapper.

Cosi Van Tuti no 3★★★
                  142mm/4 1/2 ins × 11.10mm/28
Very mild, soft. Almost insipid. Burns easily. Beginner's
cigar.

Figaro no 4★★★   108mm/4 1/4 ins × 16.00mm/41
Mild, very smooth. Burns well. Cool smoke. Good cigar
for beginner.

Papageno no 5★★★★
                  110mm/4 15/16 ins × 10.00mm/25
Surprisingly full bodied for a cigarillo. Not for beginners.

PALMAS★★★   108mm/4 1/4 ins × 16.00mm/41
Attractive, dark natural wrapper. HTL binder. Full-
bodied with good flavours. Touch of honey on palate.
PIKKOLO★★   90mm/3 9/16 ins × 8.50mm/21
PIKKOLO FILTER★   90mm/3 9/16 ins × 8.50mm/21
Filter, HTL wrapper, redish HTL binder. More a ciga-
rette. Smooth.
PORTORICO★★★   92mm/3 5/8 ins × 11.70mm/29
Good wrapper. Medium to full bodied. Spicy and
vegetal aromas. Gets stronger and harsher.
REGALIA MEDIA   108mm/4 1/4 ins × 16.00mm/41
ROSITAS ESPECIALES★
                  100mm/3 15/16 ins × 12.80mm/32
HTL wrapper and binder. Robust.
ROZET   116mm/4 9/16 ins × 11.10mm/28
SAMBA★   67.50mm/2 5/8 ins × 8.50mm/21

Brazilian tobacco. HTL binder. Coffee with touch of sweetness on palate. Quick smoke.

SENOR   92mm/3 5/8 ins × 11.70mm/29
SIBONY MIDI★★   110mm/4 15/16 ins × 10.00mm/25

Fairly full bodied. Spicy. One dimentional.

SIBONY MINI   90mm/3 9/16 ins × 9.00mm/23
SLIM JIM DUNKEL   140mm/5 1/2 ins × 9.00mm/23
SLIM JIM HELL★★   140mm/5 1/2 ins × 9.00mm/23

Filler is blend of tobacco from Cuba and Brazil. HTL wrapper. Meduim-bodied. Lots of flavour.

SPEZI★   100mm/3 5/16 ins × 12.80mm/32

HTL wrapper and binder. Full-bodied. One dimensional. Slightly harsh. Smoke for a smoke's sake.

TIPARILLO   125mm/4 15/16 ins × 10.70mm/27
VEDEDIGER   100mm/3 7/8 ins × 16.00mm/41
★VIRGINIER★★   205mm/8 1/16 ins × 10.50mm/26

Strong, with touch of harshness. Burns easily. Has dung and rum aromas.

★SPEZIAL VIRGINIER★★

                    205mm/8 1/16 ins × 10.50mm/26

Similar to virginier. A good conversation piece.

WACHAUER★★★   115mm/4 9/16 ins × 11.60mm/29

Plastic filter tip. Attractive wrapper. Medium bodied. Smooth. Good flavour.

WALLSTREET

Machine-made. Quality: superior. Wrapper from Sumatra. Filler is a blend of tobacco from Cuba, Java and Brazil. Medium to full bodied. Launced 1995. Available through most of Europe.

CLASSIC CORONA★★★★★

                    150mm/5 15/16 × 18.00mm/47

Medium strength, but full flavour. Dusty finish. Good daytime smoke.

PANETELA★★★★   145mm/5 11/16 ins × 11.10mm/28

Easy draw. Slow burning. Shows some character.

CIGARARILLO★★★★★   90mm/3 1/2 ins × 9.00mm/23

Rich, spicy floral aroma. Medium to full bodied. Smooth. Good quick smoke.

ZINO DRIE   150mm/5 7/8 ins × 18.00mm/46

★ Copy of American cowboy's "charoot". Has short filler and HTL binder. Made of dark fined Virginia tobacco. Has natural reed right through the centre, which is withdrawn and used as a wick to light it.

BELGIUM

Cigarillos account for about 90 percent of local cigar sales.

CORPS DIPLOMATIQUE
Machine-made.
Deauville
Panetela — wrapped in tissue. Sumatra wrapper. Java & Brazilian filler.
After Dinner 10's

J. CORTES
Machine-made. All tobacco.

Long Filler No 1	140mm/5 1/2 ins x 15.1mm/38
Long Filler No 2	127mm/5 ins x 15.1mm/38
Club	114mm/4 1/2 ins x 11.9mm/30
Grand Luxe	101mm/4 ins x 9.9mm/25
High Class	127mm/5 ins x 15.1mm/38
Milord	108mm/4 1/4 ins x 11.9mm/30
Royal Class	133mm/5 1/4 ins x 11.9mm/30
Mini	89mm/3 1/2 ins x 7.5mm/19

BRAZIL

Large producer of tobacco used predominantly in German cigar industry. Most famous is Bahia, north of Brazil. Commercial tobacco industry started by Portuguese who shipped the best quality to Lisbon and used lower grades for exchange of slaves imported from Africa. In 1962 total production peaked at over 400 000 bales, with Germany, Switzerland, Holland, Denmark, France, United Kingdom and Belgium consuming around 230 000 bales. Present production is about 80 000 bales.

Despite adverse weather conditions in some growing regions the 1995/1996 crop showed an increase in both quantity and price.

CANONERO
Hand-made. Quality, superior. Launched early 1996. Connecticut shade wrapper. Brazilian binder and filler. Distributed by Diamente Intl, Kentucky, USA.

No 1	190mm/7 1/2 ins x 19.84mm/50
No 2★★★★	140mm/5 1/2 ins x 19.84mm/58

Meduim bodied. Good flavour with hint of spice. Well balanced. Elegant. A daytime smoke.

No 3★★★★★	127mm/5 ins x 20.6mm/52

Meduim bodied, rich, good balance. Much more character than one expects from a Brazilian cigar. A classy daytime smoke.

No 4*****   178mm/7 ins x 18.3mm/46

Meduim strength and integrated flavours. Elegant. For the connoisseur.

No 10****   165mm/6 1/2 ins x 16.67mm/42

A bit milder than the thicker ring gauges. Good finish. Elegant, well made. Daytime smoke.

No 20   140mm/5 1/2 ins x 16.67mm/42

DON PEPE
Hand-made. All Brazilian tobacco. Made by Suerdieck.

Double Corona	191mm/7 1/2 ins x 19.84mm/50
Robusto	127mm/5 ins x 19.84mm/50
Half Corona	114mm/4 1/2 ins x 14.3mm/36
Slim Panetela	133mm/5 1/4 ins x 11.9mm/30

ELYSEE
Hand-made. Feature is luxury leather bound boxes of 25.

Elysee No 7-50	190mm/7 1/2 ins × 19.84mm/50
Elysee No 7-46	178mm/7 ins × 18.26mm/46
Elysee No 6-50	153mm/6 ins × 19.84mm/50
Elysee No 6-42	153mm/6 3/4 ins × 16.67mm/42
Elysee No 5-42	146mm/5 3/4 ins × 16.67mm/42

FIDELIO BUNDLES

Fidelio Bundle No 11
Fidelio Bundle No 22
Finlandia Little Cigars

IRACEMA-BRAZIL
Muritiba
Mara Longo

SUERDIECK
Hand-made. Dark — Brazilian wrapper. Light — Sumatran wrapper. Not for the connoisseur.

Fiesta	152mm/6 ins × 12.00mm/30
Valencia	152mm/6 ins × 12.00mm/30
Caballero	152mm/6 ins × 12.00mm/30
*Mandarim Pai	127mm/5 ins × 15.08mm/38
Brasilia	133mm/5 1/4 ins × 12.00mm/30
Nips	152mm/6 ins × 12.70mm/32
Finos	147mm/5 3/4 ins × 18.26mm/46
Fiesta	160mm/6 1/4 ins × 12.00mm/30
Corona Brasil Luxo	140mm/5 1/2 ins × 17.86mm/45
Corona Imperial Luxo	140mm/5 1/2 ins × 17.86mm/45

Mata Fino Especiale   133mm/5 1/4 ins × 16.67mm/42
Panatella Fina   136mm/5 3/8 ins × 14.29mm/36
Sumatran leaf (light wrapper)

SUERDIECK CIGARILLOS
Machine-made. See also German section. Brazilian leaf — dark wrapper. Has 10 percent of Brazilian cigar and cigarillo market.

Arpoador   113mm/4 1/2 ins × 9.30mm/23
Nina   165mm/6 ins × 8.73mm/22
Palomitas   89mm/3 1/2 ins × 12.70mm/32
Copacabana Sumatra   140mm/5 ins × 11.51mm/29
Brasillia Petit   79mm/3 1/8 ins × 8.73mm/22

SUERDIECK—Premium Cigars
Hand-made
Corona Brasil Luxo   140mm/5 1/2 ins × 17.86mm/45
Corona Imperial Luxo

                      140mm/5 1/2 ins × 17.86mm/45
Mata Fina Esp.   133mm/5 1/4 ins × 16.67mm/42
Panatella Fina   147mm/5 3/8 ins × 14.29mm/36

ZINO
Hand-made.
Zino Santos   152mm/6 1/2 ins × 13.49mm/34
Zino Par Favor   102mm/4 ins × 12.00mm/30

CANARY ISLANDS

Main producer is CITA, subsidiary of giant Spanish monopoly, Tabacalera.

CASANOVA
Hand-made. Connecticut wrapper. Brazilian binder. Filler, blend of tobacco from Caribbean. International distribution by Distabacasa, Distribuidora de Tabaccos Canarios, Las Palmas, Canary Islands.
Churchill   178mm/7 ins × 19.1mm/48
Sublime   165mm/6 1/2 ins × 17.5mm/44
Superfino   165mm/6 1/2 ins × 16.67mm/42
Consul   140mm/5 1/2 ins × 19.1mm/48

CONDAL
Hand-made
No 1   168mm/6 5/8 ins × 16.67mm/42
No 3   143mm/5 5/8 ins × 16.67mm/42
No 4   132mm/5 1/4 ins × 16.67mm/42
No 6   160mm/6 1/4 ins × 13.89mm/35
Inmenso   184mm/7 1/4 ins × 16.67mm/42

DON XAVIER
Hand-made. Imported into USA by Marcas Miguel
Tobacco, Dallas, Texas.

Panetela	191mm/7 1/2 ins x 15.5mm/39
Panetela	143mm/5 5/8 ins x 15.5mm/39
Lonsdale	168mm/6 5/8 ins x 16.67mm/42
Lonsdale	143mm/5 5/8 ins x 16.67mm/42
Corona	178mm/7 ins x 18.3mm/46
Corona	168mm/5 5/8 ins x 18.3mm/46
Churchill	191mm/7 1/2 ins x 19.84mm/50
Robusto	118mm/4 5/8 ins x 19.84mm/50

DON PISHU
Hand-made. Connecticut wrapper.

Macintosch	178mm/7 ins x 19.84mm/50
Tenerife	171mm/6 3/4 ins x 19.1mm/48
Hierro	165mm/6 1/2 ins x 19.84mm/50
Rare	152mm/6 ins x 19.1mm/48
Canary Island	146mm/5 3/4 ins x 19.1mm/48
Lanzarote	165mm/6 1/2 ins x 18.3mm/46
Tu y Yo	127mm/5 ins x 19.84mm/50
Gomera	165mm/6 1/2 ins x 16.67mm/42
Fuerte Ventura	140mm/5 1/2 ins x 18.3mm/46

DUNHILL
Hand-made. Long filler. Connecticut wrappers. Have a
black and white band.

Lonsdale Grande	190mm/7 1/2 ins × 16.67mm/42
Corona Grande	165mm/6 1/2 ins × 16.67mm/42
Corona Extra	145mm/5 11/16 ins × 19.84mm/50
Panetela	155mm/8 1/8 ins × 12.00mm/30
Corona	140mm/5 1/2 ins × 16.67mm/40

DUNHILL CANARY ISLAND CIGARS
Hand-made. Cameroon wrapper. Canary Islands filler
and binder. Distributed in USA by Lane Ltd.

Coronas	140mm/5 1/2 ins × 17.07mm/43
Coronas Extra	140mm/5 1/2 ins × 19.84mm/50
Corona Grandes	165mm/6 1/2 ins × 17.07mm/43
Lonsdale Grandes	190mm/7 1/2 ins × 16.67mm/42
Panetelas	152mm/6 ins × 12.00mm/30

LA REGENTA
Hand-made. Long filler. Connecticut shade wrappers.

Emperador	190mm/7 1/2 ins × 20.64mm/52
Gran Corona	184mm/7 1/4 ins × 18.26mm/46
Findos	178mm/7 ins × 14.29mm/36

Premier	178mm/7 ins × 16.67mm/42
No 1	165mm/6 1/2 ins × 16.67mm/42
No 2	165mm/6 1/2 ins × 18.26mm/46
No 3	140mm/5 1/2 ins × 16.67mm/42
No 4	130mm/5 1/8 ins × 16.67mm/42
Olimpicas	155mm/6 1/8 ins × 14.29mm/36
Elegantes	152mm/6 ins × 11.51mm/29
Rothschild	113mm/4 1/2 ins × 19.84mm/50

LA FAMA

Hand-made. Quality, superior. Made by CITA, Tabacos de Canarias.

Fama Platas	165mm/6 1/2 ins x 16.3mm/41
Gran Fama	165mm/6 1/2 ins x 16.3mm/41
Fama Coronas	130mm/5 1/8 ins x 15.9mm/40

MONTE CANARIO

Hand-made. Imported into USA by Marcas Miguel Tobacco, Dallas, Texas.

Nuncios	171mm/6 3/4 ins x 17.5mm/44
Imperiales	165mm/6 1/2 ins x 16.67mm/42
No 3	146mm/5 3/4 ins x 16.67mm/42
Panetelas	152mm/6 ins x 15.1mm/38

OH QUE BUENO

Hand-made. Connecticut wrapper. Indonesian binder. Filler, blend of tobacco from Dominican Rep. and Brazil.

No 1	178mm/7 ins x 16.3mm/41
Corona	133mm/5 1/4 ins x 16.3mm/41

PENAMIL

Hand-made. Cameroon wrapper. Dominican binder. Filler blend from Dominican Rep., Mexico and Brazil. Distributed in USA by Swisher Intl.

No 5	143mm/5 1/3 ins × 16.27mm/41
No 6	149mm/5 7/8 ins × 16.27mm/41
No 16	181mm/7 1/8 ins × 152mm/38
No 17	169mm/6 2/3 ins × 16.27mm/41
No 18	181mm/7 1/8 ins × 17.46mm/44
No 25	190mm/7 1/2 ins × 17.86mm/45
No 30	195mm/7 2/3 ins × 17.86mm/45
No 50	153mm/6 ins × 19.84mm/50
No 57	190mm/7 1/2 ins × 19.84mm/50

COSTA RICA

BAHIA

Hand-made. Quality: superior. Nicaraguan tobacco. Distributed by Tony Borhani Cigars.

Double Corona	216mm/8 1/2 ins x 19.8mm/50
Churchill	175mm/6 7/8 ins x 19.1mm/48
Esplendido	152mm/6 ins x 19.8mm/50
Robusto	127mm/5 ins x 19.8mm/50
No 3	152mm/6 ins x 18.3mm/46
No 4	140mm/5 1/2 ins x 16.67mm/42

FLORENTINO
Hand-made. Distributed in USA by Arango Cigar.

Viajante	209mm/8 1/4 ins × 19.84mm/50
Churchill	178mm/7 ins × 19.05mm/48
No 1	178mm/7 ins × 17.46mm/44
No 2	152mm/6 ins × 17.46mm/44
Toro	152mm/6 ins × 19.84mm/50
Presidente	190mm/7 1/2 ins × 19.84mm/50

PINTOR

Viajante
Churchill
No 1
No 2
No 4
No 5
No 6

DENMARK

Denmark is largest consumer of cigars per capita in the world.

CHRISTIAN OF DENMARK
Machine-made. Dry cigars. Dominican, Java and Brazil filler. Java binder and Sumatran wrapper.

Mini Cigarillos****	89mm/3 1/2 ins
Smooth. Plenty of flavour. Well-made cigarillo.	
Long Cigarillos	102mm/4 ins
Midi	95mm/3 3/4 ins

DAVIDOFF CIGARILLOS
Machine-made. Superior quality. All tobacco.

Davidoff Mini Cigarillos****	88mm/3 1/2 ins
Rich, smooth, elegant.	
Davidoff Mini Light****	88mm/3 1/2 ins
Mild, good flavour, smooth, elegant.	
Davidoff Long Cigarillos	114mm/4 1/2 ins

NOBEL CIGARS

Largest cigar maker in Europe. Launched in 1898. Sold

400 million cigars (all brands) in 1990/91. Machine-made. (Dry cigars).

Petit Sumatra★★★★   89mm/3 1/2 ins
Rich, full flavoured, smooth. Elegant.
Medium Panetela Sumatra
                      89mm/3 1/2 ins × 8.73mm/22
Grand Panetela Sumatra
                      140mm/5 1/2 ins × 11.11mm/28
Petit Corona   95mm/3 3/4 ins × 12.70mm/32
Petit Lights   89mm/3 1/2 ins

DOMINICAN REPUBLIC

The Dominican Republic has become the largest seller of premium cigars to the United States, exporting in 1994 around 67 million cigars. Figure for first five months of 1995 was 30.47 million.

After Fidel Castro came to power in Cuba in 1959, later expropriating businesses, many previous owners fled with little or no possessions except Cuban seed tobacco, to various countries which they thought had similar soil and climatic conditions to those of Cuba. Such countries included Honduras, Nicaragua, Dominican Republic, Jamaica and even the Canary Islands.

In the 1960s and 1970s, there was little development in the Dominican cigar industry, until in 1976 the American company General Cigar, established a leaf processing facility for all types of leaves, particularly wrappers. The Dominican Republic previously exported about five million cigars to the United States. When General Cigar became a fully-fledged cigar manufacturing operation in 1979, these exports rose to 11 million.

Between 1979 and 1981 the other American giant, Consolidated Cigar, moved its activities from the Canary Islands to La Romana on the Dominican Republic's south east coast, and sales to the United States then exploded to 33 million cigars.

During this period the country changed from a tobacco processor to a producer of premium, hand-rolled cigars and started to gain a reputation as important supplier of quality hand-made products.

In 1995 the Dominican Republic exported almost 83 million cigars to the United States, this accounting for an estimated 43 percent of imports into the USA of premium cigars. Main tobacco growing area is Cibao River Valley, close to capital Santiago. Other important tobacco growing area is Real Valley. The island's tropical climate, predominantly hot days and high humidity, as well as its fertile soil, is ideal for growing tobacco.

Despite the Dominican Republic's importance as a producer of filler and binder tobacco leaf, the country continues to import such leaf from Cameroun and Nicaragua while leaf for wrappers is bought from Cameroun, Connecticut in the United States, Ecuador and Mexico. In 1980s unsuccessful attempts were made to grow wrappers from Connecticut wrapper seed. However, in 1992 Carlos Fuente Jr., son of legendary Carlos Fuente Sr., started growing good quality shade wrapper from Cuban seed.

In Cuba the *torcedor* or cigar roller, combines the different leaves to form the filler, before rolling it in a binder and then applying the delicate wrapper.

In the Dominican Republic workers, called bunchers, roll the binder around the filler to create the bunch for the *torcedor* or roller to apply the wrapper and thus finish the cigar. In some factories a team consists of three rollers to two bunchers. In Consolidated Cigar factory teams comprise six rollers and four bunchers.

Strict quality control is employed in most Dominican factories. Many smokers do not believe any non-Cuban cigar can compete with Havanas. There is certainly a difference in taste, with Dominicans being, generally, milder than Havanas. However, the local industry is striving to improve the tobacco it uses, by experimenting with different combinations of imported leaf to provide the best flavour.

As mentioned under "Strength of Different Tobacco" in the chapter on "Smoking for Pleasure" tobacco from the Dominican Republic could be described as smooth, honeyed, earthy, floral and spicy flavours, mild and slow burning. It is popular in the USA and probably rates in strength, on a scale from one to five, as a two or three.

Main producers are: Tabacalera Arturo Fuente, making about 28 million cigars annually (Arturo Fuente, Ashton, Cuesta Rey, Don Carlos, Hemingway, Opus, La Unica); Consolidated Cigars, about 35 million (Don Diego, Flamenco, Henry Clay, H. Upmann, La Corona, Nat Sherman, Primo Del Rey, Santa Diamiana); General Cigar, about 16 million (Canaria D'Oro, Macanudo Partagas, Temple Hall, Ramon Allones; MATASA, about six and a half million (Jose Benito, JR, Romeo & Julietta); Tabacos Dominicanos, about nine million

(Avo, Davidoff, Griffin's, PG, Troya). The brands shown are those owned by the respective producers as well as private labels and is not exhaustive.

ADANTE
Hand-made. Short filler. Mexican wrapper. Binder and filler from Dominican Rep. Mild. Distributed in USA by Lignun-2 Inc.

No 405 Petit Corona	113mm/4 1/2 ins × 16.67mm/42
No 504 Corona	140mm/5 1/2 ins × 16.67mm/42
No 603 Palma Fina	160mm/6 1/4 ins × 13.49mm/34
No 702 Cetro	152mm/6 ins × 16.67mm/42
No 801 Elegante	168mm/6 5/8 ins × 17.07mm/43

AGUILA
Hand-made. Connecticut shade wrapper. Dominican binder and filler. Distributed in USA by F&K Cigar.

Coronita	140mm/5 1/2 ins × 15.87mm/40
Brevas 44	190mm/7 1/2 ins × 17.46mm/44
Brevas 46	165mm/6 1/2 ins × 18.26mm/46
Brevas 49	178mm/7 ins × 19.84mm/50
Brevas 50	190mm/7 1/2 ins × 19.84mm/50
Petit Gordo	120mm/4 3/4 ins × 19.84mm/50

ANDUJAR
Hand-made. Connecticut shade wrapper. Dominican binder and filler.

Samana	152mm/6 ins × 15.08mm/38
Vega	127mm/5 ins × 19.84mm/50
Azuo	228mm/9 ins × 18.26mm/46
Macorix	165mm/6 1/2 ins × 17.46mm/44
Romana	127mm/5 ins × 9.92mm/25
Santiago	190mm/7 1/2 ins × 19.84mm/50

ARTURO FUENTE
Hand-made. Cameroun wrapper. Quality: superior. Binder and filler from Dominican Republic, Brazil, Mexico and Nicaragua. There is also a range of machine cigars made in Tampa, Florida. Medium to full flavoured. Good value. Old-established tobacco family which since 1900, has owned factories in Tampa, Honduras, and Nicaragua and now for the past 15 years in Dominican Republic.

While I was in the United States, the industry was full of news of destruction by fire of one of family's tobacco warehouses—the sixth fire in their history. Third factory planned to open in 1995. In 1995 had 85 acres under cultivation, with option to buy another 25-acre farm. In 1994 sold over 10 million cigars across Arturo Fuente range. Same year family exported over 24 million cigars spread over seven brands.

Sold about 10 million Arturo Fuente cigars in 1994. Price range $1-95 to $3+. Late 1995, early 1996 plan to introduce series with Conecticut shade wrapper. Distributed in USA by FANCO, a joint venture between Fuente family and Newman family's M&N, whose main brand is Cuesta Rey.

One of few manufacturers who use as many as four different types of tobacco in their filler blends. Each cigar model has a different blend.

Hemingway Masterpiece★★★★★
228mm/9 ins × 20.64mm/52
Figurado shape. Dark oily wrapper. Full-bodied. Spicy with coffee undertones. Rich. Cigar for special occasion.

Hemingway Classic★★★★   178mm/7 ins × 19.05mm/48
Figurado shape. Meduim bodied. Good flavour and balance between strength and flavour. Good daytime smoke. For connoisseur and novice alike.

Hemingway Signature★★★★★
152mm/6 ins × 18.65mm/47
Figurado shape. Dark oily wrapper. Smooth. Spicy with leathery undertones. Wonderful smoke.

Hemingway Short Story★★★★★
102mm/4 ins × 17.86mm/45
Figurado shape. Meduim to full-bodied. Rich. Spicy, coffee flavours. Well-made. Hedonistic delight.

Chateau Fuente Royal Salute
193mm/7 5/8 ins × 21.43mm/54

Canones   216mm/8 1/2 ins × 20.64mm/52

Double Chateau Fuente★★★★★
172mm/6 3/4 ins × 19.84mm/50
Meduim to full-bodied. Spicy. Cool. Good balance cigar for connoisseur. Well-made. After dinner smoke.

Dantes★★★★★   178mm/7 ins × 19.84mm/50
Dark oily wrapper. Packs plenty of punch and flavour. Long finish. Ideal after dinner cigar.

Churchill★★★★   184mm/7 1/4 ins × 19.05mm/48
Rich, full flavour. Meduim bodied. Spicy with touch of coffee. Good after lunch cigar.

Corona Imperial★★★★   165mm/6 1/2 ins × 19.05mm/46
Slightly hard draw. Good burning qualities. Medium strength. Integrated herbasceous aromas. Well-made.

Flor Fina 8-5-8★★★★   152mm/6 ins × 18.65mm/47
Subtle aroma. Spicy. Touch of sweetness. Mild. Dry

finish. Good burning. Well-made.
Chateau Fuente★★★★   113mm/4 1/2 ins × 19.84mm/50
Woody. Spicy. Elegant. Good daytime smoke.
Cuban Corona   133mm/5 1/4 ins × 17.86mm/45
Seleccion Privada No.1

172mm/6 3/4 ins × 17.46mm/44
Don Carlos Robusto★★★★★

127mm/5 ins × 19.84mm/50
Dark oily wrapper. Full-bodied. Rich, spicy. Well-made.
Delight to smoke after dinner.
Rothschild   113mm/4 1/2 ins × 19.84mm/50
Panetela Fina★★★★   178mm/7 ins × 15.08mm/38
Meduim-bodied. Good balance and finish. Daytime
smoke.
Spanish Lonsdale ★★★★★

165mm/6 1/2 ins × 16.67mm/42
Dark oily wrapper. Rich. Smooth. Firm draw.
Herbasceous, spicy flavours. Well-made.
Petit Corona★★★★   127mm/5 ins × 15.08mm/38
Firm draw. Good burning. Smooth. Hint of sweetness.
Well-made. Daytime smoke.
Fumas★★★★   178mm/7 ins × 17.46mm/44
Meduim strength. Full flavours. Slightly spicy. Extra
girth improves draw.
Curley Head Deluxe   165mm/6 1/2 ins × 17.07mm/43
Curley Head   165mm/6 1/2 ins × 17.07mm/43
Don Carlos No 3★★★★ 140mm/5 1/2 ins × 17.46mm/44
Dark oily wrapper. Meduim to full-bodied. Smooth.
Good daytime smoke.
Brevas Royale★★★★   140mm/5 1/2 ins × 16.67mm/42
Well-made. Smooth. Spicy. Good daytime smoke.

ASHTON
Hand-made. Quality: superior. Connecticut shade
wrapper. Cuban seed, Dominican binder and fillers.
Mild and aromatic. Launched in 1985. Owned by
Ashton Products.
Churchill   190mm/7 1/2 ins × 20.64mm/52
Prime Minister   175mm/6 7/8 ins × 19.05mm/48
8-9-8   165mm/6 1/2 ins × 17.46mm/44
Panetela   127mm/6 ins × 14.29mm/36
Corona   140mm/5 1/2 ins × 17.46mm/44
Cordial   127mm/5 ins × 12.00mm/30
Magnum   127mm/5 ins × 19.84mm/50
Elegante   165mm/6 1/2 ins × 35

ASHTON AGED MADURO
Hand-made.

No 60	190mm/7 1/2 ins × 20.64mm/52
No 50	178mm/7 ins × 19.05mm/48
No 40	152mm/6 ins × 19.84mm/50
No 30	172mm/6 3/4 ins × 17.46mm/44
No 20	140mm/5 1/2 ins × 17.46mm/44

ASHTON CABINET SELECTION (Vintage Limited Edition).
Hand-made. Selected Connecticut shade wrapper. Aged for one year. All are shaped cigars featuring a rounded head and Perfecto-style foot. Among best of vintage cigars. Introduced in 1988.
Cabinet

No 1	228mm/9 ins × 20.64mm/52
No 2	178mm/7 ins × 18.26mm/46
No 3	152mm/6 ins × 18.26mm/46

ASHTON EUROPE CIGARS

Petit	79mm/3 1/8 ins Cigarillo
Coronita	82mm/3 1/4 ins × 12.00mm/30
Senorita	89mm/3 1/2 ins × 12.00mm/30
Dutch Corona	111mm/4 3/8 ins × 13.89mm/35
Royal	147mm/5 3/4 ins × 16.67mm/42

AVO
Hand-made. Quality: superior. Connecticut shade wrapper. Cuban seed binder. Filler is blend of four tobaccos. Elegant pale pink, gold, black and white band. Made by Tabacos Dominicanos.

These cigars were created by a renowned musician Avo Uvezian. While a young man was official pianist to the late Shah of Iran. Imported and distributed exclusively internationally by Davidoff of Geneva. Sold over 1.4 million cigars in 1995.

Avo No 1★★★★   172mm/6 3/4 ins × 16.67mm/42
A good example of lonsdale shape. Ideal to follow a meal.
Avo No 2★★★★   152mm/6 ins × 19.84mm/50
Well-made. Good flavour. Long finish. Daytime smoke.
Avo No 3★★★★   190mm/7 1/2 ins × 20.64mm/52
Good wrapper. Spicy with dusty finish.
Avo No 4★★★   198mm/7 ins × 15.08mm/38
Hard draw, difficult burning qualities. Harsh finish.

Avo No 5	172mm/6 3/4 ins × 18.26mm/46
Avo No 6	165mm/6 1/2 ins × 14.29mm/36
Avo No 7	152mm/6 ins × 17.46mm/44

Avo No 8   133mm/5 1/2 ins × 15.87mm/40
Avo No 9   120mm/4 3/4 ins × 19.05mm/48
Especiales   223mm/8 ins × 19.05mm/48
Pyramide★★★★   178mm/7 ins × 21.43mm/54
Well-made. Spicy, leathery flavours. Meduim-bodied.
Satisfying. A cigar for special occassion.
Belicoso   152mm/6 ins × 19.84mm/50
Petit Belicoso   120mm/4 3/4 ins × 19.84mm/50

AVO "XO"
Hand-made. Quality: superior. Connecticut shade
wrapper. Cuban seed binder. Filler is blend of four
tobaccos. Elegant peach, gold, black and white band.
Imported and distributed exclusively innternationally by
Davidoff of Geneva.
Maestoso★★★★   178mm/7 ins × 19.05mm/48
Medium-bodied. Smooth. Spicy, leathery. Dayting
smoke or to follow light lunch.
Fantasia★★★★   152mm/6 ins × 20.64mm/52
Full-bodied. Spicy earthy flavours. Well made. Cigar for
special occasion.
Preludio★★★★★   152mm/6 ins × 15.87mm/40
Full-bodied. Good balance between strength and
flavour. Integrated. Spicy, herbascious aroma. Good
daytime cigar or to follow meal. Cigar for the connois-
seur.
Notturno   152mm/6 ins × 17.46mm/44
Intermezzo   140mm/5 1/2 ins × 19.84mm/50
Allegro   127mm/5 ins × 15.08mm/38
Serenata   114mm/4 1/2 ins × 13.5mm/34

BAUZA
Hand-made. Quality: superior. Made by Tabacalera A
Fuente. Owned by Mike's Cigars, Miami, USA. Named
after Cuban born owner, Oscar Boruchin. Cameroon
wrappers. Mexican binder. Medium-bodied. Premium
priced.
Fabulosos   190mm/7 1/2 ins × 19.84mm/50
Grecos★★★★★   140mm/5 1/2 ins × 16.67mm/42
Dark brown, oily wrapper. Good flavour. Smooth. Cigar
for connoisseur.
Jaguar★★★★★   165mm/6 1/2 ins × 16.67mm/42
Medium to full-bodied. Rich, spicy.
Casa Grande★★★★★   172mm/6 3/4 ins × 19.05mm/48
Full flavours. Hint of coffee. Good finish.
Florete★★★   175mm/6 7/8 ins × 13.89mm/35
Hard to draw. Touch of spice on palate. Slightly harsh
burn.

Petit Corona   127mm/5 ins × 15.08mm/38
Robusto★★★★★   140mm/5 1/2 ins × 19.84mm/50
Beautiful natural maduro oily, smooth wrapper. Lots of
flavour. Touch of cinamon. More flavour than normally
associated with Dom. Republic. New style.
Presidente   190mm/7 1/2 ins × 19.84mm/50
Medalla d'Oro No 1   175mm/6 7/8 ins × 17.46mm/44

BUTERA ROYAL VINTAGE
Hand-made. Connecticut wrapper. Binder from Dominican Republic. Owned by Butera Pipe Co.

Bravo Corto   113mm/4 1/2 ins × 19.84mm/50
Cetro Fino   165mm/6 1/2 ins × 17.46mm/44
Dorado 652   152mm/6 ins × 20.64mm/52
Capo Grande   190mm/7 1/2 ins × 19.05mm/48

BUTERA ROYAL VINTAGE
Hand-made. Connecticut shade wrapper. Dominican
binder and filler. Owned by Butera Pipe Co.
Bravo Corto   114mm/4 1/2 ins × 19.8mm/50
Cedro Fino   165mm/6 1/2 ins × 17.5mm/44
Dorado 652   152mm/6 ins × 20.6mm/52
Capo Grande   190mm/7 1/2 ins × 19.1mm/48
Fumo Dolce   140mm/5 1/2 ins × 17.5mm/44
Mira Bella   171mm/6 3/4 ins × 15.1mm/38

CABALLEROS
Hand-made with distinctive dark Connecticut wrappers.
Churchill   178mm/7 ins × 19.84mm/50
Rothschild   127mm/5 ins × 19.84mm/50
Petit Corona   140mm/5 1/2 ins × 16.67mm/42
Corona   147mm/5 3/4 ins × 17.07mm/43
Double Corona   172mm/6 3/4 ins × 19.05mm/48

CABANAS
Hand-made by Consolidated Cigar. Connecticut shade
wrapper. Binder and filler from Domincan Republic.
Exquisitos   165mm/6 1/2 ins × 19.05mm/48
Corona Grande   152mm/6 ins × 19.05mm/48
Premier   168mm/6 5/8 ins × 16.67mm/42
Lonsdale   168mm/6 5/8 ins × 16.67mm/42
Corona   140mm/5 1/2 ins × 16.67mm/42
Royale★★★★   143mm/5 5/8 ins × 18.26mm/46
Medium-bodied. Earthy. Lacks sublety.

CACIQUE
Hand-made. Available with Connecticut and Cameroon
wrappers. Owned by Tropical Tobacco.
Jaragua   172mm/6 3/4 ins × 14.29mm/36

Tainos	152mm/6 ins × 16.67mm/42
Siboneyes	172mm/6 3/4 ins × 17.07mm/43
Caribes	175mm/6 7/8 ins × 18.26mm/46
Incas	178mm/7 1/2 ins × 20.64mm/50
*Azteca	120mm/4 3/4 ins × 20.64mm/50
**Apache	152mm/6 ins × 20.64mm/50

*Available in maduro wrapper only.
**Available in maduro and Connecticut wrapper.

CANARIA D'ORA

Hand-made. Quality: superior. Cameroun wrapper. Dominican, Jamaican and Mexican filler and binder. Light, sweet tasting. Owned by General Cigar.

Supremos★★★★★   178mm/7 ins × 17.86mm/45
Slow, even burning. Spicy with honeyed undertones. Medium to full-bodied. Ideal to follow meal that is not too spicy.

Lonsdale★★★   165mm/6 1/2 ins × 16.67mm/42
One dimensional. Slightly harsh and becomes bitter towards the end. Medium-bodied, vegetal finish on palate.

Fino★★   152mm/6 ins × 12.30mm/31
Medium to full-bodied. Not size for inexperienced smoker. Becomes tiring to smoke.

Immensos★★★★★   140mm/5 1/2 ins × 19.45mm/49
Smooth silky claro wrapper. Multi-layered flavours with honeyed undertones. Smooth. Ideal to follow meal.

Corona★★★★   140mm/5 1/2 ins × 16.67mm/42
Smooth, oily claro wrapper. Mild. Flavour little one dimensional.

Rothschild★★★   108mm/4 1/2 ins × 19.84mm/50
Maduro, almost oscuro wrapper. Slow, even burn. Honeyed overtones on palate. Surprisingly dull finish for this size.

Babies★   108mm/4 1/2 ins × 12.70mm/32
Hard draw. Little flavour.

Vista   160mm/6 1/4 ins × 12.70mm/32

CARLOS TORAÑO

Hand-made. Connecticut shade wrapper. Dominican filler and binder. Available in Europe and USA. Owned by Toraño Cigars, Miami.

Carlos I	152mm/6 ins × 19.8mm/50
Carlos II	171mm/6 3/4 ins × 17.1mm/43
Carlos III	191mm/7 1/2 ins × 20.6mm/52
Carlos IV	146mm/5 3/4 ins × 17.1mm/43
Carlos V	152mm/6 ins × 18.3mm/46
Carlos VI	178mm/7 ins × 19.1mm/48

| Carlos VII | 121mm/4 3/4 ins × 20.6mm/52 |
| Carlos VIII | 165mm/6 1/2 ins × 14.3mm/36 |

CARRINGTON

Hand-made. Quality: superior. Connecticut shade warpper. Dominican binder and filler. Made by Tobacos Dominicas for House of Oxford.

| I | 190mm/7 1/2 ins × 19.8mm/50 |
| II★★★★ | 152mm/6 ins × 16.67mm/42 |

Medium-bodied. Spicy. Smooth and creamy.

III	178mm/7 ins × 14.3mm/36
IV	140mm/5 1/2 ins × 15.9mm/40
V★★★★	175mm/6⅞ ins × 18.3mm/46

Good draw. Burns evenly. Ash tends to fall off easily. Touch of cinamon. Ideal for beginners.

| VI★★★★ | 114mm/4 1/2 ins × 19.8mm/50 |

Good texture. Subtle. Mild to medium-bodied. Well made. Daytime smoke.

| VII | 152mm/6 ins × 19.8mm/50 |
| VIII (pyramid) | 175mm/6⅞ ins × 23.8mm/60. |

Note the gigantic ring gauge.

CASA BLANCA

Hand-made. Quality: superior. Connecticut shade and maduro wrappers. Filler both from Dominican Republic and Brazil. Binder is Mexican. Originally created for use in US White House and was the cigar offered at the inauguration dinner of Ronald Reagan. Jeroboam and Half Jeroboam have massive 66 ring gauges. Exclusive to Santa Clara, N.A.

| *Jeroboam★★★ | 254mm/10 ins × 26.19mm/66 |

Because of size most smokers would find this too tiring to finish. Smooth.

*Half Jeroboam	127mm/5 ins × 26.19mm/66
*Magnum	178mm/7 ins × 23.81mm/60
*Presidente	190mm/7 1/2 ins × 19.84mm/50
*De Luxe	152mm/6 ins × 19.84mm/50
*Lonsdale★★★★	165mm/6 1/2 ins × 16.67mm/42

Easy draw. Even burn. Mild to medium-bodied.

| Corona★★★★ | 140mm/5 1/2 ins × 16.67mm/42 |

Good oily wrapper. Herbaceous. Smooth. Good cigar for beginner.

| Panetela | 152mm/6 ins × 14.29mm/36 |
| Bonita | 102mm/4 ins × 14.29mm/36 |

*Also available in maduro wrapper.

CASA MARTIN

Hand-made bundles. Available with Cameroon and

Connecticut wrapper. Owned by Tropical Tobacco.
Named after owner, Pedro Martin.

Petit Coronas	133mm/5 1/2 ins × 16.67mm/42
Seleccion Especial	172mm/6 3/4 ins × 14.29mm/36
Regulares	152mm/6 ins × 17.07mm/43
Numero Uno Plus	172mm/6 3/4 ins × 17.46mm/44
Matador	152mm/6 ins × 19.84mm/50
Majestad	190mm/7 1/2 ins × 19.84mm/50
*Fumas	178mm/7 ins × 17.46mm/44
*Cazadores	160mm/6 1/4 ins × 17.46mm/44
*Grandes	181mm/7 1/2 ins × 15.87mm/48
*Emperador	203mm/8 ins × 19.84mm/50
Numero Cuatro	133mm/5 1/2 ins × 16.67mm/42
Pinceles	178mm/7 ins × 12.00mm/30
Palma Fina	178mm/7 ins × 14.29mm/36
Numero Dos	147mm/5 3/4 ins × 16.67mm/42
Cetros	152mm/6 ins × 17.46mm/44
Rothschild	120mm/4 3/4 ins × 19.84mm/50
Numero Uno	172mm/6 3/4 ins × 17.07mm/43
Toros	152mm/6 ins × 19.84mm/50
Churchills	175mm/6 7/8 ins × 18.26mm/46
Presidentes	190mm/7 1/2 ins × 19.84mm/50
Viajantes	216mm/8 1/2 ins × 20.24mm/52

*Short filler.

CHAIRMAN'S RESERVE by H. Upmann
Hand-made. Quality: superior. Launched towards end
1996. Made by Consolidated Cigar. Super premium
line.

Torpedo	
Robusto	121mm/4 3/4 ins × 19.84mm/50
Churchill	171mm/6 3/4 ins × 19.1mm/48
Double Corona	178mm/7 ins × 19.84mm/50

CHAMBRAIR
Hand-made. Quality: superior. Made specially for restaurants in Germany.

Ceremonial★★★   190.5mm/7 1/2 ins × 19.7mm/50
Comment: Mild and aromatic. Palate slightly sweet.

Elite★★★★   184.0mm/7 1/4 ins × 18.9mm/48
Comment: Rich and full-bodied flavour.
Moreau★★★★
Comment: Dark wrappers. Full-bodied and herbacious
flavours.
Elegance★★★★   171.5mm/6 3/4 ins × 17.30mm/43
Comment: Tightly rolled. For the experienced smoker.
Plaisir★★★★   171.5mm/6 3/4 ins × 13.80mm/35

Comment: Has character and powerful flavours. For the experienced smoker.

Faible★★★ 139.7mm/5 1/2 ins × 16.90mm/43

Comment: Mild & elegant. Ideal for beginners.

Finesse★★★ 127.0mm/5 ins × 11.80mm/28

Comment: Very light with finesse. Cigar for ladies and beginners.

Mademoiselles★★★★
124.0mm/ 4 13/16 ins × 8.00mm/20

Comment: Blend of four different tobaccos. Mild with herbaceous flavour. The name suggests it is made for ladies.

CIBAO
Hand-made. Distributed in USA by Indian Head Sales.

Magnum	254mm/10 ins × 19.84mm/50
Especiales	203mm/8 ins × 19.84mm/50
Piramid	178mm/7 ins × 21.4mm/54
Elegantes	178mm/7 ins × 17.46mm/44
Diamates	165mm/6 1/2 ins × 13.89mm/35
Churchills	172mm/6 3/4 ins × 18.26mm/46
Brevas	133mm/5 1/4 ins × 19.84mm/50
Corona Deluxe	140mm/5 1/2 ins × 17.07mm/43

COHIBA
Hand-made, by General Cigars. Not yet widely available. Same name as flagship brand made in Cuba. Dominican version unbanded.

Robusto	140mm/5 1/2 ins × 19.84mm/50
Corona Especiale	165mm/6 1/2 ins × 16.67mm/42
Esplendido	178mm/7 ins × 19.45mm/149

CONNISSEUR SILVER LABEL
Hand-made. Bundles. Honduran wrapper. Distributed in USA by Indian Head Sales.

Corona	133mm/5 1/4 ins × 17.07mm/43
Brevas	152mm/6 ins × 19.84mm/50
Elegantes	178mm/7 ins × 17.46mm/44
Especiales	203mm/8 ins × 19.84mm/50
Diamantes	228mm/7 ins × 13.89mm/35
Churchills	190mm/7 1/2 ins × 19.84mm/50

CREDO DOMINICAN
Hand-made. Connecticut shade wrapper. Binder is aged Dominican leaf. Filler is blend of Dominican Olor and Piloto Cuban leaf for medium strength. Owned by Credo and distributed exclusively in USA by Hollco Rohr.

Pythagoras   178mm/7 ins × 21.43mm/50
Magnificent   175mm/6 7/8 ins × 18.26mm/46
Arcane   127mm/5 ins × 19.84mm/50
Anthanor★★★★   147mm/5 3/4 ins × 16.67mm/42
Easy draw. Even burn. Medium-bodied. Good early morning smoke or ideal for casual smoker.
Jubilate   127mm/5 ins × 13.49mm/34

CUBITA
Created for European market, where smokers prefer full body and rich aroma. Connecticut wraper. Binder and filler from Dominican Republic. Made by MATASA. Distributed in USA by S.A.G. Imports.

$2000   178mm/7 ins × 19.84mm/50
$8-9-8   172mm/6 3/4 ins × 17.07/43
$500   133mm/5 1/2 ins × 17.07mm/43
$1   223mm/8 ins × 15.08mm/38

CUESTA-REY CABINET SELECTION
Hand-made. Quality: superior. Mild. Founded in 1884 by Angel LaMadrid Cuesta, Spanish cigar maker who did apprenticeship in Cuba. Partner was Peregrino Rey. Then owners' surnames provided name of company. In 1985 bought by Newman family's M&N company in USA. In 1995 celebrated 100th anniversary; marked by launch of new brand, Diamond Crown. M&N first US company to wrap cigars in cellophane. Made by Tabacalera Arturo Fuente. Available in both light-natural and maduro wrapper.
Cabinet No 1884   172mm/6 3/4 ins × 17.46mm/44
Cabinet No 95★★★★   160mm/6 1/4 ins × 16.67mm/42
Mild. Well-balanced. Elegant. Good daytime.
Cabinet No 898   178mm/7 ins × 19.84mm/50
Cabinet No 2   178mm/7 ins × 14.29mm/36

CUESTA-REY CENTENNIAL COLLECTION
Hand-made. Quality: superior. Owned by Newman family's M&N company in USA. Made by Tabacalera Arturo Fuente.
Dominican No 1   216mm/8 1/2 ins × 20.64mm/52
Dominican No 2★★★★   184mm/7 1/4 ins × 19.05mm/48
Easy draw. Even burn. Medium-bodied. Smooth. Elegant, although finishes rather flat. Daytime smoke. Ideal for occasional smoker.
Dominican No 3   178mm/7 ins × 14.29mm/36
Dominican No 4★★★★   165mm/6 1/2 ins × 16.67mm/42
Easy draw. Medium-bodied. Spicy with touch of coffee. Good balance between strength and flavour.

Dominican No 5   133mm/5 1/2 ins × 17.07mm/43
Dominican No 7   114.3mm/4 1/2 ins × 19.8mm/50
Dominican No 60   152.4mm/6 ins × 19.8mm/50
Captiva (aluminium tube)
                157mm/6 3/16 ins × 16.67mm/42
Aristocrat (Glass Tubes)
                184mm/7 1/4 ins × 19.05mm/48
Rivera   177.8m/7 ins × 14.3mm/36
Individual   216mm/8 1/2 ins × 20.64mm/52
Cameo   107.9mm/4 1/4 ins × 12.7mm/32

DAVIDOFF
Hand-made. Quality: superior.
Range owned by Max Oettinger Company of Basel, Switzerland and made in Dominican Republic.

New milder Davidoffs, made in the Dominican Republic by Tabacos Dominicanos (Tabadom Factory) in Santiago, must be judged in their own right. Have Connecticut shade wrappers and Dominican filler leaves and are extremely well made. Range includes four different blends. Cigars aged at factory for three weeks before shipment. Have strict colour grade standards. Sell about six million cigars a year world-wide.

Davidoff, highly respected marque named, in 1969, after Zino Davidoff, doyen of cigar industry in Europe, and son of Henri Davidoff, cigarette maker and merchant who, in 1911, immigrated to Switzerland from Russia. Made in Cuba until 1992.

Young Zino grew up working in his father's tobacco store in Lausanne before going to tobacco plantations in Bahia, Brazil and Cuba, to gain practical experience in all aspects of cigar-making.

On return developed business, later opening shop on corner of Rue de Rive and Rue de La Fontaine in fashionable Geneva, which the Mecca of Europe's rich and famous.

In 1970 Zino Davidoff, then 65, sold to large import-export Max Oettinger Company based in Basel, Switzerland. This company founded in 1875 and one of earliest importers of cigars from Havana, Brazil and Jamaica into France, Germany and Switzerland.

Davidoff remained in business to assist Ernst Schneider, present head of company. Internationalised business by opening additional shops. Now has chain of 45 stores (some corporate owned, some franchised). Davidoff range of cigars, bearing famous white and gold band, synonymous with top-quality, vying with

Montecristo and later Cohiba. Some sizes were produced at prestigious El Laguito factory in Havana, but majority made at Hoyo De Monterrey factory.

During eighties, conflict developed between state-owned Cubatabaco and Davidoff over quality. This coincided with 1982 launch of Cohiba, first post-revolutionary truly Cuban quality cigar. Observers believe Cubans gave Cohiba brand priority to detriment of Davidoff range.

In 1990 Davidoff announced no further production in Cuba switching to Santiago in Dominican Republic.

Cubatabaco maintained it had right to use Davidoff name, but in 1991 court determined Cuban Davidoffs could only be sold until stocks exhausted and, in any event, no later than end of 1992.

This Cuban range has scarcity value and certain sizes can still be obtained most expensively from specialist cigar merchants in London and on Continent.

In 1983, Davidoff's Zino range, made in Honduras, launched in United States. (Listed in the Honduras section.)

Davidoff Aniversario No 1★★★★
220mm/8 2/3 ins × 19.05mm/48
Good draw with even burn. Mild. Smooth. Creamy. Early morning smoke.

Davidoff Aniversario No 2
178mm/7 ins × 19.05mm/48

Davidoff No 1	192mm/7 1/2 ins × 15.08mm/38
Davidoff No 2	152mm/6 ins × 15.08mm/38
Davidoff Tubos	152mm/6 ins × 15.08mm/38
Davidoff No 3	126mm/5 1/8 ins × 12.00mm/30

Davidoff Ambassadice
117mm/4 5/8 ins × 10.32mm/26

Davidoff Grand Cru No 1★★★★
155mm/6 3/32 ins × 16.67mm/42
Elegant. Mild to medium-bodied. Spicy. Well made. Daytime smoke.

Davidoff Grand Cru No 2
168mm/5 5/8 ins × 16.67mm/42

Davidoff Grand Cru No 3★★★★
127mm/5 ins × 16.67mm/42
Carries punch. Spicy with honeyed undertones on palate. After lunch cigar.

Davidoff Grand Cru No 4
117mm/4 5/8 ins × 15.87mm/40

Davidoff Grand Cru No 5 102mm/4 ins × 15.87mm/40

Davidoff 1000	117mm/4 5/8 ins × 13.49mm/34
Davidoff 2000	127mm/5 ins × 16.67mm/42
Davidoff 3000	178mm/7 ins × 13.10mm/33

Davidoff 4000★★★★★ 155mm/6 3/32 ins × 16.67mm/42
Beautiful oily wrapper. Slow burning. Spicy with touch of honey. Well made.

| Davidoff 5000 | 143mm/5 5/8 ins × 18.26mm/46 |

Davidoff Special "R" (Royal)
124mm/4 7/8 ins × 19.84mm/50

Davidoff Special "T" (torpedo)★★★★★
15.20mm/8 ins × 19.84mm/50
Slow burning smooth smoke. Benefits from thick girth. Wonderful intergrated aroma and flavours. Well-made cigar for connoisseur.

Davidoff Double "R"★★★★★
19.00mm/7 1/2 ins × 19.84mm/50
Beautiful colorado claro wrapper. Slow burning. Spicy herbascious aroma with honeyed undertones on palate. Complex and smooth. Great cigar to end wonderful meal or celebrate special occasion.

DIANA SILVIUS
Hand-made. Quality: superior. Connecticut shade wrapper. Dominican filler and binder. Mady by Tobacalera Fuente for Diana Silvius, Charasmatic owner of Up Down Tobacco Shop in Chicago.

Diana Churchill★★★★ 179mm/7 ins × 19.8mm/50
Medium to full-bodied. Flavour improves. Well balanced. To follow meal.

| Diana 2000 | 171mm/6 3/4 ins × 18.3mm/46 |
| Diana Corona | 165mm/6 1/2 ins × 16.67mm/42 |

Diana Robusto★★★★ 124mm/4 7/8 ins × 20.6mm/52
Needs 1/2 ins (1cm) to get benefit of its full flavour. An elegant cigar for the connoisseur. Daytime smoke or to follow lunch.

DIAMOND CROWN
Hand-made. Quality: superior. Five-year-old Connecticut shade wrapper. Dominican filler and binder. Up to seven leaves used in the filler. This blend took three years to perfect in creating full-flavoured cigars that are not too overpowering. Finished cigars are cedar-aged for 12 months. Relaunch of an old brand, to commemorate M & N's 100th anniversary in 1995. One of most expensive non-Cuban ranges on market. Made by Tobacatera Arturo Fuente. Owned by M & N.

| No 1 | 216mmmm/8 1/2 ins × 21.4mm/54 |
| No 2 | 191mm/7 1/2 ins × 21.4mm/54 |

No 3	165mm/6 1/2 ins × 21.4 mm/54
No 4	140mm/5 1/2 ins × 21.4mm/54
No 5	114mm/4 1/2 ins × 21.4mm/54

DOMINICAN ORIGINAL

Hand-made. Bundles. Connecticut shade wrapper. Dominican binder and filler. Exclusive to Mike's Cigars, Miami.

Minatures	108mm/4 1/4 ins × 12.7mm/32
Cetros	152mm/6 ins × 17.5mm/44
Churchill	175mm/6 7/8 ins × 18.3mm/46
Fat Tub	254mm/10 ins × 26.2mm/66
Gorilla	127mm/5 ins × 26.2mm/66
King Kong	216mm/8 1/2 ins × 20.6mm/52
Monster	178mm/7 ins × 23.8mm/60
No 1	165mm/6 1/2 ins × 16.67mm/42
No 2	140mm/5 1/2 ins × 16.67mm/42
Palma Fina	178mm/7 ins × 14.7mm/37
Piramides	152mm/6 ins × 22.2mm/56
Presidents	191mm/7 1/2 ins × 19.84mm/50
Robusto	114mm/4 1/2 ins × 19.84mm/50
Toro	152m/6 ins × 19.84mm/50
Torpedo	178mm/7 ins × 19.84mm/50

DOMINICAN PRIVATE STOCK

Hand-made. Exclusive to Brick-Hanauer Co.

Viajante	216mm/8 1/2 ins × 20.64mm/52
President	178mm/7 ins × 19.84mm/50
Toro	152mm/6 ins × 19.84mm/50
Elegante	178mm/7 ins × 17.07mm/43
Numero Uno	172mm/6 3/4 ins × 17.07mm/43
Cetros	152mm/6 ins × 17.07mm/43
Numero Cuatro	133mm/5 1/2 ins × 17.07mm/43
Palma Elite	178mm/7 ins × 15.08mm/38

Dominican Guarantee Seal

This brand is also provided with a private label, if required.

DOMINICANA SUPERBA

Hand-made bundles. Tobacco all from Dominican Republic. Exclusive to H. J. Bailey Co.

No 1	216mm/8 1/2 ins × 20.64mm/52
No 2	178mm/7 ins × 19.45mm/49
No 3	172mm/6 3/4 ins × 17.46mm/44
No 4	113mm/4 1/2 ins × 19.84mm/50
No 5	127mm/5 1/2 ins × 17.07mm/43
No 6	190mm/7 1/2 ins × 19.84mm/50

DOMINGOLD

Hand-made bundles. Cameroon wrapper. Connecticut binder and filler from Dominican Republic Packed 20 per bundle. Exclusive to Arango Cigar Co in Chicago.

Toro	152mm/6 ins × 19.84mm/50
Lonsdale	160mm/6 1/4 ins × 17.07mm/43
Rothschild	
Corona	140mm/5 1/2 ins × 17.07mm/43
President	152mm/6 ins × 18.26mm/46
Churchill	178mm/7 ins × 19.84mm/50

DOMINICAN ESTATES

Hand-made. Connecticut wrapper. Dominican filler. Mexican binder.

Double Corona	178mm/7 ins × 19.84mm/50
Corona Gorda	152mm/6 ins × 19.84mm/50
Lonsdale	165mm/6 1/2 ins × 17.1mm/43
Corona	140mm/5 1/2 ins × 17.1mm/43

DOMINICO

Hand-made bundles. Connecticut shade wrapper. Dominican binder and filler. Exclusive to Hollco-Rohr.

No 700	191mm/7 1/2 ins × 23.8mm/60
No 701	216mm/8 1/2 ins × 20.6mm/52
No 702	178mm/7 ins × 19.1mm/48
No 703	152mm/6 ins × 19.84mm/50
No 704	178mm/7 ins × 17.1mm/43
No 705	140mm/5 1/2 ins × 17.1mm/43
No 706	121mm/4 3/4 ins × 20.6mm/52

DON DIEGO

Hand-made. Connecticut shade wrappers on larger sizes. Cameroon wrappers on smaller sizes. Some sizes available in choice of double claro (AMS) or colorlab (EMS). Privados series more fully matured. Made by Consolidated Cigar. Cigars sold in Europe not same blends sold in USA.

Privada 1	172mm/6 3/4 ins × 17.07mm/43
Privada 2	168mm/6 5/8 ins × 19.84mm/50
Privada 3	168mm/6 5/8 ins × 15.08mm/38
Privada 4	147mm/5 3/4 ins × 16.67mm/42
Imperiale	168mm/6 5/8 ins × 18.26mm/46
Grandes	152mm/6 ins × 19.84mm/50
Monarch★★★★	178mm/7 1/4 ins × 18.26mm/46

Smooth, oily dark wrapper. Medium-bodied. Hint of coffee on palate. After dinner cigar for occasional smoker.

Amatista	149mm/5 7/8 ins × 15.87mm/40

Corona	143mm/5 5/8 ins × 16.67mm/42
Lonsdales	168mm/6 5/8 ins × 16.67mm/42
Amigos	165mm/6 1/2 ins × 14.29mm/36
Grecos	165mm/6 1/2 ins × 15.08mm/38
Royal Palmas★★★	155mm/6 1/8 ins × 14.29mm/36

Burns slightly hot causing some harshness. Good draw. Hint of coffee on palate.

Petit Corona	130mm/5 1/8 ins × 16.67mm/42
Corona Major	129mm/5 1/16 ins × 16.67mm/42
Pequenos No 100	113mm/4 1/2 ins × 19.84mm/50
Pequenos No 200	113mm/4 1/2 ins × 18.26mm/46
Pequenos No 300	113mm/4 1/2 ins × 16.67mm/42
Preludes	102mm/4 ins × 11.11mm/28
Amigos EMS	165mm/6 1/2 ins × 14.29mm/36
Babies SMS	129mm/5 1/16 ins × 13.10mm/33
Coronas Bravas	165mm/6 1/2 ins × 19.05mm/48
Coronas Major Tubes EMS	
	129mm/5 1/16 ins × 16.67mm/42
Coronas EMS/AMS	143mm/5 5/8 ins × 16.67mm/42
Coronas EMS	143mm/5 5/8 ins × 16.67mm/42
Grandes EMS	152mm/6 ins × 19.84mm/50
Grecos EMS	165mm/6 1/2 ins × 15.08mm/38
Imperial EMS	186mm/7 5/16 ins × 18.26mm/46
Lonsdales EMS/AMS	168mm/6 5/8 ins × 16.67mm/42
Monarchs Tubes EMS	184mm/7 1/4 ins × 18.26mm/46
Petit Coronas EMS/AMS	
	131mm/5 1/8 ins × 16.67mm/42
Preludes EMS	102mm/4 ins × 11.11mm/28
Royal Palmas Tubes EMS	
	155mm/6 1/8 ins × 14.29mm/36

DON ESTABAN
Hand-made bundles. In natural and maduro wrappers. Cameroon wrapper. Micon binder and filler blend of tobacco from Mexico and Dominican Republic. Exclusive to H. J. Bailey Co.

Churchill	175mm/6 7/8 ins × 19.05mm/48
Puritano	147mm/5 3/4 ins × 16.67mm/42
Selector	178mm/7 ins × 15.08mm/38
Elegante	172mm/6 3/4 ins × 16.67mm/42
Emperador	152mm/6 ins × 19.84mm/50
President	190mm/7 1/2 ins × 19.84mm/50

DON JULIO
Hand-made bundles. Connecticut wrapper. Binder and filler from Dominican Republic. Owned by Swisher Intl.

| Corona Deluxe | 147mm/5 3/4 ins × 17.07mm/43 |
| Fabulosos | 178mm/7 ins × 19.84mm/50 |

Miramar	147mm/5 3/4 ins × 17.07mm/43
Private Stock No 1	160mm/6 1/4 ins × 17.07mm/43
Supremos	172mm/6 3/4 ins × 15.10mm/38

DOM MARCUS

Hand-made. Connecticut wrapper. Dominican binder and filler. Old brand relaunched in 1995. Distributed by Phillips & King.

Coronas****	140mm/5 1/2 ins × 16.67mm/42

Medium-bodied. Rich flavour with hint of coffee. Well made.

Cetros	165mm/6 1/2 ins × 16.67mm/42
Naturals (tubed)	156mm/6 1/8 ins × 14.3mm/36
Double Corona	165mm/6 1/2 ins × 19.1mm/48
Toros	152mm/6 ins × 19.84mm/50
Torpedo	152mm/6 ins × 19.84mm/50
Monarch	178mm/7 ins × 18.3mm/46

DON MIGUEL

Hand-made. Sold only in Europe, although sales are not restricted. Made by Consolidated Cigars.

Lonsdale (No 1)	164mm/6 1/2 ins × 16.67mm/42
Tubos (Alum. Tube)	156mm/6 1/8 ins × 16.67mm/42
Corona (No 3)	140mm/5 1/2 ins × 16.67mm/42
Petit Corona (No 4)	131mm/5 1/6 ins × 16.67mm/42
Grecos	165mm/6 1/2 ins × 15.10mm/38

DON LEO

Hand-made. Quality: superior. All Dominican tobacco. Launched 1996. Made by a family of tobacco farmers, Puros de Villa Gonzalez, newest cigar factory in Santiago. Distributed by House of Oxford.

Cetro	165mm/6 1/2 ins × 17.5mm/44
Churchill	191mm/7 1/2 ins × 19.84mm/50
Corona	140mm/5 1/2 ins × 16.67mm/42
Robusto	114mm/4 1/2 ins × 19.84mm/50
Toro	152mm/6 ins × 19.84mm/50

DON VITO

Hand-made. All Dominican tobacco. Distributed by Marcos Miquel Tobacco, Dallas, Texas.

Troncas	203mm/8 ins × 19.84mm/50
Robusto	127mm/5 ins × 19.84mm/50
Virginianos	152mm/6 ins × 17.5mm/44
Lonsdale	171mm/6 3/4 ins × 16.67mm/42
Caobas	140mm/5 1/2 ins × 16.67mm/42
Padrinos	191mm/7 1/2 ins × 15.1mm/38
Alfonsitos	127mm/5 ins × 11.9mm/30

DUNHILL (VINTAGE)

Hand-made. Quality: superior. Long filler, Connecticut shade wrappers. Aged for at least 3 months before distribution. Well made, slow burning. Dominican Dunhills have a blue and white band.

All the tobacco comes from one year's harvest. Only good years are chosen. First vintage from 1986 crop went on sale in 1989. 1987 vintage sold from 1991. The 1989 vintage on sale from 1993. The current 1994 one in 1996. Limited stock still available for all vintages, except 1986.

Dunhill's also makes a hand-made range, with black bands, in the Canary Islands with Connecticut wrappers.

Brand made by Consolidated Cigar, distributed by Lane Ltd.

Cabreras (tubed)   178mm/7 ins × 19.05mm/48
Peravias (Churchill)★★★★★
                          178mm/7 ins × 19.84mm/50
(1987 vintage) Medium bodied. Smooth. An elegant cigar for the connoisseur.
Tabaras   140mm/5 1/2 ins × 16.67mm/42
Condados★★★★   152mm/6 ins × 19.05mm/48
Medium-bodied. Spicy. Smooth. Well made. Daytime smoke.
Diamantes (lonsdale) 168mm/6 5/8 ins × 16.67mm/42
Samanas (Especial)   165mm/6 1/2 ins × 15.08mm/38
Valverdes (corona)   140mm/5 1/2 ins × 16.67mm/42
Altimiras (tubed)★★★★★   127mm/5 ins × 19.05mm/48
(1989 vintage) Oily wrapper. Elegant, smooth. Earthy flavours. For discerning smoker.
Romanas (rothschild) 113mm/4 1/2 ins × 19.84mm/50
Fantinos (panetela)   178mm/7 ins × 11.11mm/28
Centenas★★★★★   152mm/6 ins × 19.84mm/50
(1994 vintage). Tapered with curly head. Good draw. Fine balance between strength and flavour. Well-made. Definitely for connoisseur.

EL SUBLIMADO

Hand-made. Quality: superior. Connecticut wrapper. Dominican binder and filler. Brand owned by young dynamic, Emmanuelle Marty, who brings femine flair to masculine world. Packed in elegant and distinctive off-white aluminium tube with green and gold band. Cognac-scented cigar, launched in 1993. Some people, including Churchill, follow practice of dipping end of cigar into glass of cognac. This inelegant practice dissolves some of the tar which has accumulated in the end of the cigar, damaging cognac's flavour, while smoke's taste remains unchanged. Many believe this is nothing more than sucking cognac from a cigar.

Some place a little cognac in their humidor, which does not appreciably alter the flavour when smoked.

Dipping leaves in cognac does affect tobacco flavours, while simple spraying has only ephemeral effect and, some believe, this does not develop desired synergy.

Therefore, patented method developed that blends flavours of tobacco and cognac, the one enhancing the other.

Cognac used is a 50-year-old "Noces d'Or" from Cognac A. Hardy & Co.

Torpedo★★★★★   178mm/7 ins × 21.43mm/54
Launched in 1995. Breaks new barriers. A stupendous cigar for the self-confident, unconventional smoker.
Churchill★★★★★   203mm/8 ins × 19.05mm/48
Mild. Smooth with distinctive character. Lots of flavour. Thicker girth of this size and Regordette does wonders. Most luxurious smoke.
Regordete★★★★★   113mm/4 1/2 ins × 19.84mm/50
Mellow with lots of distinctive flavour, but not dominated by cognac. For discerning smoker who knows what he likes and has self-confidence not to be dictated to by convention.
Corona★★★★   152mm/6 ins × 17.46mm/44
If any tighter would be hard to draw. Medium strength, smooth, good balance between strength and flavour. Cigar for discerning smoker. suffers by comparison to larger girth of other three models.

FIVE STAR SECONDS
Hand-made. Connecticut shade wrappers. Mild. Good value. Exclusive to Santa Clara NA.

No 100	165mm/6 1/2 ins × 17.46mm/44
No 200	152mm/6 ins × 17.46mm/44
No 300	140mm/5 1/2 ins × 17.46mm/44
No 400	178mm/7 ins × 19.84mm/50
No 500	152mm/6 ins × 19.84mm/50
No 600	152mm/6 ins × 13.49mm/34
No 700	127mm/5 ins × 19.84mm/50
No 800	216mm/8 1/2 ins × 20.64mm/52
No 900	172mm/6 3/4 ins × 13.49mm/34

FLAMENCO
Hand-made. Quality: superior. Not active brand but in
process of being revived. Production limited by manufacturing capacity. Made by Consolidated Cigars.

Brevas   141mm/5 9/16 ins × 16.67mm/42

FLOR DE ORLANDO
Hand-made bundles. Connecticut shade wrapper. Dominican filler and binder.

Emperador	197mm/7 3/4 ins × 19.84mm/50
Churchill	178mm/7 ins × 19.1mm/48
Governor	152mm/6 ins × 19.84mm/50
No 1	178mm/7 ins × 17.1mm/43
No 4	140mm/5 1/2 ins × 16.67mm/42
Corona	165mm/6 1/2 ins ×17.5mm/44
Panetela Extra	178mm/7 ins × 14.3mm/36
Panetela	140mm/5 1/2 ins × 13.5mm/34

FONSECA
Hand-made. Quality: superior. Cabinet selection ci-
gars. Uses Connecticut shade wrapper. Dominican
filler. Mexican binders. Owned by Manufactures de
Tabacos SA (MATASA). Same name as brand made in
Cuba, also famous Port house.

8-9-8   152mm/6 ins × 17.07mm/43
*7-9-9   165mm/6 1/2 ins × 18.26mm/46
*10-10★★★★   178mm/7 ins × 19.84mm/50
Medium-bodied. Smooth. Even burn, but fairly hard
draw. Daytime smoke.
*5-50★★★★★   127mm/5 ins × 19.84mm/50
Medium-bodied. Smooth. Coffee and honeyed
flavours. Well-made. Top cigar.
*2-2   108mm/4 1/4 ins × 15.87mm/40
Triangular★★★★★   133mm/5 1/2 ins × 22.23mm/56
Figurado. Difficult shape to make. Concentrated
flavours. Elegant. Cigar for discerning smoker.
*Also available in maduro Connecticut shade wrapper.

FONSECA "VINTAGE VITOLAS"
Hand-made. Quality: superior. Small quantities of se-
lected tobacco is further aged. Made by MATASA.
Distributed by SAG Imports.

Corona Doble	190mm/7 1/2 ins × 20.64mm/52
Corona Gorda	152mm/6 ins × 19.84mm/50
Cetro Extra	172mm/6 3/4 ins × 19.05mm/48

FRANCO

Hand-made. Connecticut shade wrapper. Dominican binder and filler. Owned by House of Oxford.

Condados	165mm/6 1/2 ins × 17.46mm/44
Eminentes	140mm/5 1/2 ins × 16.67mm/42
Gourmets	178mm/7 ins × 15.1mm/38
Magnum	190mm/7 1/2 ins × 19.84mm/50
Regios	140mm/5 1/2 ins × 19.84mm/50

GRIFFIN'S

Hand-made. Quality: superior. Connecticut shade wrappers. Made by Tobacos Dominicas in Santiago. Exclusively distributed by Davidoff.

Griffin's Don Bernado   228mm/9 ins × 18.26mm/46
Griffin's Prestige★★★★   152mm/8 ins × 19.05mm/48
Mild and elegant with good flavours, but looses interest towards end. Good daytime smoke.
Griffin's No. 100   178mm/7 ins × 15.08mm/38
Griffin's No. 200   178mm/7 ins × 17.46mm/44
Griffin's No. 300   160mm/6 1/4 ins × 17.46mm/44
Griffin's No. 400   152mm/6 ins × 15.08mm/38
Griffin's Robusto★★★★★   127mm/5 ins × 19.84mm/50
Smooth, integrated flavours. Medium-bodied. Well-made. A top cigar.
Griffin's Privilege★★★★★   127mm/5 ins × 12.00mm/30
Mild and elegant but good flavours. Well made. Good daytime smoke.
Griffin's Griffinos   95mm/3 3/4 ins × 7.14mm/18

HABONOS HATUEY

Hand-made. Connecticut shade wrapper. Dominican filler and binder. Owned by Los Liberatodores Cigars. Coral Gables. Distributed by Mike's Cigars, Miami.

Chuchills	175mm/6 7/8 ins × 19.1mm/48
Coronas	140mm/5 1/2 ins × 16.67mm/42
Lonsdale	165mm/6 1/2 ins × 17.5mm/44
Robustos	127mm/5 ins × 19.1mm/48

HENRY CLAY

Hand-made. All with maduro wrappers.
This was one of the most famous old Havana brands, created in the 19th century and named after a famous American senator. The cigars sold in Europe are not the same blends as those sold in the United States. Made by Consolidated Cigars.

J.A Leather	178mm/7 ins × 16.70mm/42
Milla Fleurs	165mm/6 1/2 ins × 19.00mm/48
Brevas Fina★★★	152mm/6 1/2 ins × 19.05mm/48

Oily, but rough dark wrapper. Smooth, but short on flavour. Good for beginner.

Londres	152mm/6 ins × 18.20mm/46
Brevas a la Conserva	143mm/5 5/8 ins × 18.26mm/46
Anitas	141mm/5 9/16 ins × 16.70mm/42
Brevas★★★★	140mm/5 1/2 ins × 16.67mm/42

Even burning. Medium-bodied. Smooth. Daytime smoke.

Largas	171mm/6 3/4 ins × 15.00mm/38
Panetelas	152mm/6 ins × 12.70mm/32
Slim Panetela	127mm/5 ins × 13.00mm/33

HUGO CASSAR DIAMOND SELECTION
Hand-made. Connecticut shade wrappers. Binder and filler from Dominican Rep. Brand owned by Hugo Cassar Cigars, California.

Corona	140mm/5 1/2 ins × 16.67mm/42
Robusto	121mm/4 3/4 ins × 19.84mm/50
Grand Corona	152mm/6 ins × 18.3mm/46
Toro	165mm/6 1/2 ins × 20.6mm/52
Lonsdale	178mm/7 ins × 17.5mm/44
El Presidente	203mm/8 ins × 19.84mm/50

HUGO CASSAR MYSTIQUE
Hand-made. All Dominican tobacco

Lonsdale	178mm/7 ins × 17.5mm/44
Toro	159mm/6 1/4 ins × 19.84mm/50
Churchill	203mm/8 ins × 19.84mm/50

HUGO CASSAR PRIVATE COLLECTION
Hand-made. All Dominican tobacco.

Corona	152mm/6 ins × 16.67mm/42
Robusto	127mm/5 ins × 19.8mm/50
Torpedo	152mm/6 ins × 19.1mm/48
Toro	165mm/6 1/2 ins × 20.6mm/52
Presidente	191mm/7 1/2 ins × 19.5mm/49

H. UPMANN
Hand-made. Quality: superior. Cameroon wrappers. Central American filler. Well made, mild to medium smoke. Band reads "H. Upmann 1844" on Cuban version date replaced with "Habana". Made by Consolidated Cigar.

Amatista	149mm/5 7/8 ins × 15.87mm/40
Aperitiff	102mm/4 ins × 11.11mm/28
Churchills★★★★	143mm/5 5/8 ins × 18.26mm/46

Spicy and herbaceous flavours. Good daytime smoke or to follow light meal.

Coronas Imperiales	178mm/7 ins × 18.26mm/46

Lonsdales   168mm/6 5/8 ins × 16.67mm/42
Coronas Major Tubes 128mm/5 1/16 ins × 16.67mm/42
Coronas   141mm/5 9/16 ins × 16.67mm/42
Coronas Bravas   165mm/6 1/2 ins × 19.05mm/48
Demi Tasse   113mm/4 1/2 ins × 13.10mm/33
Director Royale   165mm/6 1/2 ins × 16.67mm/42
El Prado   178mm/7 ins × 14.29mm/36
Emperadores   197mm/7 3/4 ins × 18.26mm/46
Extra Finos Gold Tube 172mm/6 3/4 ins × 15.08mm/38
Finos Gold Tube   155mm/6 1/8 ins × 14.29mm/36
Monarch Tubes   178mm/7 ins × 17.86mm/45
Naturales Tubes   156mm/6 1/8 ins × 14.29mm/36
No. 2000 SBN   178mm/7 ins × 16.67mm/42
Pequenos No. 100★★★★

                          113mm/4 1/2 ins × 19.84mm/50
Dark oily wrapper. Spicy with coffee undertones on
palate. Medium-bodied. Satisfying.
Pequenos No. 200   113mm/4 1/2 ins × 18.26mm/46
Pequenos No. 300   113mm/4 1/2 ins × 16.67mm/42
Petit Coronas   128mm/5 1/16 ins × 16.67mm/42
Topacios SBN   133mm/5 1/4 ins × 17.07mm/43
Tubos Gold Tube   128mm/5 1/16 ins × 16.67mm/42

H. UPMANN CABINET SELECTION
Hand-made. Quality: superior. Cameroun wrappers.
Central American filler.
Columbo   203mm/8 ins × 19.84mm/50
Corsario   140mm/5 1/2 ins × 19.84mm/50
Robusto★★★★   120mm/4 3/4 ins × 19.84mm/50
Medium-bodied. Good flavours. To follow meal.

JOHN AYLESBURY EL FUMO
Hand-made. Superior quality.
Does not have the elegant "JA" band. See entry under
Germany and Honduras.
Brevas
Palomas
Exquisitos

JOHN AYLESBURY FLOR DE ORLANDO
Hand-made. Superior quality.
Has a red, white and gold "Flor de Orlando" band and
not the "JA" band. One model only. See entry under
Germany and Honduras.

JOHN AYLESBURY SANTA DOMINGA
Hand-made.
Mild and subtle. See entry under Germany and Hondu-
ras. Produced for John Aylesbury chain of cigar shops

in Germany. Also exported to USA where distributed by
F & K Cigar.

Churchill	178mm/7 ins × 18.3mm/46
Lonsdale	168mm/6 5/8 ins × 16.67mm/42
Rothschild	114mm/4 1/2 ins × 19.84mm/50
Corona	140mm/5 1/2 ins × 16.67mm/42
Panetela	152mm/6 ins × 12.27mm/32
Elegante	171mm/6 3/4 ins × 15.08mm/38

JOHN T'S

Hand-made. Tubed in bundles of 20. Untubed in boxes.
Connecticut wrapper. Dominican binder. Pipe tobaccos
filler. Distributed by Indianhead Sales.

Brown Gold	140mm/5 1/2 ins × 15.1mm/38
Cherry Cream	140mm/5 1/2 ins × 15.1mm/38
Capuccino	140mm/5 1/2 ins × 15.1mm/38
Cafe Ole	140mm/5 1/2 ins × 15.1mm/38
Amaretto	140mm/5 1/2 ins × 15.1mm/38
Magnum Amaretto	171mm/6 3/4 ins × 18.3mm/46
Magnum Brown Gold	171mm/6 3/4 ins × 18.3mm/46
Magnum Cherry Cream	171mm/6 3/4 ins × 18.3mm/46
Magnum Capuccino	171mm/6 3/4 ins × 18.3mm/46
Magnum Expresso	171mm/6 3/4 ins × 18.3mm/46

JOSE BENITO

Hand-made. Quality: good. Cameroon wrapper. Cuban
seed Dominican filler. Central American Cuban seed
binder. Medium strength. The large Magnum is one of
biggest on market. Made by MATASA, small producer
employing fewer than 70 bunchers and rollers. Owned
by Manuel Quesada, whose family has been making
cigars since 1877.

Magnum	229mm/9 ins × 25.00mm/64
Presidente	197mm/7 3/4 ins × 19.84mm/50
Churchill★★★★	178mm/7 ins × 19.84mm/50

Medium-bodied. Touch of honey. Good balance. After-
dinner cigar.

Corona	172mm/6 3/4 ins × 17.07mm/43
Panetela	172mm/6 3/4 ins × 15.08mm/38
Palma★★★★★	152mm/6 ins × 16.67mm/43

Medium-bodied. Smooth. Well-made. Appreciated by
experienced smoker and novice alike.

Petite	140mm/5 1/2 ins × 15.08mm/38
Rothschild	120mm/4 3/4 ins × 19.84mm/50
Chico	108mm/4 1/4 ins × 12.27mm/32
Havanitos	127mm/5 ins × 9.92mm/25

JOSÉ MARTI

Hand-made. Connecticut wrapper. Mild and sweet. Brand named after leader of Cuban revolution against USA in 1895, also known as Apostle of Cuba. Made by Ramón Carbonell. Distributed by Cigars by Santa Clara NA.

José Marti	190mm/7 1/2 ins × 19.05mm/48
Maceo	175mm/6 7/8 ins × 17.46mm/44
Palma	178mm/7 ins × 16.67mm/42
Robusto	140mm/5 1/2 ins × 19.84mm/50
Corona	140mm/5 1/2 ins × 15.87mm/40
Créme	152mm/6 ins × 13.49mm/34

JUAN CLEMENTE

Hand-made. Quality: superior. Connecticut shade wrapper. Ages well. Launched in Europe in 1982 and in USA in 1985. One of few Dominican-made cigars that can be sold to tourists visiting the Republic. Produces about 450 000 cigars per year. Feature is packing of 24 cigars per box.

Juan Clemente Gargantua	
	343mm/13 1/2 ins × 19.84mm/50
Juan Clemente Gigante	228mm/9 ins × 19.84mm/50
Churchill★★★★	175mm/6 7/8 ins × 18.26mm/46

Medium-bodied. Good balance between strength and flavour. Well-made. For experienced smoker and novice alike.

Corona	127mm/5 ins × 16.67mm/42
Grand Corona	152mm/6 ins × 16.67mm/42
Panetela	165mm/6 1/2 ins × 13.49mm/34
Juan Clemente Especiale	
	190mm/7 1/2 ins × 13.49mm/34
530	127mm/5 ins × 12.00mm/30
Demi Corona	102mm/4 ins × 15.87mm/40
Rothschild	124mm/4 7/8 ins × 19.84mm/50
Demi Tasse	92mm/3 5/8 ins × 13.49mm/34
Club Selection No 1	152mm/6 ins × 19.84mm/50
Club Selection No 2	113mm/4 1/2 ins × 18.26mm/46
Club Selection No 3	178mm/7 ins × 17.46mm/44
Club Selection No 4★★★★	146mm/5 3/4 ins × 16.67mm/42

Smooth with creamy flavours. Medium-bodied. Well-made. Daytime smoke.

KING

Hand-made bundles. Natural or maduro wrapper. Imported into USA by Club Imports

No 1	165mm/6 1/2 ins × 16.67mm/42

No 2	140mm/5 1/2 ins × 16.67mm/42
No 3	172mm/6 3/4 ins × 15.08mm/38
No 5	140mm/5 1/2 ins × 15.08mm/38
No 6	120mm/4 3/4 ins × 15.87mm/40
No 7★★★★	216mm/8 1/2 ins × 20.64mm/52

Rich, full flavoured. Smooth. Good value.

No 8	178mm/7 ins × 23.81mm/60
No 9	254mm/10 ins × 26.19mm/66
No 10	190mm/7 1/2 ins × 19.45mm/49
No 13	127mm/5 ins × 26.19mm/66

KISKEYA
Hand-made bundles. Connecticut shade wrapper. Distributed in USA by Tropical Tobacco.

Palma Fina	178mm/7 ins × 14.29mm/36
Numero Dos	145mm/5 3/4 ins × 16.67mm/42
*Rothschild	120mm/4 3/4 ins × 19.84mm/50
Cetros	152mm/6 ins × 17.46mm/44
Numero Uno	172mm/6 3/4 ins × 17.07mm/43
*Toros	152mm/6 ins × 19.84mm/50
Churchills	175mm/6 7/8 ins × 18.26mm/46
Presidentes	190mm/7 1/2 ins × 19.84mm/50
Viajantes	216mm/8 1/2 ins × 20.64mm/52

*Also available with maduro wrapper.

KNOCKANDO
Hand-made. Connecticut shade wrapper. Dominican binder and filler. Introduced by distillers Justerini and Brooks to go with their whiskies, particularly the well-known Knockando single malt. They are mild to medium, well matured cigars that have been well made.

No 1★★★★	175mm/6 7/8 ins × 17.86mm/45

Good draw and burning qualities. Appreciated by connoisseurs and novices alike.

No 2	165mm/6 1/2 ins × 13.89mm/35
No 3	168mm/5 5/8 ins × 15.87mm/40
No 4	190mm/7 1/2 ins × 19.05mm/48
St James	127mm/5 ins × 16.67mm/42

LA AURORA
Hand-made. Quality: superior. Established 1903. One of oldest brands made in Dominican Rep. Cameroon wrapper. Domincan binder and filler. Distributed by Miami Cigar.

Petite Corona	114mm/4 1/2 ins × 14.7mm/37
Palmas Extra	171mm/6 3/4 ins × 13.9mm/35
Corona	127mm/5 ins × 15.1mm/38
Auror No 4	133mm/5 1/4 ins × 17.1mm/43
Cetro	165mm/6 1/2 ins × 13.5mm/34

| Bristol Especiales | 165mm/6 1/2 ins × 19.1mm/48 |
| Sublimes | 127mm/5 ins × 15.1mm/38 |

LA CORONA VINTAGE SELECTION
Hand-made. Quality: superior.
This brand used to be made in the United States and is now produced by Consolidated Cigar Corporation in the Dominican Republic. They are well made, mild to medium and use Connecticut shade wrappers. Cigars sold in Europe not same blends as sold in USA. La Corona Whiffs machine-made in USA.

| Directors★★★ | 165mm/6 1/2 ins × 18.26mm/46 |

Smooth wrapper. Good draw. Creamy and smooth. Daytime smoke.

Aristocrats	155mm/6 1/8 ins × 14.29mm/36
Coronas	154mm/6 1/16 ins × 17.07mm/43
Corona Chicas	140mm/5 1/2 ins × 16.67mm/42

LAMBS CLUB
Hand-made. Ecuador wrapper. Honduran binder. Filler, blend of tobacco from Dominican Rep. and Brazil. Distributed by Finck Cigar.

Churchill	178mm/7 ins × 19.84mm/50
Corona Extra	159mm/6 1/4 ins × 17.1mm/43
Palma Extra	178mm/7 ins × 15.1mm/38
Rothschild	121mm/4 3/4 ins × 19.84mm/50
Toro	152mm/6 ins × 19.84mm/50
Chico	114mm/4 1/2 ins × 15.9mm/40

LA UNICA
Premium bundles — hand-made. Available in both light-natural and maduro wrappers. Owned by Newman family's M&N company in USA. Made by Arturo Fuente. Range also available with maduro wrappers. Good value.

| No 100★★★★★ | 216mm/8 1/2 ins × 20.64mm/52 |

Well-made. Good draw. Medium-bodied. Spicy. An undiscovered cigar.

| No 200★★★★★ | 178mm/7 ins × 19.84mm/50 |

Good balance between strength and flavour. Proof that bundle cigars need not always be lower quality. Daytime or after-dinner cigar.

No 300	172mm/6 3/4 ins × 17.64mm/44
No 400	113mm/4 1/2 ins × 19.84mm/50
No 500	133mm/5 1/2 ins × 17.07mm/43

LICENCIADOS
Hand-made. Quality: superior. Connecticut wrapper. Honduran binder. Filler from Dominican Republic. Logo

similar to Cuban Diplomaticas brand. Made by MATASA. Brand owned and distributed by Mike's Cigars, Miami.

Churchill	178mm/7 ins × 19.84mm/50
Excellentes	171mm/6 3/4 ins × 17.1mm/43
Expresso★★★★★	114mm/4 1/2 ins × 13.9mm/35

Full-flavoured. Smooth. Well-made cigar for experienced smoker. Good, quick smoke to follow meal.

No 4	146mm/5 3/4 ins × 17.1mm/43
Panetela Linda	178mm/7 ins × 15.1mm/38
Presidentes	203mm/8 ins × 19.84mm/50
Soberanos	216mm/8 1/2 ins × 20.6mm/54
No 200	146mm/5 3/4 ins × 17.1mm/43
No 300	171mm/6 3/4 ins × 17.1mm/43
No 400	152mm/6 ins × 19.84mm/50
No 500	203mm/8 ins × 19.84mm/50
Toro★★★★	152mm/6 ins × 19.84mm/50

Medium-bodied. Smooth. Refined flavour improves. Daytime smoke or to follow meal.

Wavell	127mm/5 ins × 19.84mm

LEON JIMENES

Hand-made. Connecticut shade wrapper. Made by La Aurora since 1903. Distributed by Miami Cigar.

No 1★★★★	190mm/7 1/2 ins × 19.84mm/50

Good draw. Mild, but rich flavours that improve.

No 2	178mm/7 ins × 18.65mm/47
No 3	165mm/6 1/2 ins × 16.67mm/42
No 4★★★★	143mm/5 5/8 ins × 16.67mm/42

Medium-bodied. Good balance. Well-made. Elegant.

No 5	127mm/5 ins × 15.08mm/38
Robusto	140mm/5 1/2 ins × 19.84mm/50

LOS LIBERTADORES

Hand-made. Connecticut wrapper. Dominican filler and binder. Owned by Los Libertadores Cigars, Coral Gables, Florida.

Mambises	175mm/6 7/8 ins × 19.1mm/48
Insurrectos	133mm/5 1/2 ins × 16.67mm/42
Exiliados	191mm/7 1/2 ins × 15.1mm/38
Macheteros	102mm/4 ins × 15.9mm/40
Alcade	165mm/6 1/2 ins × 17.5mm/44
Maceo	127mm/5 ins × 19.1mm/48
Figurado	165mm/6 1/2 ins × 20.6mm/52
Diplomaticos	127mm/5 ins × 11.9mm/30
Belicoso Reserva Especial	
	140mm/5 1/2 ins × 20.6mm/52
Robusto Reserva Especial	127mm/5 ins × 19.1mm/48

Churchill Reserva Especial
175mm/6 7/8 ins × 19.1mm/48

MATASA Seconds

Hand-made. Quality: superior. Connecticut wrappers. Mild. Overruns of some famous brands. Made by MATASA. Exclusive to Santa Clara MA.

Corona	152mm/6 ins × 17.07mm/43
No 2	165mm/6 1/2 ins × 17.07mm/43
No 4	140mm/5 1/2 ins × 16.67mm/42
Palma Fina	178mm/7 1/2 ins × 14.29mm/38
Palmita	127mm/5 ins × 14.29mm/38
Super Fino	152mm/6 ins × 14.29mm/36

MATCH PLAY

Hand-made. Quality: superior. Connecticut shade wrapper. Binder and filler from Ecuador. Distributed by Dormie Imports, Portland, Oregan.

Cypress	12.06mm/4 3/4 ins × 19.40mm/50
St. Andrews	159mm/6 1/4 ins × 17.1mm/43
Turnberry	152mm/6 ins × 19.84mm/50
Prestwick	175mm/6 7/8 ins × 18.3mm/46
Olympic	191mm/7 1/2 ins × 19.84mm/50
Troon	178mm/7 ins × 21.4mm/54

MONTECRISTO

Hand-made by Consolidated Cigar. Quality: superior. Full-bodied, rich flavours not normally associated with cigars made in Dominican Republic. Good alternative for lovers of Havanas. Only available in selected stores. Not sold outside USA. Be advised that there is a brand, Monte Cristi, in the Dominican Republic which has no connection to the authorised, registered brand.

Churchills★★★★★ 178mm/7 ins × 19.05mm/48
Oily dark wrapper. Packed full of flavours. Has punch, but also finesse. Well-made. They don't get much better than this.

No 1 165mm/6 1/2 ins × 17.46mm/44
Tubos 155mm/6 1/8 ins × 16.67mm/42
No 2 Torpedo★★★★ 152mm/6 ins × 19.84mm/50
Honeyed and woody undertones on finish. Good burning qualities. Becomes richer and stronger, but still remains mild. Would prefer slightly easier draw. Good daytime smoke. Much milder than Cuban version.

No 3 140mm/5 1/2 ins × 17.46mm/44
Robustos★★★★★ 120mm/4 3/4 ins × 19.84mm/50
Beautiful, smooth, oily redish wrapper. Spicy, leathery aroma. Elegant, well-made cigar for connoisseur.

MONTESINO

Hand-made. Quality: superior. Connecticut shade wrapper. Dominican and Brazilian filler. Nicaraguan binders. Milder than Arturo Fuerte range. Wrapper colours often not evenly matched in box. Good value. Made by Arturo Fuente. Distributed by FANCO.

Gran Corona	172mm/6 3/4 ins × 19.05mm/48
No. 1	175mm/6 7/8 ins × 17.07mm/43
No. 2★★★★	160mm/6 1/4 ins × 17.46mm/44

Medium-bodied. Smooth. Spicy. Good balanced and finish. Daytime smoke.

No. 3	172mm/6 3/4 ins × 14.29mm/36
Diplomatico★★★★★	140mm/5 1/2 ins × 16.67mm/42

Good draw. Slow, even burning. Smooth. Spicy and earthy. Well-made. For discerning smoker.

Napoleon Grande★★★★★ 178mm/7 ins × 18.26mm/46

Medium-bodied. Smooth. Well-balanced. Connoisseur's cigar. Also wonderful introduction for beginner.

Fumas 172mm/6 3/4 ins × 17.46mm/44

MONTECRUZ

Hand-made Filler. Cameroon wrapper. Dominican binders. Cuban seed tobacco and Brazilian filler.

When the Menendez family, former owners of Montecristo brand, left Cuba they started a factory in the Canary Islands making Montecruz, with labels similar to Montecristo. In the mid-1970s the operation was taken over by Consolidated Cigar Corporation and moved to the Dominican Republic. Well made. Matured medium to full flavoured. First cigar imported in USA with a Cameroun wrapper.

Individuales	203mm/8 ins × 19.84mm/50
Colossus	165mm/6 1/2 ins × 19.84mm/50
Senores	146mm/5 3/4 ins × 13.9mm/35
Robusto	114mm/4 1/2 ins × 19.8mm/50
Tubo (A/tube)	152mm/6 ins × 16.67mm/42
Tubulares (A/tube)	155mm/6 1/8 ins × 14.29mm/36
Junior	124mm/4 7/8 ins × 13.10mm/33
Chicos	99mm/3 3/8 ins × 11.11mm/28
No 200	184mm/7 1/4 ins × 18.26mm/46
No 201	155mm/6 1/8 ins × 15.08mm/38
No 205	178mm/7 ins × 16.67mm/42
No 210	165mm/6 1/2 ins × 16.67mm/42
No 220	140mm/5 1/2 ins × 16.67mm/42
No 230	127mm/5 ins × 16.67mm/42
No 240	120mm/4 3/4 ins × 17.46mm/44
No 250	165mm/6 1/2 ins × 15.08mm/38

No 255	178mm/7 ins × 14.29mm/36
No 265	140mm/5 1/2 ins × 15.08mm/38
No 270	120mm/4 3/4 ins × 13.89mm/35
No 275	178mm/7 ins × 12.7mm/32
No 276	152mm/6 ins × 12.7mm/32
No 277	127mm/5 ins × 12.7mm/32
No 280	178mm/7 ins × 13.10mm/33
No 281	152mm/6 ins × 13.10mm/33
No 282	127mm/5 ins × 16.67mm/42

MONTERO

Hand-made. Connecticut wrapper. Dominican filler and binder. Boxes of 20. Owned by Tropical Tobacco. Named after vic-president of company, Ralph Montero.

Torpedo	178mm/7 ins × 21.4mm/54
Presidente	191mm/7 1/2 ins × 19.84mm/50
Churchill	175mm/6 7/8 ins × 18.3mm/46
Toro	152mm/6 ins × 19.84mm/50
Cetro	152mm/6 ins × 17.5mm/44
Robusto	127mm/5 ins × 19.84mm/50

MORENO MADURO

Hand-made.Mexican maduro wrappers. Binder from Dominican Rep. Fill blend of tobacco from Brazil and Dominican Rep. Made by Consolidated Cigar. Exclusive to Phillips & King.

No 445	140mm/5 1/2 ins × 17.46mm/44
No 326	152mm/6 ins × 14.29mm/36
No 426	165mm/6 1/2 ins × 16.67mm/42
No 486	152mm/6 ins × 19.05mm/48
No 507★★★★	178mm/7 ins × 19.84mm/50

Rich, spicy and honeyed flavours. Good draw. Well-made.

NAT CICCO'S SUPREMOS DOMINICANOS

Hand-made bundles. Quality: good. All Dominican Rep. tobacco. Distributed in USA by Phillips & King.

Grandiosos	228mm/9 ins × 23.81mm/60
Exquisitos	184mm/7 1/4 ins × 19.84mm/50
Sabrosos	152mm/6 ins × 19.05mm/48
Lindos	113mm/4 1/2 ins × 19.84mm/50
Deliciosos	165mm/6 1/2 ins × 17.07mm/43

NAT SHERMAN CITY DESK SELECTION

Hand-made. Quality: superior. Mexican maduro wrapper. Dominican binder and blend of Dominican and Mexican filler. Medium to full bodied. Orange, red and gold band.

Named after famous newspapers in days when tough

cigar-smoking editors wearing green visors, with shirtsleeves held up by garters, brought news to the masses in classic style.

Gazette	152mm/6 ins × 16.67/42
Dispatch	165mm/6 1/2 ins × 18.26mm/46
Telegraph★★★★	152mm/6 ins × 19.84mm/50

Mild, and mellow. Touch of sweetness on palate. Gets rounder as you smoke. Daytime smoke or to follow light meal.

Tribune	190mm/7 1/2 ins × 19.84mm/50

NAT SHERMAN EXCHANGE SELECTION

Hand-made. Quality: superior. Connecticut shade wrapper. Binders from Mexico and fillers from Dominican Republic. Mild. Dark green, red and gold band.

Second generation, Joel Sherman, is proud of family's deep New York roots and, accordingly, all brands named after famous New York landmarks. Each one has different colour band for identification.

Named after celebrated New York telephone exchanges of the past.

Academy No 2	127mm/5 ins × 12.30mm/31
Murray Hill No 7	152mm/6 ins × 15.08mm/38
Butterfield No 8	165mm/6 1/2 ins × 16.67mm/42
Trafalgar No 4	152mm/6 ins × 18.65mm/47
Oxford No 5★★★★	178mm/7 ins × 19.45mm/49

Mild. Delicate flavours with nutty aroma. An elegant cigar.

NAT SHERMAN GOTHAM SELECTION

Hand-made. Quality: superior. Connecticut shade wrapper. Dominican Olor binder and blend of Dominican and Cuban seed filler. Mild. Grey, red and gold band.

Named after addresses synonymous with Sherman heritage. Each box covered in leather.

No 65 (Where Joel was born)	152/6 ins × 12.70mm/32
No 1440 (First store)	160mm/6 1/4 ins × 17.46mm/44
No 711 (First Fifth Ave store)★★★★★	
	152mm/6 ins × 19.84mm/50

Good balance between flavour and strength. Mild, integrated flavours, mellow and smooth. Thicker girth probably helps this blend. Great cigar.

No 500 (Present Fifth Ave store)	
	178mm/7 ins × 19.84mm/50

NAT SHERMAN LANDMARK SELECTION

Hand-made. Quality: superior. Cameroon wrapper.

Mexican binder and Dominican filler. Black, red and gold band.

Named after places that needed no address to true New Yorker. Just name of hotel, jazz club, special building would identify address not normally found in tourist guides.

Metropole	152mm/6 ins × 13.49mm/34
Hampshire	140mm/5 1/2 ins × 16.67mm/42
Algonquin	172mm/6 3/4 ins × 17.07mm/43
Vanderbilt★★★★	127mm/5 ins × 18.65mm/47

Elegant well-made, mild cigar. Smooth with herbacious aroma. Excellent cigar for someone looking for light-ness.

Dakota	190mm/7 1/2 ins × 19.45mm/49

NAT SHERMAN MANHATTAN SELECTION

Hand-made. Quality: superior. Mexican wrapper and binder. Dominican filler. Medium bodied with lots of flavour. Chocolate, red and gold band.

Named after small communities in Manhattan.

Beekman	133mm/5 1/4 ins × 11.11mm/28
Tribeca	152mm/6 ins × 12.30mm/31
Chelsea	165mm/6 1/2 ins × 15.08mm/38
Gramercy	172mm/6 3/4 ins × 17.07mm/43
Sutton★★★★	140mm/5 1/2 ins × 19.45mm/49

Lovely aromatic, leathery aromas. Tangy finish. More flavour than Landmark Vanderbilt. Good daytime smoke.

NAT SHERMAN METROPOLITAN SELECTION

Hand-made. Quality: superior. Connecticut shade wrapper. Dominican binder and filler. Medium-bodied. Royal blue, red and gold band. Named after great New York private clubs leaving legacy of buildings reflecting permanence and discreet good taste.

Anglers	140mm/5 1/2 ins × 17.1mm/43
Nautical (pyramid)	178mm/7 ins × 19.1mm/48
University★★★★★	152mm/6 ins × 19.84mm/50

Good draw and even burning. Good balance. Flavour develops after half inch (one cm). Medium-bodied. Elegant daytime smoke for connoisseur.

Explorers (pyramid)★★★★

140mm/5 1/2 ins × 19.84mm/50

Mild. Good subtle flavours. Burns evenly. Elegant. Daytime smoke.

Metropolitan (torpedo)	mm/7 ins × 23.8mm/60

NAT SHERMAN VIP SELECTION

Hand-made. Quality: superior. Connecticut shade wrapper. Dominican binder and blend of Dominican and Brazilian filler. Medium to full bodied. Purple, red and gold band.

Named after famous New York personalities.

Zigfeld "Fancytale"	172mm/6 3/4 ins × 12.70mm/32
Morgan	178mm/7 ins × 16.67mm/42
Astor★★★★	113mm/4 1/2 ins × 19.84mm/50

Herbacious, spicy aromas. Strength is little ahead of flavour. Not as elegant as Landmark Vanderbilt and Gotham No 711.

Carnegie	152mm/6 ins × 19.05mm/48

NUDE DOMINICAN

Hand-made bundles. Distributed in USA by Indian Head Sales.

60	127mm/5 ins × 12.00mm/30
38	133mm/5 1/4 ins × 17.07mm/43
40	133mm/5 1/4 ins × 19.84mm/50
56	152mm/6 ins × 17.07mm/43
54	160mm/6 1/4 ins × 17.46mm/44
50	172mm/6 3/4 ins × 17.07mm/43
48	175mm/6 7/8 ins × 18.26mm/46
58	178mm/7 ins × 12.00mm/30
52	178mm/7 ins × 14.29mm/36
32	178mm/7 ins × 17.46mm/44
44	190mm/7 1/2 ins × 19.84mm/50
42	203mm/8 ins × 19.84mm/50

ONYX

Hand-made. Quality: good. Mexican maduro wrapper. Java binder. Dominican and Mexican filler. Launched in 1992. Made by Consolidated Cigar.

No 642	152mm/6 ins × 16.67mm/42
No 646	168mm/6 5/8 ins × 18.26mm/46
No 650★★★★	152mm/6 ins × 19.84mm/50

Good flavour with chocolate undertones. Good balance.

No 750★★★★	190mm/7 1/2 ins × 19.84mm/50

Medium-bodied. Rich and smooth. Touch of sweetness.

No 852	203mm/8 ins × 20.64mm/52

OLAR

Hand-made. Connecticut wrapper. Filler and binder from Dominican Republic.

Cacique	194mm/7 5/8 ins × 21.4mm/54
Colossus	184mm/7 1/4 ins × 19.1mm/48
Lonsdale	162mm/6 1/2 ins × 16.67mm/42
Paco	152mm/6 ins × 19.84mm/50
Rothschild	114mm/4 1/2 ins × 19.84mm/50
Momento	140mm/5 1/2 ins × 17.1mm/43

OPUS X

Hand-made. Quality: superior. Unique Dominican shade wrapper. Pioneered by Carlos Fuente Jr. Dominican filler and binder. Super premium range. Pride of Fuente family. Among most expensive non-Havana cigars on market. Plans were to sell only 500 000 cigars in 1996. Made by Arturo Fuente. Distributed in USA by FANCO (joint venture between Fuente and M&N).

| Petit Lancero | 159mm/6 1/4 ins × 15.5mm/39 |
| Perfecxion No 5★★★★★ | 124mm/4 7/8 ins × 15.9mm/40 |

Medium-strength. Full flavours. Hint of coffee and nutmeg. Smooth. Wonderfully balanced. Do not be misled by its size, quick satisfying smoke for connoisseur.

Fuente Fuente	143mm/5 5/8 ins × 18.3mm/46
Reserva D'Chateau	178mm/7 ins × 19.1mm/48
Double Corona★★★★★	194mm/7 5/8 ins × 18.3mm/46

Dark oily wrapper. Packed with flavour. Good balance. Hell of a cigar! They do not get much better than this.

| Robusto | 133mm/5 1/4 ins × 19.84mm/50 |
| Perfecxion No 2★★★★ | 162mm/6 3/8 ins × 20.6mm/52 |

Beautiful Colorado wrapper. Medium-bodied. Good flavour, but doesn't have punch of *parejos* (parallel-sided) cigars. Tends to fade towards the end. Extremely well-made.

ORO DE CUBA

Cameroon or maduro wrappers. Distributed in USA by Brick-Hanauer Co.

El Falcon	133mm/5 1/2 ins × 17.07mm/43
El Flamingo	172mm/6 3/4 ins × 13.89mm/35
El Pantero	165mm/6 1/2 ins × 17.46mm/44
El Aquila	178mm/7 ins × 17.07mm/43
El Pasofina Tube	133mm/5 1/2 ins × 16.67mm/42
El Tigre	152mm/6 ins × 19.84mm/50
El Leon	178mm/7 ins × 19.45mm/49

OSCAR

Hand-made. Quality: superior. Connecticut shade wrapper. Dominican filler and binder. Brand owned by Dominican Cigar Imports and named after owner, Oscar Rodriguez.

| Don Oscar | 229mm/9 ins x 18.3mm/44 |
| Supreme★★★★ | 203mm/8 ins x 19.1mm/48 |

Full-bodied. Spicy with good finish.

Prince	127mm/5 ins x 11.9mm/30
No 100	178mm/7 ins x 15.1mm/38
No 200	178mm/7 ins x 18.3mm/44
No 300	159mm/6 1/4 ins x 18.3mm/44
No 400	152mm/6 ins x 15.1mm/38
No 500	140mm/5 1/2 ins x 19.84mm/50
No 600	114mm/4 1/2 ins x 19.84mm/50
No 700	178mm/7 ins x 21.4mm/54
Oscarito	102mm/4 ins x 7.91mm/20

P & K GUARDSMEN

Hand-made. Java wrapper. Dominican binder. Filler, blend of tobacco from Mexico, Brazil & Dominican Rep. Brand owned by Phillips & King.

P & K Guardsmen No 1	203mm/8 ins × 20.64mm/52
P & K Guardsmen No 2	190mm/7 1/2 ins × 19.84mm/50
P & K Guardsmen No 3	152mm/6 ins × 19.84mm/50
P & K Guardsmen No 4	120mm/4 3/4 ins × 19.84mm/50
P & K Guardsmen No 5★★★★	
	178mm/7 ins × 19.05mm/48

Meduim to full bodied. Good value.

P & K Guardsmen No 6	133mm/5 1/2 ins × 17.46mm/44
P & K Guardsmen No 7	152mm/6 ins × 16.67mm/42
P & K Guardsmen No 8	152mm/6 ins × 14.29mm/36

PARTAGAS

Hand-made. Quality: superior. Fillers are mixture of Jamaican, Dominican and Mexican tobacco. They are well made, medium to full-bodied, with a touch of sweetness. Relatively expensive. Second biggest brand made by giant General Cigar. Band reads "Partagas 1845" on Cuban version date replaced with "Habana". Most names different to Cuban range.

| No 1★★★★★ | 172mm/6 3/4 ins × 17.07mm/43 |

Spicy, vegetal aroma and flavours. Well balanced between strength and flavour. Elegant. Good finish. Well-made.

| No 2★★★★★ | 147mm/5 3/4 ins × 17.07mm/43 |

Well-made elegant cigar. Slightly salty finish. For the connoisseur.

| No 3★★★★★ | 133mm/5 1/4 ins × 17.07mm/43 |

Medium bodied. Good balance between integrated flavours and strength. Earthy undertones. Elegant.

| No 4★★★★ | 127mm/5 ins × 15.08mm/38 |

Smooth silky wrapper. Medium to full bodied. This cigar gets better as you smoke. Finishes on high note.

No 5★★ 133mm/5 1/4 ins × 11.11mm/28
Hard draw, difficult burning. Not easy to smoke.

No 6★★★ 152mm/6 ins × 13.49mm/34
Medium bodied. Mildly aromatic.

No 10★★★ 190mm/7 3/4 ins × 19.45mm/49
Lacks punch. Good introduction to this size for beginner.

8-9-8★★★ (cabinet) 175mm/7 1/2 ins × 17.07mm/43
Good dark, almost maduro wrapper. Mild. Slightly sweet. Lacks punch.

Aristorcrat★★ 152mm/6 ins × 19.84mm/50
Not very aristocratic. One dimensional and boring.

Naturales★★★★ 140mm/5 1/2 ins × 19.45mm/49
Smooth Colorado maduro wrapper. Well-made. Flavour builds up after half-way. Elegant.

Maduro 160mm/6 1/4 ins × 18.65mm/47
Tubos★★★ (aluminium tubes)
190mm/7 ins × 13.49mm/34
Elegant looking cigar. Could do with more complexity.

Humitube (glass tubes)★★★
147mm/6 3/4 ins × 17.07mm/43
Mild, spicy, floral aromas. Dull wrapper. Lacks punch.

Sabroso (aluminium tubes)★★★★★
149mm/5 7/8 ins × 17.46mm/44
Full bodied. Lots of spicy, earthy flavours. Has character. Ideal to follow spicy meal.

Almirante★★★ 160mm/6 1/4 ins × 18.65mm/47
Very mild. Liquorice, coffee and honeyed flavours. Lacks punch.

Robusto★★★★★ 113mm/4 1/2 ins × 19.45mm/49
Burns easily and evenly. Subtle spicy aroma and flavours. Medium bodied. Smooth. Daytime smoke or to follow light meal.

Puritos (tins)★★★★ 107mm/4 3/16 ins × 12.7mm/32
Machine-made. Short filler. Medium bodied, floral aroma. Burns well.

Limited Reserve Royale★★★★★
147mm/6 3/4 ins × 17.07mm/43
Green and gold band. Lovely wrapper. Elegant, well-made cigar with intergrated spicy and floral aroma and flavours with coffee undertones. Good finish. For connoisseur.

Limited Reserve Regale★★★★★
160mm/6 1/4 ins × 18.65mm/47
Green and gold band. Good colorado claro wrapper.

Burns slowly and evenly. Thick girth allows lots of integrated flavours. For connoisseur.

PARTAGAS 150 SIGNATURE SERIES

Hand-made. Quality: superior. Unique 18 year old Cameroon wrapper leaf. This limited once-in-a-lifetime edition was created to commemorate 150th anniversary of Partagas brand, by Ramon Cifuentes who, pre-Castro, ran the Partagas factory in Cuba. Cigars packed in cedar boxes of 25, 50 and 100, bearing Cifuentes' signature and special Partagas 150 logo. Total production under one million. Released November 1995. For further details see 1996 edition.

PAUL GARMIRIAN — PG.

Hand-made by Tabacos Dominicanos for PG. Top price range.

P.G. Celebration	228mm/9 ins × 19.84mm/50
P.G. Double Corona	193mm/7 5/8 ins × 19.84mm/50
P.G. Magnum	178mm/7 ins × 19.84mm/50
P.G. Belicoso	165mm/6 1/2 ins × 20.64mm/52
P.G. Churchill	178mm/7 ins × 19.05mm/48
P.G. No 1	190mm/7 1/2 ins × 15.08mm/38
P.G. Corona Grande	165mm/6 1/2 ins × 18.26mm/46
P.G. Belicoso Fino	140mm/5 1/2 ins × 20.64mm/52
P.G. Lonsdale	165mm/6 1/2 ins × 16.67mm/42
P.G. Connoisseur	152mm/6 ins × 19.84mm/50
P.G. Epicure	140mm/5 1/2 ins × 19.84mm/50
P.G. Robusto	127mm/5 ins × 19.84mm/50
P.G. No 2	120mm/4 3/4 ins × 19.05mm/48
P.G. Petit Corona	127mm/5 ins × 17.07mm/43
P.G. Petit Bouquet	113mm/4 1/2 ins × 15.08mm/38
P.G. No 5	102mm/4 ins × 15.87mm/40

PETERSON

Hand-made. Quality: superior. Connecticut shade wrapper. Dominican filler and binder from Ecuador. Owned by famous piper makers, Peterson of Dublin. Made by Cuervo Y Hermano. Distributed in USA by Hollco Rohr.

Presidente★★★★★	190mm/7 1/2 ins × 19.8mm/50

Meduim-bodied. Touch of spice. Smooth. Good balance. Well-made cigar with finesse.

Churchill	178mm/7 ins × 19.1mm/48
Toro	152mm/6 ins × 19.8mm/50
Corona	146mm/5 3/4 ins × 17.1mm/43
Petit Corona	127mm/5 ins × 17.1mm/43
Robusto	120mm/4 3/4 ins × 19.8mm/50

| Tres Petit Corona | 114mm/4 1/2 ins × 15.1mm/38 |

PETER STOKKEBYE

Hand-made. Connecticut shade wrapper. Dominican binder. Brazilian and Cuban seed tobacco filler. Very mild. Distributed in USA by Arango Cigar.

Santa Maria	178mm/7 ins × 19.84mm/50
Santa Maria No. 2	172mm/6 3/4 ins × 15.08mm/38
Santa Maria No. 3	133mm/5 1/2 ins × 17.07mm/43

PLAYBOY by DON DIEGO

Hand-made. Quality: superior. Licensed to carry Playboy Rabit logo. Made by Consolidated Cigar. Super premuim line. Launched towards end 1996.

Double Corona	152mm/6 ins × 20.6mm/52
Robusto	127mm/5 ins × 19.84mm/50
Churchill	146mm/5 3/4 ins × 19.84mm/50
Gran Corona	171mm/6 3/4 ins × 19.1mm/48
Lonsdale	165mm/6 1/2 ins × 16.67mm/42

PLEIADES

Hand-made. Connecticut shade wrapper. Dominican binder and filler. Brand owned by Swisher Intl.

Aldebran	216mm/8 1/2 ins × 19.84mm/50
Saturne	203mm/8 ins × 18.26mm/46
Neptune	190mm/7 1/2 ins × 16.67mm/42
Sirius	175mm/6 7/8 ins × 18.26mm/46
Orion	147mm/5 3/4 ins × 16.67mm/42
Uranus	175mm/6 7/8 ins × 13.49mm/34
Antares	133mm/5 1/2 ins × 15.87mm/40
Pluton	127mm/5 ins × 19.84mm/50
Perseus	127mm/5 ins × 13.49mm/34
Mars	127mm/5 ins × 11.11mm/28

POR LARRANAGA

Hand-made. Connecticut shade wrappers. Dominican binders and fillers blend of Dominican and Brazilian leaf. Brand owned in USA by Consolidated Cigar. Band carries words "La Romana", while Cuban version has word "Habana".

Fabulosos	178mm/7 ins × 19.84mm/50
Cetros	175mm/6 7/8 ins × 16.67mm/42
Nacionales	140mm/5 1/2 ins × 16.67mm/42
Delicados	165mm/6 1/2 ins × 14.29mm/36
Robusto	127mm/5 ins × 19.84mm/50
Petit Cetro	127mm/5 ins × 15.10mm/38

PRIMO DEL REY

Machine-bunched & hand-finished. Brazilian wrapper.

Label similar to Montecruz. Made by Consolidated Cigar.

*No 100	113mm/4 1/2 ins × 19.84mm/50
*Aguilas	203mm/8 ins × 20.64mm/52
*Almirantes★★★★	152mm/6 ins × 19.84mm/50

Dark oily wrapper. Spicy with coffee undertones. Good finish. After dinner smoke.

**Cazadores	154mm/6 1/16 ins × 17.46mm/44
Chavon	165mm/6 1/2 ins × 16.27mm/41
*Churchill	165mm/6 1/2 ins × 19.05mm/48
Cortos	102mm/4 ins × 11.11mm/28
*Panetela Extras	151mm/5 15/16 ins × 13.49mm/34
*Panetelas	136mm/5 3/8 ins × 13.49mm/34
*Presidentes	157mm/6 13/16 ins × 17.46mm/44
Reales	155mm/6 1/8 ins × 14.29mm/36
Seleccion No 1	157mm/6 13/16 ins × 16.67mm/42
**Seleccion No 2	160mm/6 1/4 ins × 16.67mm/42
*Seleccion No 3	157mm/6 13/16 ins × 14.29mm/36
**Seleccion No 4	140mm/5 1/2 ins × 16.67mm/42
Seleccion No 5	147mm/5 3/4 ins × 15.48mm/39
*Soberanos	190mm/7 1/2 ins × 19.84mm/50

*Maduro wrappers.
**Maduro and Colorado wrappers.

PRIMO DEL REY CLUB SELECTION
Hand-made. Quality: superior. Connecticut shade wrapper, different to standard range.

Nobles	160mm/6 1/4 ins × 17.46mm/44
Aristocrats	172mm/6 3/4 ins × 19.45mm/48
Regals★★★★	178mm/7 ins × 19.84mm/50

Attractive wrapper. Good balance between strength and flavour. Well made. Mild, smooth. Good daytime smoke or after light meal.

Barons	203mm/8 1/2 ins × 20.64mm/52

PRIVATE STOCK
Hand-made. "Seconds" from Tobacos Dominicanos SAFactory. Brand owned by Davidoff. More affordable price range.

No 1	197mm/7 3/4 ins × 19.05mm/48
No 2	152mm/6 ins × 19.05mm/48
No 3	165mm/6 1/2 ins × 13.10mm/33
No 4	147mm/5 3/4 ins × 15.08mm/38
No 5	147mm/5 3/4 ins × 17.07mm/43
No 6	133mm/5 1/4 ins × 18.26mm/46
No 7	120mm/4 3/4 ins × 17.07mm/43
No 8	117mm/4 5/8 ins × 13.89mm/35

No 9	117mm/4 5/8 ins × 10.32mm/26
No 10	102mm/4 ins × 15.87mm/40
No 11	117mm/4 5/8 ins × 19.84mm/50

QUORUM
Hand-made. Connecticut shade wrappers. Dominican binders. Originally made in Canary Islands.

Chairman	190mm/7 1/2 ins × 19.84mm/50
President	184mm/7 1/4 ins × 18.26mm/46
No 1	168mm/6 5/8 ins × 16.67mm/42
Corona	143mm/5 5/8 ins × 16.67mm/42
Rothschild	113mm/4 1/2 ins × 19.84mm/50
Whillo	178mm/7 ins × 14.29mm/36
Trumph	108mm/4 1/4 ins × 16.67mm/42

RAMON ALLONES
Hand-made by General Cigar. Quality: superior. Cameroun wrappers. Made by General Cigar. Binders from Mexico and fillers from Mexico, Jamaica and Dominican Republic. Mild. Names different to Cuban range. Bands do not include the word "Habana". Made by General Cigar.

Ramonitos	113mm/5 1/8 ins × 12.70mm/32
Redondos★★★	178mm/7 ins × 19.45mm/49

Fairly hard draw. Mild to medium bodied. Little flavour. Lacks character.

A★★★★ 178mm/7 ins × 17.86mm/45

Smooth. Mild but rich flavours. Hint of coffee. A sophisticated smoke for the connoisseur.

B★★★★ 165mm/6 1/2 ins × 16.67mm/42

Rich, earthy flavours. Touch of coffee. Smooth. Slow burning. Well made.

D★★★★ 127mm/5 ins × 16.67mm/42

Beautiful colorado maduro wrapper. Spicy, floral aroma. Hint of coffee on palate. Elegant, sophisticated smoke.

Crystals (glass tubes)★★★★

165mm/6 3/4 ins × 16.67mm/43

Beautiful dark brown wrapper. Elegant. Good finish. Ideal to follow a meal.

Trumps (cabinet)★★★★★

172mm/6 3/4 ins × 17.07mm/43

Beautiful dark oily wrapper. Integrated flavours. Mild. Smooth. Well made.

REPUBLICA DOMINICA
Hand-made. Bundles. Indonesian wrapper. Mexican binder. Dominican filler. Made by Consolidated Cigar.

No 1	204mm/8 ins × 20.6mm/52
No 2	191mm/7 1/2 ins × 19.84mm/50
No 3	152mm/6 ins × 19.84mm/50
No 4	127mm/5 ins × 19.84mm/50
No 5	178mm/7 ins × 19.1mm/48
No 6	168mm/6 5/8 ins × 17.5mm/44
No 7	152mm/6 ins × 16.67mm/42
No 8	175mm/6 7/8 ins × 15.1mm/38

RIGOLETTO

Hand-made. Connecticut shade wrapper. Filler and binder from Dominican Republic. Made by Arturo Fuente Ltd. Distributed in USA by M&N.

Black Magic	190mm/7 1/2 ins × 18.26mm/46
Black Arrow	160mm/6 1/4 ins × 17.46mm/44
Dominican Lights	160mm/6 1/4 ins × 19.05mm/48

ROLLERS CHOICE

Hand-made in distinctive presentation. Made by MAJASA. Distributed by SAG Imports.

RC Double Corona	178mm/7 ins × 19.84mm/50
RC Lonsdale	165mm/6 1/2 ins × 18.26mm/46
RC Corona	152mm/6 ins × 17.07mm/43
RC Fine	133mm/5 1/2 ins × 16.27mm/41
RC Robusto	127mm/5 ins × 19.84mm/50
RC Pequeno	108mm/4 1/4 ins × 15.87mm/40

ROMEO Y JULIETA

Hand-made. Quality: superior. Cameroon wrappers. Dominican and Cuban seed filler. Well made. Medium bodied. Until recently was also made in Honduras and Cuba. No longer made in Honduras. Made in MATASA factory in Santiago free-trade zone. The range made in Cuba also include a Churchill and a Romeo. The bands do not include the word "Habana". Owned in USA by Hollco Rohr.

Monarcas	203mm/8 ins × 20.64mm/52
*Churchills	178mm/7 ins × 19.84mm/50
Presidentes	178mm/7 ins × 17.07mm/43
*Rothschild	127mm/5 ins × 19.84mm/50
Palmas	152mm/6 ins × 16.67mm/43
*Cetros	165mm/6 1/2 ins × 17.46mm/44
Coronas	140mm/5 1/2 ins × 17.46mm/44
Delgados★★★★	178mm/7 ins × 16.67mm/43

Earthy aroma. Gentle cigar with finese. Well-made. Ideal for novice.

| Brevas | 143mm/5 5/8 ins × 15.1mm/38 |

Panetelas	133mm/5 1/4 ins × 13.89mm/35
Chiquitas	108mm/4 1/4 ins × 19.84mm/50
*Romeo (torpedo)	152mm/6 ins × 18.26mm/46

*Available with maduro wrapper.

ROMEO Y JULIETA VINTAGE

Hand-made. Quality: superior. Connecticut shade wrapper. Filler blend of Cuban seed and Dominican Binder is aged Mexican leaf. Packed in Spanish cedar box, fitted with French Credo humidifier.

Vintage I	152mm/6 ins × 17.07mm/43
Vintage II	152mm/6 ins × 18.26mm/46
Vintage III	113mm/4 1/2 ins × 19.84mm/50
Vintage IV	178mm/7 ins × 19.05mm/48
Vintage V	190mm/7 1/2 ins × 19.84mm/50

ROYALES
Hand-made.

No 1	203mm/8 ins × 20.64mm/52
No 2	190mm/7 1/2 ins × 19.84mm/50
No 3	152mm/6 ins × 19.84mm/50
No 4	127mm/5 ins × 19.84mm/50
No 5	168mm/6 5/8 ins × 17.46mm/44
No 6	152mm/6 ins × 16.67mm/42
No 7	175mm/6 7/8 ins × 15.08mm/38

ROYAL DOMINICANA

Hand-made. Quality: superior. Connecticut wrapper. Mild to medium. Exclusive to Santa Clara, N.A..

Churchill	190mm/7 1/2 ins × 19.84mm/50
Corona	152mm/6 ins × 18.26mm/46
Nacional	140mm/5 1/2 ins × 17.07mm/43
No 1	172mm/6 3/4 ins × 17.07mm/43
Super Fino	152mm/6 1/2 ins × 13.89mm/35

ROYAL JAMAICA

Hand-made. Quality: good. Cameroun wrapper. Java binder. Maduro wrappers from Brazil. Formerly made in Jamaica. Mild.

Ten Downing Street	178mm/7 ins × 17.86mm/45
*Giant Corona	190mm/7 1/2 ins × 19.45mm/49
Goliath	228mm/9 ins × 17.86mm/45
Double Corona	178mm/7 ins × 17.86mm/45
*Churchill	203mm/8 ins × 20.24mm/51
*Corona Grande	165mm/6 1/2 ins × 16.67mm/42
Royal Corona	152mm/6 ins × 15.87mm/50
Director 1	152mm/6 ins × 17.86mm/45
New York Plaza	152mm/6 ins × 15.87mm/50

Tube No 1	165mm/6 1/2 ins × 16.67mm/42
Doubloon	178mm/7 ins × 12.00mm/30
Navarro	160mm/6 1/4 ins × 13.49mm/34
*Buccaneer	140mm/5 1/2 ins × 12.00mm/30
Park Lane	152mm/6 ins × 18.65mm/47
*Corona	140mm/5 1/2 ins × 15.87mm/47
Petit Corona	127mm/5 ins × 15.87mm/40
Churchill Minor	113mm/4 1/2 ins × 19.45mm/49
Pirate	113mm/4 1/2 ins × 12.00mm/30
Goucho	
Rapier	

*Maduro wrapper.

SANTA DAMIANA
Hand-made. Quality: superior. Connecticut shade wrapper. Mexican binder. Filler, blend of Dominican and Mexican tobacco. Mild. Launched in 1992 by Consolidated Cigars.

Seleccion No. 100	172mm/6 3/4 ins × 19.05mm/48
Seleccion No. 300	140mm/5 1/2 ins × 18.26mm/46
Seleccion No. 500	127mm/5 ins × 19.84mm/50
Seleccion No. 700	165mm/6 1/2 ins × 16.67mm/42
Seleccion No. 800	178mm/7 ins × 19.84mm/50
Seleccion No. 200	140mm/5 1/2 ins × 16.67mm/42
Seleccion No. 400	127mm/5 ins × 16.67mm/42
Seleccion No. 600	113mm/4 1/2 ins × 14.29mm/36

Brand relaunched in 1995 in four sizes with traditional names and blue and gold band, essentially for UK market. Has different blend to "Seleccion" range.

Churchill	178mm/7 ins × 19.05mm/48
Carona	140mm/5 1/2 ins × 16.67mm/42
Petit Corona*****	127mm/5 ins × 16.67mm/42

Medium bodied. Good flavour and balance. Elegant. Well-made. For discerning smoker.

Panetela	114mm/4 1/2 ins × 14.29mm/36

SANTIAGO
Hand-made. Connecticut wrapper. Dominican filler and binder.

No 1	171mm/6 3/4 ins × 19.1mm/48
No 2	178mm/7 ins × 14.3mm/36
No 3	165mm/6 1/2 ins × 18.3mm/46
No 4	140mm/5 1/2 ins × 18.3mm/46
No 5	127mm/5 ins × 15.9mm/40

SAVINELLI EXTREMELY LIMITED RESERVE
Hand-made. Connecticut wrapper. Dominican binder

and filler. Small production. Owned by famous maker of pipes.

No 1 Churchill	184mm/7 1/4 ins x 19.1mm/48
No 2 Cosona Extra	168mm/6 5/8 ins x 18.3mm/46
No 3 Lonsdale	159mm/6 1/4 ins x 17.1mm/43
No 4 Double Corona	152mm/6 ins x 19.84mm/50
No 5 Extraordinaire	140mm/5 1/2 ins x 17.5mm/44
No 6 Robusto	127mm/5 ins x 19.5mm/49

SILLEMS LAS TERENAS
Hand-made. Connecticut wrapper. Dominican binder and filler. Launched 1996. Exclusive to F&K Cigar Co.

Carabella	16.83mm/6 5/8 ins x 16.67mm/42
Hidalgo	15.24mm/6 ins x 19.84mm/50
Baraja	11.43mm/4 1/2 ins x 19.84mm/50
Levantado	19.05mm/7 1/2 ins x 19.84mm/50
Talamquera	14.29mm/5 5/8 ins x 16.67mm/42

SOSA
Hand-made. This brand was introduced 20 years ago by Juan Sosa. Wrapper from Ecuador and Connecticut. Binder from Honduras. Filler from Dominican Rep. Distributed by Antillian Cigar, Miami.

Magnum	190mm/7 1/2 ins × 20.64mm/52
Piramides No 2	178mm/7 ins × 25.00mm/64
Churchill	176mm/6 15/16 ins × 19.05mm/48
Lonsdale	165mm/6 1/2 ins × 17.07mm/43
Governor	152mm/6 ins × 19.84mm/50
Brevas	133mm/5 1/2 ins × 17.07mm/43
Wavell	120mm/4 3/4 ins × 19.84mm/50
Sante Fe	152mm/6 ins x 13.9mm/35

SOSA FAMILY SELECTION
Hand-made. Connecticut shade wrapper. Dominican filler and binder. Owned by Antillian Cigar.

No 1	171mm/6 3/4 ins x 17.1mm/43
No 2	159mm/6 1/4 ins x 21.4mm/54
No 3	146mm/5 3/4 ins x 17.5mm/44
No 4	127mm/5 ins x 15.9mm/40
No 5	127mm/5 ins x 19.8mm/50
No 6	159mm/6 1/4 ins x 15.1mm/38
No 7	152mm/6 ins x 19.8mm/50
No 8	171mm/6 3/4 ins x 19.1mm/48
No 9	197mm/7 3/4 ins x 20.6mm/52
Intermezzo	127mm/5 ins x 12.7mm/32

SPECIAL CARIBREAN
Hand-made. Quality: superior. Connecticut wrapper. Very mild.

Corona	140mm/5 1/2 ins × 17.07mm/43

Churchill	178mm/7 ins × 19.05mm/48
Fino	152mm/6 ins × 13.89mm/35
Nom Plus	140mm/5 1/2 ins × 19.84mm/50
Port Au Prince	194mm/7 5/8 ins × 20.64mm/52
No 1	194mm/7 5/8 ins × 17.07mm/43
No 2	162mm/6 3/8 ins × 16.67mm/42
No 898	165mm/6 1/2 ins × 17.86mm/42

SPECIAL CORONAS
Hand-made. Quality: superior. Ecuador wrappers. Made exclusively for Santa Clara, N.A. Mild to medium flavour. High quality construction.

Pyramides	178mm/7 ins × 21.43mm/54
No 754 Light	178mm/7 ins × 21.43mm/54
No 2 Light	165mm/6 1/2 ins × 17.76mm/45
No 54 Light	152mm/6 ins × 21.43mm/54
No 4 Light	140mm/5 1/2 ins × 17.86mm/45
Victoria Obesquio	190mm/7 1/2 ins × 20.64mm/52

SPECIAL JAMAICA
Hand-made. Connecticut shade wrapper. Mild. Sweet. Made in Jamaica until 1985. Exclusive to Santa Clara, N.A.

Rey del Rey	228mm/9 ins × 23.81mm/60
Mayfair	178mm/7 ins × 23.81mm/60
Pyramid	178mm/7 ins × 20.64mm/52
Churchill	178mm/7 ins × 20.64mm/52
Nobles (flared)	178mm/7 ins × 19.84mm/50
Bonita Obsequio	152mm/6 ins × 19.84mm/50
A	165mm/6 1/2 ins × 17.46mm/44
Fancytale Shape	165mm/6 1/2 ins × 17.07mm/43
B	152mm/6 ins × 17.46mm/44
C	140mm/5 1/2 ins × 17.46mm/44
D	152mm/6 ins × 19.84mm/50
Pica	127mm/5 ins × 12.70mm/32

TABAQUERO
Hand-made. Quality: superior. Connecticut wrapper. Dominican filler and binder. Exclusive to Indian Head Sales.

No 850	203mm/8 ins × 20.84mm/50
No 746	178mm/7 ins × 18.3mm/46
No 650	152mm/6 ins × 20.84mm/50
No 644	152mm/6 ins × 17.5mm/44
No 638	152mm/6 ins × 15.1mm/38
No 542	127mm/5 ins × 16.67mm/42

TOPPER CENTENNIAL

Hand-made. Connecticut wrapper. Dominican filler. Mexican binder. Launched to mark founding of company in 1896. Owned by Topper Cigar Co.

Churchill	191mm/7 1/2 ins × 20.6mm/52
Toro	152mm/6 ins × 20.84mm/50
Lonsdale	171mm/6 3/4 ins × 17.1mm/43

TRESADO

Hand-made. Quality: good. Medium flavour. Well made. Mild. Indonesian wrapper. Dominican binder and filler.

No 100	216mm/8 1/2 ins × 20.64mm/52
No 200	178mm/7 ins × 19.05mm/48
No 300	165mm/6 ins × 18.26mm/46
No 400	168mm/6 5/8 ins × 17.46mm/44
No 500	140mm/5 1/2 ins × 16.67mm/42

TROYA

Hand-made. Quality: superior. Connecticut shade or maduro wrappers. Havana seed binder, long fillers. Made by Tabacos Dominicos. Brand owned in USA by Lignum-II. Still made in Cuba with "Habana" on band.

No 81 Torpedo	178mm/7 ins × 21.43mm/54
No 72 Executive	197mm/7 3/4 ins × 19.84mm/50
No 63 Churchill	175mm/6 7/8 ins × 18.26mm/46
No 54 Elegante	178mm/7 ins × 16.67mm/43
No 45 Cetro	160mm/6 1/4 ins × 17.46mm/44
No 36 Palma Fina	178mm/7 ins × 14.29mm/36
No 27 Corona	140mm/5 1/2 ins × 16.67mm/42
No 18 Rothschild	113mm/4 1/2 ins × 19.84mm/50

TROYA CLASICO

Limited production. Long filler, double selection. Connecticut shade wrapper.

Executive	197mm/7 3/4 ins × 19.84mm/50
Corona	133mm/5 1/2 ins × 20.64mm/52

VUELTABAJO

Hand-made. Connecticut shade wrapper. Dominican binder and filler. Brand owned by Hollco Rohr.

Gigante	203mm/8 1/2 ins × 20.64mm/52
Churchill	178mm/7 ins × 19.05mm/48
Robusto	113mm/4 1/2 ins × 20.64mm/52
Lonsdale	178mm/7 ins × 17.07mm/43
Toros★★★★	152mm/6 ins × 19.84mm/50

Good flavour. Elegant. After dinner cigar.

Corona	147mm/5 3/4 ins × 16.67mm/42

ECUADOR

PRIMERA BUNDLES
Hand-made. Distributed in USA by Phillips & King.

No 1	178mm/7 ins × 16.67mm/42
No 2	149mm/5 7/8 ins × 17.46mm/44
Toro	127mm/5 ins × 17.07mm/43

GERMANY

In 1950 there were more than 300 cigar factories in Germany. Today although fewer than 10, cigar making (mainly cigarillos) is major industry. In 1995 exports to USA doubled to 4.988 million cigars over 1994. Cigar consumption in Germany has fallen in past 30 years from five billion to around one billion — about 5 percent of the total tobacco market.

AL CAPONE
Machine-made. Distributed by Swisher Intl.

Sweet	82mm/3 1/4 ins
Pockets	70mm/2 3/4 ins

BRANIFF GOLDEN LABEL
Machine-made. Tobacco from Sumatra. Short filler. Dry cigar.
Cigarillo★★   75mm/2 15/16 ins x 8.3mm/21
Good integrated flavours.

CANDLELIGHT DRY CURED
Machine-made. Light green wrapper cured with heat to fix chlorophyll in leaf. Slightly sweet taste.
Mini
Senorita
Panetela
Corona Slim
Block Corona

CLUBMASTER
Machine-made. Quality: good. Produced by Arnold André-Zigarrenfabrik, largest cigar producer in Germany. Part of gaint Ebas Group which was established in 1989 as result of merger between Dutch companies, La Paz and Willem II and Arnold André. Key markets: Germany, Belgium and France. Known mainly for its Brazil cigar type. Mild and aromatic.
Export/Export Light   75mm/3 ins × 8.8mm/22

Superior Sumatra/Brazil*   75mm/3 ins × 8.8mm/22
Slightly harsh.
Superior Mild Sumatra/Brazil 75mm/3 ins × 8.8mm/22
Finos Sumatra/Brazil   90mm/3 9/16 ins × 9.00mm/23
Selectos Sumatra/Brazil 92mm/3 5/8 ins × 9.00mm/23
Elegantes Sumatra/Brazil

107mm/4 3/16 ins × 10.70mm/27
Long Sumatra/Brazil

145mm/5 11/16 ins × 81.80mm/22
Panatelas Sumatra/Brazil

145mm/5 11/16 ins × 11.00mm/28
Half Corona Sumatra/Brazil

125mm/4 15/16 ins × 13.80mm/35

DANNEMANN
Machine-made. Established 1873 by Geraldo
Dannemann in Brazil. Made with Brazilian and Sumatra
tobaccos. Homogenised (HTL) wrapper. In 1994
launched vigerous marketing campaign in USA where it
is distributed by Swisher Intl. One of largest producers
of cigarillos in world. Employs nearly 500 people in
Germany and has about 33 percent share of local cigar
market.
Lonja (Brazil/Sumatra)****

136mm/5 3/8 ins × 9.92mm/25
Mild. Good balance. Spicy. Morning smoke. Ideal for
beginners.
Speciale (Brazil/Sumatra)**

74mm/2 7/8 ins × 9.92mm/25
Mild, pleasant aroma.
Imperial (Sumatra/Brazil)

108mm/4 1/4 ins × 9.92mm/25
Pierrot (Sumatra leaf/Brazil)

9.84mm/3 7/8 ins × 11.11mm/28
Menor (Sumatra)

9.84mm/3 7/8 ins × 11.11mm/28
Moods   73.2mm/2 7/8 ins × 7.9mm/20

IRACEMA
Machine-made.

Iracema Autentico Fuma 133mm/5 1/4 ins × 17.46/44
Iracema Macumba   165mm/6 1/2 ins × 16.67/42
Iracema Mata Fina   210mm/8 1/4 ins × 17.46mm/44
Iracema Santo Amoro   89mm/3 1/2 ins × 9.95mm/25

JOHN AYLESBURY
Hand-made. Good quality. Tobacco from Brazil,
Sumatra and Indonesia.

This group is based in Germany where it manufactures a range of cigars from Brazilian and Sumatran leaf. It also imports range of hand-made cigars from Dominican Republic and Honduras with "John Aylesbury" label.

Unique feature of this company is that distribution in Germany is guaranteed through a chain of 44 individually owned specialist cigar shops, with each shop owner having a share in the manufacturing business.

This brand is exported to the United States.

(See also "John Aylesbury" in Dominican Republic and Honduras sections.)

JOHN AYLESBURY

Feinschmecker No 1 (Indonesian leaf)
Feinschmecker No 2 (Indonesian leaf)
Feinschmecker No 3 (Indonesian leaf)
These sizes are repeated using Brazilian leaf.

JOHN AYLESBURY (all from Sumatra leaf)

No 22
No 23
No 24
Corona
Jubilee
Half Corona Number 1
Number 9
Pedito
Grandola
Tubo
Los Finos No 506
Los Finos No 509
Los Finos No 510
Half Corona

The above sizes are repeated using Brazilian leaf.

JOHN AYLESBURY CIGARILLOS
Machine-made.

No 1 (Brazilian & Sumatran leaf)
Mild and small (Sumatran)
Black and small (Brazilian)
Speciales (Brazilian)
Senoritas (Sumatra and Brazilian)
Longos (Sumatran and Brazilian)
Light Slenders (Sumatran)
Dark Slenders (Brazilian)

Twenty one (Sumatran and Brazilian)
Japura (Brazilian)

JOHN AYLESBURY LOS FINOS
Machine-made.

Rondo (Sumatran)
No 501 (Sumatran and Brazilian)
No 502 (Sumatran and Brazilian)
Mini Cigarillo (Sumatran and Brazilian)

JOHN AYLESBURY SIR JOHN'S
Mini (Sumatran, Brazilian and Cuban)
Aromatic (Sumatran and Brazilian)
Selection 100 (Sumatran and Brazilian)
Selection 400 (Cuban)

SUERDIECK (see also Brazil)
Machine-made.

Mandarim (Sumatra & Brazilian wrapper)

H O L L A N D

Holland is the largest global manufacturer of cigars accounting for nearly half the world's production. It makes close to three billion (including cigarillos). About 95 percent is made by four companies: Agio, about one billion (of which 500 million are their own brands); Ebas, about 900 million; Henri Winterman, about 650 million and Ritmeester, about 130 million. Of the total production about 50 percent is cigarillos. In 1995 exports to the USA increased from 3.26 million the previous year to 5.7 million. Local consumption is around 455 million pieces (decline of 3.3 percent on 1994) for a population of only 15 million. The country has a highly developed marketing infrastructure. There are still about 2 000 good tobacco shops, of which around 200 are top, specialist shops.

In 1995, for second year running, cigarillos accounted for more than 50 percent of the Dutch market.

Senoritas and tuit sizes did well at expense of larger cigars.

The industry started about 1830 on a small scale in Amsterdam. Until the Second World War most cigars were made by hand. Today, only about four brands are made that way. By 1860 there were 62 cigar makers in and around Amsterdam selling in grocery stores that specialised in colonial goods, such as coffee, tea, spices and tobacco. Now there are only two hand rollers left in Amsterdam. Harry Nak and his wife, situated opposite the famous and prestigeous Hajenius tobacco shop in what was the heart of the Amsterdam tobacco trade.

By 1900 many cigar makers had settled around the towns of Eindhoven, near the Belgian border, and Veenendal in the centre of Holland. The country was poor and there was plenty of cheap labour available. The industry built on what was, largely, a home industry.

Cigar makers would call at the factories on Saturday to collect tobacco and then during the week the whole family — husband, wife, children and grand-parents — would make cigars, with most skilful members adding the wrappers. Finished cigars were delivered to the factories the following Saturday when tobacco was collected for the next week.

Cigars were entirely hand-rolled until the 1930s, when the first machines were introduced. These only made the "bunch" (the filler wrapped inside the binder leaf). The wrapper was still applied by hand. Today the entire process is mechanised.

It was only after the end of the Second World War that the Dutch began to export cigars in earnest.

At that time there were hundreds of factories. As recently as 1963 there were still 22 cigar companies, but by 1982 the number had decreased to about 10.

Holland has created a huge industry even though it produces no tobacco itself. It has always relied on its former colonies, particularly Indonesia, for raw material. Despite this, and extremely high labour costs, Holland has been able to create this vast industry because of the concentration of production in a few large, highly mechanised and automated factories.

Amsterdam and Rotterdam used to be world centres for the trade in Indonesian and American tobacco. Today all Indonesian tobacco is sold by auction in Bremen in Germany and Cameroun tobacco in Paris.

What has certainly contributed to international popularity of the Dutch product is the variety of small cigars and cigarillos which have the taste of a true cigar and which can be smoked in a short time. Also, because of the link between disease and cigarettes, many cigarette smokers are switching to pure tobacco cigars which are less harmful as many of the damaging elements, including nicotine, have been considerably reduced.

In addition, Dutch cigars cost substantially less than a Havana and this was highlighted by Fons Maenen, export manager of the Ebas Group, who told me on a recent visit to Holland, "The Cubans make cigars for wealthy capitalists, while the Dutch make cigars for the mass market".

AGIO CIGARS
Machine-made. (Dry cigars). Available in Sumatran and dark Brazilian wrappers. Big seller in Europe.

Agio Sigarenfabrieken is one of largest cigar manufacturers in Europe. Head office is situated in Duizel, near the Belgium border. It produces about one billion cigars a year, of which about 500 million exported under own brand names to more than 100 countries outside Europe. Employs about 2 500 people world-wide. Family enterprise established in 1904 by Jacques Wintermans, grandfather of present chairman.

Rapid growth of Agio, combined with shortage of manpower in the Dutch Kempen, led to the establishment, in 1961 of a subsidiary in Geel, Belgium, where all cigars are currently produced. Increased labour costs in Holland and Belgium sparked off subsidiaries in Malta in 1973, Sri Lanka in 1985 and the Dominican Republic in 1990. These companies process binder and wrappers on bobbins for Agio and, to an increasing extent, for other cigar manufacturers as well.

The cigars are actually manufactured in the factory in Geel. Binders and filler tobacco are provided from the plant in Duizel. Final processing such as cutting, putting on the bands and wrapping in cellophane takes place in Duizel, where packing in wood or cardboard boxes is undertaken. Company has also developed and manufactured bobbin machines for its own use as well as for other manufacturers.

AGIO
Machine-made. Quality: good. Short filler. Dry cigar.

Agio Lights (Connecticut shade wrapper, light blue box)★★★★ 79mm/3 1/8 ins × 8.30mm/21
Lemony aroma. Smooth and mild.
Biddies (Brazilian wrapper, green box)★★★
99mm/3 7/8 ins × 9.10mm/23
Light bodied, but good balance between strength and flavour.
Biddies (Sumatran wrapper, blue box)★★★
99mm/3 7/8 ins × 9.10mm/23

Medium bodied. Stronger and more flavour than Brazilian wrapper.
Biddies Light (Connecticut shade wrapper, cream box)★★★★   99mm/3 7/8 ins × 9.10mm/23
Spicy flavour and aroma. Smooth and mild.

Elegant Rich & Light (Cuban shade wrapper, blue box)★★★   99mm/3 7/8 ins × 9.6mm/24
Figurado shape (*tuitcigar*). Full flavour. Medium bodied. Spicy. Also available with Sumatran wrapper.

Filter Tip (Cameroun wrapper, white box)★★
          79mm/3 1/8 ins × 8.20mm/20
Plastic tip with charcoal filler. HTL binder. Touch of sweetness. Mild. Much like a cigarette.

Junior Tip (Cameroun wrapper, white box)
          79mm/3 1/8 ins × 8.20mm/20
Mehari's Cigarillos (Cameroun wrapper, pale orange box)★★   99mm/3 7/8 ins × 9.10mm/23
Touch of sweetness. Medium bodied. HTL binder.
Mehari's Cigarillos (Brazilian wrapper)
          99mm/3 7/8 ins × 9.10mm/23

Mehari's Mild & Light (Connecticut shade wrapper, blue box)★   99mm/3 7/8 ins × 9.10mm/23
Sweet. Mild. HTL binder.

Agio Biddies (Brazilian)   85mm/3 3/8 ins × 7.9mm/20
Agio Biddies (Sumatran)
          85mm/3 3/8 ins × 7.9mm/20

BALMORAL
Machine-made. Quality: good. Short filler. Dry cigar. Owned by Agio. Heads are pre-cut.
Corona de Luxe (al. tubes)
          122mm/4 3/4 ins × 16.60mm/42
Overland   132mm/5 1/4 ins × 13.40mm/34
Coronas No 4★★★★   132mm/5 1/4 ins × 13.40mm/34
Meduim-bodied. Full creamy flavours.
Aristocrates   159mm/6 1/4 ins × 13.40mm/34
Valentine (figurado — *tuitcigar*)
          85mm/3 3/8 ins × 7.90mm/20
Cambridge (figurado — *tuitcigar*)
          99mm/3 7/8 ins × 9.60mm/24
Oxford (figurado — *tuitcigar*)
          91mm/3 9/16 ins × 12.60mm/32
Cardinal (figurado — *tuitcigar*)★★★
          106mm/4 3/16 ins × 12.60mm/32

Sumatra wrapper. Good balance between flavour and stength. Surprisingly full bodied for a small cigar.
Regentes (figurado — *tuitcigar*)

	96mm/3 7/16 ins × 14.50mm/37
Cumberland	112mm/4 3/8 ins × 10.00mm/25
Senoritas No 5	112mm/4 3/8 ins × 10.00mm/25
Highlands	111mm/4 5/16 ins × 12.20mm/31
Midlands	103mm/4 1/8 ins × 12.60mm/32
Panatella	124mm/4 7/8 ins × 12.30mm/31
Diana	85mm/3 3/8 ins × 7.9mm/20
Legende	97mm/3 1/2 ins × 7.60mm/19
Shetlands	93mm/3 11/16 ins × 9.40mm/24
Cigarillos No 3	93mm/3 11/16 ins × 9.40mm/24

CHAMBORD

Quality: superior. Made by Henri Wintermans, mainly for French market. Models No 2 and No 3, hand-made. Blend of tobacco from Cuba.

No 2	156m/6 1/8 ins × 12.7mm/32
No 3	140mm/5 1/2 ins × 16.67mm/42
No 5	124mm/4 7/8 ins × 9.10mm/23
No 7★★★★	95mm/3 3/4 ins × 7.6mm/19

Rich, surprisingly full flavour for cigarillo. Smooth. Well balanced.

COMPAENEN GREEN SERIES

Machine-made. Short filler. Dry cigar. Quality: superior. Produced for past 15 years as exclusive label to about 100 tobacco shops in Holland. Mild, elegant range. Technical committee from tobacconists select the range from various manufacturers.

Corona No 700★★★★
Smooth elegant cigar with spice and mushroom aroma. Good daytime smoke.
Corona No 720
Corona Royal No 725 (al. tube)★★★★

125mm/4 15/16 ins × 12.10mm/30

Medium-bodied with spicy aroma. Ideal to smoke with cup of espresso.
Half Corona No 730
Panetela No 760★★★★
Cigar for connoisseur. Smooth and elegant.
Wilde Havana No 770
Foot is uncut
Senoritas No 755
Senoritas No 765

Tuitsenoritas No 790 (figurado — *tuitcigar*)★★★★
Medium-bodied. Has little strength until normal girth of
cigar is reached, then good satisfying smoke.
Cigarillos No 775
Tuit cigarillos (figurado — *tuitcigarillo*)
Mini cigarillos No 795

COMPAENEN RED SERIES

Machine-made. Short filler. Dry cigar. Quality: superior.
Produced for last 15 years as exclusive label to about
100 local tobacco shops. Fuller bodied than green
series.

Corona No 620
Wilde Havana No 670
Senoritas No 665
Wilde Cigarillos No 680
Cigarilos No 675

DE HEEREN VAN RUYSDAEL

Machine-made. 100 percent tobacco. Undusted. Superior quality. Dry cigar. Tobacco from Sumatra, Cuba and
Brazil. Sumatran Deli-sandleaf wrapper.

Recreations of old plantation cigars that made Dutch
cigars world famous more than 100 years ago. Well
constructed and beautifully presented. Mild, subtle with
woody aroma. For those that like dry cigars, this is
about as good as it gets.

There are two blends. Composition No 12 is a
somewhat understated taste, with a balanced mixture
of Java, Havana and Brazilian tobaccos — mild cigar
with pleasant aroma. Composition No 17 is a rich
aristocratic blend with a touch of freshness provided by
the Havana tobacco.

Corona Invincible Grandes XO★★★★★
　　　　　　　　164mm/6 1/2 ins × 14mm/36
Good integrated flavours and aroma. Elegant cigar to
follow meal.

Magistraat Panatella	121.5mm/6 1/2 ins × 13 mm/33
Procureur Tuitknak	108mm/4 3/16 ins × 13mm/33
Gezel Petit Panatella	117mm/4 5/8 ins × 10mm/25
Referndaris cigantto	94.5mm/3 3/4 ins × 9mm/23

Corona Commandeur★★★★★
　　　　　　　　127mm/5 ins × 16.27mm/41
Spicy aroma with rich flavour. Classy cigar to follow
lunch.
Regent senoritas★★★★　　102mm/4 ins × 15.87mm/40
Wonderful wrapper. Full-bodied and well-balanced.

Resident half corona★★★★
102mm/4 ins × 12.30mm/31
Sophisticated pre-dinner smoke.

DE HUIFKAR
Machine-bunched and hand finished. Short filler. Quality: superior. Owned by Agio. Unusual feature is that details of wrapper, binder and filler blend on inside of lid of wood box. Wrapper from Sumatra, binder from Java and filler blend of tobacco from Cuba, Brazil and Java.

La Romana	85mm/3 3/8 ins × 7.90mm/20
Paradiso	99mm/3 7/8 ins × 9.10mm/23
Palomas	99mm/3 7/8 ins × 9.60mm/24
Aristos	112mm/4 3/8 ins × 10.10mm/25
Practicus	111mm/4 5/16 ins × 12.20mm/30
Reservados★★★	115mm/4 9/16 ins × 15.00mm/38

Well made, elegant cigar. Very mild. Lacks flavour and character.

DUNHILL SMALL CIGARS
Machine-made. Quality: good. All tobacco. Sumatra wrapper. Java binder and filler. Dry cigar. Launched in 1986 and into US market in 1991.

Miniatures
Senoritas
Panatellas

HARRY NAK MINISTRO
Hand-made. Short filler. Dry cigar. Quality: superior. Harry Nak and his wife are last two hand rollers left in Amsterdam. Situated in what was heart of Amsterdam tobacco trade. Brand established 1980. Medium to full bodied.

Half Corona
Mirambo
Senoritas Grande
Panatella
Corona Subliem
Corona★★★★ 127mm/5 ins × 15.08mm/38
Medium to full-bodied. Good balance between flavour and body. Good daytime smoke.
Superclass

HENRI WINTERMAN CAFÉ CRÈME
Machine-made. Short filler. Dry cigar. Quality: good. Entire production of about 650 million exported, mainly cigarillos. Company established in Eersel, near Bel-

gium border, in 1934 to supply local market. Then, in 1950, because of severe competition from about 1 500 manufacturers, began exporting. Probably largest cigar export in world. Taken over by giant cigarette manufacturer, BAT. Operate separately because marketing of cigars different to that of cigarettes. However, uses parent company's expertise in emerging markets, such as the former Soviet Union countries and Eastern Europe. Presently exports to about 100 countries. Main markets are Australia, Ireland, Italy, Scandinavia and duty free shops.

Brand launched in 1963 to capture large sector of cigarillo market, that was growing as cigarette smokers switched to pure tobacco products. Packed in flat tins, bearing Café Crème logo, coffee cup symbol and cigar. These elements were added to the packaging to reinforce ideal partnership of the brand when enjoying a break, or a moment of relaxation. Annual sales exceed 100 million sticks.

Filter Tip (paper filter incorporated in plastic mouth-piece)	98mm/3 7/8 ins × 8.5mm/28
Mild	75mm/2 7/8 ins × 8.5mm/28
Grand Café	92mm/3 5/8 ins × 7.7mm/19
Mini/Mild	70mm/2 3/4 ins × 8.5mm/28
Plus/Mild	74mm/2 7/8 ins × 8.5mm/28
Specials	110mm/4 5/16 ins × 10.00mm/25

HENRY WINTERMAN CIGARS

Machine-made. Quality: superior. Sumatran wrapper. Java binder and filler blend of tobacco from Cuba and Brazil. Half-Corona claimed to be top selling cigar in UK.

Excellentes	160mm/6 3/8 ins × 16.67mm/42
Royales	
Cello	
Golden Panetella	
Kentucky Kings	
Half Corona	95mm/3 3/4 ins × 13.5mm/34
Long Panatella	131mm/5 5/8 ins × 11.9mm/30
Slim Panatella	143mm/5 5/8 ins × 7.9mm/20
Corona de Luxe	115mm/5 1/8 ins × 16.67mm/42
Scooters	90mm/3 1/2 ins × 7.9mm/20

JUSTUS VAN MAURIK

Machine-made. Quality: superior. Short filler. Dry cigar. Hand selected. Wrapper from Sumatra, binder from Java and filler blend of tobacco from Cuba, Brazil and

Indonesia. Brand established in 1794. Now owned by Ebas Group. Packed in varnished cedar boxes.

Grand Corona	152mm/6 ins × 16.67mm/42
Corona No 1	152mm/6 ins × 16.67mm/42
Coronation	135mm/5 5/16 ins × 16.67mm/42
After Dinner	120mm/5 11/16 ins × 14.5mm/37
Petit Corona	103mm/4 1/16 ins × 14.9mm/38
Noblesse	130mm/5 1/8 ins × 13.8mm/35

Sumatra Tuitnak (figurado)★★★★★

112mm/4 7/16 ins × 12.15mm/32

Even, slow burning. Spicy, floral flavours and aroma. Medium to full bodied, flavour gets going when full girth of cigar is reached. Great daytime smoke.

Classique	104mm/4 1/16 ins × 12.60mm/32
Petit Panetela	122mm/4 13/16 ins × 10.75mm/27
Zandblad Cigarillos	94mm/3 7/16 ins × 8.20mm/21
Caresse★★★	98mm/3 7/8 ins × 8.00mm/20

Full flavour, but mild in strength.

KAREL VAN SANTE

Machine-made. Short filler. Dry cigar. Quality: superior. Wrappers from Sumatra and fillers a blend of tobacco from Cuba, Brazil, Java and Sumatra. Karel van Sante has spent life time in Dutch cigar industry. Was, until few years ago, chief blender for Ritmeester.

Corona★★★★★   120mm/4 3/4 ins × 15.00mm/38

Attractive spicy aroma. Full bodied, well balanced cigar. Smooth.

Half Corona
Panatela
Senoritas
Petit Panatella

LA PAZ

Machine-made — Quality: good. 100 percent tobacco, undusted. Dry cigar. Uses tobacco from Sumatra, Java, Brazil and Cuba. Quality: superior. Brand established in 1814. Now owned by Ebas, which was established in 1989 as a result of merger between Dutch companies La Paz and Willem II and German company, Arnold André. Ebas produces more than one billion cigars annually, employ nearly 2 000 people in several countries.

La Paz popularised concept of wilde cigars.

Availability: Holland, France, Belgium, Germany, South Africa and duty free shops.

Foot of Wilde range is uncut, enabling smokers easily to see that the binder is pure tobacco leaf.

Mini Wilde★★★   79mm/3 1/8 ins × 7.60mm/19
Robust, full integrated flavours.
Wilde Cigarillos Havana★★★★

                         102mm/4 ins × 9.20mm/23
Good integrated flavours. Satisfying quick smoke.
Wilde Cigarillos Brazil   102mm/4 ins × 9.10mm/23
Wilde Panetela   119mm/4 11/16 ins × 10.5mm/27
Wilde Havana★★★★ 119mm/4 11/16 ins × 12.70mm/32
Pleasant cool smoke. Good value.
Wilde Brazil★★★★   119mm/4 11/16 ins × 12.60mm/32
Dark maduro wrapper. Spicy. Vegetal aroma. Full bodied and good flavour.
Wilde Corona   135mm/5 5/16 ins × 14.5mm/37
Cherie★★★   102mm/4 ins × 12.70mm/32
Mild pleasant quick smoke.
Corona Superiores CK126★★★

                         114mm/4 1/2 ins × 16.00mm/41
Good intergated flavours with a creamy finish. Good morning smoke.
Especiales CK164 (tube)

                         162mm/6 3/8 ins × 13.70mm/35

OUD KAMPEN SUMATRA CUM LAUDE
Machine-made. Short filler. Dry cigar. Quality: superior. Medium to full bodied. Brand owned by Ritmeester. Sell about 22 million cigars across the range.

Havana Grande   152mm/6 ins × 16.67mm/42
Grand Primeur   132mm/5 1/4 ins × 17.07mm/43
Alta Gracia   132mm/5 1/4 ins × 15.00mm/38
Ambassadeur   125mm/4 15/16 ins × 16.6mm/42
Corona Clasica★★★   107mm/4 3/16 ins × 15.7mm/40
Spicy, earth aroma. Mellow. Good intergrated flavours.
Amadeus   137mm/5 1/4 ins × 12.00mm/30
Delicatesse★★★   120mm/4 3/4 ins × 12.7mm/32
Good balance between strength and flavour. Refined cigar.
Havana Natura★★★   120mm/4 3/4 ins × 12.7mm/32
Wilde. Has uncut foot. Good easy daytime smoke.
Selection★★★★★   104mm/4 1/8 ins × 12.7mm/32
Full spicy, peppery aromas and flavour. Ideal morning smoke with coffee. For connoisseur.
La Reina★★★★   94mm/3 7/8 ins × 12.7mm/32
Full-bodied. Spicy aroma with mushroom on finish. For experienced smoker.

La Donna★★★★　　　115mm/4 9/16 ins × 10.5mm/27
Spicy aroma with mushrooms on finish. Good flavour
for small cigar.
La Diva　　　　　　114mm/4 9/16 ins × 10.5mm/27
Suzette　　　　　　100mm/3 15/16 ins × 9.00mm/23
Elite★★★　　　　　　92mm/3 5/8 ins × 9.25mm/24
Smooth. Full-bodied.
Jeunesse　　　　　　80mm/3 3/16 ins × 8.3mm/21

PANTER
Machine-made. Short filler. Dry cigar. Quality: good.
Owned by Agio. Brand specialises in smaller, quality
cigarillos. Exported widely. All have wrappers from
Java, except Lights and Domino Mild and high, which
have Connecticut shade wrappers and Domino
Cameroun with wrapper from Cameroun.

Sprint (HTL binder)★★★★
　　　　　　　　　　75mm/2 15/16 ins × 8.3mm/21
Leathery aroma. Mild to medium.
Small　　　　　　　75mm/2 15/16 ins × 8.3mm/21
Lights　　　　　　　75mm/2 15/16 ins × 8.3mm/21
Domino Cameroun★★　99mm/3 7/8 ins × 9.10mm/23
Flavour improves during smoke.
Domino Wild & Light　99mm/3 7/8 ins × 9.10mm/23
Tango★★★　　　　　99mm/3 7/8 ins × 9.10mm/23
Lots of flavour. Satisfying quick smoke.
Mignon　　　　　　96mm/3 15/16 ins × 10.00mm/25

P.G.C. HAJENIUS
Machine-made. Short filler. Dry cigar. Quality: superior.
Wrappers from Sumatra. Owned by Ritmeester. Previ-
ously only sold in prestigeous Hajenius shop in
Amsterdam. Now sold nationally. Export policy will be
finalised late 1995. Top brand in Holland.

Grand Finale No 1★★★★★　152mm/6 ins × 16.67mm/42
Coffee aroma and flavour. Well-bred cigar. Fit for
connoisseur. To follow a meal
Corona Superieur　132mm/5 3/16 ins × 17.00mm/43
Corona★★★★★　　125mm/4 15/16 ins × 16.5mm/42
Full flavour. Good balance between strength and
flavour. Smooth. Elegant cigar with good finish.
Grote Tuitnak (Figurado)
　　　　　　　　124mm/4 15/16 ins × 15.00mm/38
Grand Finale No 2★★★★★ 127mm/5 ins × 16.67mm/42
Rich creamy flavours and spicy aroma. Smooth.
Definitely for connoisseur.

Hajenius do Brasil No 1 (Brazilian wrapper)
             136mm/5 3/8 ins × 12.00mm/30
Petit Corona★★★★★   107mm/4 3/16 ins × 15.7mm/40
Attractive spicy aroma with creamy finish. Elegant. Soft.
Lovey daytime smoke.
Panetela Sumatra★★★★★

             137mm/5 3/8 ins × 12.00mm/30
Lots of punch and character in this cigar. Smooth.
Panalito   127mm/5 ins × 12.7mm/32
Senoritas★★★★★   104mm/4 1/8 ins × 12.7mm/32
Surprising satisfaction for small cigar. Smooth.
Signorina★★★★★   115mm/5 15/16 ins × 10.5mm/26
Elegant looking cigar that provider elegant smoke.
Full-bodied.
Klein Tuitnak (Figurado)★★★★★

             94mm/3 11/16 ins × 12.7mm/32
Amazingly rich for small cigar. Ideal to follow lunch
when time is short.
Tuit panetela (Figurado)

             114mm/4 9/16 ins × 7.5mm/19
Wilde Havana Select   120mm/4 3/4 ins × 12.7mm/32
Cigarillo★★★★★   92mm/3 1/2 ins × 9.25mm/23
Gentle spicy, woody aroma. Medium strength. Quick
smoke for connoisseur.

RITMEESTER

Machine-made. Short filler. Dry cigar. HTL binder.
Quality: good. Designed for mass market. Good value
range. Established in 1887. Reached high point in the
1930s, when torpedo shape developed. In 1937 employed 1 700 people; today, largely because of
mechanisation, figure down to about 200 employees.
Produce about 130 million cigars annually. (Five million
to South Africa, where it is the brand leader.) Popular in
USA, Europe and South Africa. Mild cigar using tobacco mainly from Java and Brazil. Today Ritmeester is
owned by Burger Söhne Company, manufacturers of
Dannemann brand, in Switzerland.

Half Corona★★   95mm/3 3/4 ins × 14.6mm/37
Dusted. Pleasant. Medium to full bodied.
PiKeur★   101mm/4 ins × 12.5mm/32
Ordinary quick smoke. Dusted.
Riant (dusted)★★   97mm/3 7/8 ins × 18.00/46
Mild but slightly harsh finish.
PiKeur Mini Light   83mm/3 1/4 ins × 7.8mm/20
Corona   117mm/4 5/8 ins × 16.30mm/41

Gracia (torpedo)★★ 108mm/4 1/4 ins × 19.8mm/50
HTL binder. Dusted.
Livarde★★★ 91mm/3 9/16 ins × 9.10mm/23
Dusted wrapper. Better burning and fuller body than
Livarde Light.
Livarde Light 91mm/3 9/16 ins × 9.10mm/23
HTL binder. Good wrapper from Sumatra. Mild.
Livarde Mini Light 83mm/3 1/4 ins × 7.80mm/20
Rozet★★ 117mm/4 5/8 ins × 10.7mm/27
Full-bodied. Bit harsh.
Royal Dutch Fresh and Mild

91mm/3 9/16 ins × 9.10mm/23
Royal Dutch Cigarillo 91mm/3 9/16 ins × 9.10mm/23
Royal Dutch Panatella 106mm/4 3/16 ins × 10.3mm/26
Royal Dutch Half Corona

95mm/3 3/4 ins × 11.6mm/29
Tip 75mm/3 ins × 8.70mm/22
Elites 136mm/5 1/8 ins × 9.70mm/25
Wilde Havana★★★★ 120mm/4 3/4 ins × 12.7mm/32
Medium bodied. Mild coffee aroma. Flavour little for-
ward. Good cigar.
Corona Delecta★★ 132mm/5 1/4 ins × 17.00mm/43
Medium to full-bodied. Not particularly elegant cigar.
Dusted.
*Quick 101mm/4 ins × 12.5mm/32
Whiff 91mm/3 9/16 ins × 9.10mm/23
*Senior★★★ 100mm/3 15/16 ins × 10.0mm/25
HTL binder. Dusted. Medium bodied. Bit one dimen-
sional.
*Junior 90mm/3 1/2 ins × 9.7mm/24
*Only available in South Africa.

SCHIMELPENNINCK

Machine-made. Quality: superior. Made from tobacco
from Brazil, Cameroun and Indonesia. Dry cigar.
Started in 1924 and named after 19th century Dutch
governor. About 90 percent of total production exported
to over 160 countries. Accounts for about 40 percent of
dry cigars sold in USA. Duet world's best selling thin
panetela. Owned by Rothmans.

Florina	99mm/3 7/8 ins
Half Corona	95mm/3 3/4 ins
Nostra	74mm/2 7/8 ins
Media	76mm/3 ins
Montego Milds	76mm/3 ins
Mono	86mm/3 3/8 ins
Vada	99mm/3 7/8 ins

Mini Tips	102mm/4 with Tip
Panatella 145 Miskleur	
Panatella 145 Miskleur naturel	
Superior Milds	
Duet	143mm/5 5/8 ins
Media Brazil	79mm/3 1/8 ins
Duet Brazil	79mm/5 5/8 ins
Mini Cigar	70mm/2 3/4 ins
Mono Brazil	86mm/3 3/8 ins
Havana Milds	76mm/3 ins
Swing	
VSOP Cigarillo de Luxe	
VSOP Senoritas de Luxe	
VSOP Duella de Luxe	
VSOP Corona de Luxe	
VSOP Grand Corona de Luxe	
VSOP Corona Royales (al. tube)	

SWISHER SWEETS
Machine-made. Owned by Swisher Intl.
Mini Cigarillo (tins)   111mm/4 3/8 ins × 11.1mm/28

VAN DER DONK
Hand-made. Short filler. Dry cigar. Quality: superior. All Sumatran wrappers. Small quantity produced. One of few remaining factories where cigars still hand-made. Established 1919 in Culemborg. Third generation still in business.

Merville (corona)
Top of range. Binder from Java. Filler, blend of four types of Cuban, four types of Java and four types of Brazilian tobacco.
Corona Corona
Developed in 1946 for gift to Sir Winston Churchill.
Havana Bouquet (corona)
Binder from Java. Filler blend of three types of Cuban tobacco.
Corona (petit corona)
Binder from Java. Filler blend of tobacco from Java, Cuba and Brazil.
Long Panetella
Extra long panetella. Binder from Java. Filler is blend of three types of tobacco from Brazil.
Subliem (figurado) (*tuitnak*)★★★★
Filler is blend of tobacco from Brazil, Cuba and Java. Mild woody aroma. Experience full flavour when full girth is reached. Elegant and smooth.

Panatella (short panetella)
Binder from Java. Filler is blend of tobacco from Java, Brazil and Cuba.
Half a Corona
Same tobacco as in Corona. Ideal for when time is short.
Cocktails
Between Panetela and Half a Corona in size. Came tobacco used.
Matta Fina
Blend of Dutch tobacco.
Vuelta
Cigarillo with same tobacco as in Havana Bouquet.

WILLEM II
Machine-made. Short filler. Dry cigar. Quality: good. Sumatran wrapper. HTL binder. Willem was founded in 1916 by the tobacco merchant Hendrik Kersten. Factory still located in Valkenswaard, small rural village in south of Holland. Cigars exported to more than 100 countries and stocked in nearly all duty-free shops. Part of Dutch Ebas Group established in 1989 as result of merger between Dutch companies, La Paz and Willem II and German company, Arnold André.

Optimum*　　　　126mm/4 15/16 ins × 15.8mm/40
Draws too easily, tends to burn bit harsh. Mild. Uninspiring.
Corona de Luxe　　126mm/4 15/16 ins × 15.8mm/40
Half Corona★★★　　94mm/3 5/16 ins × 13.7mm/35
All tobacco. Spicy, vegetal aroma. Good balance. Smooth.
Extra Senoritas　　101mm/3 15/16 ins × 12.4mm/31
Long Panetella★★★　143mm/5 5/8 ins × 9.0mm/23
Mild. Rich coffee and spice aroma. Touch of sweetness.
Whiff
WILLEM II WHIFF & MINATURE
No 30　　　　　　89mm/3 1/2 ins × 9.10mm/23
Java　　　　　　102mm/4 ins × 8.8mm/22
Indioz　　　　　96mm/3 13/16 ins × 7.6mm/19
Primo　　　　　96mm/3 13/16 ins × 7.6mm/19
Java Mini　　　　79mm/3 1/8 ins × 7.6mm/19
Indioz Mini　　　79mm/3 1/8 ins × 7.6mm/19
Petitos★★★★　　79mm/3 1/8 ins × 7.6mm/19
Good flavour. Medium body. Good, quick smoke.
Sigretto★★★　　70mm/2 3/4 ins × 9.00mm/23
Dark maduro wrapper. Surprisingly strong and full bodied for such a small cigar.

Wee Willem Mild	70mm/2 3/4 ins × 8.10mm/21
Wee Willem Extra Mild	70mm/2 3/4 ins × 8.10mm/21
Wings No 75	75mm/3 ins x 7.6mm/19
Wings No 105	105mm/4 1/8 ins x 7.6mm/19

ZINO
Machine-made — 100 percent tobacco. (Dry cigar). Available in Indonesian and dark Brazilian wrappers. Mild.

Zino Drie	147mm/5 3/4 ins × 15.87mm/40
Zino Jong Cigarillos	108mm/4 1/4 ins × 12.00mm/30
Zino Panatellas (Sumatran leaf)	
	140mm/5 1/2 ins × 7.14mm/18
Zino Panetellas (Brazilian leaf)	
	140mm/5 1/2 ins × 7.14mm/18
Zino Cigarillos (Brazilian leaf)★★★★	89mm/3 1/2 ins

Mild with good flavour.
Zino Cigarillos (Sumatran leaf)★★★★　　89mm/3 1/2 ins
More body than Brazilian leaf. Both excellent cigarillos.

HONDURAS

Honduras is the second largest exporter of premium cigars to the United States, exporting in 1995 more than 69 million. This accounted for 36 percent of imports into USA of premium cigars.

Main growing areas are hot, coastal plains around San Pedro Sula and cooler mountain regions of Santa Rosa de Copan stretching to the hilly Nicaraguan border of Danli.

Tradition dominating the cigar industry in Honduras is different from that of Cuba and the Dominican Republic. Something between the rustic yet disciplined air of Cuba's state-owned factories and the almost industrial atmosphere of the Dominican Republic.

Honduras is clearly Third World, with factories dotting the sparsely populated countryside or in small, frontier-like towns with cobblestone streets and carts pulled by bulls or horses.

Many believe that Honduran tobacco has the aroma and palate closest to that of true Cuban tobacco, although supporters of cigars from Nicaragua will deny this. Commercial tobacco operations in Honduras date back to mid 18th Century.

Most tobacco in Honduras is grown from Cuban seed introduced as early as 1941. However, blue mould has devasted huge amounts of tobacco in Central America since the early 1980s. About 25 percent of the crop of some producers was lost to this disease in 1993. A field of several acres can be overcome by this scourge in a single night once the mould is present.

To combat blue mould some growers in Honduras have altered their plant seasons from the milder, cooler months of November and December, which encourage the fungus, to the hotter, drier period in January and February. Mould is not able to prosper without the end-of-year cool nights and mornings wet with dew.

Although Honduras is not as sophisticated as the Dominican Republic most factories employ strict quality control. However, it is not unusual to find producers who expect workers to produce 600 cigars a day working in teams of bunchers and rollers. This is, more or less, similar to the Dominican Republic.

ASTRAL

Hand-made. Quality: superior. Premium Connecticut shade wrapper. Aged Honduran binder. Blend of Havana seed and Honduran long leaf filler. Superpremium with price range of $7 to $10, launched in June 1995. Distributed worldwide. Sales in 1996 nearly six million. Owned by U.S. Tobacco International. Distributed in USA by Miami Cigar.

Maestro★★★★★ 190mm/7 1/2 ins × 20.64mm/52
Good balance between strength and flavour. Not as much body as one would expect from such big cigar. Discreet aroma and flavours. Elegant. Well-made. Appreciated by connoisseur and occasional smoker alike.

Favorito★★★★ 178mm/7 ins × 19.05mm/48
Spicy aroma before lit. Medium bodied. Needs half inch or so before it starts to show its pace.

Perfeccion 178mm/7 ins × 19.05mm/48
Lujos★★★★ 165mm/6 1/2 ins × 17.46mm/44
Firm draw. Medium-bodied. Short on flavour. Smooth. Even burning.

Besos 127mm/5 ins × 20.64mm/52

ARANGO STATESMAN

Hand-made. All Honduron tobacco. Medium-bodied. Not to be confused with sister brand, Arango Sportsman, which is vanilla flavoured, machine-made in Tampa, USA. Owned by Arango Cigar Co., Chicago.

Barrister★★★ 190mm/7 1/2 ins × 18.26mm/46
Smooth claro wrapper. Burns evenly. Easy draw. Sweet vanilla finish.

| Executor | 127mm/5 ins × 15.87mm/40 |
| Counsetor | 140mm/5 1/2 ins × 17.46mm/44 |

BACCARAT HAVANA SELECTION
Hand-made. Quality: medium. Good value. Connecticut shade wrapper. Mexican binder. Cuban seed filler. Launched in 1978. Made by Tabocos Rancho Jamastran. This company own its own farms and in 1996 planted over 600 acres (300 hectares) of tobacco. Runs formal training school for rollers. Group owned by Eiroas Family. Imported exclusively into USA by Caribe in Florida.

| Polo | 178mm/7 ins × 20.64mm/52 |
| *Churchill★★★★ | 178mm/7 ins × 19.84mm/50 |

Mild, with lots of flavour. Well made.

No 1	178mm/7 ins × 17.46mm/44
Panetela	152mm/6 ins × 15.08mm/38
Petit Corona	140mm/5 1/2 ins × 16.67mm/42
*Rothschild	178mm/7 ins × 19.84mm/50
Bonita	113mm/4 1/2 ins × 12.00mm/30
Luchadore★★★★	152mm/6 ins × 17.07mm/43

Firm draw. Robust flavour with touch of sweetness.

| Platinum | 124mm/4 7/8 ins × 12.70mm/32 |

*Also available in maduro.

BANCES
6 hand-made — 6 machine-made. Good value. Made by Villazon. Machine-made in their Tampa, Florida plant and hand-made in Honduras using Havana seed wrappers.

*Presidents	8 1/2 ins × 52
*Corona Immensas	172mm/6 3/4 ins × 19.05mm/48
Crowns Maduro	147mm/5 3/4 ins × 19.84mm/50
Demitasse	102mm/4 ins × 13.89mm/35
*Uniques	140mm/5 1/2 ins × 15.08mm/38
Havana Holders	165mm/6 1/2 ins × 12.00mm/30
*Brevas	140mm/5 1/2 ins × 17.07mm/43
Palmas	152mm/6 ins × 16.67mm/42
Palmas (Boy or Girl)	152mm/6 ins × 16.67mm/42
El Prados	160mm/6 1/4 ins × 14.29mm/36
No 3	147mm/5 3/4 ins × 18.26mm/46
*Cazadores	160mm/6 1/4 ins × 17.46mm/44

*Hand-made.

BELINDA
Hand-made. Quality: superior. Wrapper from Ecuador. Binder from Honduras. Filler is blend of tobacco from

Honduras and Dominican Republic. Cigar of same name made in Cuba with word "Habana" on band. Exclusive to Santa Clara N.A.

Belinda****	165mm/6 1/2 ins × 14.29mm/36

Very mild. Ideal for women.

Breva Conserva	140mm/5 1/2 ins × 17.46/44
Cabinet	143mm/5 5/8 ins × 17.86/45
Ramon	184mm/7 1/4 ins × 18.65/47
Corona Grande	160mm/6 1/4 ins × 17.46/44
Medagla D'Oro	113mm/4 1/2 ins × 19.84/50

BERING

Machine-bunched and hand-finished. Quality: superior. First made in 1905 in Tampa's famed Ybor City. End of last decade entire operation moved to Honduras. Also produces range with maduro and candela wrappers. Now with red and gold bands only.

Torpedo	178mm/7 ins × 21.4mm/54
Barons	184.9mm/7 1/4 ins × 16.67mm/42
Casinos-Glass Tubes	181mm/7 1/8 ins × 16.67mm/42
Cazadores	160mm/6 1/4 ins × 17.86mm/45
Coronados	132mm/5 3/16 ins × 17.86mm/45
Grande	215.9mm/8 1/2 ins × 20.6mm/52
Corona Royale	152mm/6 ins × 16.27mm/41
Gold No 1	160mm/6 1/4 ins × 13.10mm/33
Hispanos****	152mm/6 ins × 19.84mm/50

Mild. Touch of cinnamon. Good daytime smoke.

Robusto	120.6mm/4 3/4 ins × 19.8mm/50
Imperials Boy/Girl	133mm/5 1/4 ins × 16.67mm/42
Imperials****	133mm/5 1/4 ins × 16.67mm/42

Fairly hard draw. Mild. Smooth. Lacks character. After dinner cigar.

Inmensas	181mm/7 1/8 ins × 17.86mm/45
Plazas****	152mm/6 ins × 17.07mm/43

Well-made. Easy draw. Spicy.

BERMEJO

Cazadores	160mm/6 1/4 ins × 18.26mm/46
Fumas	165mm/6 1/2 ins × 17.86mm/45

BEVERLY HILLS — VIP

No 535	127mm/5 ins × 13.89mm/35
No 550	127mm/5 ins × 19.8mm/50
No 644	152mm/6 ins × 17.46mm/44
No 736	178mm/7 ins × 14.29mm/36
No 749	178mm/7 ins × 19.45mm/49

BLUE LABEL
Hand-made. Bundle. All Honduran tobacco. Distributed by Mike's Cigars, Miami.

Bulvon	168mm/6 5/8 ins × 21.4mm/54
Churchill	175mm/6 1/8 ins × 19.1mm/48
Finos	179mm/7 ins × 11.9mm/30
Imperial	203mm/8 ins × 20.6mm/52
No 1	168mm/6 5/8 ins × 17.5mm/45
No 2	152mm/6 ins × 16.67mm/42
Palma	175mm/6 7/8 ins × 13.9mm/35
Presidente	190mm/7 1/2 ins × 19.84mm/50
Rothschild	121mm/4 3/4 ins × 19.84mm/50
Toro	159mm/6 1/4 ins × 19.84mm/50

CAMACHO
Hand-made. Quality: good. Cuban seed wrapper, binder and filler. Also with Connecticut shade wrapper. Made by Tabacos Rancho Jamastran (Eiroa Family). Imported exclusively into USA by Caribe in Florida.

El Cesar	216mm/8 1/2 ins × 20.64mm/52
Executives	197mm/7 3/4 ins × 19.84mm/50
Churchill★★★	178mm/7 ins × 19.05mm/48

Spicy and coffee aroma with cinnamon on palate. Starts with promise but soon loses its lustre.

No 1	178mm/7 ins × 17.46mm/44
Monarca	127mm/5 ins × 19.84mm/50
Cetros	165mm/6 1/2 ins × 14.29mm/36
Pan Especial	178mm/7 ins × 14.29mm/36
Elegante	155mm/6 1/8 ins × 15.08mm/38
Palmas	152mm/6 ins × 17.07mm/43
Nacionales	140mm/5 1/2 ins × 17.46mm/44
Cazadores	165mm/6 1/2 ins × 17.46mm/44
Conchitas	140mm/5 1/2 ins × 12.70mm/32

CAMÓRRA IMPORTED LIMITED RESERVE
Hand-made. Ecuador wrapper. Handuran filler and binder. Lauched 1995. Distributed by Camórra Cigars, Savannah.

Capri	140mm/5 1/2 ins × 12.7mm/32
Napoli	156mm/6 1/8 ins × 15.1mm/38
Roma	127mm/5 ins × 19.84mm/50
Genova	140mm/5 1/2 ins × 17.5mm/44
Venzia	165mm/6 1/2 ins × 17.5mm/44
San Remo	178mm/7 ins × 19.1mm/48
Padova	127mm/5 ins × 16.67mm/42
Verona	152mm/6 ins × 9.84mm/50

C.A.O.
Hand-made. Quality: superior. Connecticut shade wrapper. Honduran binder. Filler blend of tobacco from Nicaragua and Mexico. Made by Tabacos de Plasencia. Distributed by C.A.O. Enterprises, Nashville.

Petit Corona	127mm/5 ins × 15.9mm/40
Corona	152mm/6 ins × 16.67mm/42
Lonsdale	178mm/7 ins × 17.5mm/44
Robusto	114mm/4 1/2 ins × 19.8mm/50
Corona Gorda	152mm/6 ins × 19.8mm/50
Churchill	191mm/7 1/2 ins × 21.4mm/54
Triangulare	178mm/7 ins × 21.4mm/54

CCI GOLD SILK SELECTION
Hand-made. Connecticut wrapper. Honduran binder. Filler, blend of tobacco from Nicaragua and Honduras. Launched 1995. Small, select production. Owned by Cigar Club International.

No 1	191mm/7 1/2 ins × 19.84mm/50
No 2	178mm/7 ins × 19.1mm/48
No 3	152mm/6 ins × 19.84mm/50
No 4	159mm/6 1/4 ins × 17.5mm/44
No 5	127mm/5 ins × 19.84mm/50

CCI ROYAL SATIN SELECTION
Hand-made. Ecuador wrapper. Filler, blend of tobacco from Nicaragua and Honduras. Binder from Dominican Rep. Owned by Cigar Club International.

No 1	191mm/7 1/2 ins × 19.84mm/50
No 2	178mm/7 ins × 19.1mm/48
No 3	152mm/6 ins × 19.84mm/50
No 4	159mm/6 1/4 ins × 17.5mm/44
No 5	127mm/5 ins × 19.84mm/50

CARAMBA TWIN-PACK
Hand-made. Made by Villazon

No 1	203mm/8 ins × 17.46mm/44
No 2	190mm/7 1/2 ins × 19.84mm/50
No 3	178mm/7 ins × 14.29mm/36
No 4	165mm/6 1/2 ins × 17.46mm/44
No 5	152mm/6 ins × 19.84mm/50
No 6	140mm/5 1/2 ins × 18.26mm/46
No 7	127mm/5 ins × 16.67mm/42
No 8	152mm/6 ins × 14.29mm/36

CASA MAYAN
Hand-made

Viajaute	216mm/8 1/2 ins × 20.64mm/52

Lonsdale	165mm/6 1/2 ins × 17.46mm/44
Robusto	140mm/5 1/2 ins × 19.84mm/50
Rothschild	113mm/4 1/2 ins × 19.84mm/50
No 4	127mm/5 ins × 16.67mm/42
President	190mm/7 1/2 ins × 19.84mm/50

CAZ-BAR
Hand-made. Bundles. Short and long filler. Distributed by Miami Cigar.

Cazadores	175mm/6 7/8 ins × 17.46mm/44
Fumas	175mm/6 7/8 ins × 17.46mm/44
Churchills	190mm/7 1/2 ins × 19.84mm/50
Corona Lonsdale	140mm/5 1/2 ins × 19.84mm/50
Petit Cazadore	175mm/6 7/8 ins × 17.46mm/44

CERVANTES
Hand-made.

Churchill	184mm/7 1/4 ins × 17.86mm/45
Corona	160mm/6 1/4 ins × 18.26mm/46
Senadores	152mm/6 ins × 16.67mm/42

CHARLES FAIRMORN
Hand-made. All Honduran tobacco. Distributed in USA by F&K Cigar.

Churchill	175mm/6 7/8 ins × 19.45mm/49
Coronas	160mm/6 1/4 ins × 17.46mm/44
Elegante	172mm/6 3/4 ins × 15.08mm/38
Super Finos	113/4 1/2 ins × 12.7mm/32

CIENFUEGO
Hand-made. Name means "100 fires" after famous fires in USA. Connecticut shade wrapper. Mexican binder. Filler blend of tobacco from Mexico, Jamaica and Dominican Republic.

New York 1776	203mm/8 ins × 21.43mm/54
Washington 1814	178mm/7 ins × 20.64mm/52
Boston 1902	178mm/7 ins × 21.43mm/54
Los Angeles 1965	216mm/8 1/2 ins × 20.64mm/52
Chicago 1871	197mm/7 3/4 ins × 19.84mm/50
Atlanta 1864	152mm/6 ins × 19.84mm/50
Detroit 1805	190mm/7 1/2 ins × 18.26mm/46
Baltimore 1902	165mm/5 1/2 ins × 16.67mm/42
Richmond 1865	152mm/6 ins × 17.07mm/43
San Franscisco 1906	178mm/7 ins × 17.07mm/43

COLORADO by Don Lino
Hand-made. Quality: superior. Attractive Colorado Connecticut wrapper. Bind from Honduras. Filler blend of tobacco from Honduras and Nicaragua. Available in

both cedar boxes and 25 cigar capacity humidors. Distributed by Miami Cigar.

Lonsdale	165mm/6 1/2 ins × 17.5mm/44
Robusto★★★★	140mm/5 1/2 ins × 19.84mm/50

Easy draw. Even, slow burning. Mild, but good flavour and balance. Well-made. Daytime smoke.

Torpedo	178mm/7 ins × 19.1mm/48
Presidente	190mm/7 1/2 ins × 19.84mm/50

CLEMENTINE

Hand-made. Bundles. Ecuador wrapper. Brand owned by House of Oxford.

Inmensas	203mm/8 ins × 21.4mm/54
Churchills	178mm/7 ins × 19.1mm/48
Cetros	159mm/6 1/4 ins × 17.5mm/44
No 1	178mm/7 ins × 17.5mm/44
No 4	140mm/5 1/2 ins × 17.5mm/44
Panetelas	178mm/7 ins × 14.3mm/36
Presidente	197mm/7 3/4 ins × 19.8mm/50
Rothchild	127mm/5 ins × 19.8mm/50
Toro	152mm/6 ins × 19.8mm/50
Viajante	216mm/8 1/2 ins × 20.6mm/52

COMPETERE

Hand-made. Wrapper from Ecuador. Binder and filler from Honduras. Distributed in USA by Brick-Hanquer.

Havana Twist	178mm/7 ins × 17.46mm/44
Havana Breva	152mm/6 ins × 19.84mm/50
Churchill	178mm/7 ins × 17.46mm/44
No. 200	152mm/6 ins × 17.07mm/43

COLUMBUS

Hand-made. Quality: superior. All Honduran tobacco. Publicly launched in 1992. Previously only available for private consumption. Extremely well-made. Owned by El Tobacco Ltd, Athens, Greece. Available in Europe. Limited distribution in USA. Tubes remind one of Cuban made Montecristo and Romeo y Juliette tubes. Beautiful, consistent wrappers are feature.

Eleven Fifty	279mm/11 ins × 19.84mm/50
Double Corona★★★★★	216mm/8 1/2 ins × 19.84mm/50

Explodes with rich, creamy flavours. Burns perfectly. Extremely well-made. This cigar will make any occasion special.

Churchill★★★★★	178mm/7 ins × 18.7mm/47

Good draw. Burns perfectly. Elegant. Lots of flavour

with hint of choclate and leather. Cigar for connoisseur
or special occasion.

No 2 Torpedo	155mm/6 ins × 20.6mm/52
Tubos★★★★★	155mm/6 ins × 16.67mm/42

Smooth with rich flavours, hint of treacle. Good burning.
For connoisseur and novice alike.

Short Churchill★★★★★	127mm/5 ins × 19.84mm/50

Smooth. Creamy flavours. Did not burn quite as evenly
as others in this range. To follow meal.

Columbus Columbus	146mm/5 3/4 ins × 18.22mm/46
Perfectos	127mm/5 ins × 17.4mm/44
Especial	159mm/6 1/4 ins × 17.4mm/44
Brevas	137mm/5 3/8 ins × 16.67mm/42
Tinas	114mm/4 1/2 ins × 11.9mm/30

CONNISSEUR GOLD LABEL

Hand-made. Bundles. Distributed in USA by Indian
Head Sales.

No 1	190mm/7 ins × 17.07mm/43
No 3	190mm/7 ins × 14.29mm/36
No 4	140mm/5 1/2 ins × 16.07mm/43
Goliath	203mm/8 ins × 25mm/64
Rothschild	113mm/4 1/2 ins × 19.84mm/50
Viajante	216mm/8 1/2 ins × 20.64mm/52
Imperial	178mm/7 1/2 ins × 19.84mm/50
Gigante	203mm/8 ins × 21.43mm/54
Toro	152mm/6 ins × 19.84mm/50
Corona	152mm/6 ins × 17.46mm/44
Churchill	190mm/7 ins × 19.45mm/40

CUBA ALIADOS

Hand-made. Quality: superior. Wrapper and binder
from Ecuador. Filler is blend of tobacco from Honduras,
Brazil and Dominican Republic. Has three large beautifully-made figurado shapes. General claimed to be
world's largest commercially available cigar. Factory
located in Danli, 15 miles (24 km) from Nicaraguan
border, in abandoned motel. Rollers are in what used to
be the lobby and sorting table was once registration
desk. Word "Cuba" appears on band. Founder of Cuba
Aliados Cigars Inc., Rolando Reyes Sr, launched
Aliados brand in Cuba in 1955. Company has wholesale and retail operation in Union City, New Jersey,
USA.

General	457mm/18 ins × 26.19mm/66
Figurin (figurado)★★★	254mm/10 ins × 23.8mm/60

Mild. Little oomph for what one would expect from such a big cigar. Becomes tedious.

Valentino (figurado)	178mm/7 ins × 19.05mm/48
Piramedes (figurado)	190mm/7 1/2 ins × 23.81mm/60
Diamedes (figurado)	190mm/7 1/2 ins × 23.81mm/60
Churchill★★★★★	181mm/7 1/8 ins × 21.43mm/54

Dark oily wrapper. Medium to full-bodied. Good balance. Strong finish. Top cigar for one who appreciates good things in life.

Cazadore	178mm/7 ins × 45
Palma	178mm/7 ins × 14.29mm/36
Fuma	165mm/6 1/2 ins × 17.7mm/45
Lonsdale	165mm/6 1/2 ins × 16.67mm/42
Corona Deluxe★★★★	165mm/6 1/2 ins × 17.86mm/45

Lots of flavour. Mild. Smooth. Elegant. Good daytime smoke.

Toro	152mm/6 ins × 21.43mm/54
Number 4	140mm/5 1/2 ins × 17.86mm/45
Remedios	140mm/5 1/2 ins × 16.67mm/42
Petite Cetro	127mm/5 ins × 14.29mm/36
Rothschild	127mm/5 ins × 20.24mm/51

CUBAN TWIST

Hand-made. Mixed filler. Distributed in USA by Indian Head Sales.

No 200	127mm/5 ins × 14.29mm/36
No 400	178mm/7 ins × 14.29mm/36
No 500	152mm/6 ins × 19.84mm/50
No 600	178mm/7 ins × 18.26mm/46

DANLYS

Hand-made bundles. All Honduran tobacco. Made byTobacos de Plascencia. Distributed by House of Oxford.

Churchill	178mm/7 ins × 19.8mm/50
Luchadore★★★★	152mm/6 ins × 16.67mm/42

Medium to full-bodied. Well-made. Tends to fade.

Panetela	152mm/6 ins × 15.1mm/38
Toro	152mm/6 ins × 19.8mm/50
No 1	178mm/7 ins × 16.67mm/42
No 4	127mm/5 ins × 16.67mm/42

DON ASA

Hand-made. All Honduran tobacco. Made by US Tobacco for House of Oxford.

Blunts	127mm/5 ins × 16.67mm/42
Cetros	165mm/6 1/2 ins × 17.5mm/44
Coronas	140mm/5 1/2 ins × 19.8mm/50

Imperial	203mm/8 ins × 17.5mm/44
President	190mm/7 1/2 ins × 19.8mm/50
Rothchilds	114mm/4 1/2 ins × 19.8mm/50

DON JOSE
Hand-made bundles of 20. All available in natural or maduro wrapper. Distributed by M&N.

Valrico	114mm/4 1/2 ins × 19.84mm/50
Granada	152mm/6 ins × 17.1mm/43
Turbo	152mm/6 ins × 19.84mm/50
San Marco	178mm/7 ins × 19.84mm/50
El Grandee	216mm/8 1/2 ins × 20.6mm/52

DON LINO
Hand-made. Quality: superior. Connecticut wrapper. Binder and filler blend of tobacco from Handuras. Distributed by Miami Cigar.

Corona	140mm/5 1/2 ins × 19.84mm/50
Peticetro	140mm/5 1/2 ins × 16.67mm/42
Toros	140mm/5 1/2 ins × 18.3mm/46
No 1	165mm/6 1/2 ins × 17.5mm/44
No 3	152mm/6 ins × 14.3mm/36
No 4	127mm/5 ins × 16.67mm/42
No 5	159mm/6 1/4 ins × 17.5mm/44
Torpedo	178mm/7 ins × 19.1mm/48
Churchill★★★★★	190mm/7 1/2 ins × 19.84mm/50

Dark oily wrapper. Spicy with woodsy undertones. Good balance and finish. After-dinner cigar for connoisseur.

| Panetelas | 178mm/7 ins × 14.3mm/36 |
| Robustos★★★★ | 140mm/5 1/2 ins × 19.84mm/50 |

Smooth oily wrapper. Wet hay aroma. Creamy finish. Smooth. Well-made.

Rothchild	114mm/4 1/2 ins × 19.84mm/50
Epicures	114mm/4 1/2 ins ×12.7mm/32
Supremos	216mm/8 1/2 ins × 20.6mm/52

DON LINO ORO
Hand-made. Quality: superior. Wrapper of Cameroon seed grown in Handuras. Binder and filler from Cuban seed grown in Honduras. Distributed by Miami Cigar. More robust than Don Lino range.

No 1	165mm/6 1/2 ins × 17.5mm/44
Panetelas	178mm/7 ins × 14.3mm/36
Toro	140mm/5 1/2 ins × 18.3mm/46
Churchill	190mm/7 1/2 ins × 19.84mm/50

DON MATEO
Hand-made bundles. All Honduran tobacco. Made by Consolidated Cigar.

No 1	178mm/7 ins × 12.00mm/30
No 2	175mm/6 7/8 ins × 13.89mm/35
No 3	152mm/6 ins × 16.67mm/42
No 4	140mm/5 1/2 ins × 17.46mm/44
No 5	143mm/5 5/8 ins × 17.46mm/44
No 6	175mm/6 7/8 ins × 19.05mm/48
No 7	120mm/4 3/4 ins × 19.84mm/50
No 8	160mm/6 1/4 ins × 19.84mm/50
No 9	190mm/7 1/2 ins × 19.84mm/50
No 10	203mm/8 ins × 20.64mm/52

DOM RAMOS
Hand-made by Villazon for Hunters and Frankau, London.

Gigantes	172mm/6 3/4 ins × 18.65mm/47
Magnum	160mm/6 1/4 ins × 17.46mm/44
Gordas	113mm/4 1/2 ins × 19.84mm/50
Corona	140mm/5 1/2 ins × 16.67mm/42
Especial	175mm/6 7/8 ins × 14.29mm/36
Petit Corona	127mm/5 1/2 ins × 16.67mm/42
Tres Petit Corona	102mm/4 1/2 ins × 16.67mm/42

This range also comes in aluminium tubes and is simply named according to numbers, from Honduras No 11 through to Honduras No 18.

DON MELO
Hand-made. All Honduran tobacco. Distributed by Cigars of Honduras, Virginia.

Presidente	216mm/8 1/2 ins × 202mm/50
Churchill	179mm/7 ins × 19.5mm/49
Corona Gorda	152mm/6 ins × 17.5mm/44
Numero Dos	152mm/6 ins × 16.67mm/42
Corona Extra	140mm/5 1/2 ins × 18.3mm/46
Petit Corona	140mm/5 1/2 ins × 16.67mm/42
Nom Plus	121mm/4 3/4 ins × 20.2mm/50
Cremos	114mm/4 1/2 ins × 16.67mm/42

DON REX
Hand-made. Connecticut shade or Sumatra maduro wrappers. Launched in 1987. Available in different wrappers grown in Honduras: Connecticut seed shade Sumatran seed and maduro. Made by US Tobacco Co. Distributed by Miami Cigar.

Gigantes maduro	216mm/8 1/2 ins × 21.43mm/52
Presidentes	190mm/7 1/2 ins × 19.84mm/50

Cetros No 2★★★   165mm/6 1/2 ins × 17.46mm/44
Fairly tight draw. Lacks flavour. Daytime smoke.
Coronas   140mm/5 1/2 ins × 19.84mm/50
Panetela Largas   178mm/7 ins × 14.29mm/36
Blunts   127mm/5 ins × 16.67mm/42

DON RUBIO
Hand-made. Bundles. Wrapper from Ecuador. Binder
and filler from Honduras. Distributed by Brick-Hanauer.
No 1   178mm/7 ins × 17.07mm/43
Cazadore (Sandwich) 160mm/6 1/4 ins × 17.46mm/44
Corona Extra   140mm/5 1/2 ins × 18.26mm/46
Corona Gorda   160mm/6 1/4 ins × 17.46mm/44
Churchill   178mm/7 ins × 19.45mm/49
Grandios   203mm/8 ins × 23.81mm/60
Lindas   140mm/5 1/2 ins × 23.81mm/38
Monarchs   178mm/7 ins × 20.64mm/52
Nom Plus   127mm/5 ins × 19.84mm/50
Panatella   172mm/6 3/4 ins × 13.89mm/35
President   216mm/8 1/2 ins × 19.84mm/50
Soberanos   197mm/7 3/4 ins × 19.84mm/50
Toro   152mm/6 ins × 19.84mm/50

DOM TOMAS
Hand-made. Quality: superior. Cuban seed wrappers.
All sizes available in four wrappers: natural/colorado,
maduro and claro claro. Medium strength. Introduced in
1974. Owned by U.S. Tobacco International. Distrib-
uted in USA by Miami Cigar.
igantes   216mm/8 1/2 ins × 20.64mm/52
Imperiales No 1   203mm/8 ins × 17.46mm/44
Presidentes   190mm/7 1/2 ins × 19.84mm/50
Panetela Largas   178mm/7 ins × 14.29mm/36
Cetros No 2   165mm/6 1/2 ins × 17.46mm/44
Corona Grandes (tubed)★★★★★
                     165mm/6 1/2 ins × 17.46mm/44
Dark smooth oily wrapper. Easy draw. Burns evenly.
Ash falls off easily. Spicy, earthy. Lots of flavour.
Dignified cigar.
Supremos★★★★   160mm/6 1/4 ins × 16.67mm/42
Easy draw. Even burn. Cool. Spicy. Mild to medium
strength. Good cigar for beginner.
Panetelas   152mm/6 ins × 14.29mm/36
Coronas   140mm/5 1/2 ins × 19.84mm/50
Toros   140mm/5 1/2 ins × 18.26mm/46
Matadors   140mm/5 1/2 ins × 16.67mm/42
Rothschild   113mm/4 1/2 ins × 19.84mm/50
Epicures   113mm/4 1/2 ins × 12.70mm/32

It's a Boy/Girl   165mm/6 1/2 ins × 17.46mm/44

DOM TOMAS SPECIAL EDITION
Hand-made. Quality: Superior. Connecticut, Cuban and Dominican seed tobacco. Connecticut shade wrapper. Smooth and aromatic. Good quality. Owned by United States Tobacco Company. Distributed by Miami Cigar.

No 100	190mm/7 1/2 ins × 19.84mm/50
No 200★★★★	165mm/6 1/2 ins × 17.46mm/44

Touch of cinnamon. Fairly strong but balanced with flavour. Suitable to follow meal.

No 300	127mm/5 ins × 19.84mm/50
No 400	178mm/7 ins × 14.29mm/36
No 500★★★★★	140mm/5 1/2 ins × 18.26mm/46

Spicy. Touch of coffee. Good balance. Smooth. Good burn. After-dinner cigar. Smoke for connoisseur.

DOM TOMAS INTERNATIONAL SERIES
Hand-made. Quality: superior. Cuban seed tobacco. Distributed by Miami Cigar.

No 1	165mm/6 1/2 ins × 17.46mm/44
No 2	140mm/5 1/2 ins × 19.84mm/50
No 3	140mm/5 1/2 ins × 16.67mm/42
No 4	178mm/7 ins × 14.29mm/36

EL PARAISO

Grande	203mm/8 1/2 ins × 20.6mm/52
Presidente	190mm/7 1/2 ins × 19.84mm/50
Double Corona	178mm/7 ins × 18.26mm/46
Panetelas	165mm/6 1/2 ins × 14.29mm/36
Toro	152mm/6 ins × 19.84mm/50
Corona	147mm/5 3/4ins × 17.07mm/43
Pequenos	127mm/5 ins × 12.00mm/30

EL REY DEL MUNDO
Hand-made. Quality: superior. 25 models. Heavy bodied Havana style cigar with Ecuador Sumatra wrapper grown in the Rio Jagna region of Spanish Honduras. Made by Villazon for Santa Clara, N.A. Same name as Cuban brand, which has "Habana" on band.

Tino	140mm/5 1/2 ins × 15.08mm/38
Rothschilde★★★★	127mm/5 ins × 19.84mm/50

Rich, medium strength, full flavours. Spicy aroma.

Robusto Zavalia 127mm/5 ins × 21.43mm/54
Robusto Suprema★★★★★

      184mm/7 1/4 ins × 21.43mm/54

Dark oil wrapper. Well-made. Range of flavours. Ideal
to follow sweet dessert.

Robusto Larga	152mm/6 ins × 21.43mm/54
Robusto★★★★★	127mm/5 ins × 21.43mm/54

Cool smoke with lots of flavour. Top cigar for connoisseur. One of best in this size.

Reynita	127mm/5 ins × 15.08mm/38
Rectangulare	143mm/5 5/8 ins × 17.86mm/45
Principale	203mm/8 ins × 18.65mm/47
Plantation	165mm/6 1/2 ins × 12.00mm/30
Petit Lonsdale	117mm/4 5/8 ins × 17.07mm/43
Originale	143mm/5 5/8 ins × 17.86mm/45
Montecarlo	155mm/6 1/8 ins × 19.05mm/48
Imperiale	184mm/7 1/4 ins × 21.43mm/54
Habana Club	140mm/5 1/2 ins × 16.67mm/42
Flor del Mundo★★★★	184mm/7 1/4 ins × 21.43mm/54

Spicy. Medium to full-bodied. Lots of flavour. Smooth,
but gets bitter towards end.

Flor de Llaneza (torpedo)★★★★★

165mm/6 1/2 ins × 21.43mm/54

Varnished cabinet box of 35 cigars. Spicy aroma.
Honeyed finish. Full-bodied. If draw too hard ensure
that enough has been cut off head. Great experience
for connoisseur.

Elegante	136mm/5 3/8 ins × 11.51mm/29
Double Corona★★★★★	178mm/7 ins × 19.45mm/49

Strong, full flavoured cigar, beautifully presented in
white tissue paper. For connoisseur after rich meal.

Coronation	216mm/8 1/2 ins × 20.64mm/52
Corona	143mm/5 5/8 ins × 17.86mm/45
Corona Inmensa	184mm/7 1/4 ins × 18.65mm/47
Classic Corona	143mm/5 5/8 ins × 17.86mm/45
Choix Supreme★★★★	155mm/6 1/8 ins × 19.45mm/49

Spicy, earthy. Slow to start but good flavour soon
comes through. Elegant cigar. Good daytime smoke.

Cedar	178mm/7 ins × 17.07mm/43
Cafe Au Lait	113mm/4 1/2 ins × 13.89mm/35

ENCANTO
Hand-made.

Viajantes	216mm/8 1/2 ins × 20.64mm/52
*Churchill	178mm/7 ins × 19.45mm/49
Grandotes 1	90mm/7 1/2 ins × 18.65mm/47
Elegantes	178mm/7 ins × 17.07mm/43
Toro	152mm/6 ins × 19.84mm/50
Corona Larga	165mm/6 1/2 ins × 17.46mm/44
*Cetros	152mm/6 ins × 16.67mm/42

**Rothschild	113mm/4 1/2 ins × 19.84mm/50
Palma Fina	172mm/6 3/4 ins × 14.29mm/36
*Petit Corona	140mm/5 1/2 ins × 16.67mm/42
Luchadores	160mm/6 1/4 ins × 17.46mm/44
Princesse	113mm/4 1/2 ins × 12.00mm/30

* Natural & claro claro.
** Natural & maduro.

ESPADA
Hand-made. All Honduran tobacco.

Viajantes	216mm/8 1/2 ins × 20.6mm/52
Presidente	216mm/8 1/2 ins × 19.84mm/50
Torpedo	178mm/7 ins × 21.4mm/54
Monarch	178mm/7 ins × 20.6mm/52
Executive	197mm/7 3/4 ins × 19.84mm/50
Corona Gorda	159mm/6 1/4 ins × 17.5mm/44
Rothschild	127mm/5 ins × 19.84mm/50
Palma Fina	175mm/6 7/8 ins × 14.3mm/36

EVELIO
Hand-made. Quality: superior. Ecuadorian wrapper. Binder and filler from Honduras. Launched 1996. Made by Tabacos de Plasencia. Exclusive to House of Oxford.

Corona	146mm/5 3/4 ins × 16.67mm/42
Double Corona	194mm/7 5/8 ins × 18.7mm/47
No 1	178mm/7 ins × 17.5mm/44
Robusto	121mm/4 3/4 ins × 21.4mm/54
Robusto Larga	152mm/6 ins × 21.4mm/54
Torpedo	178mm/7 ins × 21.4mm/54

EXECUTOR

Viajante	216mm/8 1/2 ins × 20.6mm/52
No 1	165mm/6 1/2 ins × 17.5mm/44
No 4	140mm/5 1/2 ins × 17.1mm/43
Cetros	152mm/6 ins × 17.5mm/44
Churchill	178mm/7 ins × 19.1mm/48
Rothschild	114mm/4 1/2 ins × 19.8mm/50
Panetela	178mm/7 ins × 13.9mm/35
Toro	152mm/6 ins × 19.8mm/50

EXCALIBUR By Hoyo de Monterrey
Hand-made. Best quality. Connecticut shade wrappers. Cuban seed binder and filler. Medium to full bodied. Sold with Hoyo de Monterrey label in United States, but word "Excalibur" is on band. In Europe they are simply sold as Excalibur. Made by Villazon.

Excalibur I★★★★★   184mm/7 1/4 ins × 21.43mm/54
Slow burning, cool, elegant cigars. Needs a cm or two
(up to one inch) before it imparts its full, rich flavours.
Ideal to enjoy with good cognac or port.
Excalibur II   172mm/6 3/4 ins × 18.65mm/47
Excalibur III★★★★★   155mm/6 1/8 ins × 19.05mm/48
Easy draw. Even, slow burning. Smooth. Top cigar for
special occasion.
Excalibur IV   143mm/5 5/8 ins × 18.26mm/46
Excalibur V★★★★   160mm/6 1/4 ins × 17.86mm/45
Medium to full bodied. Good texture. Loses character
after half-way, unlike No 1, that improves inhances its
personality. Daytime smoke or to follow meal.
Excalibur VI   136mm/5 1/2 ins × 15.08mm/38
Excalibur VII★★★★★   127mm/5 ins × 17.07mm/43
Good earthy, spicy flavours. Smooth. Long finish.
Well-made. Ideal to follow meal.
Banquets (A/tube)   172mm/6 3/4 ins × 19.05mm/48
Minatures★★★★   76mm/3 ins × 8.70mm/22
Fairly strong, but smooth. Ideal quick smoke. A top
cigarillo.

F. D. GRAVE & SON
Hand-made. Connecticut wrapper. Honduran filler and
binder. Owned by F. D. Grave & Son in New Haven,
Connecticut. One of oldest companies in continuous
production.
Churchill   197mm/7 3/4 ins × 19.84mm/50
Corona Grande   178mm/7 ins × 20.6mm/52
Lonsdale   159mm/6 1/4 ins × 17.5mm/44

FELIPE GREGORIO
Hand-made. All Honduran tobacco. Exclusive to Cigars
of Honduras, Virginia.
*Glorioso   197mm/7 3/4 ins × 19.84mm/50
Suntouso   178mm/7 ins × 19.1mm/48
Belicoso (torpedo)   152mm/6 ins × 20.6mm/52
Sereno   146mm/5 3/4 ins × 16.67mm/42
Robusto   127mm/5 ins × 19.84mm/50
Nino   108mm/4 1/4 ins × 17.5mm/44
*Available with Maduro wrapper.

FIRST PRIMING
Hand-made. Bundles. All Honduran tobacco. Distrib-
uted by Phillips & King.
Grandees Natural   216mm/8 1/2 ins × 20.64mm/52
Largos Natural   190mm/7 1/2 ins × 19.84mm/50

FLOR DE ALLONES
Hand-made. Ecuadorian wrapper. Honduron binder.
Filler, a blend of tobacco from Honduras, Nicaragua
and Dominican Rep. Named after old Cuban brand,
Ramon Allones.

No 50	159mm/6 1/4 ins × 19.84mm/50
No 100	114mm/4 1/2 ins × 19.84mm/50
No 110	203mm/8 ins × 18.7mm/47
No 150	140mm/5 1/2 ins × 15.1mm/38

FLOR DE CONSUEGRA
Hand-made. Quality: superior. Cuban seed wrapper.
Full bodied. Exclusive to Santa Clara, Inc.

Corona	140mm/5 1/2 ins × 16.67mm/42
Corona Immensa	184mm/7 1/4 ins × 18.65mm/47
Cuban Corona	143mm/5 5/8 ins × 17.86mm/45
Lonsdale	165mm/6 1/2 ins × 16.67mm/42
Panetela	136mm/5 3/8 ins × 15.08mm/38
President	216mm/8 1/2 ins × 19.45mm/49
Robusto	113mm/4 1/2 ins × 19.84mm/50
Corona Grande	160mm/6 1/4 ins × 17.86mm/45
Corona Extra	152mm/6 ins × 16.67mm/42

FLOR DEL CARIBE
Hand-made. Bundles. Good value. Made by Villazon
for Arango. Also sold in Europe.

Presidents	184mm/7 1/4 ins × 18.26mm/46
No 1	165mm/6 1/2 ins × 17.07mm/43
Coronas	140mm/5 1/2 ins × 18.26mm/46
Petit Cetro	140mm/5 1/2 ins × 15.08mm/38

Medium to full-bodied. Hint of cinnamon. Well-made.
Ideal to follow meal. Underated-deserves being discovered. Good value. Retails for under $1.50.

FLOR DE PALICIO
Hand-made by Villazon for Phillips and King

No 1	178mm/7 ins × 15.48mm/39
No 2	152mm/6 ins × 16.67mm/42
Corona****	172mm/6 3/4 ins × 19.45mm/48

HABANA GOLD
Hand-made. Good value. Distributed by Gold Leaf
Tobacco Co. Available in two ranges: BLACK LABEL:
Sumatra wrapper. Nicaragua filler and binder. WHITE
LABEL: All Nicaragua tobacco. Dark wrapper.

Petite Corona	127mm/5 ins × 16.67mm/42
Corona	152mm/6 ins × 175mm/44
Double Corona	190mm/7 1/2 ins × 18.3mm/46
Robusto	127mm/5 ins × 19.8mm/50

Torpedo	152mm/6 ins × 20.6mm/52
Churchill	178mm/7 ins × 20.6mm/52
Presidente	213mm/8 1/2 ins × 20.6mm/52
No 2	157mm/6 1/8 ins × 20.6mm/52
Super Finos	102mm/4 ins × 7.9mm/20

H. A. LADRILLO
Hand-made. All Honduran tobacco.

Imperial	191mm/7 1/2 ins × 20.6mm/52
Triangulares	178mm/7 ins × 19.84mm/50
Fabuloso	178mm/7 ins × 19.1mm/48
Lancero	165mm/6 1/2 ins × 17.5mm/44
Robusto	127mm/5 ins × 20.6mm/52

HAVANA RESERVE By Don Lino
Hand-made. Quality: superior. All Honduran tobacco.Connecticut seed wrapper, aged for five years. Top of Don Lino range. Distributed by Miami Cigar.

No 1	165mm/6 1/4 ins × 17.5mm/44
Toros	140mm/5 1/2 ins × 18.3mm/46
Panetelas	178mm/7 ins × 14.3mm/36
Churchills	190mm/7 1/2 ins × 19.84mm/50
Torpedo	178mm/7 ins × 19.1mm/48
Rothchild	114mm/4 1/2 ins × 19.84mm/50
Robusto	140mm/5 1/2 ins × 19.84mm/50
Tubes	165mm/6 1/2 ins × 17.5mm/44

HECHO-A-MANO-CAZ-BAR
Hand-made. (Short and long filler.) Distributed in USA by H. J. Bailey Co.

Cazadores	172mm/6 3/4 ins × 17.46mm/44
Churchills	190mm/7 1/2 ins × 19.84mm/50
Corona Lonsdale	140mm/5 1/2 ins × 16.67mm/42
Fumas	175mm/6 7/8 ins × 17.46mm/44

HONDURAN GOLD
Hand-made. Bundles. Wrappers from Ecuador. Filler and binder from Honduras. Owned by Indian Head Sales.

Mayor	140mm/5 1/2 ins × 16.67mm/42
Panetelas	178mm/7 ins × 14.29mm/36
Senator	178mm/7 ins × 17.07mm/43
Governor	152mm/6 ins × 19.84mm/50
General	178mm/7 ins × 19.45mm/49
Presidente	216mm/8 1/2 ins × 20.6mm/52

HONDURAN IMPORT MADURO
Hand-made. Bundles. Sold in packs of two by 25. All

with maduro wrappers. All Honduran tobacco. Distributed by Phillips & King.

Bandidos	143mm/5 5/8 ins × 18.74mm/47
Delicosos	178mm/7 ins × 17.1mm/43
Granadas	152mm/6 ins × 19.84mm/50
Majestics	203mm/8 ins × 18.74mm/47
Petzels	114mm/4 1/2 ins × 19.84mm/50
Superbos	171mm/6 3/4 ins × 19.1mm/48

HONDURAS CUBAN TOBACCOS

Hand-made. Country of origin of tobacco used changes periodically. Made by Honduras Cuban Tobaccos Co., Danli, Honduras.

Viajantes	216mm/8 1/2 ins × 21.4mm/54
Presidente	216mm/8 1/2 ins × 20.6mm/52
Gigantes	203mm/8 ins × 21.4mm/54
Soberano	197mm/7 3/4 ins × 19.84mm/50
Corona Grande	191mm/7 1/2 ins × 18.3mm/46
Palma de Mayorca	203mm/8 ins × 15.1mm/38
Torpedo	178mm/7 ins × 21.4mm/54
Monarch	178mm/7 ins × 20.6mm/52
Churchill	175mm/6 7/8 ins × 19.5mm/49
Elegantes	178mm/7 ins × 16.67mm/42
Pincel	178mm/7 ins × 11.9mm/30
Palma Fina	175mm/6 7/8 ins × 14.3mm/36
Corona Gorda	159mm/6 1/4 ins × 17.5mm/44
Matador	152mm/6 ins × 19.84mm/50
Cetros	152mm/6 ins × 17.1mm/43
Petit Coronas	140mm/5 1/2 ins × 16.67mm/42
Lindas	140mm/5 1/2 ins × 15.1mm/38
Clasico	140mm/5 1/2 ins × 13.5mm/34
Rothschild	127mm/5 ins × 19.84mm/50
Super Fino	114mm/4 1/2 ins × 11.9mm/30
Moderno	114mm/4 1/2 ins × 10.3mm/26

HOYO DE MONTERREY

Hand-made. Quality: superior. Most names in this range different from those of Cuban range, which helps to avoid confusion. Bands maroon rather than red. Made from Cuban seed tobacco. Strong and full bodied in flavour.

Loose cigars, without Hoyo band, are sold in Europe and are a bargain. Also sold in UK under Don Ramos label. Made by Villazon.

President★★★★   216mm/8 1/2 ins × 20.64mm/52
Medium-bodied. Spicy with touch of cinnamon. Good

draw. Smooth. Big cigar. Needs 2 to 2 1/2 hours to enjoy it.

Sultan	184mm/7 1/4 ins × 21.43mm/54
Double Corona★★★★	172mm/6 3/4 ins × 19.05mm/48

Elegant cigar, smooth, medium bodied with spicy aroma, to follow meal.

Churchill★★★★	160mm/6 1/4 ins × 17.86mm/45

Good Colorado Maduro wrapper. Rich flavours with spicy and floral aroma. To follow robust meal.

Ambassador	160mm/6 1/4 ins × 17.46mm/44
Cuban Largos	184mm/7 1/4 ins × 18.65mm/47
Cetros	178mm/7 ins × 17.07mm/43
Governor★★★★★	155mm/6 1/8 ins × 19.84mm/50

Smooth, oily Colorado Maduro wrapper provides good ageing potential. Wonderful rich coffee and chocolate flavours with hint of spice. Full-bodied. Good balance between flavour and strength. Great cigar to end good meal.

Largo Elegantes	184mm/7 1/4 ins × 13.49mm/34
Delights	160mm/6 1/4 ins × 14.68mm/37
Dreams	147mm/5 3/4 ins × 18.26mm/46
Super Hoyos	140mm/5 1/2 ins × 17.46mm/44
Cafe Royale	143mm/5 5/8 ins × 17.07mm/43
No 1	165mm/6 1/2 ins × 17.07mm/43
No 55	133mm/5 1/4 ins × 17.07mm/43
Culebras	152mm/6 ins × 13.89mm/35
Margaritas	133mm/5 1/4 ins × 11.51mm/29
Petit	120mm/4 3/4 ins × 12.30mm/31
Rothschild	114mm/4 1/2 ins × 19.84mm/50
Corona	143mm/5 5/8 ins × 18.26mm/46
Demitasse	102mm/4 ins × 15.48mm/39
Sabrosos	127mm/5 ins × 15.87mm/40

HOJA DEL REGAL

Hand-made bundles. Distributed by Brick-Hanauer Co.

Slim Panetela	152mm/6 ins × 14.29mm/36
Soberano	190mm/7 1/2 ins × 19.84mm/50
Corona Gorda	165mm/6 1/2 ins × 17.46mm/44
Corona Extra	154mm/6 ins × 17.07mm/43
Rothschild	113mm/4 1/2 ins × 19.84mm/50
No 4	133mm/5 1/2 ins × 17.46mm/44
El Toro	152mm/6 ins × 19.84mm/50
Viajante	216mm/8 1/2 ins × 18.26mm/46
Corona Grande	190mm/7 1/2 ins × 18.26mm/46

HUGO CASSAR

Hand-made: Bundles. Connecticut shade wrapper.

Honduran filler and binder. Owned by Hugo Cassar Cigars, California.

No 1	121mm/4 3/4 ins × 19.8mm/50
No 2	140mm/5 1/2 ins × 18.3mm/46
No 3	171mm/6 3/4 ins × 17.5mm/44
No 4	178mm/7 ins × 19.1mm/48
No 5	171mm/6 3/4 ins x 21.4mm/54
No 6	191mm/7 1/2 ins × 19.8mm/50
No 7	203mm/8 ins × 20.6mm/52

HUGO CASSAR DIAMOND SELECTION
Hand-made. Quality: superior. Ecuadorian wrapper. Dominican binder. Filler, blend of tobacco from Mexico and Nicaragua.

Corona	140mm/5 1/2 ins × 17.5mm/44
Robusto	127mm/5 ins × 19.84mm/50
Lonsdale	168mm/6 5/8 ins × 18.3mm/46
Torpedo	152mm/6 ins × 21.0mm/53
Double Corona	159mm/6 1/4 ins × 20.6mm/52
Presidente	178mm/7 ins × 19.5mm/49
Chairman	197mm/7 3/4 ins × 19.84mm/50

HUGO CASSAR PRIVATE COLLECTION
Hand-made. Ecuador wrapper. Honduran filler and binder.

Matador	m/6 ins × 16.67mm/42
Imperiale	mm/7 ins × 17.5mm/44
Robusto	mm/4 3/4 ins × 20.6mm/52
Elegantes	mm/6 ins × 19.84mm/50
Emperador	mm/7 3/4 ins × 18.7mm/47

INDIAN
Hand-made. Ecuadorian Sumatra wrapper. Filler, a blend of tobacco from Honduras and Nicaragua. A unusual feature in the construction is a second layer of binder called the "neutralizer". The logo is the same as that of the Indian Motorcycle Co. Exclusive to Indian Tobacco Co., Beverly Hills.

Chief	191mm/7 1/2 ins × 20.6mm/52
TeePee (pyramid)	140mm/5 1/2 ins × 20.6mm/52
Warrior	152mm/6 ins × 16.67mm/42
Boxer	114mm/4 1/2 ins × 19.84mm/50
ASrrow	140mm/5 1/2 ins × 13.5mm/34

INDIAN HEAD
Hand-made. Bundles. Quality: good. Connecticut shade wrapper. Filler is blend of tobacco from Honduras and Dominican Republic. Made by Tobacos de Plascencia for Tropical Tobacco.

Princesse	113mm/4 1/2 ins × 12.00mm/30
Petit Coronas	140mm/5 1/2 ins × 13.49mm/34
Lindas	140mm/5 1/2 ins × 15.08mm/38
*Fumas	178mm/7 ins × 17.46mm/44
*Cazadores	160mm/6 1/4 ins × 17.46mm/44
Numero Cuatro	140mm/5 1/2 ins × 16.67mm/42
Pinceles	178mm/7 ins × 12.00mm/30
**Numero Dos	160mm/6 ins × 17.07mm/43
Panetelas	175mm/6 7/8 ins × 13.89mm/35
Coronas Gorda	160mm/6 1/4 ins × 17.46mm/44
**Rothchild	127mm/5 ins × 19.84mm/50
**Numero Uno	178mm/7 ins × 17.07mm/43
Palma de Mayorca	203mm/8 ins × 15.08mm/38
**Emperador	203mm/8 ins × 19.84mm/50
**Toros	152mm/6 ins × 19.84mm/50
Corona Grande	190mm/7 1/2 ins × 18.26mm/46
**Churchills	175mm/6 7/8 ins × 19.45mm/49
Monarch	178mm/7 ins × 20.64mm/52
**Soberanos	197mm/7 3/4 ins × 19.84mm/50
**Viajante	216mm/8 1/2 ins × 20.64mm/52
**Gigantes	203mm/8 ins × 21.43mm/54
Torpedos	190mm/7 ins × 21.43mm/54

*Mixed Filler

**Available with both maduro and natural wrapper.

JOHN AYLESBURY
Hand-made. Quality: superior.
Full bodied. Lacks subtlety. Well made and a good substitute for Havana. Has elegant "JA" band.
(See entry under Germany and Dominican Republic. Produced for John Aylesbury chain of cigar shops in Germany. Also exported to USA.)
Pinceles
Puritos
Panetela Larga
Morning
Panatela
Pico

JOHN AYLESBURY LA PINTURA
Hand-made. Quality: superior. Does not have elegant "JA" band.
Uno
Dos
Tres

JOHN AYLESBURY PEDRO DE ALVARADO
Hand-made. Quality: superior. Full bodied.
Grand De Luxe

Cetros
Supremos
Crenas

JOHN AYLESBURY SANTA ROSA DE COPAN
Hand-made. Quality: superior.
Has "Santa De Copan", not "JA" band.
Uno
Dos
Tres
La Douche

JOHN AYLESBURY SAN PEDRO SULA
Hand-made. Quality: superior.
Brown and cream band with a crown and words "special seleccion".
Corona
Panetela Corona
Slim Panetela

J.P.B.
Hand-made. All Honduran tobacco. Distributed by Lignum-2 Inc.

Imperiale	191mm/7 1/2 ins ×19.8mm/50
Monarch	178mm/7 ins × 18.3mm/46
Baron	178mm/7 ins × 16.67mm/42
Royal Carona	152mm/6 ins × 16.67mm/42
Regal	159mm/6 1/4 ins × 13.9mm/35
Dugae	140mm/5 1/2 ins × 16.67mm/42

J.R. ULTIMATE
Hand-made. Quality: superior. Cuban seed tobacco from Honduras for binder and filler. Cuban seed from Nicaragua for wrapper. Aged for over one year. Wide selection of colours. Made exclusively for Lew Rothman of J.R. Tobacco Corporation, USA. Originally available only through this company, but now available nation-wide. Full bodied. Well made.

Estelo Individual	216mm/8 1/2 ins × 20.64mm/52
Presidente	216mm/8 1/2 ins × 20.64mm/52
No 1	184mm/7 1/4 ins × 21.43mm/54
Cetro	178mm/7 ins × 16.67mm/42
Super Cetro	210mm/8 1/4 ins × 17.07mm/43
Slims	175mm/6 7/8 ins × 14.29mm/36
Palma Extra	175mm/6 7/8 ins × 15.08mm/38
Double Corona	172mm/6 3/4 ins × 19.05mm/48
Padrons	152mm/6 ins × 21.43mm/54
Toro	152mm/6 ins × 19.84mm/50
No 5	155mm/6 1/8 ins × 17.46mm/44
Corona	143mm/5 5/8 ins × 17.86mm/45

Corona Tubus   127mm/5 ins × 17.86mm/45
Petit Cetro   140mm/5 1/2 ins × 15.08mm/38
Rothschild★★★★   113mm/4 1/2 ins × 19.84mm/50
Rich, complex flavour. Well-made. Flavour fades
slightly towards end.
Petit Corona   117mm/4 5/8 ins × 17.07mm/43

JUAN LOPEZ
Hand-made. Bundles. All Honduran tobacco.
No 300   216mm/8 1/2 ins × 19.84mm/50
No 301   191mm/7 1/2 ins × 19.84mm/50
No 302   152mm/6 ins × 19.84mm/50
No 303   165mm/6 1/2 ins × 16.67mm/42
No 304   140mm/5 1/2 ins × 16.67mm/42

LA BALLA
Hand-made. Bundles. Maduro wrapper. All Honduran
tobacco. Exclusive to Phillips & King.
La Balla   171mm/6 3/4 ins × 18.3mm/46

LA DILIGENCIA
Hand-made. Connecticut shade wrapper. Dominican
binder. Filler blend of tobacco from Honduras, Nicara-
gua and Dominican Rep. Introduced 1995. Made by
Tabacos de Plasencia. Brand owned by Swisher Intl.
Presidente   216mm/8 1/2 ins × 20.6mm/52
Toro   152mm/6 ins × 19.84mm/50
Gran Corona   152mm/6 ins × 17.5mm/44
Churchill   178mm/7 ins × 19.1mm/48
Robusto   120mm/4 3/4 ins × 19.84mm/50

LA FONTANA VINTAGE
Hand-made. Quality: superior. Connecticut shade
wrapper. Mexican binder and Cuban seed filler. Made
by Tabacos Rancho Jamastran (Eiroa Family). Im-
ported exclusively into USA by Caribe in Florida.
Michelangelo   190mm/7 1/2 ins × 20.64mm/52
Da Vinci   175mm/6 7/8 ins × 19.05mm/48
Puccini   165mm/6 1/2 ins × 17.46mm/44
Gallileo★★★★   127mm/5 ins × 19.84mm/50
A well made cigar with spicy, floral aromas. Medium to
full bodied with smooth, integrated flavours.
Verdi★★★   140mm/5 1/2 ins × 17.46mm/44
Medium to full bodied. Distinct cinnamon finish. Day-
time smoke.
Dante★★★★   140mm/5 1/2 ins × 15.08mm/38
Rich spicy and coffee aroma. Full-flavoured. Not such
distinct cinnamon finish as on Verdi.

LA INVICTA

Hand-made. Quality: good. Medium bodied. Delicate spicy flavour. Originally made in Jamaica. Made by Villazon for Hunters and Frankau, London.

Churchill	172mm/6 3/4 ins × 18.65mm/47
Corona****	140mm/5 1/2 ins × 16.67mm/42

Pronounced cinnamon and cloves aroma and on finish. Burns well. Good after dinner cigar.

Magnum No 2	127mm/5 1/2 ins × 19.84mm/50
Magnum No 3	113mm/4 1/2 ins × 19.84mm/50
No 10	127mm/5 ins × 19.84mm/50
Petit Corona	127mm/5 ins × 16.67mm/42

LA LLORONA

Hand-made. Bundles of 20. Connecticut wrapper. Nicaragua filler. Mexican binder. Made by Consolidated Cigar.

No 1	165mm/6 1/2 ins × 16.67mm/42
No 2	140mm/5 1/2 ins × 18.3mm/46
No 3	178mm/7 ins × 19.1mm/48
No 4	206mm/8 1/2 ins × 19.84mm/50
No 5	127mm/5 ins × 20.6mm/52
No 6	171mm/6 3/4 ins × 21.4mm/54

LA NATIVE

Hand-made. Connecticut wrapper. Honduran filler and binder.

Gigantes	203mm/8 ins × 20.6mm/52
Corona Grande	191mm/7 1/2 ins × 18.3mm/46
Churchill	175mm/6 7/8 ins × 19.5mm/49
Cetras	152mm/6 ins × 17.1mm/43
Rothchild	127mm/5 ins × 19.84mm/50
Super Fino	114mm/4 1/2 ins × 11.9mm/30
Moderno	114mm/4 1/2 ins × 10.3mm/26

LA PRIMADORA

Hand-made. Bundles. Natural or maduro wrappers. Honduran wrapper. Dominican binder and filler. Brand owned by Swisher Intl.

Emperor	216mm/8 1/2 ins × 19.84mm/50
Solitaire	152mm/6 ins × 19.84mm/50
Starbite	113mm/4 1/2 ins × 19.84mm/50
Falcon	165mm/6 1/2 ins × 13.49mm/34
Excellentes	165mm/6 1/2 ins × 16.67mm/42
Petite Cetros	140mm/5 1/2 ins × 16.67mm/42

LA REAL

Hand-made. All Honduran tobacco. Distributed by Cigars of Honduras, Virginia.

| Imperials | 178mm/7 ins × 20.2mm/50 |
| Baron | 127mm/5 ins × 20.2mm/50 |

LAS CABRILLAS
Hand-made. Introduced in 1993. Connecticut shade wrapper. Mexican binder. Nicaraguan filler. Made by Consolidated Cigar.

Columbus	209mm/8 1/4 ins × 20.64mm/52
Balboa	190mm/7 1/2 ins × 21.43mm/54
De Soto	175mm/6 7/8 ins × 19.84mm/50
Ponce de Leon	172mm/6 3/4 ins × 17.46mm/44
Magellan	152mm/6 ins × 16.67mm/42
Coronado	175mm/6 7/8 ins × 13.89mm/35
Cortez	120mm/4 3/4 ins × 19.84mm/50

LA MAXIMILIANA
Hand-made. All Honduran tobacco. Distributed by Cigars of Honduras, Virginia.

Luxus	152mm/6 ins × 17.1mm/43
Fumas	179mm/7 ins × 17.5mm/44
Dulcis	140mm/5 1/2 ins × 16.67mm/42

LA VENGA
Hand-made. Wrapper from Ecuador. Honduran binder. Filler blend of tobacco from Dominican Rep., Nicaragua and Honduras. Exclusive to Arango Cigar.

Fuma	140mm/5 1/2 ins × 17.46mm/44
No 10	140mm/5 1/2 ins × 17.07mm/43
No 37	113mm/4 1/2 ins × 19.84mm/50
No 59	184mm/7 1/4 ins × 21.43mm/54
No 61	160mm/6 1/4 ins × 19.84mm/50
No 62	140mm/5 1/2 ins × 18.65mm/47
No 63	184mm/7 1/4 ins × 18.26mm/46
No 70	172mm/6 3/4 ins × 19.05mm/48
No 80	216mm/8 1/2 ins × 17.46mm/44

LEGACY
Hand-made. Bundles of 18. Wrapper from Ecuador. Binder and filler from Honduras. Brand owned by Lignum-2 Inc.

Napoleon	216mm/8 1/2 ins × 20.64mm/52
Monarch	178mm/7 ins × 20.64mm/52
Corona Grande	190mm/7 1/2 ins × 18.26mm/46
Elegante	178mm/7 ins × 17.07mm/43
Rothchild	127mm/5 ins × 19.84mm/50
Super Cetro	152mm/6 ins × 17.07mm/43

LEMPIRA
Hand-made. Bundles. Quality: good. Filler blend of

tobacco from Nicaragua, Honduras and Dominican Republic. Made by Tobacos de Plasencia for Tropical Tobacco.

Toro	152mm/6 ins × 17.07mm/50
Lanceros	165mm/6 1/2 ins × 15.08mm/38
Lonsdale	165mm/6 1/2 ins × 17.46mm/44
Robusto	127mm/5 ins × 19.84mm/50
Churchills	178mm/7 ins × 19.45mm/50
Presidentes	197mm/7 3/4 ins × 19.84mm/50

MARIA MANCINI
Hand-made. Quality: good. Medium to dark Havana seed wrappers. Exclusive to Santa Clara, N.A.

Clemenceau	178mm/7 ins × 19.45mm/49
Palma Delgado	178mm/7 ins × 15.48mm/39
Grandes	172mm/6 3/4 ins × 17.07mm/43
Coronas Largas	160mm/6 1/4 ins × 17.07mm/43
Corona Classico	127mm/5 ins × 16.67mm/43
De Gaulle	127mm/5 ins × 19.84mm/50

MAYA
Hand-made. Connecticut shade wrapper. Filler blend of tobacco from Honduras and Dominican Republic. Made by Tobacos de Plasencia for Tropical Tobacco.

*Executive	197mm/7 3/4 ins × 19.84mm/50
*Churchills	175mm/6 7/8 ins × 19.45mm/49
*Coronas	160mm/6 1/4 ins × 17.46mm/44
*Matador	152mm/6 ins × 19.84mm/50
*Robustos	127mm/5 ins × 19.84mm/50

*Available with Mexican maduro wrapper.

MEDAL OF HONOR
Hand-made. Bundle. Connecticut shade wrapper. Binder and filler from Honduras.

No 300	165mm/6 1/2mm × 16.67mm/42
No 500	190mm/7 1/2 ins × 19.84mm/50
No 700	216mm/8 1/2 ins × 20.64mm/52

MOCHA SUPREME
Hand-made. Quality: good. Havana seed wrappers. All Honduran tobacco. Made by Tobacos de Plasencia for Cigars by Santa Clara N.A. Full bodied.

Rembrandt	216mm/8 ins × 20.64mm/52
Patron	190mm/7 1/2 ins × 19.84mm/50
Lords	165mm/6 1/2 ins × 16.67mm/42
Renaissance	152mm/6 ins × 19.84mm/50
Baron de Rothschild	113mm/4 1/2 ins × 20.64mm/52
Sovereign	140mm/5 1/2 ins × 16.67mm/42

Allegro	165mm/6 1/2 ins × 14.29mm/36
Petites	113mm/4 1/2 ins × 16.67mm/42

MONTECASSINO
Hand-made. Bundles. All Honduran tobacco. Distributed by Mike's Cigars.

Cazadores	165mm/6 1/2 ins × 17.5mm/44
Imperial	216mm/8 1/2 ins × 20.6mm/52
Dicador	178mm/7 ins × 13.9mm/35
Super Diamantes	203mm/8 ins × 19.84mm/50

MONTELIMAR
Hand-made. Ecuador wrapper. Binder and filler from Nicaragua.

No 1	168mm/6 5/8 ins × 17.46mm/44
Cetros	152mm/6 ins × 16.27mm/41
Churchill	175mm/6 7/8 ins × 19.45mm/49
Elegante	175mm/6 7/8 ins × 13.49mm/35
Joya Maduro	113mm/4 1/2 ins × 20.64mm/52
Joya Natural	113mm/4 1/2 ins × 20.64mm/52
Luchadore Mad	168mm/6 5/8 ins × 17.46mm/44
Luchadore Nat	168mm/6 5/8 ins × 17.46mm/44
Presidente	216mm/8 1/2 ins × 20.64mm/52
Toro	152mm/6 ins × 19.84mm/50

MONTOYA PREMIUM
Hand-made. Bundles. Dominican wrapper. Binder and filler from Honduras. Made by Tabacos Rancho Jamastran (Eiroa Family) for Caribe in Florida.

Presidente	52mm/8 1/2 ins
Churchill	50mm/7 1/2 ins
No 1	43mm/6 7/8 ins
Rothschild	50mm/5 ins
Petit Corona	43mm/5 1/2 ins

NATIONAL BRAND
Hand-made. Bundles. All Honduran tobacco. Made by Tobacos Rancho Jamastran (Eiroa Family). Imported into USA by Caribe.

Imperial	216mm/8 1/2 ins × 20.6mm/52
Churchill	191mm/7 1/2 ins × 19.84mm/50
Lonsdale	165mm/6 1/2 ins × 16.67mm/42
Corona	140mm/5 1/2 ins × 16.67mm/42
Super Rothschild	152mm/6 ins × 19.84mm/50
Saberano	175mm/6 7/8 ins × 18.7mm/46
Royal Palm	175mm/6 7/8 ins × 14.7mm/37

NESTOR VINTAGE
Hand-made. Quality: superior. Ecuador wrapper. Hon-

duran binder and filler. Made by Tobacos de Plasencia.
Named after famous owner, Nestor Plasencia. Distributed by House of Oxford.

No 1	178mm/7 ins × 17.1mm/43
747	194mm/7 5/8 ins × 18.7mm/47
654	152mm/6 ins × 21.4mm/54
454	121mm/4 3/4 ins × 21.4mm/54

NAT SHERMAN HOST SELECTION
Hand-made. Quality: superior. Equador seed wrapper.
Honduran Cuban seed binder and filler. Full bodied.
Green, red and gold band.
Named after New York State resorts.

Hudson	124mm/4 7/8 ins × 12.70mm/32
Hamilton	140mm/5 1/2 ins × 16.67mm/42
Hunter	152mm/6 ins × 17.07mm/43
Harrington	178mm/7 ins × 17.46mm/44
Hobart★★★	127mm/5 ins × 19.84mm/50

Tends to become dusty on finish and looses flavour and
balance.

Hampton	178mm/7 ins × 19.84mm/50

NORDING
Hand-made. Quality: superior. Connecticut shade
wrapper. Nicaraguan binder. Filler, a blend of tobacco
from Dominican Rep. and Nicaragua. Exclusive to
Hollco Rohr.

Presidente	191mm/7 1/2 ins × 20.6mm/52
Corona Grande	152mm/6 ins × 19.8mm/50
Robusto	121mm/4 3/4 ins × 20.6mm/52
Lonsdale	171mm/6 3/4 ins × 17.1mm/43
Corona	140mm/5 1/2 ins × 17.1mm/43

PARTICULARES
Hand-made. Quality: superior. Filler blend of Cuban
seed and 30 percent tobacco from Dominican Republic.
Made by Tobacos de Plasencia for Tropical Tobacco.
Connecticut shade wrapper. Medium strength.

Petit	143mm/5 5/8 ins × 13.49mm/34
Numero Cuatro	140mm/5 1/2 ins × 16.67mm/42
Panetelas	175mm/6 7/8 ins × 13.89mm/35
Royal Coronas★★★	160mm/6 1/4 ins × 17.07mm/43

Full bodied and round — good cigar to follow lunch

*Rothschild	127mm/5 ins × 19.84mm/50
Supremos	178mm/7 ins × 17.07mm/43
*Matador	152mm/6 ins × 19.84mm/50
Churchills	152mm/6 7/8 ins × 19.45mm/49
Royal Coronas	160mm/6 1/4 ins × 17.07mm/43

Presidentes	197mm/7 3/4 ins × 19.84mm/50
*Viajantes	203mm/8 1/2 ins × 20.64mm/52
Executive	203mm/8 1/2 ins × 20.64mm/52

*Also available in maduro wrapper.

PADRON
Hand-made. Quality: superior. All Nicaraguan tobacco. Same range also made in Honduras where Connecticut shade wrapper is used. Distributed by Piloto Cigars, Miami.

| Padron 3000**** | 140mm/5 1/2 ins × 20.6mm/52 |

Burns well with good draw. Spicy with touch of cinnamon.

Magnum	229mm/9 ins × 19.84mm/50
Executive	190mm/7 1/2 ins × 19.84mm/50
Padron 2000	127mm/5 ins × 19.84mm/50
Churchill	175mm/6 7/8 ins × 18.3mm/46
Delicias	124mm/4 7/8 ins × 18.3mm/46
Ambassador	175mm/6 7/8 ins × 16.67mm/42
Palma	164mm/6 5/16 ins × 16.67mm/42
Londres	137mm/5 1/2 ins × 16.67mm/42
Grand Reserve	203mm/8 ins × 16.3mm/41
Panetela	175mm/6 7/8 ins × 14.3mm/36
Chicos	137mm/5 1/2 ins × 14.3mm/38

PADRON SERRIE DE ANIVERSARIO
Hand-made. Quality: superior. Limited production. See notes on Padron.

Pyramide	175mm/6 7/8 ins × 20.6mm/52
Diplomatico	179mm/7 ins × 19.84mm/50
Exclusivo****	137mm/5 1/2 ins × 19.84mm/50

Meduim bodied. Touch of cinnamon. Elegant. Daytime smoke or after lunch.

| Monarca | 165mm/6 1/2 ins × 18.3mm/46 |
| Superior*** | 165mm/6 1/2 ins × 16.67mm/42 |

Starts with good promise but flavour fades towards end. Looks so good, but disappoints.

| Corona | 152mm/6 ins × 16.67mm/42 |

PEDRO IGLESIAS
Hand-made.

Crowns	127mm/5 ins × 17.86mm/45
Regents	152mm/6 ins × 17.46mm/44
Lonsdales	165mm/6 1/2 ins × 17.46mm/44

PETRUS TABACAGE 89
Hand-made. Ecuador wraper. Filler and binder from Honduras. Exclusive to Cigars of Honduras, Virginia.

| *Double Corona | 197mm/7 3/4 ins × 20.2mm/50 |

Lord Byron	203mm/8 ins × 15.1mm/38
*Churchill	179mm/7 ins × 20.2mm/50
*No II	159mm/6 1/4 ins × 17.5mm/44
No III	152mm/6 ins × 20.2mm/50
No IV	137mm/5 3/8 ins × 15.1mm/38
*Corona Subline	140mm/5 1/2 ins ×18.3mm/46
Gregorius	127mm/5 ins × 16.67mm/42
*Rothschild	121mm/4 3/4 ins × 20.2mm/50
Chantaco	121mm/4 3/4 ins × 13.9mm/35
Duchess	114mm/4 1/2 ins × 11.9mm/30
Petrushkas	108mm/4 1/4 ins × 9.91mm/25
*Antonius (torpedo)	127mm/5 ins × 20.6mm/52
Palma Fina	165mm/6 1/2 ins × 13.9mm/35

*Available with maduro wrappers.

PLASENCIA

Hand-made. Exclusive to Indian Head Sales.

Viajante	216mm/8 1/2 ins × 20.64mm/52
Gigante	203mm/8 ins × 21.43mm/54
Elegante	203mm/8 ins × 14.29mm/36
Imperial 1	90mm/7 1/2 ins × 19.84mm/50
Churchill	178mm/7 ins × 19.45mm/49
No 1	178mm/7 ins × 17.07mm/43
No 3	178mm/7 ins × 14.29mm/36
No 4	140mm/5 1/2 ins × 17.07mm/43
Toro	152mm/6 ins × 19.84mm/50
Corona Especial	152mm/6 ins × 17.46mm/44
No 5	140mm/5 1/2 ins × 13.49mm/35
Rothchild	113mm/4 1/2 ins × 19.84mm/50

PRIDE OF COPAN

Hand-made. Quality: superior. Connecticut wrapper. Honduran binder and filler. Distributed by Davidoff.

No 1	171mm/6 3/4 ins × 19.84mm/50
No 2	152mm/6 ins × 17.5mm/44
No 3	137mm/5 3/8 ins × 15.1mm/38
No 4	149mm/5 7/8 ins × 13.9mm/35
No 5	159mm/6 1/4 ins × 11.9mm/30
No 6	121mm/4 3/4 ins × 11.9mm/30
No 7	105mm/4 1/8 ins × 9.91mm/25

PRIMO DEL CRISTO

Hand-made. All Honduran tobacco.

Generals	216mm/8 1/2 ins × 19.84mm/50
Inmensos	197mm/7 3/4 ins × 20.6mm/52
Churchills	165mm/6 1/2 ins × 19.84mm/50
Toros	152mm/6 ins × 19.84mm/50
Rothschilds	127mm/5 ins × 19.84mm/50

No 1   165mm/6 1/2 ins × 16.67mm/42
Coronas   140mm/5 1/2 ins × 16.67mm/42
Palmas Reales   203mm/8 ins × 14.3mm/36
Palmas Extra   178mm/7 ins × 14.3mm/36
Reyes   127mm/5 ins × 16.67mm/42

PUNCH
Hand-made. Quality: superior.
Havana seed wrappers. Names differ from those of
Cuban range, with exception of Presidents, Double
Corona, and Punch Punch. Bands are similar, but do
not include "Habana". Made by Villazon. Sold in UK
under La Invicta label. Made by Villazon.

Presidents★★★★★   216mm/8 1/2 ins × 20.64mm/52
Well-made, good-looking cigar. Medium strength,
smooth, integrated flavours. Cigar to be seen smoking.
Casa Grandes   184mm/7 1/4 ins × 18.26mm/46
After Dinner   184mm/7 1/4 ins × 17.86mm/45
Double Corona★★★★   172mm/6 3/4 ins × 19.05mm/48
Reminiscent of Havana maduro wrapper, smooth and
oily. Honeyed undertones. Loses its zest towards end.
Pitas★★★★★   155mm/6 1/8 ins × 19.84mm/50
Good balance between strength and flavour. Coffee
and spice aromas. Gets better. Cigar one doesn't want
to put out.
Cafe Royal   143mm/5 5/8 ins × 17.46mm/44
Punch Punch   160mm/6 1/4 ins × 17.46mm/44
Amatistas   160mm/6 1/4 ins × 17.46mm/44
No 1   165mm/6 1/2 ins × 16.67mm/43
No 75   140mm/5 1/2 ins × 17.46mm/44
Card Royal   143mm/5 5/8 ins × 17.46mm/44
Elites   133mm/5 1/4 ins × 17.46mm/44
Largo Elegantes   178mm/7 ins × 12.70mm/32
Super Rothschild   133mm/5 1/4 ins × 19.84mm/50
London Club   127mm/5 ins × 15.87mm/40
Rothschilds   113mm/4 1/2 ins × 19.84mm/50
Slim Panetela   102mm/4 ins × 11.11mm/28
Lonsdale   165mm/6 1/2 ins × 17.07mm43

PUNCH DE LUXE
Hand-made. Quality: superior.
Havana seed wrappers. Full bodied. Only the Coronas
has the same name as in the Havana range. Not for the
beginner.
Chateau Lafitte★★★★★ 184mm/7 1/4 ins × 21.43mm/54
Aristocratic, well-made cigar. Elegant with integrated
flavours. Maduro wrapper. Good after-dinner cigar for
connoisseur.

Chateau Margaux	147mm/5 3/4 ins × 18.26mm/46
Coronas	160mm/6 1/4 ins × 17.86mm/45
Royal Coronations (tube)	
	133mm/5 1/4 ins × 17.46mm/44

PUNCH GRAN CRU
Hand-made. Quality: superior.
Havana seed wrappers. Particularly full bodied. Appreciated by experienced smoker. Names not the same as Cuban range. Selected cigars. Made by Villazon.

| Prince Consorts | 216mm/8 1/2 ins × 20.64mm/52 |
| Diademas★★★ | 184mm/7 1/4 ins × 21.43mm/54 |

Discreet spicy aroma. Mild and smooth. Could do with more flavour. Lacks lustre.

| Monarcas (tube) | 172mm/6 3/4 ins × 19.05mm/48 |
| Britania★★★★ | 160mm/6 1/4 ins × 19.84mm/50 |

Well-made cigar. Good texture and integrated flavours. Good after-dinner smoke.

| Robustos | 133mm/5 1/4 ins × 19.84mm/50 |
| Superiors★★★★★ | 140mm/5 1/2 ins × 19.05mm/48 |

Lives up to its name. Full-bodied. Good balance between strength and flavour. Ideal to follow meal.

PURIOS INDIOS
Hand-made. Quality: superior. Ecuador wrapper and binder. Filler blend of tobacco from Dominican Rep., Brazil, Jamaica and Nicaragua. Launched early 1996. Brand owned and made by Rolando Reyes Sr, founder of Cuba Aliados Cigars Inc., which as wholesale and retail operations in Union City, New Jersey.

| Churchill Especial | 184mm/7 1/4 ins × 21.0mm/53 |
| Presidente★★★★★ | 184mm/7 1/4 ins × 18.7mm/47 |

Medium to full bodied. rich, spicy. Good finish. Well made. Elegant. To follow special meal.

| Nacionales | 165mm/6 1/2 ins × 18.3mm/46 |
| Piramide No 1★★★★ | 190mm/7 1/2 ins × 23.8mm/60 |

Medium-bodied. Smooth and elegant. I would prefer more "oomph" for cigar of this size.

Piramide No 2	165mm/6 1/2 ins × 18.3mm/46
Toro Especial	152mm/6 ins × 19.84mm/50
Rothschild	127mm/5 ins × 19.84mm/50
Palmas Real	178mm/7 ins × 15.1mm/38
No 4 Especial	140mm/5 1/2 ins × 17.5mm/44
Figurin	254mm/10 ins × 23.8mm/60
General	457mm/18 ins × 26.2mm/66
Petit Perla	127mm/5 ins × 15.1mm/38
No 1 Especial	178mm/7 ins × 19.1mm/48
No 2 Especial	165mm/6 1/2 ins × 18.3mm/46

RED LABEL
Hand-made. Bundles. Natural, maduro and claro wrappers. Mexican wrapper and binder. Honduran filler.

Amatista	147mm/5 3/4 ins × 17.86mm/45
Casino	216mm/8 1/2 ins × 16.67mm/42
Cetro	152mm/6 ins × 16.67mm/42
Chico	140mm/5 1/2 ins × 17.07mm/43
Churchill Round	152mm/6 ins × 19.45mm/49
El Dorado	203mm/8 ins × 17.86mm/45
Elegante	178mm/7 ins × 15.08mm/38
Emperadore	216mm/8 1/2 ins × 20.64mm/52
Londre	178mm/7 ins × 15.87mm/40
Lonsdale	172mm/6 3/4 ins × 19.05mm/48
Magnifico	184mm/7 1/4 ins × 21.43mm/54
Presidente	190mm/7 1/2 ins × 17.86mm/45
Rothschild	113mm/4 1/2 ins × 19.84mm/50
Super Cetro	160mm/6 1/4 ins × 17.46mm/44

REPEATER
Hand-made. Medium filler. Quality: good. Made by Tabacos Rancho Jamastram (Eiroa Family). Good value. Imported into United States by Caribe.

Repeater 100	140mm/5 1/2 ins × 17.07mm/43
Repeater 200	152mm/6 ins × 17.07mm/43
Repeater 300	165mm/6 1/2 ins × 17.07mm/43
Havana Twist	178mm/7 ins × 17.46mm/44
Churchill★★★	178mm/7 ins × 19.45mm/49

Little underfilled. Good integrated flavour and aroma.

RIATA
Hand-made. Bundles. Mexican wrapper and binder. Honduran filler. Made by Consolidated Cigar.

No. 100	178mm/7 ins × 12.00mm/30
No. 200	175mm/6 7/8 ins × 13.89mm/35
No. 300	152mm/6 ins × 16.67mm/42
No. 400	140mm/5 1/2 ins × 17.46mm/44
No. 500	168mm/6 5/8 ins × 17.46mm/44
No. 600	175mm/6 7/8 ins × 19.05mm/48
No. 700	120mm/4 3/4 ins × 19.84mm/50
No. 800	160mm/6 1/4 ins × 19.84mm/50
No. 900	184mm/7 1/4 ins × 19.84mm/50
It's A Boy/Girl	152mm/6 ins × 16.67mm/42

ROMEO Y JULIETA
Hand-made. Quality: superior. Havana seed wrapper. Good quality and well made. Full bodied. Reminiscent of a Havana. Also made in Dominican Republic and

Cuba. The bands do not include the word "Habana".
Brand owned in USA by Hollco Rohr.

Gigante	178mm/7 ins × 19.05mm/48
Celestiales	203mm/8 ins × 14.29mm/36
Especiales	160mm/6 1/4 ins × 17.07mm
Prado	140mm/5 1/2 ins × 16.67mm
Princessa	133mm/5 1/4 ins × 15.48mm/39
Sublime	113mm/4 1/2 ins × 19.84mm/50

ROYAL COURT
Hand-made. Bundles. Ecuador wrapper. Honduran
filler and binder. Brand owned by Lignum-2 Inc.

Petit Corona	140mm/5 1/2 ins × 15.08mm/38
Panetela	175mm/6 7/8 ins × 14.29mm/36
Cetro	152mm/6 ins × 17.86mm/43
Predidente	197mm/7 3/4 ins × 19.84mm/50
Viajante	216mm/8 1/2 ins × 20.64mm/52

ROYAL MANNA
Hand-made. Ecuador wrapper. Honduran filler and
binder. Brand owned by Brick-Hanauer.

No 1	7 ins × 17.07mm/43
No 4	5 5/12 ins × 16.67/42
Manchego	152mm/6 ins × 14.29mm/36
Churchill	190mm/17 1/2 ins × 19.84 mm/50
Laro Extra Fino Rothschild	
	203mm/8 ins × 15.08mm/38
Toros	152mm/6 ins × 19.84mm/50

SAN LUIS
Hand-made. Bundles. Mixed filler. Distributed by Indian
Head Sales.

Soberanos	191mm/7 1/2 ins × 19.84mm/50
Corona	166mm/6 1/2 ins × 17.5mm/44
Toro	152mm/6 ins × 19.84mm/50
Panetelas	166mm/6 1/2 ins × 14.3mm/36
Cetros	137mm/5 3/8 ins × 16.67mm/42

SANTA ROSA
Hand-made. Ecuador wrapper. Honduran filler and
binder.

Numero Cuatro	127mm/5 1/2 ins × 16.67mm/42
Cetros	152mm/6 ins × 16.67mm/42
Churchill	178mm/7 ins × 19.45mm/49
Corona	165mm/6 1/2 ins × 17.46mm/44
Elegante	178mm/7 ins × 17.07mm/43
Embajadore	216mm/8 1/2 ins × 20.64mm/52

Largos	172mm/6 3/4 ins × 13.89mm/35
Regulares	140mm/5 1/2 ins × 17.86mm/45
Toro	152mm/6 ins × 19.84mm/50

SAN FERNANDO
Hand-made. All Honduran tobacco. Distributed by Cigars of Honduras, Virginia.

Churchill	179mm/7 ins × 19.1mm/48
Corona	152mm/6 ins × 17.5mm/44
No 5	127mm/5 ins × 20.6mm/52

SOLO AROMA
Hand-made. Bundles. Connecticut shade wrapper. Filler blend of tobacco from Honduras and Dominican Republic. Made by Tabacos de Plasencia for Tropical Tobacco.

*Fumas	178mm/7 ins × 17.46mm/44
*Cazadores	160mm/6 1/4 ins × 17.46mm/44
Numero Cuatro	140mm/5 1/2 ins × 16.67mm/42
Numero Dos	152mm/6 ins × 17.07mm/43
Corona Gorda	160mm/6 1/4 ins × 17.46mm/44
Rothchild	127mm/5 ins × 19.84mm/50
Numero Uno	178mm/7 ins × 17.07mm/43
Panetela	175mm/6 7/8 ins × 14.29mm/36
Palma de Mayorca	203mm/8 ins × 15.08mm/38
Corona Grande	190mm/7 1/2 ins × 18.26mm/46
Churchill	175mm/6 7/8 ins × 19.45mm/49
Toro	152mm/6 ins × 19.84mm/50
Soberanos	197mm/7 3/4 ins × 19.84mm/50
Viajante	216mm/8 1/2 ins × 20.64mm/52

*Short filler.

SUPER SPECIAL
Hand-made. Bundles. Connecticut shade wrapper. Brand owned by Brick-Hanauer.

Toro	152mm/6 ins × 19.84mm/50
Churchill	178mm/7 ins × 19.45mm/49
Viajante	216mm/8 1/2 ins × 20.64mm/52
No 1	172mm/6 3/4 ins × 16.67mm/42
Cetros	152mm/6 ins × 16.67mm/42
Rothschild	113mm/4 1/2 ins × 20.64mm/52

SWISHER SWEETS
Hand-made. Short filler. All tobacco. No binder. Rough cut and hand-rolled. Unique sweet taste. Packed in resealable pouch. Good value mass market cigar. Owned by Swisher Intl.

| Outlaws★★★ | 108mm/4 1/4 ins × 11.1mm/28 |

TEÑA Y VEGA
Hand-made. Quality: superior. Cameroon wrapper.
Honduran binder and filler. Mild. Exclusive to Santa
Clara N.A.

Cetros	155mm/6 1/8 ins × 16.67mm/42
Churchill	178mm/7 ins × 19.84mm/50
Double Corona	152mm/6 ins × 19.84mm/50
No 1	172mm/6 3/4 ins × 16.67mm/42

TESOROS DE COPAN
Hand-made. All Honduran tobacco. Wrapper is Honduran grown Connecticut seed. La Ruta Maya Foundation, dedicated to preservatio of Central American
rainforests and remains of Mayans, original users of
tobacco, benefits from sale of these cigars. Distributed
by Cigars of Honduras, Virginia.

Churchill	179mm/7 ins × 20.2mm/50
Cetros	159mm/6 1/4 ins × 17.5mm/44
Toros	152mm/6 ins × 20.2mm/50
Corona	133mm/5 1/4 ins × 18.3mm/46
Yumbo	121mm/4 3/4 ins × 20.2mm/50
Lindas	mm/5 5/8 ins × 15.1mm/38

THOMAS HINDS HONDURAN SELECTION
Hand-made. Ecquador wrapper. Honduran filler and
binder. Owned by Hinds Brothers Tobacco.

Presidente	216mm/8 1/2 ins × 20.6mm/52
Torpedo	152mm/6 ins × 20.6mm/52
Churchill	178mm/7 ins × 19.5mm/49
Short Churchill	152mm/6 ins × 20.84mm/50
Supremo	178mm/7 ins × 20.1mm/43
Robusto	127mm/5 ins × 20.84mm/50
Royal Corona	152mm/6 ins × 20.1mm/43
Corona	140mm/5 1/2 ins × 16.67mm/42

TIBURON
Hand-made. Bundles. Connecticut wrapper. Mexican
binder. Dominican filler. Brand owned by Phillips &
King.

Tiger Shark	160mm/6 1/4 ins × 13.49mm/34
Great White	152mm/6 ins × 17.07mm/43
Mako	83mm/5 1/4 ins × 16.67mm/42

TOPPER
Hand-made. Honduran wrapper and binder. Filler,
blend of tobacco from Mexico and Dominican Republic.
Owned by Topper Cigar Co., established 1896.

Panetela	178mm/7 ins × 13.5mm/34
Corona	140mm/5 1/2 ins × 17.1mm/43

No 1	165mm/6 1/2 ins × 17.1mm/43
Rothschild	114mm/4 1/2 ins × 20.84mm/50
Toro	152mm/6 ins × 20.84mm/50
Churchill	191mm/7 1/2 ins × 20.84mm/50

TULAS

Hand-made. Bundles of 20. Connecticut wrapper. Nicaraguan filler. Mexican binder. Made by Consolidated Cigar.

No 1	165mm/6 1/2 ins × 16.67mm/42
No 2	140mm/5 1/2 ins × 18.3mm/46
No 3	178mm/7 ins × 19.1mm/48
No 4	216mm/8 1/2 ins × 19.84mm/50
No 5	127mm/5 ins × 20.6mm/52
No 6	171mm/6 3/4 ins × 21.4mm/54

V CENTENNIAL

Hand-made. Quality: superior. Top of range from Tropical Tobacco. Made by Tabacos de Plasencia. Connecticut shade wrapper. Mexican binder. Filler blend from five countries.

Torpedo★★★★	178mm/7 ins × 21.43mm/54

Spicy, hint of cinamon. Flavour bit light for strength. Smooth. Well made. Attractive presentation.

Presidente	203mm/8 ins × 19.84mm/50
*Churchills	178mm/7 ins × 19.05mm/48
Numero 1	190mm/7 1/2 ins × 15.08mm/38
*Numero 2	152mm/6 ins × 19.84mm/50
*Cetros	160mm/6 1/4 ins × 17.46mm/44
*Robustos★★★★	127mm/5 ins × 19.84mm/50

Lovely wrapper. Perhaps not enough flavour for the strength. Robust.

Coronas	140mm/5 1/2 ins × 16.67mm/42

*Also available in maduro wrapper.

VINTAGE HONDURAN

Hand-made. Medium to full bodied. All Honduran tobacco.

Cetro	165mm/6 1/2 ins × 17.46mm/44
Governor	152mm/6 ins × 19.84mm/50
Imperial	203mm/8 ins × 17.46mm/44
Matador	140mm/5 1/2 ins × 16.67mm/42
Panetela	152mm/6 ins × 14.29mm/36
Panetela Larga	178mm/7 ins × 14.29mm/36
President	190mm/7 1/2 ins × 19.84mm/50
Rothchild	113mm/4 1/2 ins × 19.84mm/50
Sultans	216mm/8 1/2 ins × 20.64mm/52
Toro	140mm/5 1/2 ins × 18.26mm/46

VIRTUOSO TORAÑO

Hand-made. Connecticut seed wrapper grown in Ecuador. Nicaraguan binder. Filler blend of tobacco from Nicaragua, Honduras and Mexico. Brand owned by Toraño Cigars, Miami.

Presidente	203mm/8 ins × 20.6mm/52
Double Corona	152mm/6 ins × 19.84mm/50
Robusto	121mm/4 3/4 ins × 20.6mm/52
Lonsdale	178mm/7 ins × 17.5mm/44
Cetros	152mm/6 ins × 17.1mm/43

VOYAGER

Hand-made. Connecticut shade wrapper grown in Ecuador. Binder and filler from Honduras. Brand owned by Brick-Hanauer.

Atlantis	190mm/7 1/2 ins × 18.26mm//46
Columbia	178mm/7 ins × 17.07mm/43
Enterprise	152mm/6 ins × 16.67mm/42

W & D

Hand-made Bundles. Good value. Distributed in USA by Hollco Rohr.

Presidentes	190mm/7 1/2 ins × 19.84mm/50
Cetros No 2★★★★	165mm/6 1/2 ins × 17.46mm/44

Oily mid brown wrapper. Smooth. Good balance. Good daytime smoke or after light meal.

Coronas	140mm/5 1/2 ins × 19.84mm/50
Panetela Largas	178mm/7 ins × 14.29mm/36
Blunts★★★	127mm/5 ins × 16.67mm/42

Fairly hard draw. Lacks lustre.

Gigantes	216mm/8 1/2 ins × 20.64mm/52

YAGO

Hand-made. Bundles. All Honduran tobacco. Exclusive to Miami Cigar.

Fumas	178mm/7 ins × 17.5mm/44
Cazadores	178mm/7 ins × 17.5mm/44
Churchill	191mm/7 1/2 ins × 19.84mm/50
Petit Cazadores	140mm/5 1/2 ins × 17.5mm/44

ZINO

Hand-made. Quality: superior. Named after Zino Davidoff. Connoisseur series developed in 1987 for opening of Davidoff shop in New York, full rich flavour. Mouton Cadet range very mild and specially selected from Baronne Philippe de Rothschild. Honduran series medium flavour. All high quality construction. Range of machine-made dry cigars also made in Holland.

Mouton Cadet No 1	160mm/6 1/2 ins × 17.46mm/44

Mouton Cadet No 2	152mm/6 ins × 13.89mm/35
Mouton Cadet No 3	147mm/5 3/4 ins × 14.29mm/36
Mouton Cadet No 4	130mm/5 1/8 ins × 12.00mm/30

Mouton Cadet No 5★★★★★

127mm/5 ins × 17.46mm/44

Spicy aroma with touch of cinnamon and sweetness on palate. Smooth. Well-balanced.

Mouton Cadet No 6	127mm/5 ins × 19.84mm/50
Connoisseur No 100	197mm/7 3/4 ins × 19.84mm/50
Connoisseur No 200	190mm/7 1/2 ins × 18.26mm/46
Connoisseur No 300	147mm/5 3/4 ins × 18.26mm/46
Veritas	178mm/7 ins × 19.84mm/50
Tradition	160mm/6 1/4 ins × 17.46mm/44
Elegance	172mm/6 3/4 ins × 13.49mm/34
Diamond	140mm/5 1/2 ins × 15.87mm/40
Junior	172mm/6 3/4 ins × 12.00mm/30
Princesse	113mm/4 1/2 ins × 7.94mm/20
Zino Tubos No 1	172mm/6 3/4 ins × 13.49mm/34
Classic Sumatra	120mm/4 3/4 ins × 18.65mm/47
Classic Brazil	120mm/4 3/4 ins × 18.65mm/47
Relax Sumatra	147mm/5 3/4 ins × 12.00mm/30
Relax Brazil	147mm/5 3/4 ins × 12.00mm/30
Pantellas Sumatra	
Panatellas Brazil	
Cigarrillos Sumatra	
Cigarrillos Brazil	

INDONESIA

DJARUM
Machine-made by G.A. Andron
Cigarillos

ITALY

ANTICO TUSCANO★★   152mm/6 ins × 10.00mm/25
Machine-made. Specially aged for export. Dark maduro, uneven wrapper. Unusual shape. Tightly rolled, but fairly easy draw. Sweet floral aroma before lit. Strong, but good balance with flavour. Touch of sweetness. Rugged cigar. No finesse.

JAMAICA

In 1995 Jamaica exported 15 339 million cigars to the USA, an increase of 40 percent over 1994.

8-9-8 COLLECTION
Hand-made. Connecticut shade wrapper. Dominican filler and binder. Distributed by Mike's Cigars, Miami.

Churchill	191mm/7 1/2 ins × 19.5mm/49
Corona	140mm/5 1/2 ins × 16.67mm/42
Lonsdale	165mm/6 1/2 ins × 16.67mm/45
Monarch	171mm/6 3/4 ins × 17.9mm/45
Robusto	140mm/5 1/2 ins × 19.5mm/49

CHEVERE

Hand-made. Bundle. All Jamaican leaf. Distributed by Mike's Cigars, Miami.

Kingston	178mm/7 ins × 19.5mm/49
Montego	165mm/6 1/2 ins × 17.9mm/45
Ocho Rios	203mm/8 ins × 19.5mm/49
Antonio	140mm/5 1/2 ins × 17.1mm/43
Spanish Town	165mm/6 1/2 ins × 16.67mm/42

CIFUENTES by Partagas

Hand-made. Quality: superior. Limited edition of about 150 000, named after Ramon Cifuentes, the Partagas brand in Cuba before Castro revolution. Went into Alfred Dunhill stores mid 1996. Aged for two years before boxing. Connecticut shade wrapper. Cameroon binder and filler blend of tobacco from Dominican Rep. and Mexico. Five sizes in range. At time of going to press sizes unavailable. Made by General Cigar.

FUNADORES

Hand-made. Connecticut shade wrapper. Mexican binder. Filler blend of tobacco from Jamaica, Mexico and Dominican Rep. Made by Combined Tobacco Co. for House of Oxford.

| King Ferdinand | 203mm/8 ins × 19.5mm/49 |
| Rothchild★★★★ | 165mm/6 1/2 ins × 16.67mm/42 |

Medium bodied. Spicy with hint of ginger. Daytime smoke for experienced smoker. After dinner cigar for casual smoker.

| Ultra | 152mm/6 ins × 19.84mm/50 |

GISPERT

Hand-made. US rights owned by Hollco Rohr. Old Cuban brand, which has word "Habana" on band.

Kingston Town
Port Royal
Montego Bay
Port Antonio

GUARANTEED JAMAICA

Hand-made. Bundles. Ecuador wrapper. Mexican binder. Filler, blend of tobacco from Jamaica, Mexico and Dominican Republic. Made by Combined Tobacco Co., Kingston, Jamaica.

No 1000	191mm/7 1/2 ins × 19.5mm/49
No 1002	203mm/8 ins × 19.84mm/50
No 100	165mm/6 1/2 ins × 16.67mm/42
No 200	140mm/5 1/2 ins × 16.67mm/42
No 300	171mm/6 3/4 ins × 15.1mm/38
No 600	152mm/6 ins × 19.84mm/50
No 900	152mm/6 ins × 17.9mm/45

JAMAICA BAY
Machine-bunched & hand-finished bundles. Connecticut wrapper, Mexican binder and filler blend of tobacco from Dominican Republic and Mexico. Good value. Distributed in USA by Arango Cigar.

No 100	190mm/7 1/2 ins × 19.45mm/49
No 200	152mm/6 ins × 19.85mm/50
No 300	172mm/6 3/4 ins × 17.86mm/45
No 400	165mm/6 1/2 ins × 16.67mm/42
No 500	152mm/6 3/4 ins × 15.08mm/38
No 600	140mm/5 1/2 ins × 16.67mm/42

JAMAICA GEM
Hand-made. Mexican grown Connecticut seed wrappers. Mexican binder and filler blend of tobacco from Mexico and Dominican Republic.

Petit Corona	127mm/5 ins × 15.87mm/40
Palma	172mm/6 3/4 ins × 13.49mm/34
Corona	140mm/5 1/2 ins × 15.87mm/40
Royal Corona	152mm/6 ins × 16.27mm/41
Corona Grande	165mm/6 1/2 ins × 17.07mm/43
Churchill	203mm/8 ins × 20.24mm/51
Double Corona	178mm/7 ins × 17.86mm/45
Giant Corona	190mm/7 1/2 ins × 19.45mm/49
Palmita	165mm/6 1/2 ins × 12.00mm/30

JAMAICA GOLD
Hand-made. Connecticut shade wrapper. Jamaican grown Connecticut seed wrapper. Mexican binder and filler from Dominican Republic

Prince	197mm/7 3/4 ins × 19.84mm/50
Earl	172mm/6 3/4 ins × 15.08mm/38
Baron★★★	165mm/6 1/2 ins × 17.46mm/44

Mild, little flavour. Easy draw. Daytime smoke. Good value. Ideal for novice.

Queen	160mm/6 1/4 ins × 17.07mm/43
Count	140mm/5 1/2 ins × 15.08mm/38
Duke	140mm/5 1/2 ins × 16.67mm/42
Baron	165mm/6 1/2 ins × 17.76mm/44
Dutchess	113mm/4 1/2 ins × 12.00mm/30

| King | 152mm/6 ins × 19.84mm/50 |
| Torpedo | 178mm/7 × 36 ins × 20.64mm/52 |

JAMAICA HERITAGE
Hand-made. Bundle. Ecuador wrapper. Mexican binder. Filler is blend of tobacco from Jamaica, Mexico and Dominican Republic. Distributed by Lignum-2 Inc and House of Oxford.

No 100	160mm/6 1/2 ins × 16.67mm/42
No 200	140mm/5 1/2 ins × 16.67mm/42
No 600	152mm/6 ins × 19.84mm/50
No 1000	190mm/7 1/2 ins × 19.5mm/49
No 1002	203mm/8 ins × 19.84mm/50

JAMAICAN KINGS
Hand-made. Bundles. Connecticut shade wrapper.

Petit Coronas	140mm/5 1/2 ins × 16.67mm/42
Buccaneers	165mm/6 1/2 ins × 16.67mm/42
Rapiers	178mm/7 ins × 14.29mm/36
Double Coronas	178mm/7 ins × 17.46mm/44
Imperials	190mm/7 1/2 ins × 19.84mm/50

JAMAICAN PRIDE
Hand-made by General Cigar.

Churchill	203mm/8 ins × 19.5mm/49
Double Corona	178mm/7 ins × 19.5mm/49
Imperiales	165mm/6 1/2 ins × 17.9mm/45
Lonsdales	152mm/6 ins × 17.9mm/45
Corona Deluxe	165mm/6 1/2 ins × 16.67mm/42
Corona	140mm/5 1/2 ins × 16.67mm/42
Petit Corona	127mm/5 ins × 15.5mm/39

MACANUDO
Hand-made. Connecticut shade wrapper. Quality: superior.

Originally founded in 1868. Now made by General Cigar.

Blend is the same for both countries — Connecticut shade wrapper, binder from Mexico and a blend of Jamaican, Mexican and Dominican tobacco for the filler.

Largest-selling premium cigar brand in United Stated. In Spanish Macanudo means "the greatest".

Excellent range of well-made cigars. Mild and smooth.

Vintage No I★★★★★   190mm/7 1/2 ins × 19.45mm/49
Excellent claro wrapper. Spicy, floral aromas. Creamy finish. Balanced. Well made.

Vintage No II★★★★★   165mm/6 1/2 ins × 16.67mm/42
Spicy aroma. Medium bodied. No harshness. A top
cigar.
Vintage No III   140mm/5 1/2 ins × 18.26mm/46
Vintage No IV★★★★★   113mm/4 1/2 ins × 18.26mm/46
Medium bodied. Elegant. Satisfying smoke with no
harshness. Ideal to follow a meal.
Vintage No V★★★★   140mm/5 1/2 ins × 19.45mm/49
Mild, smooth. Well made, but could just do with more
flavour.
*Vintage No VII   190mm/7 1/2 ins × 15.08mm/38
Prince Philip   190mm/7 1/2 ins × 19.45mm/49
*Sovereign   197mm/7 3/4 ins × 17.86mm/45
Baron de Rothschild★★★★

                        165mm/6 1/2 ins × 16.67mm/42
Elegant well-made cigar. Excellent for average smoker.
*Amatista★★★★   160mm/6 1/4 ins × 16.67mm/42
Good draw. Elegant, mild and smooth.
Hampton Court   147mm/5 3/4 ins × 17.07mm/43
Duke of Devon★★★★   140mm/5 1/2 ins × 16.67mm/42
Maduro wrapper. Rich aroma. Honey on palate.
*Lord Claridge★★★★   140mm/5 1/2 ins × 15.08mm/38
Mild. Elegant. Hard draw makes it difficult for beginners.
*Somerset   197mm/7 3/4 ins × 13.49mm/31
Portofino   178mm/7 ins × 13.49mm/34
Claybourne   152mm/6 ins × 12.30mm/31
*Duke of Wellington   216mm/8 1/2 ins × 15.08mm/38
Hyde Park★★★   140mm/5 1/2 ins × 19.45mm/49
Medium bodied. Lacks punch.
*Earl of Lonsdale   172mm/6 3/4 ins × 15.08mm/38
No. 800   190mm/7 1/2 ins × 19.45mm/49
No. 900 Portofino   178mm/7 ins × 14.29mm/36
No. 500   172mm/6 3/4 ins × 15.08mm/38
No. 700   165mm/6 1/2 ins × 16.67mm/42
No. 1000   140mm/5 1/2 ins × 19.45mm/49
No. 600   140mm/5 1/2 ins × 16.67mm/42
No. 400   140mm/5 1/2 ins × 15.08mm/38
Ascots (tin)★★★   108mm/4 1/4 ins × 12.70mm/32
Difficult burning. Fairly strong for small cigar.
*Trump★★★★★   165mm/6 1/2 ins × 17.86mm/45
Good balance between strength and flavour. Elegant
and smooth.
Crystal★★★★   133mm/5 1/2 ins × 19.45mm/49
Packed in glass tube. Mild. Good flavour.
Duke of Windsor   152mm/6 ins × 19.84mm/50
*Quill   133mm/5 1/4 ins × 11.11mm/28
Petit Corona★★★★   127mm/5 ins × 15.08mm/38

Mild, spicy and vegetal flavours. Smooth. A good daytime smoke.

Caviar	102mm/4 ins × 14.29mm/36

Manufacture of these cigars ceased early 1996 to make tobacco and production capacity available for more popular cigars. Most of these cigars have ring gauge of 40 or less. Showing market preserence for thicker cigars.

MARIO PALOMINO
Hand-made by Palomino Brothers Tobacco Co. Connecticut shade wrapper. Mexican binder and Jamaican filler. Distributed in USA by Topper Cigar.

Buccaneers	140mm/5 1/2 ins × 12.70mm/32
Delicado	140mm/5 1/2 ins × 12.70mm/32
Petit Corona	127mm/5 1/2 ins × 16.27mm/41
Rapier	152mm/6 ins × 12.70mm/32
Festivale	152mm/6 ins × 16.27mm/41
Cetro	165mm/6 1/2 ins × 16.67mm/42
Corona Immensa	152mm/6 ins × 18.65mm/47
Caballero	178mm/7 ins × 17.86mm/45
Presidente	190mm/7 1/2 ins × 19.45mm/49

OCHO RIOS
Hand-made. Bundle. Ecuador wrapper. Mexican binder. Filler blend of tobacco from Jamaica, Mexico and Dominican Republic. Exclusive to House of Oxford.

President	178mm/7 ins × 19.84mm/50
Toros	152mm/6 ins × 19.84mm/50
Vijantes	210mm/8 1/4 ins × 20.6mm/52
No 4	127mm/5 ins × 16.67mm/42
No 1	178mm/7 ins × 17.1mm/43

OLD HARBOUR
Hand-made. Bundles.

No 100	140mm/5 1/2 ins × 16.67mm/42
No 200	165mm/6 1/2 ins × 16.67mm/42
No 300	178mm/7 ins × 17.86mm/45
No 400	190mm/7 1/2 ins × 19.84mm/50

PRIDE OF JAMAICA
Hand-made. Connecticut wrapper. Mexican binder. Filler, a blend of tobacco from Jamaica, Mexico and Dominican Rep.

Monarch	203mm/8 ins × 19.84mm/50
Churchill	191mm/7 1/2 ins × 19.5mm/49
Magnum	152mm/6 ins × 19.84mm/50
Petit Churchill	152mm/6 ins × 17.9mm/45

Lonsdale	165mm/6 1/2 ins × 16.67mm/42
President	171mm/6 3/4 ins × 15.1mm/38
Royal Corona	140mm/5 1/2 ins × 16.67mm/42

SANTA CRUZ
Hand-made.

Monarch	190mm/7 1/2 ins × 19.45mm/49
Churchill	152mm/6 ins × 19.84mm/50
Bristol	172mm/6 3/4 ins × 17.86mm/45
Corona Grande	152mm/6 1/2 ins × 16.67mm/42
Majestic	172mm/6 3/4 ins × 15.08mm/38
Corona	140mm/5 1/2 ins × 16.67mm/42
Palmette	152mm/6 ins × 12.30mm/31

TEMPLE HALL
Hand-made. Quality: good. Connecticut shade wrapper. Mexican binder from San Andres area. Filler is blend of Jamaican, Dominican and Mexican tobacco. Subtle. Owned by General Cigar.

No 700	178mm/7 ins × 19.45mm/49
No 675	172mm/6 3/4 ins × 17.86mm/45
No 550★★★★	140mm/5 1/2 ins × 19.84mm/50

Smooth, elegant, slow burning. Good introduction to this size. Excellent daytime smoke or after unspiced meal.

| No 625 | 160mm/6 1/4 ins × 16.67mm/42 |
| No 450 Maduro | 113mm/4 1/2 ins × 19.45mm/49 |

Discreet, aromatic aroma. Slightly sweet, honeyed after taste.

| No 685 | 175mm/6 7/8 ins × 13.49mm/34 |
| No 500★★★ | 127mm/5 ins × 12.30mm/31 |

Medium bodied. Discreet, spicy aroma. Good daytime smoke.

| Belicoso★★★ | 152mm/6 ins × 19.84mm/50 |

Medium to full bodied. Mild, spicy, floral aromas. Last third has bitter finish.

No 4 Trump	190mm/7 1/2 ins × 19.45mm/49
No 1 Trump	165mm/6 1/2 ins × 16.67mm/42
No 2 Trump	140mm/5 1/2ins × 19.84mm/50
No 3 Trump	140mm/5 1/2 ins × 16.67mm/42

M E X I C O

San Andrés Valley produces finest tobacco and is centre of cigar export business. In 1995 9,68 million pieces exported to USA, up from 6,47 million in 1994. Mexican cigars are very popular in USA and offer good value for money.

AROMAS DE SAN ANDREAS
Hand-made. Packed in amber tubes. Made by Tabacos
Santa Claro.

Maximillian	190mm/7 1/2 ins × 20.64mm/52
Gourmet★★★★★	165mm/6 1/2 ins × 16.67mm/42

Spicy, coffee flavours. Good balance between strength
and flavour. Strong finish. Ideal for regular smoker.

Aficionado	152mm/6 ins × 19.84mm/50
Robusto	127mm/5 ins × 19.84mm/50

BLACK LABEL
Hand-made. Bundles. All Mexican tobacco. Distributed
by Mike's Cigars, Miami.

Acapulco	152mm/6 ins × 16.67mm/42
Cancun	203mm/8 ins × 20.6mm/52
Guadalajara	168mm/6 5/8 ins × 13.9mm/35
Jaliso	175mm/6 7/8 ins × 21.4mm/54
Monterrey	190mm/7 1/2 ins × 19.84mm/50
Robusto★★★★	121mm/4 3/4 ins × 9.84mm/50

Full-flavoured, strong, but smooth. Ideal to follow spicy
meal.

Toro	152mm/6 ins × 19.84mm/50
Veracruz	168mm/6 5/8 ins × 18.3mm/46
Tijuana	127mm/5 ins × 12.7mm/32

CRUZ REAL
Hand-made. Quality: superior. All Mexican tobacco.
Made by Tabacos y Puro de San Andres SA. Distributed
by Finck Cigar Co., San Antonio, Texas.

No 1	168mm/6 5/8 ins × 16.67mm/42
No 2	152mm/6 ins × 16.67mm/42
No 3	168mm/6 5/8 ins × 13.9mm/35
No 14	191mm/7 1/2 ins × 19.84mm/50
No 19	152mm/6 ins × 19.84mm/50
No 24	114mm/4 1/2 ins × 19.84mm/50
No 25	140mm/5 1/2 ins × 20.2mm/52
No 28	216mm/8 1/2 ins × 21.4mm/54
Ministro Special Edition	159mm/6 1/4 ins × 16.67mm/42
Emperador Special Edition	
	159mm/6 1/4 ins × 19.84mm/50
Canciller Special Edition	
	191mm/7 1/2 ins × 19.84mm/50

EL BESO
Hand-made.
Available in Natural and Maduro.

Churchill	190mm/7 1/2 ins × 19.84mm/50
Toro	168mm/6 ins × 19.84mm/50

No 1   168mm/6 5/8 ins × 16.67mm/42
Cetros   152mm/6 ins × 16.67mm/42

EL TRIUNFO
Hand-made. Distributed by Consolidated Cigars. Mexican wrapper and binder. Filler is blend of tobacco from Mexico and Nicaragua.

No. 1 Mayans   190mm/7 1/2 ins × 19.84mm/50
No. 2 Aztecs   168mm/6 5/8 ins × 19.84mm/50
No. 3 Toltecs   152mm/6 ins × 19.84mm/50
No. 4 Tulas   168mm/6 5/8 ins × 18.26mm/46
No. 5 Palenques   152mm/6 ins × 18.26mm/46
No. 6 Mitlas   168mm/6 5/8 ins × 16.67mm/42
No. 7 Pueblas   152mm/6 ins × 16.67mm/42

FLOR DE MEXICO
Hand-made. Bundles. All Mexican tobacco. Brand owned by House of Oxford.

Churchill   190mm/7 1/2 ins × 19.84mm/50
Toro   152mm/6 ins × 19.84mm/50
No 1   168mm/6 5/8 ins × 16.67mm/42
No 2   152mm/6 ins × 16.67mm/42
No 3   168mm/6 5/8 ins × 19.9mm/35
No 4   127mm/5 ins × 16.67mm/42

HOJA DE MEXICALI
Hand-made.

Lonsdale Natural   168mm/6 5/8 ins × 16.67mm/42
Royal Corona Natural   152mm/6 ins × 16.67mm/42
Soberano Natural   190mm/7 1/2 ins × 19.84mm/50
Toro Natural/Maduro   152mm/6 ins × 19.84mm/50
Viajante Natural/Maduro

                     203mm/8 1/2 ins × 20.64mm/52

HOJA DE ORO
Hand-made. Bundles. Wrapper is Mexican grown Sumataran seed. Mexican binder and filler.

100   178mm/7 ins × 19.84mm/50
101   178mm/7 1/2 ins × 19.84mm/50
103   152mm/6 ins × 19.84mm/50
104   152mm/6 3/4 ins × 17.86mm/45
105   113mm/4 1/2 ins × 19.84mm/50
106   152mm/6 ins × 17.86mm/45
107   127mm/5 ins × 17.86mm/45

HUGO CASSAR
Hand-made. Bundles. All Mexican tobacco. Owned by Hugo Cassar Cigars, California.

Tulum   121mm/4 3/4 ins × 19.8mm/50

Monterey	152mm/6 ins × 16.67mm/42
Durango	171mm/6 3/4 ins × 18.3mm/46
Veracruz	178mm/7 ins × 21mm/54
Yucatan	191mm/7 1/2 ins × 19.8mm/50
Sierra Madre	203mm/8 ins × 20.6mm/52

HUGO CASSAR PRIVATE COLLECTION
Hand-made. All Mexican tobacco.

Rothschild	114mm/4 1/2 ins × 19.84mm/50
Corona	152mm/6 ins × 16.67mm/42
Toro	165mm/6 1/2 ins × 19.84mm/50
Robusto	140mm/5 1/2 ins × 20.6mm/52
Churchill	191mm/7 1/2 ins × 19.84mm/50

KINGSTON
Hand-made. All Mexican tobacco. Distributed by Brick-Hanauer, Massachusetts.

Corona Grande	165mm/6 1/2 ins × 16.67mm/42
Giant Corona	191mm/7 1/2 ins × 19.84mm/50
Panetela Extra	164mm/6 5/8 ins × 13.9mm/35
Royal Corona	152mm/6 ins × 16.67mm/42
Rothschild	114mm/4 1/2 ins × 19.84mm/50
Toro	152mm/6 ins × 19.84mm/50
Viajante	216mm/8 1/2 ins × 20.6mm/52

MATACAN BUNDLES
Hand-made. Light brown and maduro wrappers. Mexican wrapper and binder. Filler is blend of tobacco from Mexico and Nicaragua. Distributed by Consolidated Cigars.

No 1	190mm/7 1/2 ins × 19.84mm/50
No 2	152mm/6 ins × 19.84mm/50
No 3	168mm/6 5/8 ins × 18.26mm/46
No 4	168mm/6 5/8 ins × 16.67mm/42
No 5	152mm/6 ins × 16.67mm/42
No 6	168mm/6 5/8 ins × 13.89mm/35
No 7	108mm/4 3/4 ins × 19.84mm/50
No 8	203mm/8 ins × 20.64mm/52
No 9	127mm/5 ins × 12.70mm/32

MEXICAN EMPERADOR
Hand-made. Packed in single boxes. One of biggest cigars made in Mexico.

349mm/13 3/4 ins × 19.45mm/49

MOCAMBO
Hand-made. All Mexican tobacco. Exclusive to Santa Clara N.A.

| Churchill | 178mm/7 ins × 19.84mm/50 |

Premier	168mm/6 5/8 ins × 17.07mm/43
Empires	165mm/6 1/2 ins × 15.48mm/39
Double Corona	152mm/6 ins × 20.24mm/51
Royal Corona	152mm/6 ins × 16.67mm/42

NEW YORK, NEW YORK by TE-AMO

Machine-made. Mexican grown Sumatra wrapper. Mexican binder and filler. Each size named after a famous New York street. Extremely mild. Made by Matacapan Tobacos. Distributed by Consolidated Cigars.

Park Avenue	168mm/6 5/8 ins × 16.67mm/42
Fifth Avenue	140mm/5 1/2 ins × 17.46mm/44
7th Avenue	165mm/6 1/2 ins × 18.26mm/46
Broadway	184mm/7 1/4 ins × 19.05mm/48
Wall Street	152mm/6 ins × 20.64mm/52
La Guardia	127mm/5 ins × 21.43mm/54

NUDE MEXICAN

Hand-made. Bundles. Available in claro and maduro.

900	113mm/4 1/2 ins × 19.84mm/50
902	140mm/5 1/2 ins × 20.64mm/52
904	152mm/6 ins × 16.67mm/42
906	152mm/6 ins × 19.84mm/50
908	165mm/6 1/2 ins × 14.29mm/36
910	168mm/6 5/8 ins × 16.69mm/42
912	190mm/7 1/2 ins × 19.84mm/50
914	216mm/8 1/2 ins × 19.84mm/50

ORNELAS

Hand-made. All Mexican Tobacco. LTD shape cognac treated wrappers. Five shapes treated with vanilla flavouring. Owned by Marcos Miguel Tobacco, Dallas, Texas.

LTD 40 Al Cognac	159mm/6 1/4 ins × 16.67mm/42
No 1	171mm/6 3/4 ins × 17.5mm/44
No 2	152mm/6 ins × 17.5mm/44
No 3	178mm/7 ins × 15.1mm/38
No 4	127mm/5 ins × 17.5mm/44
No 5	152mm/6 ins × 15.1mm/38
No 6	127mm/5 ins × 15.1mm/38
*Churchill	178mm/7 ins × 19.5mm/49
*Robusto	121mm/4 3/4 ins × 19.5mm/49
Cafetero Grande	165mm/6 1/2 ins × 18.3mm/46
Cafetero Chico	140mm/5 1/2 ins × 18.30mm/46
Matinee	152mm/6 ins × 11.9mm/30
Matinee Lights	121mm/4 3/4 ins × 11.9mm/30

250	232mm/9 1/2 ins × 25mm/64
No 1 Vanilla	171mm/6 3/4 ins × 17.5mm/44
No 5 Vanilla	152mm/6 ins × 15.1mm/38
No 6 Vanilla	127mm/5 ins × 15.1mm/38
Matinee Vanilla	152mm/6 ins × 11.9mm/30
Matinee Lights Vanilla	121mm/4 3/4 ins × 11.9mm/30

*Available with maduro wrapper.

ORTIZ

Hand-made by Tabacos Santa Clara.

Churchill	190mm/7 1/2 ins × 19.84mm/50
Club House	152mm/6 ins × 19.84mm/50
Double Corona	168mm/6 5/8 ins × 17.07mm/43
Magnum	152mm/6 ins × 16.67mm/42
Mexican Emperadors	349mm/13 3/4 ins × 19.45mm/49

SANTA CLARA "1830"

Hand-made. Quality: Superior. Medium flavoured. Exclusive to Santa Clara, N.A., Inc. All Mexican tobacco. Made by Tabacos Santa Clara.

No I	178mm/7 ins × 20.24mm/51
No II	165mm/6 1/2 ins × 19.05mm/48
No III	168mm/6 5/8 ins × 16.67mm/43
No IV	127mm/5 ins × 17.46mm/44
No V	152mm/6 ins × 17.46mm/44
No VI	152mm/6 ins × 20.24mm/51
No VII	140mm/5 1/2 ins × 9.92mm/25
No VIII	165mm/6 1/2 ins × 12.00mm/30

Quino.

| Premier Tubes (tubed) | 171mm/6 3/4 ins × 15.1mm/38 |
| Robusto | 113mm/4 1/2 ins × 19.84mm/50 |

TE-AMO

Hand-made. Long filler. Quality: medium. Mild and medium strength. Medium available in choice of light brown and maduro wrappers. Top selling Mexican brand in USA. Name means "I love you" in Spanish. Made by Matacapan Tabacos. Distributed by Consolidated Cigars.

Torero	165mm/6 1/2 ins × 13.49mm/35
No 4	127mm/5 ins × 16.67mm/42
Picador	178mm/7 ins × 10.72mm/27
C.E.O	216mm/8 1/2 ins × 20.64mm/52
Epicure	127mm/5 ins × 12.00mm/30
Contemplation	175mm/6 7/8 ins × 17.46mm/44

Churchill★★★   190mm/7 1/2 ins × 19.84mm/50
Very mild. Burns little hot.
Presidente★★★★   178mm/7 ins × 19.84mm/50
Spicy. Smooth. Daytime smoke. Suitable for novice.
Robusto★★★★   140mm/5 1/2 ins × 21.43mm/54
Mild. Smooth. Flavour develops. Good balance.
Torito   113mm/4 1/2 ins × 19.84mm/50
Toro   152mm/6 ins × 19.84mm/50
Figurado (torpedo)★★★★ 168mm/6 5/8 ins × 19.84/50
Mild coffee flavours. Smooth.
Caballero   178mm/7 ins × 13.89mm/35
Impulse   127mm/5 ins × 12.70mm/32
Maximo   178mm/7 ins × 21.43mm/54
Celebration   170mm/6 11/16 ins × 17.46mm/44
Satisfaction   152mm/6 ins × 18.26mm/46
Grand Piramides (pyramid))
                       160mm/6 1/4 ins × 21.43mm/54
Relaxation   168mm/6 5/8 ins × 16.67mm/42
Piramides   160mm/6 1/4 ins × 19.84mm/50
Meditation   152mm/6 ins × 16.67mm/42
Elegante   140mm/5 1/2 ins × 12.00mm/30
Intermezzo   178mm/7 ins × 21.43mm/54
Pauser   137mm/5 3/8 ins × 13.89mm/35
Following machine-made with short filler.

TE-AMO SEGUNDO
Churchill   190mm/7 1/2 ins × 19.84mm/50
Presidente   178mm/7 ins × 19.84mm/50
Relaxation   168mm/6 5/8 ins × 17.46mm/44
Satisfaction   152mm/6 ins × 18.26mm/46
Toro   152mm/6 ins × 19.84mm/50
Meditation   152mm/6 ins × 16.67mm/42
Torero   166mm/6 9/16 ins × 13.89mm/35

VERACRUZ
Hand-made.
Mina de Veracruz, Reserva Especial
                       160mm/6 1/4 ins × 16.67mm/42
Veracruz Magnum, Owner's Reserve
                       200mm/7 7/8 ins × 19.1mm/48
Flor de Veracruz Carinas118mm/4 5/8 ins × 13.5mm/34
Poemas de Veracruz (tubed)
                       160mm/6 1/4 ins × 16.67mm/42
Veracruz L'Operetta   124mm/4 7/8 ins × 13.5mm/34

NICARAGUA

Many believe that Nicaragua produces tobacco closest
to that of Cuba. Ten years of war and famine did much

to damage cigar industry. Privatisation policy of present government is successful in restoring tobacco industry to meet increased demand and fulfill country's role as major exporter of cigars. In 1993, for first time in more than decade, good crop of oily Cuban seed wrapper was produced.

In 1995 exported 3.525 million cigars to USA, up from 605 000 in 1994.

BLUE RIBBON
Hand-made.

No 500	190mm/7 1/2 ins × 20.64mm/52
No 501	152mm/6 ins × 19.84mm/50
No 502	120mm/4 3/4 ins × 19.84mm/50
No 503	160m/6 1/2 ins × 17.46mm/44
No 504	140mm/5 1/2 ins × 16.67mm/42

CASA DE NICARAGUA
Hand-made. All Cuban seed tobacco grown in Nicaragua. Distributed in USA by Indian Head Sales.

Rothschild	127mm/5 ins × 19.84mm/50
Petit Corona	140mm/5 1/2 ins × 19.84mm/50
Corona	152mm/6 ins × 19.05mm/43
Toro	152mm/6 ins × 19.84mm/50
Panetela Extra	178mm/7 ins × 14.29mm/36
Double Corona	178mm/7 ins × 17.46mm/44
Churchill	178mm/7 ins × 19.49mm/49
Presidente	190mm/7 1/2 ins × 20.64mm/52
Gigante	203mm/8 ins × 21.43mm/54
Viajante	216mm/8 1/2 ins × 19.84mm/50

FLOR DE JALAPA
Hand-made. Ecuador wrapper. Binder and filler from Nicaragua. Made by Tabacos de Plasencia. Brand owned by Swisher Intl. Introduced 1995.

Presidente	216mm/8 1/2 ins × 20.6mm/52
Toro	152mm/6 ins × 19.84mm/50
Gran Corona	152mm/6 ins × 17.5mm/44
Churchill	178mm/7 ins × 19.1mm/48
Robusto	120mm/4 3/4 × 19.84mm/50

FLOR DE NICARAGUA
Hand-made. Ecuador wrapper. Nicaraguan filler and binder.

Viajante	216mm/8 1/2 ins × 20.6mm/52
Presidente	203mm/8 ins × 21.4mm/54
Presidente Corto	184mm/7 1/4 ins × 21.4mm/54
Emperador	197mm/7 3/4 ins × 20.6mm/50
Emperador Corto	191mm/7 1/2 ins × 20.6mm/50

No 1	168mm/6 5/8 ins × 17.5mm/44
No 2	114mm/4 1/2 ins × 16.67mm/42
No 3	152mm/6 ins × 17.5mm/44
No 5	175mm/6 7/8 ins × 13.9mm/35
No 6	152mm/6 ins × 16.3mm/41
No 7	178mm/7 ins × 11.9mm/30
No 9	203mm/8 ins × 15.1mm/38
No 9 Corto	178mm/7 ins × 15.1mm/38
No 11	191mm/7 1/2 ins × 18.3mm/46
Churchill	175mm/6 7/8 ins × 19.1mm/48
Duke	152mm/6 ins × 20.6mm/50
Corona Extra	140mm/5 1/2 ins × 18.3mm/46
Consul	114mm/4 1/2 ins × 20.6mm/52
Nacional	140mm/5 1/2 ins × 17.5mm/44
Seleccion B	140mm/5 1/2 ins × 16.67mm/42
Elegante	165mm/6 /2 ins × 15.1mm/38
Corona	143mm/5 5/8 ins × 19.1mm/48
Petits	140mm/5 1/2 ins × 15.1mm/38
Senoritas	140mm/5 1/2 ins × 13.5mm/34
Piccolino	105mm/4 1/8 ins × 11.9mm/30

HABANICA

Hand-made. All Nicaragua tobacco. Full-bodied. Distributed by Cigars of Honduras, Virginia.

Serie 747	179mm/7 ins × 18.7mm/47
Serie 646	152mm/6 ins × 18.3mm/46
Serie 638	152mm/6 ins × 15.1mm/38
Serie 546	140mm/5 1/2 ins × 18.3mm/46
Serie 550	127mm/5 ins × 20.2mm/50

DON JUAN

Hand-made. Packed 8-9-8 in wooden boxes. Quality: superior. Connecticut shade wrapper. Nicaraguan binder. Filler blend of tobacco from Nicaragua and 30 per cent from Dominican Republic. Made by Tabacos de Plasencia. Distributed in USA by Tropical Tobacco. International distribution by Nica-Habano São Paulo, Brazil.

| Lindas | 140mm/5 1/2 ins × 14.29mm/38 |
| Cetros★★★★ | 152mm/6 ins × 17.07mm/43 |

Easy draw. Even burn. Medium-bodied. Elegant. Good balance. Good daytime cigar or to follow lunch.

Palma Fina	175mm/6 7/8 ins × 14.29mm/36
Numero Uno	168mm/6 5/8 ins × 17.46mm/44
Matador	152mm/6 ins × 19.84mm/50
Churchills	178mm/7 ins × 19.45mm/49
Presidents	216mm/8 1/2 ins × 19.84mm/50
Robusto	127mm/5 ins × 19.84mm/50

JOYO DE NICARAGUA

13 models, all hand-made. Quality: superior. Started in 1965. Until Nicaragua revolution in 1979 was considered one of best non-Havana brands. During revolution many tobacco fields and its factory damaged by fire. U.S. embargo in place between 1985 and 1990. Post revolution cigars not as good as those made pre-revolution. Quality improving rapidly. Medium strength. Pleasant peppery flavour.

Brand with same name made by two different factories.

Viajante★★★★★	216mm/8 1/2 ins × 20.64mm/52

Easy draw. Good burning qualities. Well balanced, smooth. A big cigar with lots of flavour. For experienced smoker.

Churchill	175mm/6 7/8 ins × 19.05mm/48
Consul★★★★	113mm/4 1/2 ins × 20.64mm/52

Easy draw. Spicy, with touch of cinnamon. Medium to full-bodied. Good balance between strength and flavour. Not particularly refined, but smooth. Daytime smoke for experienced smoker.

Corona	143mm/5 5/8 ins × 19.05mm/48
No 1	168mm/6 5/8 ins × 17.46mm/44
No 2	113mm/4 1/2 ins × 16.27mm/41
No 5	175mm/6 7/8 ins × 13.89mm/35
Petit	140mm/5 1/2 ins × 15.08mm/38

HOYO DE NICARAGUA MADURO DELUXE

Presidente	203mm/8 ins × 21.43mm/54
Toro★★★★	152mm/6 ins × 19.84mm/50

Full-bodied, rich flavours. Robust. Smooth. For experienced smoker.

Robusto	121mm/4 3/4 ins × 20.64mm/52

LA CORDOBA

Hand-made. Bundles. Distributed in USA by Brick-Hanauer.

Numero Uno	165mm/6 1/2 ins × 19.09mm/43
Numero Cuatro	140mm/43 ins × 19.09mm/43
Gorda	152mm/6 ins × 17.46mm/44
Churchill	175mm/6 7/8 ins × 19.45mm/49
Gigante	203mm/8 ins × 21.43mm/54
Monarch	184mm/7 1/4 ins × 21.43mm/54
President	190mm/7 1/2 ins × 20.64mm/52
Rothschild	113mm/4 1/2 ins × 20.64mm/52
Soberano	197mm/7 3/4 ins × 19.84mm/50
Toro	152mm/6 ins × 19.84mm/50
Viajante	349mm/8 1/2 ins × 20.64mm/52

LA FINCA

Hand-made. Quality: superior. All Nicaraguan tobacco. Full-bodied. Has good ageing potential. Made by Tabacos de Plasencia, whose brands sell eight million cigars plus a year. Distributed in USA by Cigars by Santa Clara NA. International distribution by Nica-Habano, São Paulo, Brazil.

Robusto★★★★★   140mm/5 1/2 ins × 19.5mm/49
Dark oily wrapper. Burns evenly with fairly tight draw. Rich, elegant, herbascious with chocolate undertones. Well-made. To follow meal. For discering smoker.

Romeos★★★★★   165mm/6 1/2 ins × 16.67mm/42
Beautiful wrapper. Smooth, elegant with good balance. Well made.

Corona   140mm/5 1/2 ins × 16.67mm/42
Joyas★★★★★   152mm/6 ins × 19.84mm/50
Dark oil wrapper. Even, slow burning. Mildly spicy with hint of coffee. Elegant with intergrated flavours. Classy cigar. Will make any occasion special.

Bolivares   190mm/7 1/2 ins × 19.84mm/50
Grand Finca   216mm/8 1/2 ins × 206mm/52

MICUBANO

Hand-made. All Nicarguan tobacco. Unusual feature is two bands on each cigar — one near foot. Distributed by Lane Ltd.

No 450★★★★   121mm/4 3/4 ins × 19.84mm/50
Medium-bodied. Smooth. Good balance. Well made. Daytime smoke.

542   140mm/5 1/2 ins × 16.67mm/42
650   152mm/6 ins × 19.84mm/50
644   165mm/6 1/2 ins × 17.5mm/44
748   178mm/7 ins × 19.1mm/48
852   216m/8 /2 ins × 20.6mm/52

NICARAGUA ESPECIAL

Hand-made bundles. Wrapper from Ecuador. Binder and filler from Nicaragua. Distributed in USA by Lignum-2 Inc.

Linda   140mm/5 1/2 ins × 14.29mm/38
Super Cetro   152mm/6 ins × 17.46mm/44
Matador   152mm/6 ins × 19.84mm/50
Presidente   188mm/7 3/8 ins × 19.84mm/50
Viajante   216mm/8 1/2 ins × 20.64mm/52

PURO NICARAGUA

Hand-made. Bundles. Connecticut shade wrapper.

Filler blend of tobacco from Nicaragua and Dominican Republic. Distributed in USA by Tropical Tobacco.

Lindas	140mm/5 1/2 ins × 15.08mm/38
Numero 4	140mm/5 1/2 ins × 16.67mm/42
Rothschild★★★★	127mm/5 ins × 19.84mm/50

Full-bodied and aromatic. Wrapper slightly sweet. For experienced smoker, after meal.

Panetela Especial	175mm/6 7/8 ins × 13.89mm/35
Corona Gorda	152mm/6 ins × 17.46mm/44
Numero 1	168mm/6 5/8 ins × 17.46mm/44
Toro	152mm/6 ins × 19.84mm/50
Churchill	178mm/7 ins × 19.45mm/49
Soberano	197mm/7 3/4 ins × 19.84mm/50
Viajantes	216mm/8 1/2 ins × 20.64mm/52
Gigantes	203mm/8 ins × 21.43mm/54

ROYAL NICARAGUAN

Hand-made bundles. Distributed in USA by Indian Head Sales.

Numero 2	216mm/8 1/2 ins × 20.64mm/52
Numero 4	203mm/8 ins × 21.43mm/54
Numero 6	190mm/7 1/2 ins × 20.64mm/52
Numero 8	178mm/7 ins × 19.49mm/49
Numero 10	178mm/7 ins × 17.46mm/44
Numero 12	178mm/7 ins × 14.29mm/36
Numero 14	152mm/6 ins × 19.84mm/50
Numero 16	152mm/6 ins × 17.86mm/43
Numero 18	140mm/5 1/2 ins × 17.07mm/43
Numero 20	127mm/5 ins × 19.84mm/50

SABROSO

Hand-made. Bundle. Ecuador wrapper. Binder and filler from Nicaragua. Introduced 1995. Made by Tabacos de Plasencia for Swisher Intl.

Numero Uno	120mm/4 3/4 ins × 19.84mm/50
Numero Dos	152mm/6 ins × 17.5mm/44
Numero Tres	152mm/6 ins × 19.84mm/50
Numero Quatro	178mm/7 ins × 19.1mm/48
Numero Cinco	216mm/8 1/2 ins × 20.6mm/52

SEGOVIA

Hand-made. Ecuador wrapper. Filler and binder from Dominican Rep. Exclusive to Brick-Hanauer Co., Massachusetts.

Crown Royal	178mm/7 ins × 20.6mm/52
Primo Gorda	152mm/6 ins × 16.67mm/42
Robusto	127mm/5 ins × 20.6mm/52

| Toro | 152mm/6 ins × 19.84mm/50 |
| X-O | 165mm/6 1/2 ins × 18.3mm/46 |

THOMAS HINDS NICARAGUAN SELECTION
Hand-made. All Nicaraguan tobacco. Made by Tabacos
Puros de Nicargua for Hinds Brothers Tobacco.

Torpedo	152mm/6 ins × 20.6mm/52
Churchill	178mm/7 ins × 19.5mm/49
Short Churchill	152mm/6 ins × 20.8mm/50
Lonsdale Extra	178mm/7 ins × 17.1mm/43
Robusto	127mm/5 ins × 20.84mm/50
Corona	140mm/5 1/2 ins × 16.67mm/42

TORCEDOR
Hand-made. Quality: superior. All Nicaraguan tobacco.
Made by Tabacos de Plasencia. Exclusive to House of
Oxford.

No 1	178mm/7 ins × 17.5mm/44
Churchill	178mm/7 ins × 19.84mm/50
Rothchild	127mm/5 ins × 19.84mm/50
Toro	152mm/6 ins × 19.84mm/50
Vijante	203mm/8 ins × 20.6mm/52

PANAMA

In 1995 exported 308 000 cigars to USA.

BALBOA
Hand-made. Honduran wrapper. Mexican binder. Filler
blend of tobacco from Honduras, Panama and Dominican Republic.

Viajante	216mm/8 1/2 ins × 20.64mm/52
Churchill	178mm/7 ins × 19.10mm/48
No 1	178mm/7 ins × 17.09mm/43
No 2	165mm/6 1/2 ins × 17.07mm/43
No 4	140mm/5 1/2 ins × 16.67mm/42
Palma Extra	178mm/7 ins × 14.3mm/36

HIDALGO
Hand-made bundles. Wrapper from Ecuador. Mexican
binder. Filler blend of tobacco from Panama, Honduras
and Domincan Republic. Distributed in USA by Arango
Cigar Co.

Cazadore	178mm/7 ins × 17.46mm/44
Fuma	178mm/7 ins × 17.46mm/44
Corona	140mm/5 1/2 ins × 16.67mm/42
Double Corona	178mm/7 ins × 19.05mm/48
Monarch	216mm/8 1/2 ins × 20.64mm/52

J. F. LLOPIS GOLD
Hand-made. Connecticut wrapper. Mexican binder. Filler, blend of tobacco from Honduras, Panama and Dominican Republic.

Viajante	213mm/8 1/2 ins × 20.6mm/52
Churchill	178mm/7 ins × 19.1mm/48
No 1	191mm/7 1/2 ins × 17.1mm/43
No 2	165mm/6 1/2 ins × 17.1mm/43
No 4	140mm/5 1/2 ins × 16.67mm/42
Palma Extra	175mm/7 ins × 14.3mm/36

JOSE LLOPIS
Hand-made. Bundles. Wrapper from Ecuador. Binder from Mexico. Filler blend of tobacco from Panama, Dominican Republic and Honduras. Not to be confused with J. F. Llopis brand. Distributed in USA by Arango Cigar Co.

Viajante	216mm/8 1/2 ins × 20.64mm/52
Churchill	178mm/7 ins × 19.05mm/48
No 1★★★★	178mm/7 ins × 17.07mm/43

Good burning qualities. Mild, smooth. Elegant. well-made.

No 2★★★	165mm/6 1/2 ins × 17.07mm/43

Even burning. Light-bodied. Daytime smoke. Good value.

No 4	140mm/5 1/2 ins × 17.07mm/43
Palma Extra	178mm/7 ins × 14.29mm/36
Rothschild	121mm/4 3/4 ins × 19.84mm/50
Soberano	184mm/7 1/4 ins × 20.64mm/52

PHILIPPINES

In 1995 exported 429 000 cigars to USA.

ALHAMBRA
Hand-made. Bundles. Wrapper from Philippines. Binder from Java. Filler, a blend of tobacco from Indonesia and Java.

Corona	127mm/5 ins × 16.67mm/42
Corona Grande	209mm/8 1/4 ins × 18.65mm/47
Double Grande	216mm/8 1/2 ins × 19.84mm/50
Duque	165mm/6 1/2 ins × 16.67mm/42
Especiale	165mm/6 1/2 ins × 19.84mm/50

CALIXTO LOPEZ/CARLOS V
Hand-made.
Called Calixto Lopez in the USA and Carlos V in the

United Kingdom. Havana seed wrappers. Binder and
filler from Java and Indonesia.

Czars	203mm/8 ins × 17.86mm/45
Corona Numero 1	163mm/6 3/8 ins × 17.86mm/45
Corona Exquisito	137mm/5 3/8 ins × 17.07mm/43

Lonsdale Suprema★★★★

172mm/6 3/4 ins × 16.67mm/42

Full-bodied. Rich, full-flavoured. Bold. Well-made.
Good value.

Palma Royale	184mm/7 1/4 ins × 14.29mm/36
Gigantes	216mm/8 1/2 ins × 19.84mm/50
Nobles Extrafinos	165mm/6 1/2 ins × 19.84mm/50

DOUBLE HAPINESS
Hand-made. Quality: superior. Connecticut shade
wrapper. Binder and filler from Philippines. Owned by
Splendid Seed Tobacco Co., Manila, Philippines.

Nirvana (pyramide)	152mm/6 ins × 20.6mm/52
Euphoria	165mm/6 1/2 ins × 19.84mm/50
Bliss	13mm/5 1/3 ins × 19.1mm/48
Rapture	127mm/5 ins × 19.84mm/50
Ectasy	178mm/7 ins × 18.7mm/47

FIGHTING COCK
Hand-made. Quality: superior. Java wrapper. Binder
and filler from Philippines. Owned by Splendid Seed
Tobacco Co., Manila, Philippines.

Sidewinder (pyramide)	152mm/6 ins × 20.6mm/52
Texas Red (square)	165mm/6 1/2 ins × 19.84mm/50
Smokin' Lulu (perfecto)	133mm/5 1/4 ins × 19.1mm/48
Rooster Arturo	127mm/5 ins × 9.84mm/50
C.O.D.	178mm/7 ins × 18.7mm/47

FLOR DE MANILA
Hand-made. All Philippine tobacco. Distributed by
Hugo Cassar Cigars, California.

Cetro Largo	191mm/7 1/2 ins × 15.5mm/39
Cetro	152mm/6 ins × 15.5mm/39
Churchill	178mm/7 ins × 18.7mm/47
Corona Largo	178mm/7 ins × 18.7mm/44
Corona	140mm/5 1/2 ins × 18.7mm/44
Cortado (torpedo)	
Londres	146mm/5 3/4 ins × 18.7mm/44
Panetela	127mm/5 ins × 13.9mm/35

HARROWS
Hand-made. Quality: good. Sumatra wrappers.

Londonderry	203mm/8 ins × 19.05mm/48
Camelot	178mm/7 ins × 17.07mm/43

No 1   160mm/6 1/4 ins × 19.07mm/43
Esquire   152mm/6 ins × 13.10mm/33
Regent   143mm/5 5/8 ins × 17.46mm/44

LA FLOR DE LA ISABELA
Hand-made. Quality: superior. Made in Manila by company of same name.

Coronas Largas Especiales 203mm/8 ins × 18.7mm/47
Coronas Largas   175mm/6 1/2 ins × 17.5mm/44
Coronas   140mm/5 1/2 ins × 17.5mm/44
Coronas Sumatra★★★★ 140mm/5 1/2 ins × 17.5mm/44
Dark, almost maduro wrapper. Mild to medium bodied. Good balance between strength and flavour. Smooth. Burns evenly. Daytime smoke.
Brevas★★★   130mm/5 ins × 16.3mm/41
Attractive dark wrapper. Fairly hard draw. Extremely mild and smooth. Not very exciting.
Half Coronas   100mm/4 ins × 14.7mm/37
1881★★★★★   190mm/7 1/2 ins × 16.67mm/42
Attractive wrapper. Good draw and balance. Medium-bodied with lots of flavour. Good finish. Well-made. For connoiseur. Also sold in impressive 30 cigar capacity humidor, complete with humidifier and hygrometer.

Following machine-made with short filler.
Caprichos   120mm/4 3/4 ins × 11.1mm/28
Isabela   150mm/5 7/8 ins × 16.3mm/41
Ideales   130mm/5 ins × 16.3mm/41
Brevas   130mm/5 ins × 16.3mm/41
Half Coronas   100mm/4 ins × 14.7mm/37
Conchas   115mm/5 7/8 ins × 16.3mm/41
Panetelas Largas   150mm/5 7/8 ins × 13.9mm/35
Damas   100mm/4 ins × 13.9mm/35
Panetelas   120mm/4 3/4 ins × 13.9mm/35
Cigarillos   95mm/3 3/4 ins × 9.9mm/25
Tips (with pipes)   135mm/5 5/16 ins × 11.1mm/28

TABACALERA
Hand-made. Filler from Philippines. Binder and filler from Java and Indonesia. Made by La Flor de la Isabela.

Banderilla   184mm/7 1/4 ins × 13.89mm/35
Breva★★★   133mm/5 1/4 ins × 17.46mm/44
Maduro wrapper. Good draw. Very mild, creamy flavour. Mellow. Not much character.
Corona Larga Especiale 203mm/8 ins × 18.26mm/46
Conde De Guell   168mm/6 5/8 ins × 12.00mm/38
Corona   133mm/5 1/4 ins × 16.67mm/42

Corona Larga	178mm/7 ins × 17.07mm/43
Cortado	127mm/5 ins × 17.86mm/45
Don Q	184mm/7 1/4 ins × 16.27mm/41
Gigantes	362mm/14 1/4 ins × 23.81mm/60
Panatella	133mm/5 1/4 ins × 13.49mm/34
Panatella Larga	152mm/6 ins × 13.49mm/34
El Conde De Guell Sr	178mm/7 ins × 16.27mm/41
Brevas A La Conserva	133mm/5 1/4 ins × 17.07mm/43

PUERTO RICO

DUTCH MASTERS
Machine-made by Consolidated Cigars. Short filler. Homogenised binder. Available in regular or menthol. Part of range machine-made in USA.

Cadet Regular	120mm/4 3/4 ins × 11.11mm/28
Perfecto	120mm/4 3/4 ins × 17.46mm/44
Panetela★★★	140mm/5 1/2 ins × 14.29mm/36

Floral spicy aroma. Medium to full-bodied. Smooth. Daytime cigar.

Belvedere	124mm/4 7/8 ins × 18.65mm/40
President	143mm/5 5/8 ins × 17.46mm/41
Corona Deluxe★★★	147mm/5 3/4 ins × 17.07mm/43

Natural Connecticut wrapper. HTL binder. Pierced hole in head. Spicy, cardamon and peppery aroma. Full-bodied.

Elites	156mm/6 1/8 ins × 11.5mm/29

DUTCH MASTERS COLLECTION
Machine-made. Short filler. Natural Connecticut wrapper. Homogenised binder. Made by Consolidated Cigars.

Cigarillos	120mm/4 3/4 ins × 10.75mm/27
Panetelas De Luxe	137mm/5 3/8 ins × 14.00/36
Palmas Maduro★★	

Good maduro wrapper. Pierced hole in head. Sweet, cherry, coffee aroma and flavour. Dusty finish.

MURIEL
Machine-made.

Magnum	117mm/4 5/8 ins × 18.65mm/47
Sweet Coronas	143mm/5 5/8 ins × 16.27mm/41
Air Tips Regular	127mm/5 ins × 12.3mm/31
Sweet Little Cigars	
Air Tips Pipe Aroma	127mm/5 ins × 12.3mm/31
Air Tips Menthol	127mm/5 ins × 12.3mm/31
Air Tips Sweet	127mm/5 ins × 12.3mm/31
Coronella	117mm/4 5/8 ins × 12.3mm/31

Coronella Pipe Aroma 117mm/4 5/8 ins × 12.3mm/31
Coronella Sweet 117mm/4 5/8 ins × 12.3mm/31
Sweet Minis 102mm/4 ins × 12.7mm/32

ROI-TAN
Machine-made. HTL wrapper and binder. Made by
Consolidated Cigars.
Bankers 127mm/5 ins × 16.27mm/41
Blunts 143mm/5 5/8 ins × 16.27mm/41
*Falcons 160mm/6 1/4 ins × 12.30mm/34
Panetelas 140mm/5 1/2 ins × 14.29mm/36
Perfecto Extras 127mm/5 ins × 16.27mm/41
Tips 130mm/5 1/8 ins × 10.72mm/27
*Available in "Its A Girl" and "Its A Boy" packings.

SOUTH AFRICA

Produces tobacco virtually sufficient for large local
cigarette industry. In the past unsuccessful attempts
made to produce low-priced, mass-market cigars. Late
1995 saw launch of first serious attempt by Gauteng
Cigar Factory to produce top quality hand-made cigars
from tobacco imported from Sumatra, Java and Brazil.
Consumption imported cigars in 1980 was 15 million,
but fell to around 10 million in 1994. However, sales in
1995 are expected to be substantially more. Market
leader is Ritmeester (three models) with about 50
percent of sales. Small, but discerning market for
premium hand-made cigars from Cuba, Dominican
Republic and Honduras. Biggest importer is L. Suzman
& Company.

GAUTENG

Hand-made. Quality: Superior. Dry cigar. Leaf from
Indonesia. Established in 1995 in Roodepoort, in
Province of Gauteng, near Johannesburg, by Tom and
wife, Jon, van der Marck, Hollanders, now resident in
South Africa. He has 32 years experience as tobacco
buyer and blender with Dutch, Swiss, German and
American companies. Senoritos launched in 1996.

Rolled in tradition that made Holland famous in
1940s and 1950s, now all but disappeared. This is a
range for connoisseur of dry cigars.

Amsterdam Corona★★★★★
120mm/4 3/4 ins × 15.8mm/40
Mild to medium-bodied. Good balance, flavour and
finish. Elegant. Well made.

Alkmaar Half Corona★★★★★
104mm/4 1/8 ins × 15.8mm/40
Mild to medium-bodied. Good balance, flavour and finish. Elegant. Well-made. Quick daytime smoke.
Alphen Senoritas★★★★ 100mm/3 7/8 ins × 12.30mm/31
Mild to medium-bodied. Firm draw. Good quick smoke. These have wrappers from Sumatra.
Djakarta Corona★★★★★ 120mm/4 3/4 ins × 15.8mm/40
Medium-bodied. Good flavours with coffee undertones. Long creamy finish. Well made.
Djokja Half Corona★★★★★
104mm/4 1/8 ins × 15.8mm/40
Medium-bodied. Good flavours with coffee undertones. Long creamy finish. Well made. Quick daytime smoke.
Djember Senorita★★★★
100mm/3 7/8 ins × 12.30mm/31
Medium-bodied. Firm draw. Good quick smoke.
These have wrappers from Java.

S P A I N

First cigars to be made in similar fashion to those of today were produced by the tobacco monopoly, Tabacalera, in Seville, Spain in the early 18th century. It was then that the idea of constructing a cigar with filler, binder and wrapper was invented. The process was exported to Cuba, and in 1740, a Spanish Royal Decree created a tobacco monopoly in Cuba, called Royal Trading Company (Real Compania de Comerrio de la Habana). As a result, Cuba has maintained its cigar links with Spain, even when it had strong ties with the former Soviet Union — such ties endured even with a Communist Castro in power in Cuba and a fascist Franco dictatorship in Spain.

The monopoly makes about 350 million machine-made cigars a year in Spain and hand-made ones through CITA, its subsidiary in the Canary Islands. It also imported around 28 million cigars in 1996 — about half of Cuba's exports of hand-made cigars and around 10 percent of its machine-made cigars. The value of these imported was in excess of $35 million £35 million (£25 million). Spain also imports about 75 percent of Cuba's export leaf production for use in its local industry. The value of leaf imports exceeds $70 million (£46 million).

Production of cigars in Spain is controlled by huge monopoly, Tabacalera, which is partnership of Government and private sector. Full details of its activities and output are given under heading "Tabacalera" in the section "Some Important Names in the Industry."

Because of small tax on tobacco products and the narrow profit margins, both for wholesalers and retailers, Spain has significantly low prices for Havanas.

Spain may be considered cigar-friendly country, as smoking allowed in vast majority of restaurants, all good ones having cigars for sale.

Tobacco most commonly used for cigar production are those from Cuba, Brazil, Dominican Republic, Java and Sumatra.

CARIGES
Machine-made.
No 1   152mm/6 ins × 16.67mm/42
No 2   134mm/5 1/4 ins × 16.67mm/42

DUCADOS
Machine-made.
Cigarritos (tins)   74mm/2 7/8 ins × 8.7mm/23
Panetelas   146mm/5 3/4 ins × 8.4mm/21
Extra   90mm/3 1/2 ins × 8.9mm/23
Suaves   74mm/2 7/8 ins × 8.7mm/22

ENTREFINOS
Machine-made.
Cortados   90mm/3 1/2 ins × 11mm/28
Java   90mm/3 1/2 ins × 11mm/28
Java Largos   150mm/5 7/8 ins × 11mm/28
Java Superiors   100mm/4 ins × 12.4mm/31

FARIOS
Machine made. Leading machine-made brand with about 250 million cigars, accounting for over 60 percent of Tabacelera's production.
Centenario   121mm/4 3/4 ins × 16.20mm/41
Superiores   116mm/6 3/8 ins × 16.00mm/40
No 1   120mm/4 11/16 ins ×18.30mm/46
Superiores Especinles 115mm/6 11/16 ins × 15.50mm/39
Chico   100mm/4 ins × 12.50mm/31
Purito   88mm/3 7/16 ins × 11.00mm/28
Club   90mm/3 1/2 ins × 8.70mm/22

FINOS CORTADOS
Machine-made.   90mm/3 1/2 ins × 9.50mm/24

MONTECRISTO MINI   82mm/3 1/4 ins × 7.60mm/19
Machine-made. All Cuban tobacco.

TARANTOS
Machine-made.   100mm/4 ins × 12.4mm/30

VEGAFINA
Machine-made.
Delicias   90mm/3 1/2 ins × 8.70mm/22
Mini   77mm/3 ins × 8.70mm/22

SWITZERLAND

In 1995 exported 1,436 million cigars to the USA.

DANNEMANN
Machine-made.
Lights — Sumatra   152mm/6 ins × 13.49mm/34
Lights — Brazil   152mm/6 ins × 13.49mm/34
Lights — Brazil Boy/Girl   152mm/6 ins × 13.49mm/34
Espada — Sumatra   127mm/5 ins × 17.86mm/45
Espada — Brazil   127mm/5 ins × 17.86mm/45

INDIANA SLIMS
Machine-made.
Indiana Slims   82mm/3 1/4 ins

PEDRONI
Machine-made.
Classico   92mm/3 5/8 ins × 13.5mm/34

VILLIGER
Machine-made. Made from leaf from Mexico, Domini-
can Republic, Java, Columbia and Brazil. Cuban
tobacco also used in cigars not exported to USA. Some
all tobacco while others use homogenised binder.
Today made in Switzerland, Germany and Ireland.
Produce over 450 million cigars and cigarrillos of which
nearly 100 million exported to 70 countries. Also make
pipe tobacco and bicycles.
Villiger-Kiel Mild   165mm/6 1/2 ins
Villiger-Kiel Brasil   165mm/6 1/2 ins
Villiger-Kiel Junior Mild   113mm/4 1/2 ins
Villiger-Kiel Junior Brasil   113mm/4 1/2 ins
Villiger Menorca (wood chest)
Villiger Jewels Wood chest of 28
Villiger Export   102mm/4 ins
Villiger Export Kings   130mm/5 1/8 ins
Villiger Premium No 4   102mm/4 ins
Villiger Premium No 7★★   102mm/4 ins
Full-bodied. Dusty. Slightly harsh.
Villiger Premium No 10   70mm/2 3/4 ins

Braniff No 1	89mm/3 1/2 ins
Braniff No 2	113mm/4 1/2 ins
Braniff No 3	95mm/3 3/4 ins
Braniff No 8	102mm/4 ins
Braniff Cortos Filter Light	76mm/3 ins

UNITED KINGDOM

Imports around five million Cuban cigars, some 500 000 hand-made cigars from Central America and about 27 million mass market machine-made cigars from various countries.

ALTON
Only hand-made cigar company in England. Situated in Nottingham. Use Havana wrappers and binders and Jamaican filler.

HAMLET
Machine-made. Mild. Mass market cigar.
Slim Panetelas
Special Panetelas
Panetelas
Short Panetelas

UNITED STATES OF AMERICA

UNITED STATES

Cigar industry established early 1800s. Tobacco production from Cuban seed started around 1825. Connecticut tobacco today providing some of best wrapper leaf to be found outside Cuba. In 1900 there were more than 25 000 active TP numbers (government registered tobacco product or producer numbers). Today fewer than 100 in active use. Between two World Wars there was huge influx of trained cigar makers from Cuba. Consumer market is estimated at 2.33 billion in 1994, of which about two billion, mainly machine-made, manufactured locally. Consumption peaked in 1993 at nine billion and from 1964, due to Surgeon-General's health warning on smoking, consumption, fell to around two billion in 1992. Then in 1993 and 1995 consumption increased by over 28 percent to present levels.

In 1995 imports of premium cigars rose 33·1 percent on 1994 figure.

It is estimated that past two years have seen the arrival of over five million new cigar smokers. Whereas, previously the average cigar smoker was more than 50 years old, these new smokers are aged 25 to 35, of which an important percentage are women. Year 1995 characterised by out-of-stock positions in retail shops and manufacturers holding back-orders of two to six months, particularly for bigger sizes.

For the best part of 100 years the corona-size cigar has been the most popular in the world. Today, in the USA, there is a shift to larger cigars with the robusto, churchill and torpedo shapes becoming increasingly in demand.

With the exception of a small number of manufacturers with Cuban origins, mainly in Little Havana in Miami and Union City, New Jersey, who make hand-made cigars, most of the local output is machine-made. The main producers are: Consolidated, 900 million (Antonio y Cleopatra, Dutch Masters, Muriel Roitan, Backwoods, Masters Collection, El Producto, La Corona, Harvester, Roi-Tan, Super Value, Rustlers, Supre Sweets, Super Value Little Cigars, Dutch Treats and Ben Franklin); Swisher International, 600 million (King Edward, Directors, Dexter, Landres, Keep Moving, El Trelles, Santa Fe, Swisher Sweets, Optimo, Outlaws, Dixie Made, As You Like It and Pom Pom Operas); General Cigar, 350 million (White Owl, Garcia y Vega, Tijuana Smalls, Roburt Burns and Wm. Penn); Villazon/Danby-Palicio Group, 55 million (Lord Beaconsfield, Pedro Iglesias, Villa de Cuba, Villazon Deluxe and Topstone). These manufacturers also produce hand-made cigars in other countries, principally, Dominican Republic, Honduras, Mexico and Jamaica.

Main imports into the United States are: Dominican Republic (82,556 million); Honduras (69,109 million), Jamaica (15,339 million); Mexico (9,68 million); Holland (5,167 million) and Germany (4,968 million). Figures quoted are for 1995.

AMERICAN EAGLE
Hand-made. Cameroon wrapper. Filler blend of tobacco from Dominican Rep. and Brazil. Made by Tampa Rico Cigar, Tampa.

Statesman	191mm/7 1/2 ins × 19.1mm/48
Citation	178mm/7 ins × 17.5mm/44
Centennial	165mm/6 1/2 ins × 14.3mm/36
Independence	152mm/6 ins × 16.67mm/42

ANTONIO Y CLEOPATRA
Machine-made. Short filler. Distinctive light green colour called claro claro or candela. Also known as AMS

(American Market Selection) because this was colour most cigar smokers in USA used to favour. Made by Consolidated.

Grenadiers Whiffs   92mm/3 5/8 ins × 9.52mm/24
Grenadiers Mini★★★   113mm/4 1/2 ins × 11.11mm/28
Spicy vegetable aroma. Sweet finish. Pleasant quick smoke.
Grenadiers Mini Dark
Grenadiers Mini Light
Tribunes
Panetelas Deluxe★★ 13.65mm/5 3/8 ins × 14.29mm/36
Natural Connecticut wrapper. Medium bodied spicy. Dusty finish.
Grenadiers   160mm/6 1/4 ins × 13.49mm/34
Grenadiers Boy/Girl
Classics Coronas★★   168mm/5 5/8 ins × 17.07mm/43
Natural Comnnecticut wrapper. Full bodied. Pleasant smoke.
Grenadiers Tubos   168mm/5 5/8 ins × 17.07mm/43
Grenadiers/Presidentes★★★★
Natural Connecticut wrapper. HTL binder. Good value cigar.

ANTELO
Machine-made.

No 1	172mm/6 3/4 ins × 16.27 mm/42
No 5	130mm/5 1/8 ins × 16.67 mm/42
Panatela	17.46mm/6 7/8 ins × 14.29 mm/36
Presidente	193mm/7 5/8ins × 19.84mm/50
Super Cazadore	190mm/7 1/2 ins × 18.26mm/46
Churchill	175mm/6 7/8ins × 18.26mm/46
Cetros	147mm/5 3/4 ins × 16.67 mm/42
Wavell	130mm/5 1/8 ins × 18.26 mm/46

ARANGO SPORTSMAN★★★
Machine-made in Tampa, Florida. Vanilla flavoured. Made with tobacco from Honduras, Dominican Republic and Ecuador. Be careful not to store these in same humidor as non-flavoured cigars. Mild. Owned by Arango Cigar.

No 100	147mm/5 3/4 ins × 13.49mm/34
No 200 (Boy & Girl)	160mm/6 1/4 ins × 16.67mm/42
No 300	178mm/7 ins × 18.26mm/46
No 350	147mm/5 3/4 ins × 19.05mm/48
No 400	190mm/7 1/2mm × 19.05mm/48
Little Cigars	

AS YOU LIKE IT
Machine-made by Swisher Intl.

No 18	152mm/6 ins × 16.27mm/41
No 22	113mm/4 1/2 ins × 16.27mm/41
No 32	152mm/6 ins × 17.07mm/43
No 35	133mm/5 1/4 ins × 13.10mm/33

B-H
Machine-made.

B-H Blunt	152mm/6 ins × 17.46mm/44
B-H Blunt Boy & Girl	152mm/6 ins × 17.46mm/44
B-H Corona	165mm/6 1/2 ins × 16.67mm/42
B-H Golden Corona Boy & Girl	
	165mm/6 1/2 ins × 16.67mm/42
B-H Kings	165mm/6 1/2 ins × 16.67mm/42
B-H Special No 76	165mm/6 1/2 ins × 16.67mm/42

BACKWOODS★★★
Machine-made. Connecticut Broadleaf wrapper, aged for one year. Filler blend of tobacco from Phillipines, Malawi and Mexico. Has wilde (uncut) foot. Is sealed in unique, eight pack, pouch-lined with aluminium foil to keep humidity. Looks like old-fashioned home-rolled cigar. Good value. Made by Consolidated Cigars.

Original	104mm/4 1/8ins × 10.72mm/27
Sweet Aromatic	104mm/4 1/8 ins × 10.72mm/27
Black 'n Sweet	104mm/4 1/8 ins × 10.72/27

BANCES
Machine-made. Brand established 1840. Made in Tampa by Villazon. Larger sizes hand-made in Honduras.

Crown	147mm/5 3/4 ins × 19.84mm/50
Dermitasse	102mm/4 ins × 13.89mm/35
Havana Holders	165mm/6 1/2 ins × 12.00mm/30
Palmas	152mm/6 in × 16.67mm/42
Palmas (Girl or Boy)	152mm/6 in × 16.67mm/42
No 3	147mm/5 3/4 ins × 18.26mm/46

BEN BEY
Machine-made.

Crystals	143mm/5 5/8 ins × 17.46mm/44

BEN FRANKLIN★★
Machine-made by Consolidated Cigars.
Perfectos
Blunts

BLACK HAWK
Machine-made.

Chief   130mm/5 1/8 ins × 17.86mm/45

BLACK & MILD
Machine-made. Brand owned by John Middleton Inc.
Pipe Tobacco Cigars   127mm/5 ins × 11.9mm/30

BOUQUET SPECIAL
Hand-made. Quality: superior. Owned by F.D Grave &
Son in New Haven, Connecticut. One of oldest factories
in continuous production. Founded 1884. Occupies
same building since beginning of Century.
(in glass tubes)   130mm/5 1/8 ins × 18.26mm/46

BUDD SWEET
Machine-made
Perfecto   127mm/5 ins × 17.07mm/43
Panatela   133mm/5 1/4 ins × 13.49mm/34

CABANAS
Machine-made.
Coronas   140mm/5 1/2 ins × 16.67mm/42
Exquisitos   165mm/6 1/2 ins × 19.05mm/48
Premiers   143mm/6 5/8 ins × 16.67mm/42
Royales   143mm/5 5/8 ins × 18.26mm/46
Estupendos   190mm/7 1/2 ins × 19.84mm/50
Grandes   152mm/6 ins × 19.84mm/50

CALLE OCHO
Hand-made. Quality: superior. Ecuador wrapper. Mexican binder. Filler blend of tobacco from Mexico, Nicaragua and Dominican Republic. Launched in 1996 by Carribean Cigar Factory. See details of company under "Santiago Cabana" brand in USA section. Distributed by Miami Cigar.
Ninas   127mm/5 ins × 15.1mm/38
Festivale   140mm/5 1/2 ins × 17.5mm/44
Gordito   127mm/5 ins × 19.84mm/50
Gordito Largo   152mm/6 ins × 19.84mm/50
Perfect Corona   165mm/6 1/2 ins × 16.67/42
Laquito   190mm/7 1/2 ins × 15.1mm/38
Churchill★★★★★   184mm/7 1/4 ins × 19.84mm/50
Medium-bodied. Good balance. Hint of pepper and spice. Smooth. Well made. Daytime smoke for experienced smoker.
Immenso   190mm/7 1/2 ins × 21.4mm/54
Torpedo   165mm/6 1/2 ins × 21.4mm/54
Pyramide   184mm/7 1/4 ins × 21.4mm/54
Embajador   229mm/9 ins × 23.8mm/60

CARIBBEAN FAMILY
Machine-made.

Rounds	184mm/7 1/4 ins × 18.26mm/46
Casinos	160mm/6 1/4 ins × 18.26mm46
Royales	160mm/6 1/4 ins × 13.49mm/34
Petite	120mm/4 3/4 ins × 13.49mm/34

CHARLES DENBY
Machine-made.

Invincible	140mm/5 1/2 ins × 17.07mm/43

CHAVELO
Hand-made.

No 1	175mm/6 7/8 ins × 17.46mm/44
No 2	175mm/6 7/8 ins × 17.46mm/44
Churchill	175mm/6 7/8 ins × 19.05mm/48
Presidente	162mm/7 3/8 ins × 19.84mm/50
Panatela	168mm/6 5/8 ins × 14.29mm/36

CHERRY BLEND
Machine-made. Owned by John Middleton Inc.

Pipe-tobacco cigars	127mm/5 ins × 12.30mm/30

CIBAO
Machine-made.

Brevas	133mm/5 1/4 ins × 19.84mm/50
Corona Deluxe	140mm/5 1/2 ins × 17.07mm/43
Diamantes	172mm/6 3/4 ins × 14.29mm/36
Churchills	172mm/6 3/4 ins × 18.26mm/46
Elegantes	178mm/7 ins × 17.46mm/44
Especiales	203mm/8 ins × 19.84mm/50

CONNOISSEUR GOLD LABEL
Machine-made. Natural and maduro wrappers.

Viajante	216mm/8 1/2 ins × 20.64mm/52
Gigante	203mm/8 ins × 21.43mm/54
Elegante	203mm/8 ins × 14.29mm/36
Imperial 1	90mm/7 1/2 ins × 19.84mm/50
Churchill	178mm/7 ins × 19.45mm/49
No 1 Nat	178mm/7 ins × 17.07mm/43
No 3 Nat	178mm/7 ins × 14.29mm/36
Toro Nat	152mm/6 ins × 19.84mm/50
Corona	152mm/6 ins × 17.46mm/44
No 4	140mm/5 1/2 ins × 17.07mm/43
Rothschild	113mm/4 1/2 ins × 19.84mm/50
Goliath	203mm/8 ins × 25.04mm/64

CONNOISSEUR SILVER LABEL

Especiales	216mm/8 1/2 ins × 19.84mm/50
Elegantes	178mm/7 ins × 17.46mm/44

Churchills	175mm/6 7/8 ins × 18.26mm/46
Diamantes	172mm/6 3/4 ins × 14.29mm/36
Corona	140mm/5 1/2 ins × 16.67mm/43
Brevas	133mm/5 1/4 ins × 19.84mm/50

CONQUISTADOR

No 100	165mm/6 1/2 ins × 13.89mm/35
No 300	152mm/6 ins × 17.46mm/44
No 500	168mm/6 5/8 ins × 17.46mm/44
No 700	175mm/6 7/8 ins × 19.05mm/48
No 900	120mm/4 3/4 ins × 19.84mm/50
No 1100	160mm/6 1/4 ins × 19.84mm/50
No 1300	190mm/7 1/2 ins × 19.84mm/50

CUESTA-REY
Machine-made in Tampa, Florida. Established in 1884 by Angel LaMadrid Cuesta, a Spanish cigar maker, apprenticed in Cuba. In 1985 bought by Newman family's M & N Company in USA. First company to wrap cigars in cellophane. Made in Tampa, Florida. Some styles made by hand in Dominican Republic.
Corona (Cameroon wrapper)
No 240
No 120
Palma Supreme
Caravelles

CUETO

| Machine-made. | 124mm/4 7/8 ins × 17.86mm/45 |

CYRILLA
Machine-made in Tampa by Villazon for Arango Cigar.

Nationals	152mm/6 ins × 16.67mm/42
Kings	178mm/7 ins × 18.26mm/46
Senators	190mm/7 1/2 ins × 19.05mm/48
Slims	165mm/6 1/2 ins × 14.29mm/36

DENOBILI
Machine-made.
Toscani
Toscani Longs
Twin Pack
Popular Amm

| Kings | 10.80mm/4 1/4 ins |

DEXTER LONDRES

| Machine-made. | 133mm/5 1/4 ins × 16.67mm/42 |

DIRECTORS★★★
Machine-made. HTL binder. Mild, smooth with lots of

flavour. Good value. Touch of sweetness. Owned by Swisher Intl.

Panetela	137mm/5 3/8 ins × 14.3mm
Corona	152mm/6 ins × 16.67mm/42

DON CESAR
Machine-made. Long filler.

Palma	143mm/5 5/8 ins × 16.67mm/42

DRY SLITZ
Machine-made.

DUTCH MASTERS★★★
Machine-made. Short filler. HTL binder and natural wrapper. Big seller. Made by Consolidated Cigars.

Cadet Tip	140mm/5 1/8 ins × 10.72mm/27
Cadet	
*Carona Deluxe	
President	143mm/5 5/8 ins × 16.30mm/41
Belvedere	134mm/4 7/8 ins × 18.70mm/47
*Elites	156mm/6 1/8 ins × 11.90mm/30
Panetela Deluxe	
Palma	

*HTL binder and natural wrapper. Mild. Good value.

DUTCH TREATS★★★
Machine-made. HTL binder. Made by Consolidated Cigars.

Regular	99mm/3 7/8ins × 7.94mm/20
Menthol	99mm/3 7/8 ins × 7.94mm/20
Pipe Aroma	99mm/3 7/8 ins × 7.94mm/20
Sweet	99mm/3 7/8 ins × 7.94mm/20
Ultra Lite	99mm/3 7/8 ins × 7.94mm/20

ELEGANTE
Hand-made. Connecticut shade wrapper. Dominican filler and Honduran binder. Made by Tampa Rico Cigar Co., Tampa.

Grande	203mm/8 ins × 19.1mm/48
Especial	178mm/7 ins × 19.1mm/48
Centimo	178mm/7 ins × 17.5mm/44
Panetela Larga	178mm/7 ins × 14.3mm/36
Petit Cetro	152mm/6 ins × 16.67mm/42
Queen	121mm/4 3/4 ins × 19.8mm/50

EL CANELO
Hand-made. Long filler. Some good cigars in an inconsistent range. This range is also available under

"Infiesta" and "Beck" brands. Made in St. Augustine and Miami, Florida by El Canelo.

Soberanos	203mm/8 ins × 19.84mm/50
Churchill★★★	178mm/7 ins × 19.1mm/48

Hard draw. Somewhat dusty flavour. Good-looking cigar. Daytime smoke or to follow light meal.

Fumas★★★★ 178mm/7 ins × 17.5mm/44

Smooth. Colorado maduro wrapper. Medium-strength. Hint of coffee and caramel. Good introduction to this size.

Cazadores	178mm/7 ins × 18.3mm/46
Governos★★★★	152mm/6 ins × 19.84mm/50

Medium-bodied. Good draw. Burns evenly. To follow lunch.

San Marcos★★★ 152mm/6 ins × 18.3mm/44

Fairly coarse colorado maduro wrapper. Medium-bodied. Flavours not fully integrated. Robust cigar.

No 1★★★★★ 178mm/7 ins × 17.1mm/43

Medium-bodied. Good balance. Burns evenly. Well-made elegant cigar to follow dinner.

Cetros No 2	165mm/6 1/2 ins × 16.67mm/42
Panetela No 3★★	178mm/7 ins × 14.3mm/36

Has curly head. Very mild with little character. Difficult burning.

No 4	140mm/5 1/2 ins × 16.67mm/42
St George★★★	178mm/7 ins × 11.9mm/30

Very mild, but has some flavour. Not easy to smoke due to its size.

Minatures★★★ 114mm/4 1/2 ins × 11.9mm/30

Even burning. Has punch for small cigar. Tends to become harsh. Quick smoke to follow a light meal.

EL MACCO
Machine-made.

Puritano 120mm/4 3/4 ins × 17.86mm/45

EL PRODUCTO★★★
Machine-made. HTL binder and wrapper. Promoted by comedian George Burns who, until his death at the age of 100, early in 1996, smoked an average of 10 of these cigars a day. Made by Consolidated Cigars.

Little Coronas	118mm/4 5/8 ins × 12.30mm/31
Blunts	143mm/5 5/8 ins × 16.27mm/41
Bouquets	120mm/4 3/4 ins × 17.46mm/44
Panetelas	130mm/5 1/8 ins × 15.87mm/40
Finos	124mm/4 7/8 ins × 18.20mm/46
Coronas	147mm/15 3/4 ins × 17.07mm/43
Favoritas	127mm/5 ins × 19.05mm/48

Escepcionales　　　　130mm/5 1/8 ins × 20.64mm/52
Natural wrapper. HTL binder.
Queens　　　　　　　143mm/5 5/8 ins × 16.67mm/42
Natural wrapper. HTL binder.

EL RICO HABANO
Hand-made by El Credito in Miami. See details of company under "La Gloria Cubana" brand in USA section. Wrapper from Ecuador. Binder from Nicaragua. Filler blend of tobacco from Dominican Republic and Nicaragua. Fuller bodied than Hoya Selecta.
Gran Habanero Deluxe
　　　　　　　　　194mm/7 5/8 ins × 19.84mm/50
Earthy. Smooth. Good balance. Well made. Finishes strongly.
Double Coronas　　　178mm/7 ins × 18.65mm/47
Gran Coronas★★★★　143mm/5 5/8 ins × 18.26mm/46
Rich, spicy. Well made. Fades on finish.
Lonsdale Extra　158mm/6 3/16 ins × 17.46mm/44
Coronas　　　　142mm/5 5/8 ins × 16.67mm/42
Petit Habanos　　126mm/5 ins × 15.87mm/40
Habano Club　　124mm/4 7/8 ins × 19.05mm/48
No 1　　　　　190mm/7 1/2 ins × 15.08mm/38

EL TRELLES
Machine-made.
Bankers　　　　　　152mm/6 ins × 17.07mm/43
Blunt Extra　　133mm/5 1/4 ins × 17.86 mm/45
Club House　　　　152mm/6 ins × 16.27mm/41
Kings　　　　　　　152mm/6 ins × 16.27mm/41
Tryangles Deluxe　133mm/5 1/4 ins × 17.86mm/45

EL VERSO
Machine-made.
Corona Extra　　147mm/5 3/4 ins × 18.65mm/47
Bouquet　　　107mm/4 3/4 ins × 17.86 mm/45
Commodore　　　152 mm/6 ins × 14.29mm/36
Bouquet Light Leaf　120mm/4 3/4ins × 17.86mm/45
Mellow　　　　133mm/4 1/4 ins × 11.51mm/29

EMERSON
Machine-made.
Diplomat　　　　120mm/4 3/4ins × 17.07mm/43

ERIK
Machine-made.
Natural (Filter Tipped)　　　　99mm/3 7/8 ins
Menthol (Filter Tipped)　　　99 mm/3 7/8 ins
Cherry Flavor (Filter Tipped)　　99m/3 7/8 ins

EVERMORE
Machine-made.
Original	117mm/4 5/8 ins × 17.86mm/45
Palma	152mm/6 ins × 16.67mm/42
Corona Grande	147mm/5 3/4 ins × 18.65mm/47

FARNAM DRIVE
Machine-made.
Original	130mm/5 1/8 ins × 179mm/45

FIGARO   165mm/6 1/2 ins × 15.87mm/40
Machine-made. Available in Natural and Maduro.

FLAMENCO
Machine-made.
Brevas SMS	141mm/5 9/16 ins × 16.67mm/42

GARCIA Y VEGA★★★
Machine-made. HTL binder. Natural wrapper. Mild.
Good value mass market cigar. Made by General Cigar.
*Cigarillos	108mm/4 1/4 ins × 10.72mm/27
*Chico**	108mm/4 1/4 ins × 10.72mm/27
**Tips	133mm/5 1/4 ins × 12.00mm/30
Miniatures	117mm/4 5/8 ins × 11.51mm/29
**Whiffs	95mm/3 3/4 ins × 9.13mm/23
**Bravura	136mm/5 3/8 ins × 13.94mm/34

Good looking cigar. Mild.
*Panatella Deluxe	136mm/5 3/8 ins × 13.49mm/34
*Senators	113mm/4 1/2 ins × 16.27mm/41
**Blunts	120mm/4 3/4 ins × 16.27mm/41
**Bouquets	117mm/4 5/8 ins × 17.86mm/45
**Delgado Panetela	136mm/5 3/8 ins × 13.49mm/34
*Elegantes	162mm/6 3/8 ins × 13.49mm/34
**Gallantes	162mm/6 3/8 ins × 13.49mm/34
**Presidente	147mm/5 3/4 ins × 16.27mm/41
*Napoleon	147mm/5 3/4 ins × 16.27mm/41
**English Coronas (Tubed)	
	133mm/5 1/4 ins × 16.27mm/41
**English Coronas Boy/Girl	
	133mm/5 1/4 ins × 16.27mm/41
*Granadas (tubed)	162mm/6 3/8 ins × 13.49mm/34

Difficult to smoke due to thinness. Mild. Little flavour.
**Romeros	162mm/6 3/8 ins × 13.49mm/34
Gran Coronas (Tubed)	155mm/6 1/8 ins × 16.27mm/41
**Gran Premios (Tubed)	
	155mm/6 1/8 ins × 16.27mm/41
**Crystals No 100	155mm/6 3/8 ins × 13.50mm/34

A good, simple cigar.
Crystals No 200	155mm/6 1/8 ins × 16.27mm/41

Mild, one dimensional cigar.

*Available Only In Claro wrapper.
**Available Only In Natural wrapper.

GOLD & MILD
Machine-made. Owned by John Middleton Inc.
Pipe Tobacco Cigars   127mm/5 ins 11.9mm/30

HARVESTER
Machine-made.
Perfecto
Record Breaker

HAUPTMANN'S
Machine-made.
Perfecto Light/Dark   130mm/5 1/8 ins × 17.86mm/45
Broadleaf   133mm/5 1/4 ins × 17.07mm/43
Corona   133mm/5 1/4 ins × 17.07mm/43
Panetela   147mm/5 3/4 ins × 15.08mm/38

HAVANA BLEND
Machine-made. Short filler. All tobacco, 20 percent of filler from 1959 Cuban crop. Made in San Antonio, Texas. Distributed by Hollco Rohr.
Petit Corona   121mm/4 3/4 ins × 15.1mm/38
Palma Fina   165mm/6 1/2 ins × 11.5mm/29
Coronado ★★★   127mm/5 ins × 17.1mm/43
Easy draw. Burns evenly. Full-bodied. Robust smoke.
Delicado★★★★   146mm/5 3/4 ins × 17.1mm/43
Rich, full flavours. Touch of coffee and sweetness. Smooth.
Rothschild★★★★   127mm/5 ins × 19.8mm/50
Dark, almost black wrapper. Full-bodied. Rich. Not subtle.
Doubloon   165mm/6 1/2 ins × 16.67mm/42
Churchill   178mm/7 ins × 18.7mm/47

HAVANA CLASSICO
Hand-made. Quality: superior. Ecuador wrapper. Binder from Dominican Republic. Filler blend of tobacco from Mexico, Honduras and Dominican Rep. Launched in 1996 by Carribean Cigar Factory. See details of company under "Santiago Cabana" brand in USA section. Distributed by Miami Cigar.
Puntas   127mm/5 ins × 15.1mm/38
Varadero   140mm/5 1/2 ins × 17.5mm/44
Robusto   127mm/5 ins × 19.84mm/50
Robusto Largo   152mm/6 ins × 19.84mm/50

Corona Classic	165mm/6 1/2 ins × 16.67mm/42
Double Corona	190mm/7 1/2 ins × 18.3mm/46
Churchill★★★★★	184mm/7 1/4 ins × 19.84mm/50

Full-bodied. Good balance. Complex, spicy flavours. Cool. Well-made, elegant. Ideal for regular smoker. To follow heavy meal.

Presidente	190mm/7 1/2 ins × 21.4mm/54
Torpedo	165mm/6 1/2 ins × 21.4mm/54
Pyramide	184mm/7 1/4 ins × 21.4mm/54
Malelcon	229mm/9 ins × 23.8mm/60

HAV-A-TAMPA

Machine-made. Distinctive self-contained wooden mouthpiece introduced in late 1940s. Has huge following. Owned by Havatampa Inc.

Jewel	Wood Tip
Jewel Sweet	Wood Tip
Jewel Classic	Wood Tip

HOUSE OF WINDSOR

Machine-made.

Palmas	165mm/6 1/2 ins × 13.49mm/34
Imperiales	203mm/8 ins × 17.07mm/43
Panetela	165mm/6 1/2 ins × 13.49mm/34
Sportsman	127mm/5 ins × 17.07mm/43
Crook	127mm/5 ins × 15.90mm/45
Magnate	165mm/6 1/2 ins × 17.07mm/43

IBOLD

Machine-made.

Blunt	124mm/4 7/8 ins × 17.46mm/44
Black Pete	124mm/5 7/8 ins × 4 7/8 ins × 17.46mm/44
Breva	130mm/5 1/8 ins × 20.24mm/51
Cigarillo	108mm/4 1/4 ins × 11.51mm/29

JON PIEDRO

*Jon Piedro Acapulco Breva
152mm/6 ins × 16.67mm/42
*Jon Piedro Acapulco Slims
165mm/6 1/2 ins × 14.29mm/36
Jon Piedro Acapulco Cazadores
165mm/6 1/2 ins × 17.86mm/45
Connecticut Broadleaf Rounds
165mm/6 1/2 ins × 18.26mm/46

*Natural & Claro Claro

JOSE MELENDI

Machine-made. Vega series available in Cameroon

wrappers. Named after a former master cigar blender from Cuba who established a factory in New York.

Vega I	5 3/8 ins × 14.70mm/37
Vega II	5 1/2 ins × 17.10mm/43
Vega III	6 ins × 16.67mm/42
Vega IV	6 1/2 ins × 13.50mm/34
Vega V	6 1/2 ins × 17.70mm/45
Vega VII	7 ins × 17.70mm/45
Wild Maduro	6 7/8 ins × 13.50mm/34
Rothschild Maduro	5 ins × 19.80/50

JOYA DEL REY

Numero 35	178mm/7 ins × 13.49mm/35
Numero 42	140mm/5 1/2 ins × 16.67mm/42
Numero 43	178mm/7 ins × 17.07mm/43
Numero 49	178mm/7 ins × 19.45mm/49
Numero 50	152mm/6 ins × 19.84mm/50
Numero 52	216mm/8 1/2 ins × 20.64mm/52

JUDGES CAVE
Hand-made and machine-made. Quality: superior. All Connecticut leaf. Brand established in 1884. Owned by Historic F.D. Grave & Son in New Haven, Connecticut. One of oldest company's in continuous production. Founded in 1884. Occupied same building since beginning of century.

KING EDWARD★★★
Machine-made in Georgia, USA. This is probably the biggest selling brand in the world. HTL binder and wrapper. Sold in over 60 countries. Unique blend of tobacco and flavouring, a mild, sweet cigar. Good value mass market cigar. Made by Swisher Intl.

Invincible Deluxe	140mm/5 1/2 ins × 16.67/42
Panetela Deluxe	133mm/5 1/4 ins × 14.29mm/36
Cigarillo Deluxe	108mm/4 1/4 ins × 11.51mm/29
Imperial	127mm/5 ins × 16.27mm/41
Specials	111mm/4 3/8 ins × 11.51mm/29
Tip Cigarillo	124mm/4 7/8 ins × 11.11mm/28
Wood Tip Cigarillo	140mm/5 1/2 ins × 11.51mm/29

LA CORONA
Machine-made.
Whiffs★★   92mm/3 5/8 ins × 9.52mm/24
Touch of sweetness on palate. Smooth.

LA CORONA VINTAGE
Machine-made.

Corona Chicas	140mm/5 1/2 ins × 16.67mm/42
Coronas	152mm/6 in/17.07mm/43
Aristocrats	155mm/6 1/8 ins × 14.29mm/36
Directors	165mm/6 1/2 ins × 18.26mm/46

LA FENDRICH
Machine-made.

| Favorita | 130mm/5 1/8 ins × 17.90mm/45 |
| Buds | 108mm/4 1/4 ins × 12.70mm/32 |

LA FONTANA
Hand-made.

Dante	140mm/5 1/2 ins × 17.46mm/38
Verdi	140mm/5 1/2 ins × 17.46mm/44
Galileo	127mm/5 ins × 19.84mm/50
Puccini	165mm/6 1/2 ins × 17.46mm/44
Da Vinci	175mm/6 7/8 ins × 19.05mm/48
Michelangelo	190mm/7 1/2 ins × 20.64mm/52

LA GLORIA CUBANA

Hand-made. Quality: superior. Wrappers from Ecuador. Binders from Dominican Republic. Fillers are blend of Dominican, Brazilian and American leaf. All sizes available in maduro, which is Connecticut broad leaf. Full bodied. El Credito, like many small producers, is unable, due to space and finance, to buy and store large quantities of tobacco. However, due to genius of owner, Cuban born, Ernesto Carillo, who has great understanding of characteristics of different tobacco and how they work together, is able to alter blends to achieve a consistent result. Of all the cigars I have smoked, made outside Cuba, those from La Gloria Cubana are closest in flavour, texture and quality to that of genuine Havana. To achieve this Carillo sometimes uses tobacco from Nicaragua, Dominican Republic, Brazil, Sumatra, Mexico and USA. Production in 1995 was 1.4 million cigars across range of three brands of which La Gloria Cubana was almost one million. To overcome critical shortage of skilled workers in Miami, Carillo expanded operation to Dominican Republic in 1996 by leasing two-floor, 32 000 sq ft factory, built to his specification. Annual production in Dominican Republic is expected to reach 1.5 million cigars by end of 1997.

| Crown Imperial | 228mm/9 ins × 19.45mm/49 |
| Soberano★★★★★ | 203mm/8 ins × 20.64mm/52 |

Medium-bodied. Good balance between strength and flavour. Cool. Cigar for memorable occasion.

Charlemagne	184mm/7 1/4 ins × 21.43mm/54
Double Corona	197mm/7 3/4 ins × 19.45mm/49
Churchill	178mm/7 ins × 19.84mm/50
Glorias Inmensas★★★	190mm/7 1/2 ins × 19.05mm/48

Full-bodied. Little harsh.

| Corona | 152mm/6 ins × 20.64mm/52 |
| Wavell★★★★★ | 127mm/5 ins × 19.84mm/50 |

Dark, oily wrapper. Spicy, floral aroma. Rich honeyed undertones on finish. Smooth. For the connoisseur.

| Glorias Extra | 160mm/6 1/4 ins × 18.26mm/46 |
| Coronas Extra Large★★★★ | 197mm/7 3/4 ins × 17.46mm/44 |

Medium-strength. Lots of flavour. Long finish. Connoisseur's cigar for all occasions.

Medaille D'Or No 1	172mm/6 3/4 ins × 17.07mm/43
Medaille D'Or No 2	160mm/6 1/4 ins × 17.07mm/43
Glorias	130mm/5 1/2 ins × 17.07mm/43
Minutos	113mm/4 1/2 ins × 15.87mm/40
Panetela De' Luxe	178mm/7 ins × 14.8mm/37
Medaille D'Or No 3	178mm/7 ins × 11.11mm/28
Medaille D'Or No 4	152mm/6 ins × 12.07mm/32
Torpedo No 1	165mm/6 1/2 ins × Tapered
Piramides★★★★★	184mm/7 1/4 ins × Tapered

Spicy, leathery aroma. Full bodied. Good balance between strength and flavour. Wonderful cigar to follow wonderful meal. This cigar is an occasion!

LA HOJA SELECTA

Hand-made. Connecticut shade wrapper. Dominican, Brazillian and Mexican filler. Dominican binder. Has loyal following. Originally made in Cuba. Now made in USA by El Credito in Miami. See details of company under "La Gloria Cubana" brand in USA section.

Chateau Sovereign	190mm/7 1/2 ins × 20.64mm/52
Cosiac	178mm/7 ins × 19.05mm/48
Choix Supreme	152mm/6 ins × 19.84mm/50
Palais Royals	120mmm/4 3/4 ins × 19.84mm/50
Selectos No 1	165mm/6 1/2 ins × 16.67mm/42
Cetros de Oro	147mm/5 3/4 ins × 17.07mm/43
Bel Aires	172mm/6 3/4 ins × 15.08mm/38
Geneves	165mm/6 1/2 ins × 12.7mm/32

LANCER
Machine-made.

| Havana Slims | 127mm/5 ins × 12.7mm/32 |

LA PLATA
Hand-made. Connecticut wrapper. Ecuador binder.

Filler blend of tobacco from Ecuador and Dominican Republic. Made by La Plata Cigar Co. Founded in 1947, is last large-scale cigar manufacturer in Los Angeles.

Hercules	140mm/5 1/2 ins × 21.4mm/54
Enterprise Classic	178mm/7 ins × 20.6mm/52
Grand Classic	152mm/6 ins × 17.5mm/44

LA PLATA MADUROS
Hand-made Tobacco as in standard La Platta range, but with Maduro wrapper. Made by La Plata Cigar Co.

Royal Wilshire	178mm/7 ins × 20.6mm/52
Robusto Uno	114mm/4 1/2 ins × 20.6mm/52
Magnificos	152mm/6 ins × 17.5mm/44

LORD BEACONSFIELD
Machine-made. Short filler. Homogenised binder. Honduran filler. Full flavour. Originally made for British market. Made by Villazon in Tampa, Florida.

Directors	197mm/7 3/4 ins × 18.26mm/46
Rounds	184mm/7 1/4 ins × 18.26mm/46
Lords	178mm/7 ins × 13.49mm/34
Corona Superbas	160mm/6 1/4 ins × 16.67mm/42
Lindas (girl or boy)	165mm/6 1/2 ins × 14.29mm/36
Cubanolas	140mm/5 1/2 ins × 17.46mm/44

Available with EMS, claro claro or maduro wrappers.

LORD CLINTON
Machine-made.
Perfecto

Corona Gorda	160mm/6 1/4 ins × 17.46mm/44
Churchill	178mm/7 ins × 19.45mm/49
Nom Plus	113mm/4 1/2 ins × 19.84mm/50
President	216mm/8 1/2 ins × 19.84mm/50
Toro	152mm/6 ins × 19.84mm/50

MACABI
Hand-made by Antillian Cigar, Miami. Long filler.

Super Corona	197mm/7 3/4 ins × 20.6mm/52
Double Corona	175mm/6 7/8 ins × 19.5mm/49
Corona Extra	152mm/6 ins × 19.8mm/50
Royal Corona	127mm/5 ins × 19.8mm/50
No 1	171mm/6 3/4 ins × 17.5mm/44
Media Corona	140mm/5 1/2 ins × 17.1mm/43
Belicoso Fino (triangular)	
	159mm/6 1/4 ins × 20.6mm/52

MARK IV
Machine-made.
Magnates
Maduro Supremes

MARSH
Machine-made.

Mountaineer	140mm/5 1/2 ins × 13.49mm/34
Virginian	140mm/5 1/2 ins × 14.68mm/37
Pioneer	140mm/5 1/2 ins × 14.68mm/37
Old Reliable	140mm/5 1/2 mm × 13.10mm/33
Deluxe	178mm/7 ins × 13.49mm/34

MIFLIN'S CHOICE
Machine-made.

Deluxe II	178mm/7 ins × 13.49mm/34
Corona	127mm/5 ins × 17.07mm/43
Panatela	162mm/6 3/8 ins × 12.70mm/32

MUNIEMAKER
Machine-made. All American tobacco. Brand launched in 1916 by F.D. Grave & Son in New Haven, Connecticut. One of oldest companies in continuous production. Occupied same building since beginning of century.

Regular	113mm/4 1/2 ins × 18.65mm/47
Straights	130mm/5 1/8 ins × 19.05mm/48
Longs	152mm/6 ins × 18.26mm/46
Breva 100's Oscura	130mm/5 1/8 ins × 19.05mm/48
Panetela 100's Oscura	152mm/6 ins × 13.10mm/33
Palma 100's	152mm/6 ins × 18.26mm/46
Perfecto 100's	133mm/5 1/4 ins × 18.65mm/47
Boy/Girl	113mm/4 1/2 ins × 18.65mm/47

ODIN
Machine-made.

Viking	120mm/4 3/4 ins × 16.67mm/42

OLD HERMITAGE
Machine-made.

Golden Perfecto	140 mm/5 1/2 ins × 17.86mm/45

OPTIMO**
Machine-made. Natural leaf wrapper. HTL binder. Spicy, coffee aroma. Dry finish. Mild. Mass market cigar. Made by Swisher Intl.

Diplomat	155mm/6 1/8 ins × 13.10mm/33
Admiral	152mm/6 ins × 16.27mm/41
Admiral Boy/Girl	152mm/6 ins × 16.27mm/41
Admiral Just Married	152mm/6 ins × 16.27mm/41
Coronas	133mm/5 1/4 ins × 16.67mm/42
Palmas	152mm/6 ins × 16.67mm/41
Panetela	132mm/5 1/4 ins × 13.10mm/33
Sports	113mm/4 1/2 ins × 16.67mm/4

ORO BLEND
Hand-made. All Honduran tobacco. Made by Tampa Rico Cigar, Tampa, Florida.

•24	191mm/7 1/2 ins × 19.84mm/50
•22	165mm/6 1/2 ins × 17.5mm/44
•18	140mm/5 1/2 ins × 16.67mm/42
•14	152mm/6 ins × 14.3mm/36
•10	114mm/4 1/2 ins × 11.4mm/50

PALMA LITES
Machine-made.
Palmas

PARODI
Machine-made. Dry cigar. All tobacco.

Ammezzati	89mm/3 1/2 ins
Economy	102mm/4 ins
Kings	104mm/4 1/8 ins
Avanti	113mm/4 1/2 ins
Avanti Cont'l	113mm/4 1/2 ins
Ramrod Deputy	113mm/4 1/2 ins
Ramrod Original	113mm/4 1/2 ins
Kentucky Cheroots	136mm/5 3/8 ins

PEDRO IGLESIAS
Machine-made. Short filler. Made by Villazon in Tampa.

Lonsdales	165mm/6 1/2 ins × 17.46mm/44
Regents	152mm/6 ins × 17.46mm/44
Crowns	127mm/5 ins × 17.86mm/45

PETRI

Toscani
AA Cello
Sigaretto King
Sigaretto Reg.
Squillo
Toscanelli

PHILLIES
Machine-made in Selma, Alabama by Phillies Cigar.

Perfecto	147mm/5 3/4 ins × 17.07mm/43
Titan	160mm/6 1/4 ins × 17.46mm/44
Coronas	136mm/5 3/8 ins × 16.27mm/41
Blunts	120mm/4 3/4 ins × 16.67mm/42
Panatella	140mm/5 1/2 ins × 13.49mm/34
Sport	147mm/5 3/4 ins × 17.07mm/43
Cheroot	127mm/5 ins × 12.70mm/32
King Cheroot	140mm/5 1/2 ins × 12.70mm/32
Mexicali Slim	117mm/4 5/8 ins × 12.70mm/32

Juniors	127mm/5 ins × 16/27mm/41
Sweets	147mm/5 3/4 ins × 16/67mm/43
Tips (tipped)	113mm/4 1/2 ins × 11.11mm/28
Tip Sweet (tipped)	113mm/4 1/2 ins × 11.11mm/28

POLLACK
Machine-made.

| Crown Drum | 140mm/5 1/2 ins × 13.10mm/33 |

PRINCE ALBERT
Machine-made. Owned by John Middleton Inc.

Soft & Sweet Vanilla	127mm/5 ins × 11.9mm/30
Traditional	127mm/5 ins × 11.9mm/30
Cool Mint	127mm/5 ins × 11.9mm/30

R.G. DUN
Machine-made.
Admiral
Babies
Bouquet
Cigarillo

RED DOT
Machine-made.

| Perfecto | 127mm/5 ins × 16.67mm/42 |
| Panetela | 133mm/5 1/4 ins × 13.50mm/34 |

RICO HAVANA BLEND
Hand-made. Long filler. Ecuador wrapper. Dominican binder and filler. Made by Tampa Rico Cigar Co., Tampa, Florida.

Rough Rider	229mm/9 ins × 19.84mm/50
Churchill	203mm/8 ins × 19.1mm/48
Double Corona	178mm/7 ins × 19.1mm/48
Plaza	178mm/7 ins × 17.5mm/44
Corona	152mm/6 ins × 16.67mm/42
Panetela	178mm/7 ins × 13.5mm/34
Mercedes	152mm/6 ins × 11.9mm/30
Duke	121mm/4 3/4 ins × 19.84mm/50
Habanero	114mm/4 1/2 ins × 16.67mm/42

RIGOLETTO CIGARS
Machine-made in Tampa. Two models hand-made in Dominican Republic. Made by M & N, Tampa.

Londonaire	159mm/6 1/4 ins × 17.10mm/43
Black Jack	137mm/5 3/8 ins × 18.30mm/46
Natural Coronas	152mm/6 ins × 16.67mm/42
Palma Grande	152mm/6 ins × 16.30mm/41

ROBERT BURNS
Machine-made in Dotham, Alabama. Short filler. Homogenised binder. Mass market cigar made by General Cigar.
Cigarillos★★   113mm/4 1/2 ins × 10.72mm/27
Quick burning. Hint of sweetness.
Black Watch   140mm/5 1/2 ins × 16.27mm/41

ROLANDO BLEND
Hand-made. Connecticut shade wrapper. Dominican filler and binder. Made by Tampa Rico Cigar Co, Tampa.
Numero No 2   190mm/7 1/2 ins × 19.1mm/48
Numero No 3   152mm/6 ins × 20.2mm/50
Numero No 4   152mm/6 ins × 17.1mm/43
Robusto   121mm/4 3/4 ins × 20.6mm/52
Pyramid   165mm/6 1/2 ins × 13.5mm/34
Perfecto   178mm/7 ins × 17.5mm/44

ROSEDALE
Machine-made.
Perfecto
Londres

RUM RIVER
Machine-made.
Crooks Rum
Crookettes Rum

RUM RUNNER
Hand-made. Long filler with sweet rum flavour. Launched late 1996 by Caribbean Cigar Factory in Miami.
Bucaneer   140mm/5 1/2 ins × 17.5mm/44
Pirate   178mm/7 ins × 18.3mm/46

RUSTLERS★★
Machine-made. Filler tipped. HTL wrapper and binder. Very mild, sweet. Made by Consolidated Cigars.
Black 'n Cherry   99mm/3 7/8 ins × 9.13mm/23
Sweets   99mm/3 7/8 ins × 9.13mm/23
Menthol   99mm/3 7/8 ins × 9.13mm/23

SFS SPECIAL SELECTION
Machine-made.
Almond Liqueur
Cafe Cubano (Coffee)

SAN FELICE
Machine-made.
Original

SAN LUIS
Machine-made

Soberanos	190mm/7 1/2 ins × 19.84mm/50
Corona	165mm/6 1/2 ins × 17.46mm/44
Toro	152mm/6 ins × 19.84mm/50
Panetelas	165mm/6 1/2 ins × 14.29mm/36
Panetelas Boy	165mm/6 1/2 ins × 14.29mm/36
Panetelas Girl	165mm/6 1/2 ins × 14.29mm/36
Cetros	136mm/5 3/8 ins × 16.67mm/42

SANTA FE
Machine-made.

Biltmore	152mm/6 ins × 16.27mm/41
Fairmont	152mm/6 ins × 16.67mm/43
Panetela	133mm/5 1/4 ins × 13.10mm/33
Patties	140mm/5 1/2 ins ×16.67mm/42

SANTIAGO CABANA
Hand-made. Quality: superior. Ecuador wrapper. Mexican binder. Filler blend of tobacco from Honduras, Nicaragua and Dominican Rep. Launched late 1995. Made by Caribbean Cigar Factory. First major manufacturer of hand-made cigars to open in USA in post 30 years. Main factory in Miami. Has shops with manufacturing facilities in Key Largo, Key West and Miami South Beach. Company founded by former air traffic controller, Kevin Doyle and financial adviser and venture capitalist, Mike Risley to seek listing on Yew York Stock Exchange. Company presently employs about 40 cigar rollers. Has plans, during 1996, to open another factory in trade free zone in Dominican Republic. This brand named after Santiago Cabana, Cuban cigar roller who created range. Distributed by Miami Cigar.

Chicas (torpedo)	127mm/5 ins × 15.1mm/38
Caribe	130mm/5 1/2 ins × 17.5mm/44
Robusto	127mm/5 ins × 19.8mm/50
Lancero	190mm/7 1/2 ins × 15.1mm/38
Double Corona	190mm/7 1/2 ins × 18.3mm/46
Churchill	184mm/7 1/4 ins * 19.8mm/50
Presidente	190mm/7 1/2 ins × 21.4mm/54
Torpedo★★★★★	165mm/6 1/2 ins × 21.4mm/54

Medium to full-bodied. Good balance. Spicy, nutty flavours. Good finish. Well-made cigar for special occasion.

Corona★★★★★   165mm/6 1/2 ins × 16.67mm/42
Spicy with touch of nutmeg. Medium-bodied. Good

balance. Smooth. A well-made elegant cigar for connoisseur.

SAN VICENTE BLEND
Hand-made. All Honduran tobacco. Made by Tampa Rico Cigar Co., Tampa, Florida.

Supremo	165mm/6 1/2 ins × 17.5mm/44
Panetela	152mm/6 ins × 14.3mm/36
Matador	140mm/5 1/2 ins × 16.67mm/42
Presidente	203mm/8 ins × 19.8mm/50
Rothchild	127mm/5 ins × 19.8mm/50

SELLO DE ORO
Mixed filler.

Fumas
Cazador
Super Cazador

SUPER VALUE PIPE TOBACCO CIGARS★★
Machine-made by Consolidated Cigars.
Black 'n Cherry
Black 'n Sweet

SUPRE VALUE LITTLE CIGARS★★
Machine-made by Consolidated Cigars. Good value mass market cigar.

Menthol	99mm/3 2/8 ins × 7.94mm/20
Cherry	99mm/3 7/8 ins × 7.94mm/20
Sweet	99mm/3 7/8 ins × 7.94mm/20
Ultra Mild	99mm/3 7/8 ins × 7.94mm/20

SUPRE SWEETS★★
Machine-made by Consolidated Cigar. Short filler. Mild and slightly sweet. Good value mass market cigar.

Tip Cigarillo	130mm/5 1/8 ins × 10.72mm/27
Cigarillo	120mm/4 3/4 ins × 11.11mm/28
Perfectos	120mm/4 3/4ins × 17.46mm/44
Little Cigars	99mm/3 7/8 ins × 7.94mm/20

SWISHER SWEETS★★
Machine-made. Short filler. HTL wrapper and binder. One of America's top selling brands. Unique blend of tobacco and flavouring, creating a mild, sweet cigar. Made by Swisher Intl.

Kings	140mm/5 1/2 ins × 16.67mm/42
Perfecto Slims	127mm/5 ins × 16.27mm/41
Coronella	127mm/5 ins × 11.11mm/28
Cigarillo	111mm/4 3/8 ins × 11.51mm/29
Tip Cigarillo	124mm/4 7/8 ins × 11.11mm/28

Wood Tip Cigarillo   124mm/4 7/8 ins ×11.51mm/29

TAMPA NUGGET
Machine-made. Mass market cigar.

Sublime Perfecto	120mm/4 3/4 ins × 17.07mm/43
Blunt Blunt	127mm/5 ins × 17.07mm/43
Panetela Panatela	140mm/5 1/2 ins × 14.29mm/36
Tip Regular Cigarillo	127mm/5 ins × 11.11mm/28
Tip Sweet Cigarillo	127mm/5 ins × 11.11mm/28
Juniors Miniature	113mm/4 1/2 ins × 12.30mm/31
Juniors Panetela	113mm/4 1/2 ins × 12.30mm/31

TAMPA SWEET
Machine-made. Mass market cigar. HTL wrapper and binder.

Perfecto	4 3/4 ins × 17.07mm/43
Cheroot	4 3/4ins × 12.30mm/31
Tip Cigarillo	5 ins × 11.11mm/28

TIJUANA SMALLS
Machine-made. HTL wrapper and binder. Made by General Cigar.

Aromantic	89mm/3 1/2 ins × 8.33mm/21
Cherry★★	89mm/3 1/2 ins × 8.33mm/21

Aromatic and sweet.

Regular★	89mm/3 1/2 ins × 8.33mm/21

One dimensional. Much like mild cigarette.

TIPARILLO
Machine-made.

Mild Blend	108mm/4 1/4 ins × 10.32mm/26
Sweet Blend	108mm/4 1/4 ins × 10.32mm/26
Aromatic	108mm/4 1/4 ins × 10.32mm/26
Menthol	108mm/4 1/4 ins × 10.32mm/26

TOPPER
Machine-made by Topper Cigar Co.
Old Fashioned Perfecto
                          124mm/4 7/8 ins × 17.46mm/44
Old Fashioned Extra Oscuro

Breva	140mm/5 1/2 ins × 17.86mm/45
Ebony	140mm/5 1/2 ins × 17.46mm/44
Grande Corona	152mm/6 ins × 17.46mm/44

TOPSTONE
Machine-made. Long filler. All Connecticut leaf. Made by Villazon.

Directors	197mm/7 3/4 ins × 18.26mm/46
Grande	147mm/5 3/4 ins × 18.26mm/46

Bouquet	140mm/5 1/2 ins × 18.26mm/46
Oscuro	140mm/5 1/2 ins × 18.26mm/46
Extra Oscuro	140mm/5 1/2 ins × 18.26mm/46
Supremes	152mm/6 ins × 16.67mm/42
Panetela	152mm/6 ins × 15.48mm/39

TOPSTONE — NATURAL DARKS

Machine-made. Connecticut broad leaf. Maduro. Long filler. Made by Villazon in Tampa, Florida.

Executives	184mm/7 1/4 ins × 18.65mm/47
Coronas	160mm/6 1/4 ins × 17.46mm/44
Panetela	152mm/6 ins × 15.48mm/39
Breva	140mm/51/2 ins × 18.26mm/46

TOPSTONE

Machine-made. Connecticut broadleaf. Long filler. Made by Villazon.

Supreme	152mm/6 ins × 16.67mm/42
Extra Oscuro	140mm/5 1/2 ins × 18.26mm/46
Grande	147mm/5 3/4 ins × 18.26mm/46
Panetela	152mm/6 ins × 15.48mm/39
Bouquet	140mm/5 1/2 ins × 18.26mm/46
Oscuro	140mm/5 1/2 ins × 18.26mm/46
Directors	197mm/7 3/4 ins × 18.65mm/47

TORQUINO

Hand-made. Long filler. Triangular bundles. Ecuador wrapper. Mexican filler and binder. Made for Brick-Hanauer Co., Massachusetts.

Breva Corona	146mm/5 3/4 ins × 17.1mm/43
Classic Corona	178mm/7 ins × 17.1mm/43
Delicioso	178mm/7 ins × 20.6mm/52
Torquino	178mm/7 ins × 19.84mm/50
Privada No 1	152mm/6 ins × 18.3mm/46
Pyramide	165mm/6 1/2 ins × 23.8mm/60
Rothschild	114mm/4 1/2 ins × 19.84mm/50
Toro	152mm/6 ins × 19.84mm/50
Torpedo	178mm/7 ins × 21.4mm/54

VILLA DE CUBA

Machine-bunched with homogenised binder. Made by Villazon in Tampa. Available since early 1930s.

Corona Grande	184mm/7 1/4 ins × 17.86mm/45
Majestics	162mm/6 3/8 ins × 17.07mm/43
Brevas	147mm/5 3/4 ins × 17.46mm/44

VILLAZON DELUXE

Machine-made. Medium filler. Made by Villazon.

| Chairman | 197mm/7 3/4 ins × 17.07mm/43 |

| Cetros | 182mm/7 3/16 ins × 17.46mm/44 |
| Senators | 172mm/6 3/4 ins × 17.46mm/44 |

VILLAZON DELUXE AROMATICS
Machine-made. Short filler. Made by Villazon in Tampa, Florida.

| Commodores | 152mm/6 ins × 16.67mm/42 |
| Panetela | 147mm/5 3/4 ins × 13.49mm/34 |

WHITE OWL
Machine-made. Short filler. Homogenised binder. A top seller in USA. Launched in 1902. Made by General Cigar.

Coronetta	117mm/4 5/8 ins × 11.51mm/29
Demi-Tip	108mm/4 1/4 ins × 12.70mm/32
Miniatures★★★	117mm/4 5/8 ins × 11.49mm/34

Medium-bodied. Good flavour for cigarillo. Good quick smoke.

| Panetela Deluxe★★ | 133mm/5 1/4 ins × 13.49mm/34 |

Uninspiring. Smooth.

Invincible(Boy/Girl)	136mm/5 3/8 ins × 16.67mm/41
New Yorker	143mm/5 5/8 ins × 16.67mm/41
Ranger	162mm/6 3/8 ins × 13.49mm/34
Blunts★★	120mm/4 3/4 ins × 16.67mm/41

Mild. Good finish. Touch of sweetness.

WILLIAM ASCOT
Machine-made in Tampa.
Palma (Natural, Maduro, Claro claro)
Rounds
Panetela

WILLIAM PENN
Machine-made. HTL wrapper and binder. Made by General Cigar.

| Willow Tips | 108mm/4 1/4 ins × 10.32mm/26 |
| Braves★ | 117mm/4 5/8 ins × 11.51mm/29 |

Medium-bodied. Sweet. One dimensional.

| Perfecto | 116mm/5 3/8 ins × 16.27mm/41 |
| Panetela | 133mm/5 1/4 ins × 13.49mm/34 |

WINCHESTER
Machine-made.
Winchester Little Cigars
Winchester Menthol Little Cigars
Winchester Sweets 100's Little Cigars
Winchester 100's Little Cigars

WOLF BROTHERS
Machine-made.

Rum Crooks   140mm/5 1/2 ins × 12.00mm/30
Crooks Sweet Vanilla
Nippers   83mm/3 1/4 ins

World Directory Index

Identifying brands with countries

Aus — Austria
Bel — Belgium
Bra — Brazil
CI — Canary Islands
CR — Costa Rica
Den — Denmark
Dom — Dominican Republic
Ecu — Ecuador
Ger — Germany
Hol — Holland
Hon — Honduras
Ind — Indonesia

It — Italy
Jam — Jamaica
Mex — Mexico
Nic — Nicaragua
Pan — Panama
Phi — Philippines
PR — Porto Rico
SA — South Africa
Spa — Spain
Swi — Switzerland
UK — United Kingdom
USA — United States

ADANTE — Dom
AGIO — Hol
AGUILA — Dom
AIRPORT — Aus
AL CAPONE — Ger
ALHAMBRA — Phil
ALTON — UK
AMERICAN EAGLE — USA
ANATOL — Aus
ANDUJAR — Dom
ANTELO — USA
ANTICO — It
ANTONIO Y CLEOPATRA — USA
ARANGO — Hon, USA
ARLBERG — Aus
AROMAS DE SAN ANDREAS — Mex
ARTURO FUENTE — Dom
ASHTON — Dom
ASTRAL — Hon
AS YOU LIKE IT — USA
ATTACHE ROYAL — Aus
AVO — Dom

B-H — USA
BACCARAT HAVANA SELECTION — Hon
BAHIA — CR
BACKWOODS — USA
BALBAO — Pan
BALMORAL — Hol
BANCES — Hon, USA
BANIFF GOLDEN LABEL — Ger
BAUZA — Dom
BELINDA — Hon
BEN BEY — USA
BEN FRANKLIN — USA
BERING — Hon
BERMEJO — Hon
BEVERLY HILLS — Hon
BLACK & MILD — USA
BLACK HAWK — USA
BLACK LABEL — Mex
BLUE RIBBON — Nic
BOUQUET — USA
BUDD SWEET — USA
BUTERA ROYAL VINTAGE — Dom
CABALLERO — Aus

362

DOMINICAN — Dom
DOMINICAN ESTATES — Dom
DOMINICANA — Dom
DOMINICO — Dom
DON ASA — Hon
DON CESAR — USA
DON DIEGO — Dom
DON ESTEBAN — Dom
DON JOSE — Hon
DON JUAN — Nic
DON JULIO — Dom
DON LEO — Dom
DON LINO — Hon
DON MARCUS — Dom
DON MATEO — Hon
DON MIGUEL — Dom
DON MILO — Hon
DON PEPE — Bra
DON PISHU — CI
DON RAMOS — Hon
DON REX — Hon
DON RUBIO — Hon
DON TOMAS — Hon
DON VITO — Dom
DON XAVIER — CI
DOUBLE HAPINESS — Phi
DRY SLITZ — USA
DUNHILL — CI, Dom, Hol
DUTCH MASTERS — PR, USA
DUTCH TREATS — USA
8-9-8 COLLECTION — Jam
EL BESO — Mex
EL CANELO — USA
ELEGANTE — USA
EL MACCO — USA
EL PARAISO — Hon
EL PRODUCTO — USA
EL REY DEL MUNDO — Hon
EL RICO HABANO — USA
EL SUBLIMADO — Dom

EL TRELLES — USA
EL TRIUNFO — Mex
EL VERSO — USA
ELYSEE — Bra
EMERSON — USA
ENCANTO — Hon
ERIK — USA
ESPADA — Hon
EVELIO — Hon
EVERMORE — USA
EXCALIBUR — Hon
EXECUTOR — Hon
FALSTAFF — Aus
FARNAM DRIVE — USA
F. D. GRAVE & SON — Hon
FELIPE GREGORIO — Hon
FIDELIO — Bra
FIGARO — USA
FIGHTING COCK — Phi
FIRST PRIMING — Hon
FIVE STAR SECONDS — Dom
FLAMENCO — Dom, USA
FLIP — Aus
FLOR DE ALLONES — Hon
FLOR DE CONSUEGRA — Hon
FLOR DE JALAPA — Nic
FLOR DEL CARIBE — Hon, Ind
FLOR DE MANILA — Phi
FLOR DE NICARAGUA — Nic
FLOR DE ORLANDO — Dom
FLOR DE PALICIO — Hon
FRANCO — Dom
FLORENTINO — CR
FONSECA — Dom
FUNADORES — Jam
GARCIA Y VEGA — USA
GAUTENG — SA

LA AURORA — Dom
LA BALLA — Hon
LA CORDOBA — Nic
LA CORONA — Dom, USA
LA DILIGENCIA — Hon
LA FAMA — CI
LA FENDRICH — USA
LA FONTANA — Hon, USA
LA FINCA — Nic
LA FLOR DE LA ISABELA — Phi
LA GLORIA CUBANA — USA
LA HOJA SELECTA — USA
LA INVICTA — Hon
LA LLORONA — Hon
LA MAXIMALIANA — Hon
LAMBS CLUB — Dom
LA NATIVE — Hon
LANCER — USA
LA PAZ — Hol
LA PLATA — USA
LA PRIMADORA — Hon, USA
LA REAL — Hon
LA REGENTA — CI
LAS CABRILLAS — Hon, USA
LA SIESTA — Dom
LAS LIBERTADORES — Dom
LA UNICA — Dom
LA VENGA — Hon
LEICHTE BRUNS — Aus
LEGACY — Hon
LEMPIRA — Hon
LEON JIMENES — Dom
LICENCIADOS — Dom
LIVARDE — Aus
LORD BEACONSFIELD — USA
LORD CLINTON — USA
MACABI — USA

MACANUDO — Jam
MADRIGAL — USA
MARIA MANCINI — Hon
MARK IV — USA
MARIO PALOMINO — Jam
MARSH — USA
MASTERS COLLECTION — Nic
MARTINEZ Y CIA — USA
MATACAN — Mex
MATASA — Dom
MATCH PLAY — Dom
MAYA — Hon
MEDAL OF HONOR — Hon
MEXICAN EMPERADOR — Mex
MEXICAN SEGUNDOS — Mex
MICUBANO — Nic
MIFLIN'S CHOICE — USA
MINTERO — Dom
MOCAMBO — Mex
MOCCA — Aus, Hon, Ind
MONTE CANARIO — CI
MONTECASSINO — Hon
MONTECRISTO — Dom
MONTECRUZ — Dom
MONTELIMAR — Hon
MONTESINO — Dom
MONTOYA — Hon
MORENO MADURO — Dom
MOZART — Aus
MUNIEMAKER — USA
MURIEL — PR
NAT CICCO — Dom
NATIONAL BRAND — Hon
NAT SHERMAN — Dom, Hon
NESTOR — Hon
NEW YORK — Mex

ROLLER'S CHOICE — Dom
ROMEO Y JULIETA — Dom
ROSEDALE — USA
ROSITAS — Aus
ROYAL COURT — Dom
ROYAL DOMINICANA — Dom
ROYALES — Dom
ROYAL JAMAICA — Dom
ROYAL MANNA — Hon
ROYAL NICARAGUAN — Nic
ROZET — Aus
RUM RIVER — USA
RUSTLERS — USA
SABROSO — Nic
SAMBA — Aus
SAN FELICE — USA
SAN FERNANDO — Hon
SAN LUIS — Hon, USA
SANTA CLARA — Mex
SANTA CRUZ — Jam
SANTA DAMIANA — Dom
SANTA FE — USA
SANTA ROSA — Hon
SANTIAGO — Dom
SANTIAGO CABANA — USA
SAN VICENTE BLEND — USA
SAVINELLI — Dom
SCHIMMELPENNICK — Hol, USA
SEGOUIA — Nic
SELLO DE ORO — USA
SENOR — Aus
SFS SPECIAL — USA
SIBONEY — Aus
SILLEMS LAS TERENAS — Dom
SLIM JIM — Aus
SOLO AROMA — Hon

SOSA — Dom
SPECIAL CARIBBEAN — Dom
SPECIAL CORONAS — Dom
SPECIAL JAMAICA — Dom
SPEZI — Aus
SUERDIECK — Bra, Ger
SUPER — Hon
SUPER VALUE — USA
SUPRE SWEETS — USA
SWISHER SWEETS — Hon, USA
TABACALERA — Phi
TABAQUERO — Dom
TAMPA NUGGET — USA
TAMPA SWEET — USA
TE-AMO — Dom, Mex
TEMPLE HALL — Jam
TENA Y VEGA — CR, Hon
TEREROS DE CUPAN — Hon
THOMAS HINDS — Hon, Nic
TIBURON — Hon
TIJUANA — USA
TIPARILLO — Aus, USA
TOPPER — Dom, Hon, USA
TOPSTONE — USA
TORCEDOR — Nic
TORQUINO — USA
TRESADO — Don
TROYA — Dom
TULA — Dom
VAN DER DONK — Hol
V CENTENNIAL — Hon
VEDEDIGER — Aus
VERACRUZ — Mex
VILLA DE CUBA — USA
VILLAZON — USA
VILLIGER — Swi

Books on Cigars and Related Subjects

ENGLISH

Annis
> Fact and Fancy About Cigars (Gradiaz-Annis & Company, Tampa, FL, 1967)

Anon
> Know The Cigar (EP Publishing Ltd, Yorkshire, 1973)

Back
> The Pleasures of Cigar Smoking (Rutledge Books Inc., New York, 1971)

Bati
> The Cigar Companion. A Connoisseur's Guide (Running Press Book Publishers, Philadelphia, PA, 1993; 2d edition, October 1995)

Butcher
> The Cigar. A Little Book About A Man's Smoke (Standard Press Publishers, Orange, NJ, 1949)

Cigar Institute of America
> All About Cigars (New York, 1967)
> The Story of Cigars (New York, 1942, 1943)

Crawford
> The Havana Cigar (Hunters & Frankau, London, 1971, 1975, 1980)

Davidoff
> The Connoisseur's Book of The Cigar (McGraw-Hill Book Company, New York, 1969, 1984)

Edmark
> Cigar Chic: A Woman's Perspective (The Summit Publishing Group, Arlington, Texas, 1995)

Finn
> Zen and The Art of Cigar Connoisseurship (The Great Colombo and Zanzibar Merchant Exchange, London, 1990)

Garmirian
> The Gourmet Guide to Cigars (Cedar Publications, McLean, VA, 1990, 1992)

Gérard Père et Fils
    The Connoisseur's Guide to Havana Cigars (Editions Solar, Paris, 1992)

Graves
    Cigars and The Man (Martins Cigar Shippers, London, 1930)

Hacker
    The Ultimate Cigar Book (Autumngold Publishing, Beverley Hills, CA, 1993)

Hauge et al.
    101 WAYS to Answer the Request WOULD YOU PLEASE PUT OUT THAT # (!&*!$ CIGAR (Simon & Schuster, Inc, New York, 1987)

Hunters & Frankau
    A Short Appreciation of Havana Cigars (London, 1977)

Hunters & Frankau
    Havanas. A Unique Blend of Sun, Soil and Skill (London, 1993)

Innes
    The Book of The Havana Cigar (Orbis Publishing Ltd, London, 1983)

Jiménez
    The Journey of The Havana Cigar (Empresa Cubana del Tabaco, Havana, 1988)

LeRoy & Szafran
    The Illustrated History of Cigars (Harold Starke Publishers, London, 1993)

Morera, Chase & Colbert
    Havanas (Hunters & Frankau, London, 1993.)

Perelman
    Perelman's Pocket Cyclopedia of Cigars, 1995 Edition (Los Angeles, CA, 1994); 1997 Edition, 1995, 1996)

Rothman
    Cigar Almanac (Education Systems and Publications, Belleville, NJ, 1979)

Rudman
    Rudman's Complete Pocket Guide to Cigars (Good Living Publishing, RSA, 1995 ed, Feb '95; 1996 revised ed, Oct '95; 1996 ed reprint, Dec '95) Third ed, Sept '96

Scott
How to Select and Enjoy Premium Cigars . . . and Save Money! (Coast Creative Services, San Diego, CA, 1994)

Vallens
Facts on Cigars For Up-to-Date Smokers (Gene-Vall Cigar Company, New York, 1912, 1914 and 1923)

West
All About Cigars: A Handbook for Tobacconists (Trade Publications Ltd, London, 1962)

Wolfson
Cigar Connoisseur. Foreplay and Reference Guide (Sausalito, CA, 1994)

DUTCH

Kroonenberg
Tijd Voor Een Sigaar (Boxtel, Amsterdam, 1991)

FRENCH

Bati
Le Cigare. Guide de l'Amateur (Éditions Soline, Paris, 1995)

Belaubre
Cigares. De l'Initiation à la Maîtrise (Champerard Productions, 92150 Soresnes, 1990)

Davidoff
Histoire du Havane (Éditions Daniel Briand, 31000 Toulouse, 1981)

—

Le Livre du Connaisseur de Cigare (Robert Laffont, Paris, 1967)

des Ombiaux
Eloge du Tabac. Traitè du Havane (Le Divan, Paris, 1924)

—

Petit Traitè du Havane (des Presses d'Oscar Lamberty Èditeur, Bruxelles, 1920)

Gérard Père et Fils
Guide de l'Amateur de Havane (Éditions Solar, 75285 Paris, 1990)

l'Univers du Havane (Éditions Solar, 75285 Paris, 1995)

Innes
Le Havane. Histoire et Voluptè (Éditions Claude Lattes, 75006 Paris, 1983)

LeRoy et Szafran
La Grande Histoire du Cigare (Éditions Flammarion, 75278 Paris, 1989)

Marsan
Le Cigare. Guides Utiles a Ceux qui Veulent Vivre la Belle Vie (La Nouvelle Societe d'Édition, Paris, 1929)

GERMAN

Anon
Das Taschenbuch des Zigarrenrauchers. Zigarrenrauchen Mit Genuss (Wilhelm Heyne Verlag, München, 1968)

Bati
Zigarren. Der Guide für Kenner und Geniesser (Wilhelm Heyne Verlag, München, 1994)

Brückner
Zigarren-Brevier. Wie Kenner Geniessen (F. Englisch Verlag, 6200 Wiesbaden, 1984)

Davidoff
Zigarren-Brevier Oder Was Raucht der Connaisseur (Paul Neff Verlag KG, Wien, 1967; Wilhelm Heyne Verlag, München, 1975)

Forster
Bei Einer Zigarre zu Lesen (Mercator-Verlag Gert Wohlfarth, 41 Duisburg, 1963)

Gorys
Die Kunst, Zigarren zu Rauchen (Ernst Heimeran Verlag, München, 1966)

Hacker
Die Welt der Zigarre (Wilhelm Heyne Verlag, München, 1995)

Herchenröder
Meine Braune Geliebte. Ein Zigarrenbrevier (C. W. Niemeyer Verlag, 325 Hamelin, n.d.)

LeRoy u. Szafran
Die Grosse Geschichte der Zigarre (Christian Verlag, München, 1989)

ITALIAN

Bozzini
Il Signor Sigaro. Dal Toscano Agli Avana Sceglieri, Conservarli, Fumarli (Gruppo Ugo Mursia Editore, S.p.A., 20124 Milano, 1982)

Davidoff
L'Amatore del Sigaro (Gruppo Ugo Mursia Editore, S.p.A., 20124 Milano, 1983)

LeRoy e. Szafran
Le Grande Storia del Sigaro (Arnoldo Mondadori Editore, S.p.A., Milano, 1989)

Plenizio
Davidoff, le Mei Storie e i Miei Sigari (Multigrafica Editrice, Roma, 1983)

SPANISH

Jiménez
El Viaje del Habano (Empresa Cubana del Tabaco, Habana, 1980)

CIGAR COLLECTIBLES

American Antique Graphics Society
Official Price Guide of CIGAR LABEL ART (Medina, OH, 1993)

Art Gallery of Windsor
NICO. A Selection of Original Painted Designs for Cigar Boxes Labels (1895-1920) (1982)

Barnes & Dunn
The Cigar-Label Art Visual Encyclopedia, Volume I (Lake Forest, CA, 92630, 1995)

Chemung County Historical Soc. Museum
The Golden Age of THE CIGAR and the Cigar Box, 1880-1920, (Elmira, NY, 1983)

Davidson
The Art of the Cigar Label (The Wellfleet Press, Secaucus, NJ, 1989)

Dunn
Cigar Label Art Price Guide. Inner & Outer Label Price Trends (Mission Viejo, CA, 1994)

Faber
Cigar Label Art (Centúry House, Y.I.Y. Museum, Watkins Glen, NY, 1949)

Faber
Smokers, Segars and Stickers (Century House, Y.I.Y. Museum, Watkins Glen, NY, 1949)

Hyman
Handbook of American Cigar Boxes (Arnot Art Museum, Elmira NY, 1979)

Jiménez
Marquillas Cigarreras Cubanas (Ediciones Tabapress, Madrid, 1989)

Terranova & Congdon-Martin
Antique Cigar Cutters and Lighters (Schiffer Publishing Ltd, Atglen, PA, April 1996)

MISCELLANEOUS

Cabrera Infante
Holy Smoke (Harper & Row Publishers, New York and London, 1985)

Finn
Poet of the Cigar (Sancho Panza Press, London, 1982)

MAGAZINES

Cigar Aficonado
(M. Shanken Communications Inc. 387 Park Ave South, New York, NY 10016. Fax: (1) (212) 684-5424. Quarterly. $16.95 (one year))

Smoke
(Lockwood Trade Journal Company Inc., 130 West, 42nd Street, New York, NY 10036. Fax: (1)(212) 827-0945, Quarterly. $14. (one year))

Cigar Monthly
(SCCM Publications Inc. 1223 Wilshire Blvd., 241 Santa Monica, CA 90403. Fax: (1)(310) 576-0776. Monthly. $18. (one year))

European Cigar-Cult-Journal
  (Falstaff-Verlag, Opening 1/E/4, A-1010 WIEN,
  Austria. Fax: (43) (1) 587-65 74 75. Quarterly.
  Published in German)

L'Amateur de Cigare
  (L'Amateur de Cigare, 22 rue des Reculettes
  75013, Paris, France. Fax: (33)(1) 433 14115.
  Quarterly. Published in French)

Cigar, das Europäische Cigarrenmagazin
  (Salz & Pfeffer AG. Postfach 351, 8401 Winterhur,
  Switzerland. Fax: (41)(52) 22 40132. Quarterly.
  Published in German)

Comments, suggestions and possible additions are
welcome for the next edition.

Feel free to contact Theo Rudman at:

P.O. Box 5223, Helderberg, 7135, South Africa.
Telephone: (27)(21) 905-3600
Fax: (27)(21) 905-2188